I0754956

THE

BLACK MAN OF THE SOUTH,

AND

THE REBELS;

OR,

THE CHARACTERISTICS OF THE FORMER, AND THE RECENT OUTRAGES OF THE LATTER.

BY

CHARLES STEARNS,

A Northern Teacher, Missionary, and Planter, and an eye-witness of many of the scenes described.

"The dark places of the Earth are full of the habitations of cruelty,"

"While every prospect pleases,
And only man is vile."

FOR SALE BY

AMERICAN NEWS CO., NEW YORK.

N. E. NEWS COMPANY, BOSTON.

1872.

TABLE OF CONTENTS.

PART I.

CHAPTER XXXVII.

CHAPTER XXXVIII.

CHAPTER XXXIX.

END OF PART I.

PART II.

MEANS NECESSARY TO BE ADOPTED TO PROMOTE THE ELEVATION OF THE FREEDMEN.

CHAPTER I.

CHAPTER II.

CHAPTER III.

CHAPTER IV.

CHAPTER V.

CHAPTER VI.

CHAPTER VII.

INTRODUCTION.

It is not the purpose of the writer of these pages to portray a favorable view only of those whose claims are here advocated. The dark shades, as well as the light ones, in the character of the freedmen will be painted; not with a more sombre hue than the facts will justify, nor with a disposition to magnify the faults of those so recently existing only as brutes, in the eyes of the law, and of public opinion South, but with an earnest desire to draw the attention of the philanthropists of our Nation, to the absolute necessity of doing something to remove from our midst the hideous evil here portrayed.

Let not any hater of the proscribed race endeavor to draw consolation from these pages, for his own unchristian feelings towards the members of that race. Least of all, let any energetic worker in their behalf, as he reads these pages exclaim, "Well, if such is their character, why should I labor any more for them?"

While I shall not "extenuate" the faults of those I plead for, I shall not "set down aught in malice," but shall sedulously endeavor to present a "plain, unvarnished" statement of facts, for the consideration of my readers. I am aware that it is customary to present "rose-colored" views of those in whose behalf you plead; but with me it will be the very misery I shall depict, moral as well as physical, that I shall rely upon to re-awaken public interest in the victims of this depravity and woe.

"*Les Miserables*" shall plead for help, not by having exhibited the bright and shining traits in their characters, but rather, by having exposed to public view the shocking faults indigenous to their former condition, and in their very helplessness, uttering such a wail of anguish as shall touch all hearts imbued with the spirit of mercy. It is not the righteous I call upon you to save, O ye disciples of Jesus, but those morally "bruised and mangled" ones, whose "lost and ruined" condition, so excited the sympathy of him who "came to save" the sons and daughters of woe, who were "plunged" into this "gulf of dark despair."

Far be it from me to attempt to judge the precise criminality of those whose faults I may portray. I leave that task to Him who searcheth all hearts, and can discover in the worst sinner, "glimmering sparks" of goodness, unperceivable by human eyes.

Once for all, let me say to those moral buzzards who are continually on the wing in quest of carrion, if such persons should venture to peruse these pages: feast not upon the moral delinquencies herein described, for whose existence in all probability you may be partially accountable; for if you and others had not stoutly opposed the abolition of Slavery, the faults you now gloat over, and make an excuse, for your satanic hatred of the black man, would have had many years less time in which to mature, and attain to their present hideous dimensions.

We are all responsible for the black man's depravity,

for we all aided in consigning him to that eternal tomb of all virtues and graces — American Slavery. The degradation of the colored man, instead of being an argument in favor of his enslavement, is the strongest possible one, why every vestige of that servitude should be removed from him "as far as is the East from the West," and the North from the South pole.

All well meaning persons who peruse these pages may not agree with the author's conclusions; but every one will be forced to admit that the safety of the Nation, as well as the happiness of the forlorn individuals themselves, demands the removal from among us, of so "dangerous a class," by the redemption of the race from their present partial bondage.

Like the Phœnix of old, rising from the ashes of its former life, a new spectacle shall yet greet the eyes of wondering millions; even that of our Nation, which had grown old and become decrepid, while holding the sceptre of despotism, now, as the "sun of righteousness" dawns upon its former prostrate form; slowly arising, casting away its grave clothes, and brushing from its eyebrows the cobwebs of its musty abode, until at length it emerges into new life, clothed in resplendent robes of truth and beauty, and becomes "fair as the moon, clear as the sun, and terrible as an army with banners," having been "renewed, rejuvenated and disenthralled by the universal genius of emancipation," and its legitimate successor, the free and full citizenship of all classes and conditions of humanity.

CHAPTER I.

DESIGN OF THE WORK.

For some years the author has been of the opinion that the great desideratum for the colored population of the South was the ownership of land; and through their successful supply of this prime necessity of man's nature, the furnishing also the toiling millions of the North with the same grand element of pecuniary welfare. Far be it from him to decry other efforts for the elevation of this long injured race, but it will be his object to portray in these pages, as clearly as he is able, first, the necessities of the Southern freedmen, and then to show that these necessities cannot be effectually provided for, without making him among other things, the industrious owner of the land he cultivates.

This little treatise will not be written in the interest of any party or sect, but solely with a view to meet this question: How can the freedman be elevated, so as to render emancipation a blessing to him rather than a curse? It is not for him to say, that even without the freedman's elevation, Slavery had better not have been abolished; but he would most emphatically aver, that emancipation is to *him* a boon of but little value, unless it shall lead in reality to his exaltation in the scale of moral and intellectual life, far above the point he occupied while a chattel-slave. I am aware that many good men have said, "We have given him his freedom, now let him shift for himself." In the words of a distinguished but eccentric philanthropist, it should now be with him, "'root hog, or die,' as it was with myself, in my early days." This philosopher fails to inform us how the hog can obey this injunction, if he has been so unfortunate as to *lose his snout*, to continue the *elegant* simile.

It is true that the black man possesses all the natural powers that we possess; but it is also true that of our own race, a Caspar Hauser affords a melancholy proof of the fact, that the most boasted powers, by disuse, may fail entirely. Every one must acknowledge that his own experience verifies this assertion. The most splendid attainments are rendered nugatory by a failure to apply them to the actual duties of life. Even godlike religion, that ally of heaven in its efforts to draw the race to its celestial throne, loses its power entirely, when long allowed to slumber; and there is no virtue or human attainment but becomes shorn of all its beauty, by being buried in the earth. *Action* is the great law of the Universe, in reference to all the complicated machinery of heaven's devising, for the promotion of man's welfare.

In the slave's case, but few of his faculties were ever exercised. He was a living skeleton, a walking frame of bones and ligaments, wholly destitute of blood or flesh; a corpse without vitality enough to remind the beholder of its former life; a mass of inorganic matter, loosely thrown into one heterogeneous compound resembling a human being. Having only recently heard the voice addressed to him, and saying, "Lazarus, come forth," how can he be expected to walk the earth with that god-like tread, belonging to those who have never experienced a like moral death? As well expect the tottering limbs of a child in its first essays in the art of walking, to evince the strength of a full grown man, as he treads with ease the ruggedest of mountain paths! A lame man, just arising from a rheumatic couch of years' existence, needs the friendly support of a pair of crutches, to enable him to equal in pedestrian efforts, even a young child. How much more does the newly emancipated slave need assistance, comfort, strength and love, in his new-born attempts to imitate the full grown sons of liberty around him?

In all that the author shall say concerning the demerits of the freedmen, let it be distinctly borne in mind that he is only describing the effects of slavery. Let no friend of the black man shudder at what he may deem the too terrific picture drawn of him; but let him remember that it is only the portraiture of Slavery that is here given. If one of the black man's enemies shall recoil at the recital of his woes, let him remember that he and his friends are the cruel authors of all this degradation, unless he can truly say he never, by word or deed, did aught to uphold the monster — American Slavery.

I wish to describe the black man as he is, not for the purpose of drawing upon him the maledictions of others, for God knows that he has received enough of them, but in order that the great heart of the lovers of our race may be filled with new detestation of Slavery, as well as be aroused to more thorough action in behalf of its former miserable victims.

If I should describe the freedman as he is sometimes

described, it would only prove that my pen was being used in a partizan sense, and not in the interests of truth alone. A splendid portraiture of him, as only an injured martyr, possessing all the virtues and none of the vices of our common manhood, would enstamp itself as a brilliant falsehood, and destroy at once all the author's claims to veracity; for as "an evil tree *cannot* bring forth good fruit," so cannot the product of Slavery be other than a loathsome corpse of mental and moral degradation.

I must draw a *true* picture of what I have seen and heard in this Sodom of America. I cannot prevaricate or embellish, lest the feelings of good people should be wounded. I utterly disclaim all intention of trampling upon the sensibilities of any Northern or Southern colored man, who has outgrown the terrific effects of Slavery. As far as heaven is from hell, so far in moral and intellectual grandeur, do great numbers of the colored race, especially at the North, tower above the unfortunate creature so lately a plantation Slave. As the Apostle says, "Such were some of you, but ye are washed, ye are sanctified, ye are justified in the name of the Lord Jesus, and by the Spirit of our God."

With these remarks in explanation of my design, I shall proceed to present the reader with a *condensed narrative* of my *personal experience among the freedmen*, after which I shall endeavor to draw *a portraiture* of *the prominent characteristics* of *the black men in Georgia*, with *descriptions* of the *institutions* and *practices obtaining among them*, and animadversions upon their *persecutions*, together with *authentic accounts* of the *outrages experienced by them*, and a *history* of *Ku Kluxism.* I shall then specify the *various measures deemed necessary* for the *black man's redemption*, the *reasons* for this *redemption*, and the encouragements for laboring to bring it about.

The one end and aim of the writer will be in all that he shall say of "saint and sinner," of rebel and of freedmen, of white men and of black men, to adhere closely to the truth, whatever that shall be, and where-ever it shall lead.

CHAPTER II.

THE AUTHOR'S MOTIVE IN COMING SOUTH, WITH REMINISCENCES OF KANSAS AND COLORADO.

Long before Slavery ceased to be the controlling spirit of this Nation, it was my opinion that when its power came to an end, it would be the duty of abolitionists to labor for the elevation of its former victims. It was therefore with no ordinary feelings of interest that I listened to the bugle blast of war that echoed over the Alleghanies, and whose sound crossed the tops of those lofty summits, near whose base I was laboring, when first was heard those electrifying notes, in the Spring of 1861.

I was then an inhabitant of Central City, Colorado Territory, having emigrated there from Kansas, a few months previously. For six years I had resided in Kansas, and humbly endeavored to do my part in swelling the tide of public opinion, that should finally banish Slavery from that virgin soil. The success of our friends, in delivering that "garden of Eden" from Slavery's blackened touch is well known to all Americans. Suffice to say, that not a tithe of the horrors of that short but sanguinary warfare will ever be fully known, to any but the actors in those scenes, until the great day of final account. For one, I may be pardoned in saying that "free Kansas" prepared the way for "free America." If we had not succeeded then, it is not to be supposed that the great war that resulted in the abolition of Slavery would have occurred. On the plains of Kansas, in the years 1856 and 1857, was in reality decided the great conflict, which resulted in the emancipation of nearly four millions of human beings. Yea, more, if success had not then crowned our efforts, the whole North would have been bound hand and foot, and tied to the slave-car, which was then seeking to ride triumphantly through our Nation.

The "Border Ruffians" so regarded the issue, there to be decided, and marshalled their hosts from every nook and corner of the dismal South, and paraded them upon our fair plains. The character of our foe may be ascertained by reading the history of the bloodiest scenes of our late war, such as the burning of Lawrence, the massacre at Fort Pillow, and the satanic treatment of our soldiers confined in the various Southern prisons. Kansas soil drank the blood of some of these fiends in human shape, and therefore there were a few less persons to perpetrate these horrors on a larger scale; but those who did thus survive became better qualified to engage in the wholesale butcheries of the war, from the delightful lessons of carnage they had taken in their Kansas school.

But the chivalry were at length defeated, mainly through the aid received from Eastern friends, and from the glorious Republican party, then in its infancy. With John C. Freemont at its head, it was not ashamed to espouse our feeble cause, and send men and money, to sustain our sinking spirits. Would to God that now in the days of its unwonted prosperity, it might not forget its "first love," and its former noble eschewing of the fatal sop of expediency, that now bids fair to control its movements, and fatally poison its already partially emasculated system.

I well remember in those days of our extreme peril, when the streets of Lawrence were daily filled with wagons from the country, carrying their affrighted occupants to abodes of safety, that our Spartan friends resisted with indignation the proposition made by some faint-hearted Eastern friends, that the settlers of Kansas should yield to the dreadful odds against them, and proceed to Fort Leavenworth, and throw themselves upon the mercy of the commander there. "Never, while a drop of blood remains in our veins," was the universal shout, as this recommendation was read from one of the leading Eastern papers that advocated our rights. This incident is stated that the reader may have a faint idea of our perilous condition.

But I am not now writing of Kansas, and I must leave the recapitulation of these scenes for some future occasion, merely adding that under God, two men did more to rescue us from our forlorn plight, than any others; and those two men were *John Brown* and "*Jim*" *Lane.* Gov. Robinson, James Montgomery, and a host of others performed their work well and faithfully; but John Brown and Jim Lane acted as *scarecrows* to drive the hosts of robber-birds from our fair domain. The presence of either of these men was enough to drive hundreds of the enemy from our borders. Under the valiant lead of the former, aided by the wise counsels of Charles Robinson, about two hundred men in Lawrence successfully defended that village in September, 1856, against the attack of twenty-three hundred enrolled men from Missouri. This I know to be the case, for I was one of the humble actors in that memorable scene, and was permitted to accompany the only cannon we had, as one of twelve men, under the lead of John Brown, who followed fifty men with "Sharps' rifles" in their persuit of the one hundred and fifty horsemen, the advance guard of the whole army, as they turned and fled rapidly, at the second or third fire of fifteen or twenty of our horsemen.

On arriving in Central City, I found that my work had not ceased. Very early we were met by the myrmidons of secession, who formed a plan to capture our little city, and thus cut off the communication of our government with California, which act would have been accomplished, if it had not been for the untiring zeal of Gov. Gilpin, who, without waiting for orders from Washington, commenced the organization of the "1st Colorado Regiment," and with the aid of the citizens, armed and equipped its members. Soon after this, the bulk of the secession leaders left our territory; and during the remainder of the war, Colorado was intensely loyal. I am sorry to be obliged to add, that for thus disregarding "red tape" formalities, Gov. Gilpin's decapitation followed in the wake of that of many others, who, like Gen. Wool, Freemont, &c., were laid upon the shelf, for their too hasty steps, in bringing the rebels into subjection. The "conductors of the war" at Washington, doubtless imagined that strict obedience to military regulations, was far more important than any immediate good, however great, that might result, from a negligence of these orders.

Those who resided near the actual conflict, can faintly realize the breathless interest with which every mail from the East was watched by us Coloradians. At one time, the Secessionists stirred up the Indians on the plains against us, so that for months we had no communication with the East, except by telegraph, and by way of California. But at length the dove of peace lit upon the Capitol of our Nation, and a stray olive leaf from her mouth was wafted to our mountain homes: and a glad shout of unutterable joy arose from our canons, and swept across our mountain tops. With some of the inhabitants of Colorado, the notes of these shouts were pitched to a higher key, by their mixing with them the still gladder sound of *free America*, "Babylon the great is fallen." I am free to confess that I could not have shouted for joy, unless I had felt that the "Sons of God" were also thus shouting, and the "morning stars were singing together," of freedom having become the glad portion of the *sable* sons and daughters of America, as well as of those hitherto more highly favored. If emancipation had not been the result of the war, I should have considered it a miserable failure, and an unjust attempt to coerce men into sustaining a form of government which they despised.

But emancipation being the fruits of the war, no lover of his race can for a moment regret its existence, or wish that the doctrine of State rights was still standing upon its former firm pedestal. But I am sorry to say that the Anti-Slavery cause did not number among its friends all those Coloradians engaged in fighting for the Union. When President Lincoln's emancipation proclamation first reached our ears, I was so elated with the news, that I ran to the newspaper office, to talk with the editor, on the glorious theme; and on my way thither, I passed the recruiting tent of an artillery officer. I looked in for a moment, and the officer, perceiving my excitement, enquired eagerly after the war news. "O," said I, "the slaves are all free, and are going to fight for the Union. *Isn't* that glorious?" Judge of my surprise, when the officer, seizing his sword, excitingly exclaimed, "By G—d, I will break this sword across my knees, and throw up my commission, rather than fight in the same army with 'niggers.'" But the officer failed to keep his rash promise, and preserved his sword unbroken, and months afterwards, was found humbly petitioning the government to be restored to his command, of which he had been deprived for some other reasons.

As an index of the strongly loyal feelings of our citizens, I will relate an incident that occurred on the death of the lamented Lincoln. The news of this sad event reached us at about 10 o'clock of the forenoon following the foul murder, and intense beyond all description was the excitement everywhere. Stout men, whose hearts had not quailed during the war, now trembled exceedingly. "Mens' hearts were failing them from fear" all around, while a strong determination was everywhere apparent, to meet this new calamity with a general outpouring of blood and treasure, if necessary. I question whether a more loyal crowd could have been found, even in Boston, than that which filled our streets during the whole of the day, and part of the day following.

A hair-brained Secessionist, partly under the influence of liquor, in an unguarded moment, exclaimed, "I am glad of it; he deserved to be shot." Almost in the twinkling of an eye, the poor unfortunate was seized by the indignant bystanders, and hurried before an impromptu tribunal assembled in the theatre. The fury of the populace knew no bounds, but "in wrath they remembered mercy," and determined that the rash youth should have a fair trial by a jury of our best citizens. A distinguished physician and orator of the place volunteered to defend him, and the testimony was patiently listened to, as well as the pleadings of his lawyer; and after the verdict, the culprit was allowed to speak in his own behalf. With tearful eyes, he pleaded for mercy, not on his account, but on that of his absent mother and sisters. The jury sentenced him to have one side of his head shorn, and to leave the place within a certain number of hours; and I believe, to receive thirty lashes on his bare back. It was at first proposed that these should be applied by a Negro; but this part of the sentence was revoked, at the earnest solicitation of the culprit's friends. Quite a number of the crowd still favored his being shot; but during the debate that ensued on this proposition, a telegram arrived from the military commander of the district at Denver, ordering the prisoner to be sent to him. This request was gladly complied with, and after another hearing of the case, the guilty man was sentenced to carry a heavy bag of sand six or eight hours a day, for thirty days in succession.

It will thus be seen, that all mining regions are not quite so rough as Eastern people imagine. And here let me say, that during my residence of four and a half years in Central City, the heart of the mining regions of Colorado, fewer violations of law occurred than in any other community where I have resided for the same length of time. My place of business was in a very public position, and during the whole of the time I was there, was entirely unprotected by bars or shutters; and although the front consisted mainly of glass, it was never injured in the slightest degree. I will also add, that I never met with a more intelligent population than those with whom it was my daily lot to associate; so that I can cheerfully recommend Central City as one of the most desirable places of residence with which I am acquainted, forming a very delightful contrast to the "valley of the shadow of death," where I at present reside, and of which I am about to speak.

But pleasant as was my life in Colorado, I determined to leave it for other duties, requiring, as I well knew, strong resolution and firmness of soul. As the title of this chapter is in part, "my motive in coming South," I may be pardoned for stating it more fully.

During the war, my wife and I had resolved that if it resulted in the abolition of Slavery, *we* would go South, and do what we could, for the perfect development of the colored race. But before we could mature our plans, the angel of death visited our abode, and called upon her who had so zealously labored for freedom in Kansas, and for the entire overthrow of Slavery elsewhere, to follow his noiseless steps into the land of unutterable beauty and perfect liberty.

She was born and reared among slaveholders, being a native of Kentucky; but for many years she had been an uncompromising abolitionist; and as her peaceful spirit joyfully obeyed the summons of God's "grim messenger," she dropped a regretful tear, at the thoughts of being prevented from joining in bodily form, her husband, in his future efforts for those whose freedom she had so ardently desired, as well as a joyful one at the thoughts of the so far glorious consummation of her wishes. Is it too much to suppose that she still watches with interest the progress of those benign efforts, and does not hesitate to pronounce her benediction upon those making them?

Some six months after this sad event, I left Colorado, for the future scene of my labors — the "sunny South," taking in my way, my native state, my dear and well beloved Massachusetts. Previous to leaving Colorado, I wrote for publication in Boston the following sketch of my plan: "I wish to proceed to some portion of the South, and there labor for the accomplishment of *three* things for the colored people. First, their *education* and moral improvement; secondly, their *right to vote;* and thirdly, the making them the *owners of the land* they cultivate." The pages of this book will show what amount of success I have been favored with, in the prosecution of this threefold enterprise.

I was full of enthusiasm on all of these points, and little dreamed of the almost insurmountable obstacles I should meet with. It is well for us that the future is not often revealed to us, for the knowledge of its trials would often deter us from engaging in many a holy undertaking. I am free to confess, that if I had then known what I know to-day, I should not have been likely to have engaged in this almost Quixotic enterprise. Little did I dream of the nature of the evil I had to contend with. I indeed foresaw violent opposition on the part of the rebels; but I did not comprehend the depths of degradation I must sound, before I could reach the *terra firma* of principle, in the hearts of the black race.

I corresponded with distinguished friends of the freedmen, who agreed that the work I proposed was a very necessary one, but entreated me not to risk my life in so rash an enterprise, little imagining that the greatest injuries I should receive, would be at the hands of those who made the loudest profession of attachment to me, for my labors in their behalf. Suffice it to say, that a voice far more potent than those of my friends, seemed to say, "Go into the land so recently cursed by Slavery, and there do my bidding." Having for many years been in the habit of following the leadings of God's spirit, I dared not any longer "confer with flesh and blood," but immediately made preparations for obeying what seemed to me "the heavenly vision." I did not expect supernatural inspiration, but only a fulfillment of those Scripture declarations, in reference to spiritual guidance, so often quoted in the writings of the Quakers and early Methodists, "There is a spirit in man, and the inspiration of the Almighty giveth understanding"; "Acknowledge the Lord in all thy ways, and he shall direct thy steps"; "As many as are led by the Spirit of God, *they are the sons of God*."

Accordingly I disposed of my effects in Colorado, and bid adieu to friends and to a prosperous and agreeable business, and took up my line of march for the East, *en route* for the South. The journey across the plains was performed in a covered wagon, drawn by four mules, and occupied eight weeks, during which time we ate and slept in the wagon. I was accompanied in this journey by my only child, a girl three years of age, whose innocent prattle beguiled many a weary hour, although it was no slight task to provide for her comfort, the whole of this task devolving upon me.

I did not reach the South, however, until nearly a year after my departure from the Rocky Mountains, during the lapse of which time I found ample employment, in combating the pernicious views of Andrew Johnson, in reference to the management of the Southern people.

CHAPTER III.

THE AUTHOR'S ARRIVAL AT THE SOUTH.

We took passage at New York, in the Steamship San Salvador, about the first of May, 1866, and landed at Savannah three days afterwards, in good health and spirits. We were accompanied by a lady, who wished to unite with me in the important undertaking of elevating the freedmen, and by Mr. Henry F. Parker, of Reading, Mass., who had been for many years identified with the Anti-Slavery cause at the East, and had performed important and heroic labors for the slave at the West. We had been intimate in Colorado, where he had signalized himself by his entire devotion to the Union cause; and his deep interest in all that related to the welfare of our embryo-community. He had been elected first president of the Miner's district, where he resided, and was a member of the first Territorial Senate. His object in visiting the South, was mainly a benevolent one; to gather facts respecting the condition of the freedmen, and to discover if any opening presented itself, where he could labor for their welfare. On board the steamer, we had many opportunities to gain information respecting the South. We saw several Yankee residents of the South, and a number of its natives; as well as several New York adventurers, on a tour of speculation, to ascertain the amount of goods that could be advantageously disposed of, for the benefit of their New York employers. These latter gentry of course, were not disposed to regard our enterprise very favorably; but from others we learned much that was valuable, in reference to both rebels and freedmen.

Some of these gentlemen were bound for Jacksonville, and enlarged upon the merits of that locality as a favorable one for the prosecution of our enterprise. A company of Boston friends had formed a settlement at New Smyrna, near Enterprise, in Florida; and we much desired to visit that locality; but on conversing with Capt. Hawks, in Charleston, on the subject, we came to the conclusion that the hardships of a frontier life, fifty miles from a market, would not compensate for any superior advantages it might possess in the way of fine scenery, delightful climate, and its multitude of sweet oranges. Since our residence at the South, we have learned that this colony proved a failure, and we felt thankful that we had not linked our fortunes with its founders. It was not our object to found a colony, but simply to purchase a large farm or plantation, and divide its products among those who performed the labor, on the principle that "the laborer is worthy of his hire."

It was our purpose, to test the practicability of the co-operative principle, in carrying on a large farm; as it had been previously tested in the various mechanical arts. For many years, the author's attention had been drawn to the vast discrepancy between the profits of labor, and of capital; and he had long desired to solve the problem of an equitable distribution of these profits, so as to allow to labor its legitimate share. Not wishing to urge upon others what might prove, after all an

Eutopian idea, he wished to show by actual experiment that business could be successfully conducted on the co-operative plan, in this country, as well as in Europe. Without intending to digress from my narrative, I may be permitted to state my convictions upon this point.

Co-operation, is heaven's great law. No result in Nature is attained except under its operations. It is the same in art. Schools, colleges, the erection of lofty piles of architectural beauty, the construction of magnificent vessels, the building of railroads without number; all prove the truth of this principle. "No man liveth unto himself, and no man dieth unto himself." But it is also a principle of Nature, that, "how can two walk together except they be agreed;" so that *harmony of purpose* is the first pre-requisite to successful co-operation. The family relation is shorn of a large share of its unutterable blessings, when discord creeps in to that sacred enclosure; and a harmonious and well balanced child, can never be the result of a two-fold life of jarring and petulancy.

Many co-operative establishments have been commenced without securing this fundamental principle of harmony, and consequently have burst asunder, by the restless fury of their own internal elements.

Therefore there can be no successful co-operation between men of totally diverse natures. With these ideas fresh in the minds of our readers, they can see the reason for the gradual change of the author's plans for the welfare of the freedmen, of which, more will be said hereafter.

We visited several plantations in different parts of South Carolina and Georgia, and finally determined to purchase one of about fifteen hundred acres, situated in Columbia County, Georgia, about eleven miles from the pretty city of Augusta. Of this Columbia County we knew but little, but have since learned, that it was always considered one of the most turbulent counties in the state, although a very wealthy one. There were but comparatively few of the so-called "poor whites" in the county, most of the plantations being large, some of them containing four thousand acres.

The location selected seemed a very healthy one, and as there was on the farm everything in readiness for farming operations, and the crops were all planted, it seemed a very desirable selection, although the price was somewhat higher than we had designed to pay, and we were obliged to run in debt for a portion of the "purchase money."

The hands were already at work, under the direction of a Southern overseer, whose services I was advised to secure for the remainder of the year — which advice I complied with, and hired him to carry on the farm, in the manner he was used to, for the remainder of the year, reserving all innovations for some future time. This overseer's name was Prince, and he had served as a soldier in the confederate army, and was quite destitute of sympathetic feelings towards the blacks.

As it may interest the reader I will endeavor to describe the place, as it was when we first purchased it, premising that all parties concerned seemed well satisfied with the purchase.

CHAPTER IV.

DESCRIPTION OF "HOPE ON HOPE EVER" PLANTATION.

Imagine the worst roads ever travelled over by a New Englander, comprising seven long hills, skirted by deep gullies, and abounding in rocks of large and small dimensions, over and through which it required the skill of an expert in the art of driving, to safely pick his way, without damage to beast or carriage. The country through which these roads passed, was monotonous in the extreme, and almost utterly destitute of those marks of thrift, and gladsome cultivation, that a ride of that length almost anywhere at the North, would present to your view. Rail-fences, old and dilapidated buildings, and rough cultivation, greeted your eye constantly; relieved only by great numbers of majestic trees, and occasionally by the sight of a fine mansion some distance from the road.

Just before you reach the dwelling on "Hope On Hope Ever Plantation" (a name we afterwards gave the place in one of our darkest hours,) you come to two lanes, one running in a Southerly, and the other in a Northerly direction from the main road. The former, extended through a portion of the plantation, and the other divided it from the land of a rebel neighbor. On the right hand side of the road, and West of the last mentioned lane, you beheld ten or twelve Negro-houses, with a small plat of ground attached to each. To the credit of the former owner of the place, it must be said, that these houses were very comfortable abodes; and presented quite a pretty appearance, as you passed them on the road. They were arranged in three rows, of three and four in a row; and each of them had a good-sized brick chimney on the outside, and had once been whitewashed. They were separated from the highway, by a high rail-fence; and from the yard belonging to the dwelling house of the whites, by a good picket fence. On the South side of the road, opposite "the quarters," as the negro-houses were termed, was a huge unsightly building called a barn, surrounded by a high fence to protect the enclosure from depredations, the entrance to which, was through a large gate, which was kept locked at night, and usually through the day. What style of architecture this barn was designed to perpetuate the memory of, I know not; but should presume it was one in vogue prior to the building of Noah's ark. It consisted of a huge frame, surrounded by what were termed stables, and a shed for wagons. The outside of these stables faced away from the barn, and toward the road on the North side of the barn, to which road the building came in close proximity. The architect, or owner of this building, had evidently been a strong believer in the modern doctrine of thorough ventilation for working animals, although his building was otherwise of so ancient a design, for, from top to bottom the boards were six or eight inches apart, all around the three sides of the building devoted to stock. Luckily in this "sunny land" we are not cursed with the icy blasts of a Northern winter, or the poor mules would not have long survived to tell the story of their wrongs.

The high fence around the "lot," as the barn-yard was termed, was composed of strips of board of all sizes and lengths, nailed promiscuously upon the cross pieces of the fence. The yard adjacent to this barn, was so constructed as to admit the water that might collect from great rains to find its way easily to the gutter bordering the highway, its projectors forgetting that vast quantities of valuable manure also found their way from the premises along with the streams of water. This "lot" was bordered by quite a number of other buildings, some of them rather old, but one, used for storing corn, was in an excellent state of preservation, and would hold several thousand bushels of corn — with which it was often filled, in the days of Slavery. The barn would hold thirty or forty thousand bundles of fodder, twenty-five thousand of which had been recently stored therein. At a short distance from the lot, situated on one side of the lane, running Southerly from the main road, was another large barn, somewhat dilapidated; and on the other side, an excellent building, termed the "granary," used for thrashing and storing grain, and containing the requisite machinery for thrashing wheat, which thrashing was performed by horse power.

Leaving the barns on your left, you now approached the "big house," as the blacks termed it, which was situated on the right hand side of the road, and at a respectful distance therefrom. It was surrounded by a yard, containing about an acre and a half of ground, and twenty-five or thirty shade trees, principally mulberry, china-berry and cedar, with a few tall slim trees, with a very smooth bark, having in their high branches a profusion of most beautiful red flowers, which appeared in July, and lasted to nearly the close of the year. It was a long time before I could ascertain correctly, from black or white persons, the name of these trees; but I afterwards ascertained they were termed the *leger-streamer* tree. All around the yard was a substantial, unpainted picket fence.

When my wife and I first beheld the dwelling-house, our impulse was to have it razed to the ground as speedily as possible; but after consideration satisfied us, that poor as it might look to our New England eyes, it was in reality no mean structure, and would answer for a shelter for our heads a long time, as it really has done, and also for sheltering at one time nearly fifty human beings. It was two stories high, with three solid brick chimnies on the outside, containing nearly as many bricks as would suffice to build a decent brick house in New England, and a good brick foundation. During the fifty years it had maintained its present grim position, it had remained wholly innocent of paint, wherewith to embellish its exterior; but it did not stand "alone in its glory" in this respect, for a large majority of the Southern plantation houses are in a similar predicament. The house was built of hard pine, in the massive style peculiar to the South, and contained eleven rooms, including the hall and attics, most of which were extremely large, and very high studded. Its interior exhibited no signs of decay, notwithstanding it had never been graced with a very large amount of paint. There was not a particle of plastering in the house, but good substantial board ceilings overhead, as well as at the sides, usurped the usual places of lath and plaster. The ceiling overhead, of the parlor, was well painted.

This house has now become endeared to us, by so many pleasant recollections, and joyful as well as sad experiences, that we should regret exceedingly to see it displaced by a finer looking one. Behind the house were various other buildings, used severally for a smoke-house, meal-house, carriage-house, pigeon-house, milk-house, &c, &c. Just back of the house, was a fine garden, containing three-fourths of an acre of land; and between it and the highway was about an acre and a quarter more of unenclosed land, which was also used as a garden. The garden proper was surrounded with a good picket fence, similar to the one surrounding the yard, and contained thirty or forty fruit trees, principally peach. A few pear trees, and a number of plum trees stood in the plat adjoining the garden. A short distance west of the garden were the gin-house and packing-screw, both good sized and substantial buildings: and a little distance north of the garden was the blacksmiths' shop.

The buildings were skirted on the North by a pleasant ravine, through which coursed a gentle, murmuring brook, finding its way among a plentiful supply of large and small rocks, and bordered on each side by a profusion of trees, affording a delightful and romantic retreat from the scorching rays of midsummer. In front of the house, and easily seen from its windows, were several slight elevations of rolling land, from the moderate summits of which a beautiful view of the surrounding country could be obtained. West of the house, stretching in seemingly an illimitable distance, were a large portion of the broad acres that composed the farm. About one half of the farm was still in woods, a large portion of which were the primitive oak and hickory of that region, and the remainder, pines of various sizes, the "second growth" of those lands after having once been cultivated. These pines were the "short leaf" pine, in distinction from the "long leaf" pines, composing the original forests of the "piny woods" region.

The original oak lands produce pines for their "second growth," and the original pine lands yield as *their* second product a bountiful supply of oaks; a fact that surprised *me*, but it may be true elsewhere. The farm was well watered by quite a number of brooks and creeks, and supplied with several splendid springs, besides a never-failing well of the purest and best water in existence. On the farm were at least three moderate water privileges; and two mills and a distillery had once blessed and cursed the plantation.

I beg the reader's pardon for occupying so much time in this lengthy, and to him perhaps uninteresting description of our plantation. I have done so, in order that the scenes hereafter described may be more vividly impressed upon him, from being connected in his mind with a "local habitation."

CHAPTER V.

FIRST DAY OF THE AUTHOR IN HIS NEW HOME.

It was on Saturday night, in the midst of a driving storm of wind and rain when we reached our new home. We had floundered through the mud of one of the worst roads of Christendom, and narrowly escaped destruction by driving off a precipice on our way out; the thick darkness of the night being only relieved by occasional flashes of lightning, one of whose friendly gleams had shown us our danger just in season to escape therefrom. The roads had not been repaired for *several years*, as we afterwards learned, and they were nearly impassable; another legitimate fruit of the all pervading evil-genius of Slavery. Our driver had left us to attend to his weary horses, and with the rain still pouring upon us, we knocked in vain for admittance to our house. The papers about the property had all been properly arranged, and the amount due amply secured by mortgage; but still there was no response to our importunate knocking.

Was not this a fitting prelude to our future labors? Were we not even then, doomed to "call and be refused?" It seems now as if our first reception was somewhat typical of the future, in its lack of response to our urgent entreaty for admittance. Our calls were at length heeded, and the burly form of a stout "overseer" made its appearance; to whom was delivered a letter from the former owner of the place, and we then received a cordial welcome.

But, as with all Southerners "Rome was not built in a day," so it took time to build a fire and make us comfortable in the uninhabited house; and still longer to prepare our supper. And such a supper! It cannot be well described! But being hungry, uninviting as were the viands set before us, we all contrived to force down a small portion of them, and then proceeded to "improvisate" a bed. What with the aid of our carriage cushions, coats and shawls and a few sheets and blankets we had brought in our baggage, we contrived to pass the night in some small degree of comfort.

We found a good feather bed, and some dingy sheets on a bedstead in the dining-room; but the fastidiousness of some of the party led them to prefer a harder bed on the floor, which should have the merit of less filth at least; as that could be swept tolerably clean with the aid of a good broom we had taken the precaution to purchase in town. We had also purchased a small supply of provisions, which we thought would suffice for our table, as soon as we could "get the hang" of the Southern mode of cooking.

The next morning did not catch us napping, but we were up and stirring long before there were any signs of life around us, except the continual howling of one of the many half-starved dogs, that are so omnipresent on every Southern plantation. It is due to the credit of the former owner to state, that he was in no wise responsible for this dismal state of affairs, as he did not reside upon the plantation, but was engaged in business in Augusta. But it did not probably occur to him, that having sold us the place in good faith, it was his duty to have made it somewhat comfortable at any rate.

Amid the darkness of the night, the filthiness of the house was partially concealed from us; but the first rays of old Sol's pure light dispelled all our ideas of having a comfortable home, until we had made it ourselves. Such a sight rarely meets the eyes of a Northern house-keeper. The room was ten or eleven feet high, twenty by twenty-five feet in size, and ceiled all around and above as before described, without ever having seen any paint or paper. It contained four windows, of eight by ten glass, and four doors, of a massive character. The floor of this room had been washed probably at the beginning of Methusalah's life; certainly not often since. The only articles of furniture were a heavy, black-looking table, a bedstead, two or three old chairs, and something in the shape of an old-fashioned side-board, innocent of paint or varnish, but containing five good drawers, and a small cupboard. As soon as sufficient daylight allowed us, my wife, Etta, peered into the recesses of this mysterious piece of furniture, evidently pleased at the idea of having found a receptacle for our provisions, in the almost utter absence of closet or pantry on the premises, when she suddenly exclaimed, "O, Charles, look here!" I sprang to her side, expecting that a huge spider or a rat had bitten her finger, when I, too, exclaimed, "O, how can we live here?" as I beheld the sight before me. Words would fail me, to describe the condition of this cupboard! But we closed our exploration of its deficiencies, until another meal had been prepared for us, by *Margaret*, the cook. This meal was a slight improvement on the former, as Etta had made a forage into the kitchen, and managed to introduce into the most important cooking utensil of the habitation, viz: a large bake-pan, a few of the savory viands we had brought with us; but she sedulously concealed from my knowledge all the addition to her stock of housekeeping information, which she had derived from this surreptitious visit to forbidden premises; as she said afterwards, she did not wish to spoil my appetite for my breakfast, as she would have done, by revealing to me the hidden depths of corruption she had partially explored.

This kitchen was one half of a large sized negro-cabin, standing a few rods from our dwelling, and between that and the negro "quarters," forming one side of the enclosure to the yard, until it met the picket-fence, before described. A short distance from this cabin, appeared the only really good thing there was on the premises, viz., our excellent well.

The food was cooked (excuse the word) in the aforesaid kitchen, and then brought across the yard, in sunshine and in rain, to the house. It never occurred to the originators of this style of living, that food thus exposed to the elements, lost a large portion of its palatableness, during this lengthy journey, and that it must be either cooked regardless of science or cleanliness, or the lady of the house must endure the heat of the noonday sun quite often, during the transit of a single dinner.

But to return to the cupboard. As soon as breakfast was over, Etta proceeded to the door of our dining-room, and called out "Margaret," in a pleasant tone, but no Margaret appeared. At length, after repeated calls of this pretty name, its worthy bearer entered the house, and commenced hustling off the dishes from the breakfast table, and "toting" them out to the polluted kitchen. "You need not do that, Margaret," said my wife. "Why, missis, you's not gwine to eat again from them ar dirty dishes, is you?" replied Margaret; and her whole nature seemed shocked at the idea. "No, Margaret," quietly responded my wife, "but I want you to wash them here."

If Margaret had heard a loud clap of thunder, she could not have been more overcome with surprise, and she exclaimed, with a distressed air, "Gwine to wash dishes in dis ere room; dis ar the gemman's sittin'-room, and ye gwine to turn it into de kitchen?" Margaret was a woman of great independence of character, outspoken and fearless. She was none of your "Miss Nancy" kind of a woman, eternally agreeing with whatever proposition was made to her, and never having a mind of her own. If circumstances had favored, she might have led a military company to battle; or at any rate, rivalled any of her loud-mouthed white sisters, in their furious denunciations of human wrongs. She was withal, extremely sensitive, as well as jealous of her honor, her rights and prerogatives; and she was determined that not one of her rights should be infringed upon, with her consent.

She was dressed in a coarse cotton gown, which had once been meant for white, but was now of a dingy brown color. This dress did not quite reach her ankles, and could not have contained over two breadths. Around her head was twined, in true negro style, a large yellow cotton handkerchief, with a few white spots upon its surface. Like all the negro women, she was as straight as an arrow, affording an agreeable contrast to the deformities of the modern fashionable belle. Her complexion was of no mongrel hue, but of the "simon-pure" black, without any discount.

Etta repeated her order in mild tones, but it was unheeded. Then and there Margaret threw down the gauntlet, and staking her all upon her ability to consummate her purposes, she declared she was "gwine to be cook ob dis ere house, and Ise want no white woman to trouble me;" and growing eloquent at the thought, she dropped everything, and planting herself in the middle of the floor, she delivered herself as follows: "You white folks spose, cause you white, and we all black, that us dunno noffin, and you knows eberyting;" and snatching her yellow turban from her head, she flourished it in her hands, and cried out at the top of her voice, "Now missus, youse one bery good white woman, come down from de great North, to teach poor we to read, and sich as that; but we done claned dishes all our days, long before ye Yankees hearn tell of us, and now does ye suppose I gwine to give up all my rights to ye, just cause youse a Yankee white woman? Does ye know missus that we's free now? Yas, free we is, and us ant gwine to get down to *ye*, any more than to them ar rebs."

What would have been the effect of this harangue upon the quiet spirit of my wife, I am not able to state, if the rough voice of the overseer had not then been heard, as he rushed through the yard, and into the house, and seizing Margaret by the neck of her dress, he dragged her out of the room in a very unceremonious manner; exclaiming, "Shut up you d——n black wench, or I'll beat your brains out;" and turning to us, he blandly said, "Never mind her, Mrs. Stearns; these niggers have no more sense or manners than a mule; but I'll teach her not to insult white people."

Thus early commenced that systematic disobedience

to our orders that we have encountered at every step of our intercourse with the blacks: but of this, more hereafter.

Margaret thus subdued, soon returned as mild as a lamb, and proceeded to wash the dishes according to Etta's orders, occasionally wincing, it is true, at the oft-repeated words, "Margaret, you haven't washed that plate clean."

But another battle was doomed to be fought, and Margaret this time came off victorious, Mr. Prince having absented himself from the plantation, to attend to other business. Margaret was ordered to wash out the sideboard; but she absolutely and flatly refused, as it was Sunday, and she wasn't hired to do such work on Sunday. If there had been any other conceivable place where our provisions could have been placed, the cleaning of that cupboard would have been deferred until Monday; but such not being the case, Mrs. Stearns was compelled to clean a portion of it herself, leaving the remainder until Monday morning, when Margaret appeared, ready for any emergency.

It was not from any love for the Sabbath that Margaret thus rebelled, but because as she said, "Sunday was her day, and black folks don't work on Sunday."

During the whole of this day, we were watched with the utmost interest by the hands on the place. The singularities of their new mistress were being discussed all around by the women; and Margaret's fervid eloquence was plainly at work, preparing for the revolt of Monday morning. One woman only, approached us in a friendly manner; and she came with a dish of nice plums, that grew on the place. Her name was Laura, and although black, she seemed possessed with the notion of her superiority to the sable crowd around her, the reason of which was made known to us a few days after, when we learned that she was a white man's mistress.

Monday morning came, and with it the information from Mr. Prince, that the hands had all refused to go to work. This seemed strange; for the gentleman of whom we had purchased the place, had assured us that they would go right on and work just the same as if he had not sold out. But such an idea as that looked to them altogether too much like the days of Slavery, when masters often sold land and slaves altogether. They wanted their pay for what they had done, they said; and they would not work without a new contract. Serious consequences might have ensued, if I had not immediately proceeded to the scene of revolt, and addressed them as follows: "Dr. S. has sold this place to me, and has informed Mr. Prince in this letter, that he wishes you to work, as you have done, and the contract he has made with you will be kept to the letter. You are to be paid one half of your wages at the end of every month, and the balance at the end of the year; but if you now violate this contract, you will not be able to recover any of your wages at the end of the year. You can all do as you please; Dr. S. is responsible to you for what you have already done, but for no more." Mr. Prince then stepped forward, and told them he was satisfied, and was going to work for Mr. Stearns, until the end of the year, and all who intended to do the same, he wished to go to work immediately, that I might know what to depend upon. "Black Bob," a tall, jet black, and dark-eyed negro, who seemed to act as a kind of leader, after meditating a few moments, stepped forward and said, "Well, boys, we may as well go to work I reckon;" and taking his hoe, he started for the field, followed by the remainder, some fifteen hands in all. Thus ended the second revolt upon our plantation.

CHAPTER VI.

LIGHT UPON THE PROPER METHOD OF MANAGING THE FREEDMEN.

Previous to visiting the South, the author entertained sundry impracticable notions, respecting the superiority of moral means over brute force, in managing men, which were all destined to be put to immediate flight, by the cogent reasoning of those stars of intellect, with whom he came in contact, during his journey; and he was therefore well prepared to hear the decided opinion of his overseer upon this question, he unhesitatingly affirming the negative of the proposition, that "our weapons are not carnal, but mighty through God, to the pulling down of the strong holds of Satan."

On board the steamer from Savannah to Charleston, he became acquainted with one of these unbelievers in the potency of truth: and he was assured by him that it was impossible to manage the "nigger" in any other way than by force. I mentioned to him that all my past experience in controlling men, assured me that kindness was more potent than force; and I could not see why the same rule, that had worked so well elsewhere, should not answer with the negroes.

Sitting in a little room on deck, where he had been invited by the captain of the steamer, and throwing his head back against the wall, and elevating his feet upon the next chair, he took a long inspiration from a fragrant Havana, and deliberately puffing the smoke from his mouth, he looked me full in the face, as if to satisfy himself of my sanity, and then said, in the most oracular manner imaginable, "Can't do it, can't do it, sir. Impossible, impossible." Then after taking another whiff at his cigar, and breaking off its burnt end, with the tip of his little finger, he turned towards me, and with a look of deep compassion, said, "My friend, you seem to be a novice in the art of managing niggers. Did you ever carry on a farm at the South?" I responded, "No sir," and he replied, "I thought as much. Now listen to me, and I will give you some good advice." Saying this, he touched with the tip of his finger my organ of benevolence, and said, "Don't let that organ control you, in your dealings with the niggers. Your ideas are good, very good, sir, with most men, but they will never answer in carrying on a Southern plantation. Now mark my word, sir; if you attempt to manage your hands by kindness, you will most assuredly come out of the 'little end of the horn.'" He then said his opportunities for ascertaining these facts had been very numerous; for, although not a Southerner himself, he had travelled quite extensively at the South, and knew whereof he affirmed.

I thanked him politely for the deep interest he manifested in my welfare, and I retired to a private corner of the boat, to meditate upon his advice. "Can it be," I said to myself, "that the gospel rule applies only to men who have always been free? Must there be one rule for white men, and another for colored ones?" I must confess that I was somewhat staggered in my opinions, by the deep earnestness of the man, and his professions of thorough acquaintance with the former victims of Slavery, as well as by his seeming interest in the welfare of my scheme.

Before I reached my plantation, I heard the same ideas advanced, but not by Northern men. I expected of course, to hear the Southerners take that side of the question. Every one, however, seemed to be interested in my success, and to wish to warn me of the quicksands into which I should step, if I tried to manage the negroes with kindness; so that the opinions of Mr. Prince did not astonish me in the least. "Why did you deal so roughly with Margaret yesterday?" I enquired of him. "Roughly," said he; "that's the way to deal with them; they are nothing but brutes, any how."

It was in vain that I assured him that they were human beings like ourselves. "They may be human," said he, "but they have a d—n queer way of showing it. I have had to do with 'niggers' all of my life, and I know how to manage them better than you do, Mr. Stearns." He was respectful enough in his manner towards me, but was evidently miffed that I, a green Yankee, who perhaps had not seen a dozen "niggers" in my life, should presume to criticize his way of managing those whom he had been accustomed to control all of his life.

I endeavored to argue the question with him, and finally gave him to understand that I was going to introduce a new *regime*, and try the efficacy of the law of love. He looked puzzled, scratched his head, and exclaimed, "Well, you can try it, if you wish: the plantation is yours; but I'll tell you once for all, you'll get no work out of the lazy cusses, unless you force them to it." "Well," said I, "let us try for a while the efficacy of kindness, and see what its effects will be."

Accordingly on the following Sunday, I had them all assembled in Peter's cabin, and told them my plans, and how I wished to govern them. I am not sure that they fully understood me, for they looked puzzled and yet somewhat pleased, as if a new evangel had been declared unto them. Perhaps the reader may desire to know my present opinion, after the lapse of nearly six years since the commencement of this experiment. Of course, no Christian can deny the full force of the blessed precepts of his glorious Lord and Master. To deny their potency, would be to blot out of existence the most splendid summary of moral duties the world has ever seen, and consign us back to that darkened age, when Moses' law of retaliation was the only acknowledged rule of action, by those trying to obey God. We cannot thus retire from the light of Christianity, and take refuge among the "moles and bats" of an inferior dispensation, when men's minds had not been educated into a development of man's higher nature. "Life for life, wound for wound, burning for burning, stripe for stripe," said Moses; but Jesus saith, "I say unto you, resist not evil, but if a man smite thee on one cheek, turn to him the other also." Jesus was speaking of retaliatory punishment, and not of private injury. It was the Mosaic law that he was attacking, and showing how it was to be superseded by "a new commandment, that ye love one another;" and he was not alluding to the right method of defending ourselves when attacked. At least, so it seems to me. But be that as it may, it is plain that he abjured the law of force, as expounded by Moses, who manifestly was actuated by a strict sense of justice, even-handed and fair, in what now seems some of his sanguinary regulations. It is therefore plain, that Christ's system requires kindness in our dealings with refractory individuals. Love is to be the motive in our punishment of criminals.

Now, although it is plain, that the Southern blacks are provoking in their conduct, as the case of Margaret shows; yet it is equally plain, that force alone should not be used in controlling them. My opinion, after a long and thorough trial, is, that a mixture of moral and physical means is necessary in governing them; the moving spring of which in all cases, should be overpowering *love.* Sometimes a fond parent punishes a refractory child severely. This he does, with love in his heart, and unfeigned sorrow at the sad necessity for his treatment, arising from the obstinacy of his child. He will not strike the child in the heat of passion; but calmly reason with it, and as a last resort, inflict bodily pain upon the offending little one.

Precisely so must it be with the Southerners, in their treatment of the blacks. The first step on their part is to love them. The next to reason with them; and as a last resort to punish them perhaps severely. I am free to confess that moral means alone, will not effectually control the unruly blacks. Their natures are too low at present to understand these motives; and like the whites, in their relations to our government, they construe kindness into cowardice and take advantage of the absence of punishment. Like Topsy, they defy the Miss Ophelias', and tauntingly say, "La, me, you can't hurt a misquetoe."

But this by no means justifies the absurd practice of every man judging for himself, as to the degree of punishment necessary to be inflicted upon offending men. The remedy is, for the *law* to decide for us. The establishment of *law* at the South, is the *one thing needed for the welfare of all classes.* When the blacks do wrong, let the *law* punish them, and not private individuals; and when the whites abuse the blacks let the law punish them also. It is absolutely necessary to punish the blacks for disobedience; but the *law* can only do this effectually and fairly.

But I am digressing from my narrative, and I must return to our domestic arrangements. During the week, my wife ransacked the house from garret to cellar; discovering all of its many deficiencies, and endeavoring to put everything to rights, as well as she could; but I thought I saw on her brow at the close of each day, new indications of deeper and more thorough disgust. I playfully enquired if she did not like her magnificent home, and she at length replied, "I don't see what there is to like in this hateful abode. It is all hateful from beginning to end; however, we must make the best of it, and try and put up with the poor creatures." It may be necessary to state, in order to account for some of her feelings, that while my wife detested Slavery, she was not an extravagant lover of the colored race. She said she wished them to "keep at a respectful distance" from her; but she would like to do them all the good she could. A trifling incident that occurred on the first day of her house cleaning, seemed an index of what we were to expect afterwards; and therefore affected her unpleasantly. Strange to say, we had neither of us heard of the innate propensity of the blacks to purloin from others; and therefore at first, admitted them to our house freely. She had placed a piece of soap used in cleaning, on one of the chairs which stood near an outside door, and on looking around for it, it was not to be found anywhere. Two individuals only had been in the room since it was first deposited in the chair; and they were Margaret and Black Bob. They both positively denied having seen the soap, although afterwards, each accused the other of having stolen it; and Margaret was especially incensed at the mean act of Bob, saying, "dese yer niggers, allers will steal, but I'se an honest woman, Missus. I neber steals." It was a matter of small consequence, only as it developed the existence of this terrible propensity on the part of the blacks. Stealing is no name for this trying vice. It is wholesale robbery of everything in their power to help themselves to; except articles of whose value they are ignorant. But I will not anticipate my story, except to say, that whenever I saw the overseer, he was dangling a huge bundle of keys; which unlocked all the buildings to which he had access, about twenty in all. To preserve these keys from loss was no mean achievement, if by chance any one became detached from the well guarded bunch. Then, there were our house keys, — some one of which was always getting lost; so that it was a herculean task to keep the whereabouts of each particular key, especially when several children became a part of the household; for it was about the last thing our blacks, little or big, ever thought of doing, to put everything in its proper place. The task of preserving every key intact and ready for all demands for its use, was one of the most annoying ones, of all that were allotted to us. Volume upon volume, as it were, of instruction upon this point, had to be given, before they could be made to comprehend that divine law, of "a place for everything, and everything in its place."

Margaret would go muttering about the house, as she was reproved the ninety-first time, for laying the meal house key on the cooking table, instead of hanging it on its appropriate nail, in words like these; "Dese ere white folks the most 'ticular ones me ever seed; dey beats old Missus all hollow, all the time makes such fuss 'bout that ole key; spec's I shan't stay wid 'em long."

Margaret was always threatening that if we did not like her cooking, and her ways in general, that she would leave; which is another peculiarity of some of these people. They seemed to evince but little desire to get rid of bad habits; thinking their own ways were all right.

Under the house was a sort of cellar; but it contained nothing but filth and rubbish. The milk was kept in a small house a few yards from the dwelling, in the shade of a large cedar tree; and was never carried into the cellar. The only purpose for which the cellar was used, as far as I could learn, was for a kennel for the dogs; to whose character I have already alluded. I think there were over twenty of these poor creatures upon the plantation; rendering the night hideous with their continual howlings, at every noise that at all disturbed their slumbers. But a new experience awaited us.

Reader, did you ever live among fleas, those tenacious friends of Southern dogs? Sitting one night in our dining-room, which was directly over that portion of the cellar where "most these dogs did congregate," suddenly I felt an indescribable kind of biting on one of my ankles. Supposing it was a mosquitoe, I essayed to brush it from me with my hands, when I felt it immediately on my other ankle; then on the side of my foot, then on the calf of my leg, then on my back, then on one arm, and then on the other; and yet after diligent search I could discover nothing but the place where it had been. "Horrors of horrors!" said I to Mr. Prince, who was sitting near me laughing out of one corner of his mouth, "what have you here, noiseless mosquitoes? or what?" and then remembering my Kentucky experience twenty-five years previously, I said, "O, you have ticks here, do you?"

Mr. Prince could restrain himself no longer, and he burst into an immoderate fit of laughter, after recovering from which, he exclaimed, "fleas! Mr. Stearns, nothing but fleas! they will do no harm."

"But how are we to get rid of them?" I asked.

"O, grin and bear them," he replied; "everybody at the South has fleas;" and so it proved.

By night and by day, when you sit down and when you rise up, everywhere and at all times, these omnipresent little tormenters essay to worry the life out of you. Tongue cannot tell the torment of my poor wife, at the constant bites of these ferocious insects, who seemed to prey more voraciously upon delicate female flesh, than upon the coarser texture of the masculine gender. Mr. Prince declared he never minded it at all, but "they do torment some people tremendously."

On diligent enquiry, however, I ascertained that if the dog kennel below was broken up, that some at least of our neighbors would leave us; and so I proceeded to clean out this "Augean stable." We removed about twenty wheel-barrow loads of dirt from the cellar; then strewed over its bottom some fine straw, and covered that with a sprinkling of sulphur, and set the whole on fire. It was somewhat of a hazardous undertaking, for one of the negroes, a year or two previously, in trying the same experiment, for a different object, however, had burned down one of the negro houses, and lost his life; but the fleas must be got rid of, or we could not live there much longer; so after taking every precaution to extinguish the fire, if it burned too fiercely, we resolved to attempt the task, and we succeeded admirably. The fleas vanished into thin air, and for a season we were delivered from our reckless tormentors. The cellar was also rendered sweet, and fit to be used for our milk and churning.

For the benefit of those similarly afflicted, I would state that there grew in our, as in most Southern gardens, a bountiful supply of double tansy, small sprigs of which, scattered over your bed at night, and placed inside of your under garments, and in your boots by day, will drive away these horrible tormentors of the human frame. It takes an expert to kill these hungry little creatures. Many a time have I rubbed the life out of one of them, as I supposed, and the little creature, after enduring this terrible mauling, would spring up, shake its tiny frame, and jump away as lively as ever; having not only the nine fabulous lives of a cat, but literally ninety and nine. Some of our family could never succeed in crushing the life out of one of them, and I was enabled to do so, only after taking lessons from old hands in the business.

CHAPTER VII.

OUR FIRST SUNDAY SCHOOL.

Just one week after our first Sunday, as already described, we assembled the whole plantation in Peter Freeman's cabin, the largest on the place, and organized them into a Sunday school. Not a man, woman, or child knew a letter of the alphabet, how to count, or indeed any nameable thing about which we asked them. They knew absolutely nothing about the country in which they lived; not even the name of the man who gave them their freedom. They had heard of Gen. Sherman, and of the North; but what it was, they could not tell. The only Washington of which they had ever heard, was one in an adjoining county, to which led the road that passed our house. They knew that they lived in Columbia County, and that "Karlina" was not far off; and this was the sum total of their geographical knowledge.

With this "darkness that might be felt," we had to cope. We had some freedmen's papers with us, containing the alphabet; and with them we commenced our first intellectual training of these poor creatures, over whose stunted intellects the dark night of Slavery had hovered so fearfully. To look at the poor children was enough to wring tears from a heart of stone. Some of them had only the vestige of clothing upon them; and one little urchin was as entirely destitute thereof as when first born into the world; and all bore in their imbruted countenances the unmistakable marks of extreme stupidity. As I saw them, and gazed upon their almost idiotic faces, I said to myself, "Is it possible that God can have created them, as well as us?" I did not at all wonder that some persons had been disposed to deny their humanity: they looked so destitute of all intelligence.

At a later period of our abode here, we saw a lad from a darker county than even ours, whose looks forcibly reminded me of those of our children when we first came among them; precisely that idiotic stare and shame-facedness, when you questioned them. It seemed to have been the settled purpose of their masters to reduce these poor creatures as nearly to the condition of brutes, as would consist with their interest. It was indeed important that they should know how to hoe corn, and "chop out" cotton; but further knowledge than this, there did not seem to be much necessity for.

This ignorance cannot be imagined by those who have never witnessed its direful presence. Imagine one in the form of a human being, with all his exterior appendages perfect, but his mind an utter blank, "dead, twice dead, and plucked up by the roots." If we had never hated Slavery before, we certainly did after beholding its terrific effect, upon these poor imbruted ones. Our very language had to be interpreted to them, by selecting such words as were familiar to them, and clothing our ideas in them alone; a task that greatly increased the labor of instructing them. Often, when you supposed you had made an idea so plain that a dog could almost understand it, on questioning them, you found that they had not comprehended it at all.

Once, in expatiating upon the joys of the future life, and dwelling on the fact that we must certainly leave this world sooner or later, I made the remark, "You have all got to leave this country, and a heavenly one is before you, if you are righteous, and keep the commandments of God." At the close of the meeting, some one not present ran up to me and said, "Mr. Stearns, is it true that you said Gen. Sherman was coming, and going to take us all to the North, by force?" And thus my striking appeal, as I regarded it, was lost upon them.

At another time, my meaning was so grossly misapprehended, that their interpretation of it did not bear the faintest resemblance to what I had intended to say. But not only were they ignorant of theology, and dull in the exercise of the reflective faculties, but still more in their use of the perceptive ones, being especially deficient in the faculty of memory. Their cruel masters seemed to have sought to close every avenue of knowledge against them, even in reference to the simplest tasks of life, aside from their daily labor. The children, and many of the adults, did not know their right hands from their left, *literally*. They did not know their own ages, nor those of their children, except that they were born in planting time, picking cotton time, or about Christmas. They did not know the names of the months, or how many days there were in each month.

They knew nothing of the points of compass, of distances, or of weights and measures. If you asked them how much ground they supposed there was in a certain enclosure containing perhaps three-fourths of an acre, they would usually guess that there were two or three acres. Of the age of the world, of course they had not the faintest idea, whether it was hundreds of years, or millions of years old. It astonished them to learn that the earth was round, and required great confidence on their part in their new teachers, to believe so strange an assertion; and the idea that the earth moved around the sun, was utterly incomprehensible to them.

Such utter and complete ignorance I had never dreamed of; and I suppose some of my readers are even now doubting my veracity. But let me repeat, that in all of my descriptions of these evils, I purposely fall short of the truth, rather than to be guilty of the slightest exaggeration, as it is my only purpose to write of things as they really were. After five and a half years residence among them, I am happy to say, that in no respect do they seem the same individuals that they were on my first arrival. Of course, I do not feel satisfied with the result of so few years' labor; but I can happily perceive a vast difference between those days and to-day.

And here let me say, that the difference between the plantation negroes and those dwelling in large towns, is almost heaven wide. In Augusta, especially, the colored people, by associating so much with their employers in the way of business, and especially by picking up information from travellers, had attained to a respectable degree of knowledge on common things; but in the dark and dismal country, it was far different. Those whose labors at the South have been confined to cities, can never fully appreciate the greatness of our task.

On religious subjects they were just as ignorant as on common affairs; but as their religion will be treated upon separately and minutely, I will omit further reference to that, except to say, that if the most degraded heathen understood Christianity, then did these people comprehend what it is to be a Christian.

The order of exercises afterwards adopted in our Sunday school was something as follows: Commencing at half past one or two o'clock P. M., we devoted one hour to teaching the alphabet; and as soon as any had mastered that, lessons in reading were given to them, from Parker and Watson's National Primer. Then another hour was devoted to various oral exercises, such as geography, arithmetic, history, spelling, and any subject of general information that might be suggested at the time. Then half or three-quarters of an hour was devoted to the simplest religious instruction, using afterwards the interesting lesson papers, furnished us by the Trinity Methodist church of Springfield, Mass: and formerly a series of questions and answers drawn up by the teacher, and sometimes question-books, sent us from the North; but the latter were generally too much above the comprehension of our scholars, to be used without much explanation.

Understanding the importance of fixing their attention upon the lessons, we adopted the plan of having them repeat in concert, passages from the Scriptures, usually from the Psalms, and then questioning them as to what they had repeated, and explaining its meaning. Another oral exercise was, for a class to read in the Bible, and then require the remainder of the school to tell what the class had read, thus securing their attention during the reading. We always required each class, at the close of their lessons, to tell in their own language what they had been reading about, so as to fasten in their memories the information given in the books. We occasionally introduced into our exercises the practice of marching around the room in single file, the scholars repeating after the teacher the multiplication table, some verses from Scripture, and singing a Sunday school hymn, adapted to that purpose. At this time, several of the larger scholars were allowed to carry little Union flags, and sometimes each scholar carried a beautiful flower in his or her hand. We almost always closed these exercises by reading a pretty story from one of the many invaluable Sunday school papers, with which we were liberally furnished by various Northern Sunday schools; and once a month, each scholar who had been punctual at school during the month, received one of these little picture-papers, which they prized very highly.

After all of these exercises were finished, the whole occupying about two and a half hours, our regular meeting was commenced, which was conducted like religious meetings elsewhere, with singing, prayer, reading of Scripture, with explanations, and a sermon.

Oftentimes at the close of our exercises, the blacks continued their meetings for an hour, in their own way, engaging in singing, religious dancing, &c., until the setting sun gave notice of the time to adjourn.

It may be asked why all these services were crowded into one afternoon, without an intermission. The reply to this question is, that it was the choice of the blacks to have a long meeting of a diversified nature, in preference to coming at different hours, and we found from experience that if an intermission was allowed, many of the scholars or hearers would not return until the remainder of the exercises were nearly closed, so great was their want of punctuality. Besides, the bulk of our scholars were from neighboring plantations, and if an intermission at noon was given, our hands complained of their being obliged to furnish refreshments for many of the crowd, which the slender state of their own larders, rendered quite a hardship. So all things considered, it was deemed best to allow them the morning to themselves, to fix up their houses and arrange their dresses, and only require of them attendance upon our services in the afternoon. Occasionally, there were other services in the neighborhood, during the forenoon, and this arrangement gave those who wished, an opportunity to attend them, and afterwards to come to our meeting.

At the final close of the public services, many of the learners made personal visits to the teacher, asking of him every variety of questions, and often expressing much gratitude for our labors in their behalf.

During the week succeeding our first meeting, our hearts were made glad by the arrival on our plantation of Mr. Holmes Parker, a son of the gentleman who had accompanied me from the North, but had returned home. Young Mr. Parker entered into the spirit of our work with great enthusiasm, and faithfully seconded all of our efforts in behalf of the colored people, as well as originated many himself. Without his timely presence, the dreary summer hours, after my wife and child's absence, could not have been so well endured, for we had no more society, as far as our white neighbors were concerned, than if we had lived among the Hottentots.

Mr. P. spent all his leisure hours in teaching the blacks, evenings, and at other times, and in giving them much valuable instruction in reference to business matters, and he became a general favorite among them.

At this first meeting, I took occasion to tell them of the new relations they sustained to mankind, and that the eyes of the world were upon them, watching their conduct; their enemies, so as to say that freedom was a curse, and their friends, so that they could refute the accusations of their enemies, who declared that they would not work, now that they were free. I conjured them to act so as to disprove all these accusations of their enemies, and to show to the world that they were worthy of the great boon of freedom.

While thus discoursing to them, a pair of eyes belonging to a pale face were fastened eagerly upon me, and not recollecting at first to whom they belonged, I began to hesitate and weigh well each word as I uttered it, supposing that a "rebel" had come in to "spy out the land"; but I was agreeably surprised on discovering that they looked out from a soul full of interest in the great experiment we were all trying. The person who thus confronted me was Mr. Josiah Sherman, who had rode from his plantation sixteen miles distant, with his accomplished lady, to become acquainted with the only Northern man of whom he had heard, who was engaged in the same business with himself. He was from Washington, Co. N. Y., and had come South the previous Fall, and engaged in farming, not long after. Mr. S. made a short address to our sable auditory, in harmony with the views already presented.

Our next meeting was held under the large trees in our dooryard, and was numerously attended by the hands from other plantations. By this time, I had been able to manufacture a large blackboard, on which my friend Holmes, drew in good style the letters of the Alphabet; and all became interested in learning them.

Some of the scholars learned quite easily, and others experienced much difficulty in remembering them. The tenor of my remarks to them at this second meeting was, to show them that it was for their interest in this world to do right; that "godliness was great gain."

We were now fairly underway with one portion of our "panaceas" for the ills the blacks were afflicted with. At noon and at night, at nearly every cabin door could be seen a little knot of these crushed ones, with a little paper or book in their hands, doing their best to master the alphabet and its succeeding mysteries.

But we were not destined thus to encroach upon the time-honored customs of our Southern friends, without receiving some severe rebukes. It was not long before threatening messages came to us, that if we did not desist from teaching the negroes, we should be abused in some way, the exact character of which we were left to imagine. The expressions used in the messages sent to us were: "Tell that d—n Yankee that if he does not leave off teaching the niggers, we will come some night and *give him hell.*" Not knowing but that some of these gentry, from their intimate acquaintance with the place, might be able to control some of its fiery elements, we began to "shake in our shoes."

Once, a man rode by the place, and delivered the message in "*propria personæ:*" at another time, it came second-handed. Mr. Parker, having fought in the first Colorado Regiment, with the red man of the forest, and being a good marksman, did not seem to fear the rebels so much; but I, having been all of my life a "man of peace," comparatively, rather dreaded an encounter with them; but nevertheless, I nerved myself up for the contest, and replenished my excellent breach-loading rifle with fresh ammunition, and we stood ready to meet our foe. We took the precaution, however, to chain at night all the gates opening into our yard, and obtained the services of a number of valiant dogs; and then with guns on our shoulders, we spent many a weary night, in parading our front yard, my friend and I, alternating, in this arduous duty. A few times, we gladly availed ourselves of the offers of the blacks, to aid us in guarding our premises; but after a few trials, we found that the poor fellows were so overcome with their daily labors in the field, that they slept at their posts in the night, and we concluded to dispense with their services.

Some of our neighbors informed us that they did not disapprove of our labors, and an excellent physician living near us declared that he had always been in favor of educating the negroes. Another neighbor said he had "nothing against my doing it, but he did not wish to do it himself."

At length a friendly overseer from a neighboring plantation called to see us, and assured us of his sympathy in our efforts; but on my inviting him to come and join our school, he said, "I should like to come, as far as I am concerned, but I do not dare to do so, from fear of the planters about." I expressed to him my surprise at the blindness of the planters on this subject, saying that, "it seems to me that the labor of an intelligent man is worth nearly double that of an ignorant one"; and I asked him why he supposed they were so much opposed to my efforts. This was his reply, "*verbatim et literatim.*" "They are mad because they lost their slaves, and they say, 'd — n them, if they are educated, they will know as much as we know.'" I cannot vouch for the correctness of this remark; I only repeat it as he gave it to me. My own opinion is, that they did not fear this equality so much as they pretended; for, as I told one of them, "You know more than they do now, and if you keep on learning, and they do the same, how can they ever overtake you?" This must be so apparent to them, that I think they had another reason for their opposition to these meetings, viz: they entirely misapprehended me and my motives in coming to their neighborhood, and doubtless regarded me as a political emissary from the North, come to instill into the minds of the blacks false notions of political and social equality. If they had ever come to my meetings, and listened to my remarks, I think they must have approved of them. Probably they did not wish their former slaves to become so enlightened as to pass from their control; but I do not think the Southern people as a whole, at all comprehend the earnest desire existing in Northern minds, to teach and instruct all their fellow men, in whatever portion of the earth they may reside; the spirit of unselfish love is so foreign to the natures of the large majority of Southerners. I am the more inclined to this opinion from the fact that at one time a gentleman happened to pass the place while I was speaking, and he stopped, and sat on his horse and listened attentively for a long time, while I addressed the blacks on their new duties as freedmen, and told them the North set them free, in order that they might secure their services in bringing the war to a close. I had heard that this gentleman was a regular "fire-eater," and so, when at the close of my discourse, he approached me, I prepared myself for a severe rebuke; but I was surprised to hear him say to me, "I have been very much interested in your remarks; I like them very much." I have often met this gentleman since on the highway, and he always greets me with a pleasant smile, totally unlike the frigid manner with which I am met by most of my Southern acquaintances.

The Rev. Dr. Parker, formerly pastor of Shawmut Avenue Baptist church of Boston, was once listened to attentively by several very rabid rebels, as he discoursed on my place, on the duties of the freedmen; and they all declared at the close that they were much pleased with his remarks, and he was invited to preach in a white church not far distant, which invitation however, was afterwards revoked.

I am sure, if the Southerners had attended our meetings constantly, they would have regarded me as their best friend, as I am in reality; for if my directions to the negroes had been obeyed, they would never have had any trouble with them. I call on high heaven to witness, that instead of having tried to "stir up" the blacks against them, it has been my unceasing endeavor to create an opposite feeling in their minds. Instead of fanning the flame of discontent already burning briskly in their hearts, I have sedulously endeavored to throw "oil upon the troubled waters," both from principle and from expediency. I am, and always have been, in favor of returning "good for evil," and of endeavoring to restrain the worst of men, and to govern them by and with the law of kindness, instead of administering to them punishment with a "cat-of-nine-tails."

But I am digressing from my narrative. I shall have something to say hereafter about the rebels and their treatment of the blacks, and the methods we should use for the protection of the latter. The kind and fatherly protection of the law in all of its majesty, should be the heavenly ægis, placed before all classes, to protect them alike, from the abuses of their fellows; and this law should be administered with rigid and impartial justice, as well as dictated by kind and heavenly feelings.

CHAPTER VIII.

VISIT TO SOME OF THE NEGRO CABINS, AND APPEARANCE OF THE FARM IN GENERAL.

Our own domicil having been made tolerable comfortable, and measures adopted for the intellectual and moral improvement of those around us, we next turned our attention to their physical condition. Summoning all our resolution, we first commenced a tour of exploration of the negro cabins, eleven in number.

Our first visit was to the cabin of Susan; a stout woman of about forty-five years of age, whose husband was a carpenter, and worked away from the plantation, but came home every Saturday night, and sometimes oftener. They had several grown children, and two younger ones; a boy of about eleven, named Glenn, and a little girl about four years old named Georgiana. Susan related to me some of her experience in slavery. She said, that when her babe was only a month old, her mistress had whipped her with three hundred lashes on her bare back, because her boy had taken off his shoes, contrary to the orders of her mistress.

She said her mistress was much harder with her than her master; not an uncommon occurrence at the South, I afterwards found. In those days, Susan did all the cooking, bringing and cutting the wood herself, and milking the cows; and after breakfast, she was obliged to go into the field and work until it was time to get dinner. She then prepared the dinner, and afterwards cleared away the dinner table; and then worked in the field again until night, when she was called to the house to cook the supper; and her day's labors were not finished until nearly eleven o'clock at night.

When I entered her cabin, she said, "I am right glad to see you, for it 'pears like as if Georgiana would never mend. Please, sir, come in and tell me what to do for her."

I entered an inner room, with hardly a ray of light penetrating it, except what came through the open door as we passed in; and there was Georgiana, sure enough, not very likely to get well under the treatment she was receiving. The one great bugbear of the South in the way of disease, is the chills and fever; and to guard against the former, the poor child was rolled and wrapped up in old quilts, dirty blankets, and parts of dresses, until she was completely saturated with perspiration. Her head also was closely covered; this being a well known peculiarity of the blacks, to keep their heads warm, even if their feet are cold. The child was in a burning fever, and in addition to the bedding, her body was clothed in the thickest garments belonging to her mother, and all to keep off the chills. I felt of her head and pulse, and found that she was alive.

"Can you help her any, Mr. Stearns?" said her anxious mother. "Her pa says, he wishes you would try and see if you could do anything for her."

I pulled off the bedclothes, opened the window shutter, and ordered some cold water brought, with which I bathed her freely, to show her mother how it was to be done; ordered a wet cloth to be put on her head, and a free circulation of air to be kept up in the room. I then returned to our house and soon re-entered Susan's cabin, with a small black case of little pills of all kinds, from which I selected a few of the "fever pills," and telling Susan of their wonderful virtues, I left them with her, with directions for their use. Then thinking it would be a favorable time to commence a housekeeping reform on the place, I availed myself of my rights as a "doctor," and examined her house quite thoroughly, and ordered all the offal and rubbish which I everywhere saw, to be removed instantly, if she expected her child to recover. I cannot now remember everything I saw there; but I well recollect that old vessels containing a variety of unhealthy smelling substances, abounded in different parts of her room, Under the bed of the child, there seemed to be a deposit of old bones, which she was saving I think for soap grease; and from every corner of the house, came an unsavory smell, enough of itself to make a well person sick.

Susan went to work with alacrity to purify her room, and when I visited it the next day, the change was complete, not only in the room but in the health of Georgiana. "O, she's a heap better," said Susan, "'pears like them pills have saved her life. I'm so much obliged to you Mr. Stearns, please lemme have some of them to keep." I was of course pleased to witness my success as a physician, so soon. Whether the great improvement was due to the pills, or to my sanitary prescriptions, I am not able to say; but the pills became very famous from that day, and soon my supply was exhausted.

The cabins were generally destitute of most articles of furniture, except an old broken chair or two, and a wooden bench. Such a thing as sitting down to a table to eat, was utterly unknown to them at that time; each one taking his hoe-cake in one hand, and a slice of fried pork in the other. It was seldom that anything in the shape of food, but these two articles was seen in their houses. They had for their rations three pounds of pork, and one peck of meal a piece, per week. The overseer told me this was a plenty for them, and "a greater variety of food, would render them unfit for work." "See how fat they look!" said he, pointing to a few specimens of the well fed ones, who were standing near. I could not reconcile it, however, to my conscience, to give them nothing else; and on enquiry, I found they liked molasses exceedingly, and I purchased a barrel, and gave them a regular allowance of that, the remainder of the time they worked for wages. My conscience at first, was not quite clear in the matter of their food; until one day I observed a bag of something in the possession of the man who drove me into town, and on asking what it was, I learned that it was meal, that he had left from his rations; which he was intending to sell. It seemed that a peck of meal per week, was more than one person could eat; but when a man, his wife and six children are obliged to live on two pecks, on the allowance for a man and his wife; then some of the children are likely to go to bed supperless. Still they seemed to prefer even this short allowance to their slavery fare; saying, that they often went hungry then, and it was of no advantage to them. "Now," they said, "if we don't take extra rations, we save our money for clothes." How human beings can enjoy good health on so meagre a diet, I cannot see; but the great majority of the hands did actually enjoy better health under this strict regime, than when afterwards it was so arranged that they could have a more generous diet. I tried to persuade them to receive double the number of pounds of rice or beans in lieu of a part of their pork; but not one would accept of the offer. Every negro garden abounds in that universal Southern esculent, the *collard;* a plant closely resembling the cabbage, but cooked in the form of "greens;" and used nearly the whole year. This article is devoured eagerly by the Southern people, both white and black; and is not despised by even the Northern residents.

The blacks also have their "patches," where they raise corn of their own, sweet potatoes, and a variety of other vegetables, of which they could get two or three crops in a season. The corn they boil whole, and also use it in the form of roasting ears. The sweet potatoes are banked up in the Fall, and last until late in the Spring, if proper care is taken of them, never opening a bank on a chilly day.

Susan's cabin was a fair example of the whole, and I will not exhaust the reader's patience by repeating a description of the same scene. Occasionally we found one a little more aristocratic than the rest, and the cabin of such an one was somewhat neater; but evidently none had ever lived among the Quakers, or dreamed of such a thing as household neatness. Many of them had chickens, cats and dogs running and lying in and around their houses, and several were the envious owners of large hogs, who roamed over the premises at will, seeming to have an undisputed right to obtain a living, at the expense of the crops around them.

They evidently had availed themselves of Horace Greeley's advice to their owners, and were in no danger of dying from starvation, from want of "rooting."

I cannot here forbear relating an amusing incident that occurred at a later day of my sojourn among the colored people. A party had visited me at my dwelling, to lay before me some petty grievance they were suffering at the hands of the overseer. After listening with patience, I told them I would endeavor to rectify the abuse; and I wished whatever trouble they had, they would always come and tell me, for I meant to see that justice was always done to them. Thus encouraged, Frank, a fine specimen of a man, came forward, and with true eloquence depicted their former condition as slaves, and then wound up with the following appeal to my benevolence. I had previous to this forbidden them to keep hogs, except at a distance from their houses, on account of the bad odor arising from so many hog-pens near the dwelling-houses. Lifting up his hands, he exclaimed, in pathetic style, "Mr. Stearns, you say you are our friend, and you wish to elevate us, and I don't doubt your word; now tell us, how *can we be elevated without hogs?*" Saying this, he retired from the front rank of the crowd, as if his argument was unanswerable, and awaited my reply. I could not resist the inclination to laugh aloud at the incongruity of the idea of *hogs* and *elevation* being connected with each other; but at length recovering my equanimity, I said to him, "Frank, I have known the owners of hogs who loved them so much as to give them a part of their own houses; and yet they were the most degraded of persons. Now if you wish to become truly elevated, I would advise you to think less of eating pork, and more of learning your letters." Frank was not particularly fond of his books.

After visiting the remainder of the cabins in the quarters, we re-entered our yard, and stopped for a moment to call upon our cook, in her own domains. Margaret tried to appear pleasant, but it was evident that she did not relish the idea of a white man's coming to her cabin, to spy out its defects. I did not remain long, as I had concluded the way to get along with Margaret was, not to tread upon her toes too much. With all of her roughness, she liked kind words, and especially those savoring of flattery. Said I, "Margaret, I have been visiting the black peoples' cabins, and I thought you would feel slighted, if I did not call upon you, also." This somewhat smoothed off the sharp points of her porcupine nature, and as she shuffled around, with her shoe heels dragging on the floor, according to her custom, she said, "I'se been cook for de white folks all my life. I knows how folks ought to live, I does. I ant like dem ar niggers down in de quarters." But like many others of our own race who boast the most, Margaret fell short, rather than exceeded others, in the matter of personal cleanliness. Indeed, I concluded that if I was to eat of her cooking, I should hereafter pay but very few visits to the place where the food was prepared; at least, not without blind-folding my eyes.

The fire-place of her cabin was of unusual dimensions, and contained a bountiful supply of fuel, some of which was nearly six feet in length, and it all rested upon huge rocks, placed in the fire-place, in room of andirons. A large shelf over the fire-place served for a place of general deposit for whatever article happened to be in the way, and contained among other things a dirty rag, used for a dish-cloth, a small pile of dusty cotton, a lot of rusty nails, some pieces of pork rind, bits of biscuit and of corn bread, a quantity of egg-shells, a small piece of tobacco, and an old pipe. Of course, at a casual glance, I could only see a small portion of the articles there deposited.

"You need not look at dat ar shelf. Massa, dem's my private property," exclaimed Margaret; and with a sweep of her capacious hand, she brushed them all into her apron, and walked away with a triumphant air, before I could tell her I had no wish to disturb her property.

Numerous little chickens were picking up the dough scattered over the floor; and two old hens stood on the table, eating out of the wooden dish, in which she mixed our corn cakes. A hungry dog was crouched in one corner, feasting upon a portion of a shoulder of pork; and five little half naked urchins, were licking with their fingers the various pots and kettles that stood in the room. The table on which she prepared our food, was an immense one, and served for cupboard and pantry, as well as for mixing Johnny-cake, and washing dishes. To call it a dirty table, would be far from describing its true character. It was literally black with filth, and could not have been washed since its first appearance on the plantation.

On the table were the following articles; first, the unwashed tin milk pail; secondly, a bag of meal with a sifter on its top; thirdly, a large piece of bacon from which she had just sliced her morning meal; then dishes without number, all, more or less cracked or broken, and the wooden dish, containing ours and the hens' food, a tin pan of bones, half a dozen iron spoons, as many forks with their tines broken; and several knives whose blades had been used in hacking up her rather tough, and sometimes bony articles of food. On one end of the table, were lying several pieces of kindling wood, and by their side, a large pine knot, used for a flambeau in the night.

Under the table there was lying an old hat belonging to Richard her husband; five or six old shoes, and a horse collar made of shucks. Near them, stood a basket of chips, a dirty pail filled with slops for a favorite hog, and a large tin pan of ashes; and in close proximity to them a pile of tin pans, and various pots and kettles half filled with dirty water, out of which the ragged children were regaling themselves, occupied a corner of the spacious fireplace.

The room contained three old chairs, and hanging on the back of one of them, was Margaret's sun bonnet, rather cleaner than her dress. When we entered the room, Margaret was cooking some eggs for our dinner by boiling them *hard* in a tea kettle. On our asking her if she was not afraid she was cooking them too much, her reply was, "You done said yesterday dem eggs wasn't half done, and I thought I'd please you to-day." This was her peculiarity. If to-day there was too much soda in the corn bread, to-morrow there would be none. If the potatoes were half done yesterday, to-day they would be burned up or boiled to pieces. Of such a thing as a happy medium in her cooking, Margaret had never dreamed. If the coffee was too hot to-day, to-morrow it would be stone cold; and so with everything.

It was evident that she considered it entirely beneath

her dignity to touch the floor of her cabin with a broom or mop; and it now needed a sharp hoe, to make an impression upon its surface. The sides and top of the room were black with smoke, and innumerable cobwebs hung in graceful festoons all around the walls. Evidently she and the spiders did not often fall out with each other.

One of the boards of the floor was a little cleaner than the others, which was accounted for by its being a kind of trap door, that opened upon the nests of three or four hens, under the house, from which most of the eggs for our dinners were taken. The reader's pardon is asked, for this lengthy description of unimportant matters. It is given, not for the purpose of burlesquing Margaret, or any other of the poor creatures so lately delivered from Slavery's iron grasp, but in order to present a true picture of the effects of Slavery, and of the condition of some of the freedmen.

We come now to the general appearance of the farm. If there is one word more applicable than another to the whole of Southern life, it is that expressive Yankee term, *shiftlessness*. Almost everything connected with the South, partakes of the opposite of what Yankees term, *thriftiness*. There is one everlasting ship-shod way of doing everything that is accounted worthy of doing at all. When a Yankee first reaches the South, his impulse is to set everything to rights, and he begins re-arranging and re-modelling all around him; but as often as he re-arranges, some one else returns things to their old places, and restores the partially disturbed reign of chaos, until at length he yields to the irresistible power around him, and abandons his reformatory labors as hopeless. It is, as when in the midst of a driving storm of wind and rain—you button your coat tightly around you, and press on valiantly towards your home, occasionally gasping for breath, until a more furious blast than ever sweeps over you, and the rain descends more piteously than before; and then you crouch before the angry elements, and gladly rush for protection to a stalwart tree you discover near you. It is of no use to war with these angry elements of carelessness and stupidity, you exclaim, and you soon become metamorphosed into a careless, ease-loving Southerner. Why this difference exists, I know not. That such is the case any Southerner can satisfy himself, by spending a few weeks among the average of Northern towns and villages, and then comparing them with his own. Even when a tree falls on the highway at the South, it sometimes remains there for years, while at the North it would be removed in a few days. Our farm was no exception to this all prevalent spirit. Not a tool or utensil of any kind was in its place at all times, unless such a place was anywhere and everywhere. The moment a negro has done using a tool, he drops it instanter; and if you wish to know where a certain tool is to be found, you should only ascertain if possible who used it last, and where he used it; and on going to that place, you will probably find it, half-rusty and besmeared with dirt.

Our yard, which was once beautifully arranged with trees and flowers, had become a receptacle for every nameable thing used on a farm, all of which were scattered about promiscuously. Old wheels stood against the trees, near the door of our dining-room. Broken plows and hoes were strewn all around. Wagons and parts of wagons stood where they had been last used.

Every part of the yard was cut up with wagon tracts; trees had been run against, and partially divested of their bark; and some of them had been hacked by careless urchins, and some cut nearly down. A huge meat-block stood not far from the side entrance to our house, on whose broad surface the colored women of the place were in the habit of "*batting*" their clothes; a process which consists in lifting the garments from the kettle of warm water, and shaking some of the water from them, and then pounding them partly dry with a heavy paddle. This made the water fly all around, and was good sport for the younger ones. At times, in the absence of a paddle, the clothes would be struck several times with great force against the meat-block. Once I saw a young girl perform this operation of "batting" upon the back of another girl, for want of a convenient block.

A large fire was built in our yard, in front of the kitchen, on washing day, and a huge iron kettle placed over it, and around it was a squad of women, doing their washing. The dirty water stood in puddles all around, and the children and hogs played in them, for their amusement. When the washing was over, the tubs of dirty water were left standing in the yard. This nuisance was a sore one to abate, and it took a long time to bring about its removal. I am sorry to be obliged to say, that if "order is heaven's *first* law," it was the last one that any one on our plantation thought of obeying. Oh, what a battle we were obliged to fight, with these elements of disorder! What sickness of soul came upon us, when we saw that disorder was destined to reign forever on "Hope On Hope Ever" plantation!

To-day, although the change is great, yet one's nerves

are continually shocked by the numerous evidences yet apparent, of the reign of this evil genius. No man can be trusted. If you keep all of your tools under lock and key, and lend them only when you think they will be taken care of, in nine cases out of ten, you must spend considerable time in searching for the loaned article. Innumerable tools, and a vast amount of property are thus annually wasted, on every plantation, I presume; for I know of no reason for supposing that our negroes were worse than others; unless they took advantage of my known desire, not to be unkind to them. When I reached our place, we had three complete sets of carpenter's tools; but hardly had a year elapsed, before more than half of them had vanished. It was so in relation to everything else. If a board fell from a building, there it always remained, until some one else than a black man ordered it replaced; or it had been used for fuel. Fences were blown down, and thus remained. Wagons were broken, and no one would ever tell you; and unless you happened to discover the injury, the destruction of the wagon would be complete.

During my residence here, I have seldom if ever, known a black man to come and tell me that any damage had been done to any of my property. I suppose this is another of the fruits of slavery.

What did the slave care for the destruction of his master's property? *He* would not suffer any more, if everything went to "rack and ruin" around him. Sometimes I am tempted to think that the negroes take an insane delight in seeing property wasted; but I am inclined to think it is not so, but that their carelessness arises from this habit of utter indifference to the welfare of the white man; a natural fruit of slavery.

But be that as it may. It is a source of constant

annoyance to every orderly person; not only in the field and out of doors, but above all in the house. Here the goddess of disorder holds her especial throne; as if to mock all the puny efforts of white women, to present a pleasant spectacle to their husbands and visitors. But I will not anticipate my story. Suffice it to say, that the one grand and everlasting source of misery to every Yankee resident of the South, must be the entire and overwhelming destruction of all of his ideas of *order in the house.* To have your home, that should be a paradise of neatness and heavenly order, turned into a "den of thieves," and become the "habitation of every foul thing," is almost like a transition from heaven to hell; but it is a fate from which I can see no possible way of escape, except by banishing from your house the whole horde of Southern servants, and substituting therefor, those of Northern origin, and Northern habits.

Etta fought against it for awhile, and then started for the North, to recruit her exhausted strength, and pour her griefs into the ears of sympathizing Northern friends. She only remained at the plantation about a month from the time of her first arrival; during which time, she maintained an unmitigated warfare against all of this disorder and anarchy. She and Margaret, were almost always at "swords' points," in the matters of cooking, and household arrangements. After she left, Mr. Parker and I concluded to accept Mr. Prince's advice in reference to the fleas; and "grin and bear" Margaret's deficiences, as the grace of God might enable us, trusting to the future, for an end of our miseries.

Mr. Parker especially ingratiated himself with her finely, by occasionally complimenting her personal appearance; particularly when she "came out" with a new turban. I had less patience with her; but between us both we managed to get along with her during the summer. When it was time for the eggs to be cooked, Holmes would take his watch and stand at the door of our dining-room, and call to Margaret, and tell her the exact moment to put the eggs in, and then to take them out; always allowing for several seconds to elapse between the hearing of the last order and the final taking them out of the tea kettle. It was impossible for Margaret to understand how to make good "Johnny-cake," although she knew how to cook corn bread, after their own fashion, which is merely to mix meal and water together, with a little salt. At last I determined to see for myself how she mixed the ingredients I had prepared for her, the proportions of which I had obtained from a copy of "Beadle's dime cook-book," which I luckily found among my old books. I proceeded to her domain and soon found that she had failed to prepare the dough as I told her, she using too much water; which is another peculiarity of the colored people, never to be exact in anything. I seized the meal, soda and cream tartar and molasses, and mixed up a cake myself, and had the satisfaction of having a palatable corn cake for breakfast that day, and as often afterwards as I could thus superintend the cook. This was the more necessary, for Margaret understood no more the art of making flour bread or biscuit, than she did the mysteries of Algebra or Euclid. When remonstrated with for her failure to use the ingredients in their right proportions, her invariable reply was, "What's de use ob being so 'ticular, old massa and missus neber said anyting if de corn bread wasn't so good ebery time," and then she would mutter over to herself, words like these, "dem Yankees is a darn sight meaner than de old rebs; it's no use to try to suit 'em."

CHAPTER IX.

SOUTHERN FARMING, AND ITS RESULTS.

In everythiug that relates to farming operations, the Southern people are at least fifty years behind the times; and the old story of the man's carrying the pumpkins from his field one at a time, with a stone in the other end of his bag to balance the pumpkin, because his father had always done so, applies admirably to the Southern system. It's enough for the blacks to know that, "My ole massa" always ploughed in a particular manner, to justify them in so doing. Such an innovation as deep ploughing, looks like sacrilege to them.

When I suggested to my overseer the propriety of ploughing a piece of ground with a two-horse plough, and harrowing it in well after the Northern style, he replied that the wheat would never come up, if ploughed in that style. I determined, however, to try the experiment, and procured four double ploughs, manufactured in Boston, and set the men to work with them; but they all declared it would ruin the ground, the mules, and the crops; but I persisted, and they persisted also, and *would not* plough deep, saying, "Them ar ploughs is no account, Mr. S.: we can do noting wid 'em." Not understanding much about ploughing myself, I failed to see "where the shoe pinched," even after a thorough examination of the ploughs, and therefore hitched up my mules, and drove fifteen miles, to a Northern farmer's, who gave me the requisite information, and I returned and endeavored to have the ploughs altered according to my friend's directions. In this I was almost as unsuccessful as in the matter of deep ploughing; for no one of the hands or the overseer, could possibly divine how to take the ploughs to pieces and put them together again. After many ineffectual attempts, Mr. Prince came to me and declared that the "pesky things" were of "no manner of account," and advised me to throw them aside, and fall back upon the good old-fashioned single ploughs, such as "we all know how to use;" and with a truly conservative air that would have done credit to a Northern politician of the antediluvian age, he said, "Mr. S., I never did like any of these new-fangled notions; the old paths of our fathers are the best for me to travel in."

Nothing daunted, however, I proceeded to the field, and after diligently examining the ploughs, I succeeded in making the desired alterations, adjusting the length of the share to that of the beam, and increasing or lessening the pitch of the share, according to the directions given me, and again set the hands to work. They grumbled a good deal at the extra labor thus imposed upon them, as holding one of these double ploughs in its proper position was no mean task, in comparison to the easy one of guiding their own miniature ploughs; but they saw I was determined, and they at length yielded, asserting all the time that the seed would never come up, if ploughed in so deeply. At first, I could not comprehend their meaning; but I afterwards ascertained that the Southern way of sowing grain, was to scatter the seed upon the unploughed surface, and then plough it in, or to sow after the ground was ploughed, and then simply drag a bush over it, to cover it up. I told him to go on with the ploughing, and when it was finished, to try his bush according to his old practice. Afterwards we procured a harrow, and prepared the ground in Northern fashion.

With the ground prepared in Southern style, it was impossible to reap the grain with a machine, owing to the gross inequalities of the surface. A few planters had begun to realize the importance of deep ploughing, but the negroes dislike it exceedingly, on account of the extra labor required.

The hoes used on the plantation were about four times as heavy as Northern ones, requiring great strength of arm to strike a heavy blow with them ; but after diligent testing the practical workings of the two kinds of hoes, we were obliged to conclude that, with the blacks as laborers, our Northern hoes would be comparatively useless, as they would not apply the quick motion to them that it was necessary, to produce good results ; and they would break those slim blades in a very short space of time. Their method of hoeing, is to lift slowly the ponderous hoe, with its long and large handle, and then let it fall by its own weight, trusting to the force thus acquired to make a suitable impression on the soil, they believing it required less labor to perform that operation, than to strike a sprightly blow, with a lighter implement. Nearly all of the tools used at the South are of the same ponderous character, except the ploughs, and they are as light as vanity. After passing over a field that the blacks called broken up for planting, in some cases you would hardly find traces of the plough ;

and with such cultivation, the wonder is that any crops at all are raised.

The ploughs used in this locality are first, the "rooter," which is a narrow and long blade three or four inches wide, and ten or twelve long, and is used in breaking up the ground early in the Spring; secondly, the "turn or shovel plough," which is considerably longer than the rooter, but does not penetrate the ground so far. This is used for "breaking up" when the ground is tolerably soft, and for breaking out the middles after the corn and cotton are planted; thirdly, the "wing plough," one side of which projects some from the main portion of the plough, but is not quite so large as the "turn plough." This is used where the object is to throw the dirt one side, so as to fall upon the plant, as in "siding" corn and cotton; and fourthly, "the sweep," or shallow plough, which is a nondescript in the way of a plough. It consists of two narrow strips of iron, reaching in a slanting direction from the point of the plough, to each end of a similar strip, crossing the plough stalk, and having another bar, reaching from the middle of the cross piece, to the apex of the plough. It is used for extremely shallow ploughing, and is designed to run through the corn and cotton previous to "laying by" the crop, so as simply to cut off the tops of the weeds and not stir the soil much.

A failure to avail ourselves of this simple plough, at one time, cost us the loss of one of our finest fields of corn; a deeper plough having been used for the last ploughing, which laid bare the roots of the corn, and the whole field withered away. It is hardly necessary for me to advise Northern farmers coming South, to avoid introducing all of their Northern notions about farming; until they have listened to the reasons on the part of the Southerners for their mode of operation. Conceit always results unfavorably to its possessor, be his conceit of Southern or Northern origin. To be sure, taken as a whole, the Northern system of farming is immeasurably superior to the Southern one; but there are some Southern practices absolutely necessary to be adopted, in order to insure success; as for instance, this one of the shallow ploughing, the *last* time the corn is ploughed.

Quite earnest discussions are often held among the hands, in regard to the relative merits of the different kinds of ploughs; each debater contending earnestly for the one he had been in the habit of using, during the days of slavery. The corn is ploughed three times, and the cotton four or five times. About the first of February, they commence breaking up the ground for corn, except on the "bottoms," where this work is often delayed until May. Corn planting commences about the first of March, and continues until early in April; at which time the planting of cotton commences, the ground having been well prepared previously. The corn is planted in furrows five feet apart, the hills being four feet from each other, in the furrows. But *one* good stalk of corn is usually allowed to grow in a hill, and one of these stalks usually produces but *one ear* of corn. This corn frequently reaches the height of ten or twelve feet, and sometimes grows still higher. The average product of corn to the acre, in this section, is seldom over ten bushels, and oftener much less; although the bottom lands frequently produce twenty-five or thirty bushels to the acre. The best manure for corn is cotton seed; a large pile of which, after being covered with dirt, is left exposed to the rain a month or two, and is thus "rotted," so as to prevent the seed from germinating. A small handful of this is put into each hill, and the corn is dropped upon it.

Various kinds of fertilizers are also used on both corn and cotton, and their use is annually increasing, the crops frequently being doubled by them, while the extra cost is only about a third more than that of ordinary cultivation. Of course, every Northern man can see where his true interest lies in his farming operations here. The corn is usually hard enough to feed the mules by the first of August, but not sufficiently hard to grind, until about a month afterwards. It usually remains in the field until some time in October; that is, the portion spared by the numerous thieves, who revel in luxury in the neighborhood of every corn-field, after the corn is hard enough to grind; and these thieves invariably select the largest and finest ears, leaving the "nubbins" for the impoverished owner. The fodder is stripped from the stalks, the tops of which are left standing, about the middle of August, and sometimes earlier, according to the heat of the summer. This fodder is the chief reliance of the farmer, for supplying the mules with a substitute for hay, the latter article being used but little on a Southern plantation, and generally fed only to cattle.

My overseer gravely informed me that the mules would not eat it; but on trial, I found that he was mistaken. Nearly all of the hay used in this region is imported from the North and West, although I can see no good reason why the cultivation of grass cannot be successfully introduced. We cut twenty tons of wild hay during one season; and I am of the opinion that the cultivation of grass would prove far more profitable than that of corn.

Cotton is planted from the tenth to the middle of April. When delayed until May, the crop is considered unreliable. Early in March, the preparation of the cotton ground commences, by ploughing it and raising it into beds about twenty inches wide, which is called "bedding up" the cotton ground. When the time comes for planting, the bed is opened in the middle, with a small plough, which is followed by a hand on foot, who carries the seed in a bag, slung across his shoulders, and drops it in, liberally or otherwise, according to the abundance of seed, generally using about four bushels to the acre. He is followed by another hand, with a mule, dragging a narrow board, about eighteen inches in length, and a little hollow in the middle, over the bed, in the direction the furrow runs, which is the process for covering the seed. Four men and two mules will thus plant from eight to twelve acres in a day. The first cotton plant makes its appearance in less than two weeks after planting, and sometimes in one week. As soon as it is possible, after the cotton is up, the hands pass over it rapidly, "chopping" it out, which consists in destroying with a hoe the superfluous plants, leaving only one in every eight or ten inches. About the same time, the first ploughing commences; usually by the middle of May. As soon as the cotton is thoroughly "chopped out," it is time for the second ploughing to commence. After a great rain, all the force of the plantation is required, for the extirpation of the weeds and grass; and from the time these first appear until August, there is a regular battle going on for the mastery, between the weeds and grass, and the tillers of the soil. It is not an uncommon thing for the tillers to be defeated in this contest, and to retire ingloriously from the field, leaving it in the possession of the wiry grass and stalwart weeds. This is by no means a necessary fate, to any but laggards in the business; but when it does take place, the sight is melancholy enough. The first blossom usually appears about the first of July, and from that time until the middle of September is the time for making cotton. All that blossoms after the latter date is considered nearly worthless, as it cannot fully mature previous to the frosts in November, it taking six weeks from the first appearance of the blossom for the boll to mature.

Owing to the rapid opening of the bolls from the heat, the first cotton is picked as early as the middle of August, and cotton picking continues from that time until after Christmas, many of the bolls opening slowly long after the frosts, producing an inferior article of stained cotton.

The appearance of the fields, when the cotton is in full bloom, is extremely beautiful; but we found it almost impossible to ascertain from the blacks whether the yellow blossom fell from the plant, or turned into a red one; and we could only be sure of the truth by actual experiment, which showed us that this change so anomalous in the botanic world, actually takes place. This fact speaks volumes in reference to the depth of the intellectual degradation of the black man. During his whole life, he had witnessed the blossoming of this cotton, and had worked among it, but had never noticed whether a cotton blossom fell upon the ground, or turned into another color. The blossoms are first white, pink, or pale yellow; and on the second or third day, according to the hour of their blossoming, fall to the ground, after, having changed to a purplish red color, leaving in their place a tiny boll. The blossom appears either early in the morning, or a little after sunset.

We found it almost impossible to ascertain the date of any past occurrence in relation to the crops. No one could tell what time last year they planted, ploughed or reaped. The only rotation of crops practised, is a change from corn to oats, and from oats to cotton. Clover is unknown as a fertilizer, or even as a grass. No grass seed is ever sown. Oats are sown from October to February, and are usually cut in June, and used as fodder; although when used the allowance of corn is usually curtailed.

Wheat is produced in limited quantities. My overseer objected to raising it, because it had to be harvested at a time, when the labor of all the hands was needed elsewhere; but wheat from this region finds its way to the New York market two weeks earlier than from any other state, and therefore its production might be made a paying business. It is not often, under the present system of cultivating it, that a farmer in this region obtains over ten bushels of wheat to the acre. I am safe in saying that nine-tenths of all the flour used in this part of the state, is manufactured from imported wheat.

The great staple of Georgia, must always be cotton, for no other crop is so likely to stand our severe droughts, and even that sometimes yields to their terrific influence.

Sweet potatoes are cultivated extensively, and form a main article of diet from October to about April, at which time they become quite scarce. It is very difficult to preserve them from rotting, however, even that length of time; and still more difficult to keep them from being appropriated by the vile thieves that prowl around every Southern plantation. Early in March a bed is prepared for bedding seed potatoes, by manuring it well, then sprinkling a little dirt on the top of the manure and then laying the small potatoes on the bed, almost as close as they can be laid together; or not over an inch apart, at the farthest. About four inches of dirt is then put over them, and in about six weeks, they are ready for transplanting; which has to be done when the ground is quite moist. Succeeding transplantings are made of portions of the *vine*, by tying up one end of the part detached from the whole vine, and inserting the other in the ground. The Sweet potato grows in beds, similar to the cotton beds, and needs continued cultivation to produce a good crop. Sometimes as many as one hundred bushels are produced from an acre. The average price is not far from one dollar a bushel during the winter months, but late in the spring they are frequently sold as high as two dollars.

Hogs are generally allowed to run at large, and woe be to the unlucky owner of a corn field, not protected by a substantial fence; or whose fence has been destroyed by the ruthless wagoners, who use rails for their camp fires whenever they find them; and particularly those of a Northern man, who may help himself if he can. These hogs when dressed, usually average in weight about one hundred pounds; and are generally deficient in that fatness that a Northern butcher expects to find in every porker offered him for sale.

Farming in Georgia, is on the whole not a very profitable business, since slavery was abolished. I have often been told by planters, that all their profits then consisted in the increase of slaves, and since the abolition of slavery, they had made nothing. Certain it is, that for various reasons, the expense of raising cotton is nearly doubled since freedom; which can be thus explained,

During the days of slavery it cost to feed and clothe a hand about sixty dollars a year; and that hand would produce on an average, four bales of cotton, and perhaps one hundred bushels of corn. The cost of feeding a mule would be about one hundred and fifty dollars a year, and incidental expenses say fifty dollars, to every two hands; so that two hands and a mule would cost three hundred and twenty dollars per annum, and would produce eight bales of cotton, and two hundred bushels of corn. The corn was worth about two hundred dollars, leaving one hundred and twenty as the actual cost of eight bushels of cotton, or fifteen dollars per bale. The average weight of a bale of cotton is four hundred and fifty pounds, so that the cost of cotton per pound, was less than three and a half cents. To this must be added the wages of the overseer, the planters' family expenses, and the interest on the capital invested. If a planter made fifty bales of cotton, and it sold for ten cents a pound, he cleared fifteen hundred dollars, which would no more than cover these expenses.

Now, after paying the hands, including their rations, one hundred and fifty dollars per year, and the product of these hands being reduced from four bales per hand, to not over three, and from one hundred bushels of corn, to seventy-five, the actual cost of cotton, amounts to twelve cents a pound; but adding fifteen hundred dollars as before for interest, family expenses, and overseer's wages, the cost would be twenty cents a pound, in lieu of the *ten cents* that it cost before.

The present cost can be stated thus. Two hands and one mule will cultivate thirty-five acres of ground; the yield of which, if one half is planted in corn, and the other half in cotton, will be one hundred bushels of corn, and six bales of cotton. The hands and mule with incidentals will cost five hundred dollars. Six bales of cotton will weigh twenty-seven hundred pounds, which after deducting one hundred and fifty dollars for the corn, from the five hundred dollars, will leave thirteen cents a pounds as the actual cost, exclusive of the three items above mentioned. Add these, and you have nearly twenty cents a pound, as the lowest possible sum for which cotton can be raised, with profit to the owner. This estimate as will be perceived, leaves the planter absolutely nothing to "lay by for a rainy day," except what he may derive from other articles beside the corn and cotton; all of which amount to but little, except to lessen the expenses of provision for his family. In former days, great numbers of hogs were raised, but now the larger part of pork consumed on plantations, is purchased at the nearest market town, at an average price of about fifteen cents a pound.

All of these expenses can of course be lessened by dispensing with the overseer's services and with the labor of several hands; results which are to sure to follow the great change from Slavery to freedom, and which have already followed very extensively as far as the overseers are concerned, comparatively few planters, now employing one.

The planters' sons are also serving their apprenticeship in the field, and even the refined daughters of well-to-do farmers are engaged in the humble, but of course honorable, duties of the dairy; a change that will prove alike beneficial to all classes concerned. If the result of the abolition of Slavery shall be to accustom the boys on the plantation to do their own work, and thus become self-reliant and self-supporting, it will prove far better for them than the imaginary enjoyment of ruling over others, and being dependent upon them for the performance of every act of labor. Future generations of white Southerners will thus have occasion to bless the Yankees for conferring upon them the invaluable boon of emancipation; instead of echoing the terrific curses that now fall from the lips of the young aristocracy, upon the heads of Union men, for being the cause of what they consider their degradation.

Freedom will also result in the destruction of the landed aristocracy, whereby a few individuals monopolized all the land. It now being impossible for the planter to amass great wealth by this extensive cultivation, it will be for his interest to sell off large portions of his land, and thus place the blessings of land ownership within the reach of that large class of the Southern people, the "poor whites," whose living has been hitherto a very precarious one. We already see those who owned no land previous to the war, now renting or buying small farms, and managing them without much if any hired help. Thus will be gradually adopted the system of self-reliant labor, which has accomplished so much for the Northern people.

Here let me entreat our Northern friends not to be too eager to obtain their cotton goods at a low price, but to remember that the Southern planter has the same right to live that you have, and in this transition state from Slavery to freedom, he must be aided rather than trampled upon, as he undoubtedly has been, by the odious

tax of two and a half cents a pound levied on cotton by our government, during the first two years of my sojourn here. What evil genius prompted our government thus to render itself more unpopular than ever at the South, it is difficult to divine! It is true, that all classes, black and white, Northern and Southern, alike felt its onerous nature, and the loud clamors for its removal happily resulted in its abolition.

CHAPTER X.

THE FOURTH OF JULY, AND THE FREEDMAN'S BUREAU.

On the Sunday previous to the fourth of July, I addressed quite a large congregation, under our shade trees, on the character of this jubilee. To my surprise, I found the utmost ignorance prevailing, respecting it, not one in the audience seeming to have the faintest idea why it was celebrated. Peter Freeman, in whose cabin our first Sunday school had been held, and who had been held up to me by our overseer as a model hand, and who had manifested an unusual desire to learn, since our arrival, was the only one who comprehended it at all. With his eyes brightening, and an unusual look of intelligence passing over his dusky countenance, he said, in reply to my question, "I know. I think I can tell." "Well, Peter, what is the 4th of July celebrated for?" said I. With a feeling of vast superiority over the ignorant ones around him, he exclaimed, with great decision, "It is the birthday of Washington."

No other one could reply at all to my question. Their ignorance on this point was only a sample of their utter inability to understand the commonest political problem. A great change in this respect had taken place, however, by the time they were called upon, to cast their first ballots; and they became as great proficients in political matters, as they were dolts at this time. Peter's information exceeded that of others present, for they did not even know who George Washington was, with the exception of "Yellow Bob," a light mulatto, who had travelled in Virginia with his master, and had seen, as he said, "pictures hanging in rooms, of a man they called Washington;" but Georgia negroes had not even "hearn tell" of the father of his country.

I can attribute the cause of this political ignorance to nothing but an apprehension on the part of the slaveholders, that if they instructed the negroes in the principles of American freedom, the enquiry might arise in their minds, "Why are not we free, also?" and that therefore the only safe way was to keep them in blissful ignorance of all these historical facts. The blacks informed me that they never had a holiday given them on the 4th of July before, and they were well pleased when I told them I should not require them to work on that day. Accordingly all hands went to town, taking with them my largest wagon and six mules, and joined in the celebration there. They returned at night, in high spirits, having enjoyed it much. A few days afterwards, when in town, I was informed by the Agent of the Freedmens' Bureau that he caused a large U. S. flag to be flung to the breeze, so that its folds fell across the sidewalk in front of their office, and that nearly every lady who had occasion to pass that way, turned from the sidewalk into the street, rather than walk under the hated flag, and yet in spite of all these demonstrations, Andrew Johnson was contriving ways and means to smuggle these rebels back into the Union. And the rebels themselves felt indignant at his ill success, having forgotten their eager desire not long before to escape from the Union. I had not been long at the South, before it became apparent to my mind that the day that saw the rebel states again members of our Union, as states, would be an evil one for our country. What sense was there in restoring to our embrace those who had bitten us so terribly, and were seeking to do so again? But madness ruled the hour, and the welfare of the whole country was lost sight of in the desire to acquire the reputation of magnanimity, forgetting that it is the duty of all men "to be *just* before being generous."

I must do the Southerners justice to say, however, that at that time the great masses were evidently more intent on repairing their pecuniary fortunes, than their political ones, and that if the people had been left to themselves, I question if a tithe of the outrages since committed, would have ever occurred. But politicians and newspaper editors inflamed the Southern mind and re-instilled the evil genius of rebellion into the hearts of those who were sick of the war and would like to have remained quiet. As is well known, during the first year after the surrender, outrages were much more infrequent than they have been since. Johnson and those pusillanimous Republicans who followed in his wake, re-echoing his drunken sentiments, are in a great measure responsible for what afterwards happened.

Of all the appliances used by our government for healing the diseased condition of the body politic South, not one of them worked so admirably, as that much abused agency the "Freedman's Bureau." Woe be to that portion of the Republican party, who in an evil hour yielded to the demands of the Democrats for its overthrow. Of all the men who have labored directly for the reconstruction of the South, none deserve a greater meed of praise than Gen. Howard, for his unwearied efforts to sustain this noble institution. The fact of its having aroused the ire of the South, was only an argument in its favor. Abuses might have crept in to its management, but the institution was alike beneficial to both master and freedman; and not a few of the former had the good sense to acknowledge the truth of this assertion.

I have seen something of the workings of this admirable institution, have had to submit to its supervision myself; and my testimony is unequivocably in favor of its wonderful adaptation to the wants of the whole Southern community. After the purchase of my plantation, I applied to the Bureau for their endorsement of the transfer to myself of the contract between the former owner and the hands, and they endorsed it as follows, "the transfer of this contract, was made before me, and I approve it, Mr. Charles Stearns agreeing to fulfil the contract from the 26th of May, 1866," and it was signed by the proper officers. This contract was fully as favorable to the employer as it was to the freedman. This fact will effectually disprove the oft-repeated assertion, that the Bureau only sought to protect the freedmen without the least regard to the rights of the employers.

But some supervision of this kind was absolutely necessary to protect the freedman, as will appear from the following fact. An elderly colored man, one day came to me with the complaint, that his boys had been severely whipped by their employer. "Why did you give him permission to whip your boys?" I enquired, after having perused the documents he handed me, which he called their contract.

"I did not say any such thing," said he in great surprise.

"It is here in the contract," said I, and I read to him a clause conferring upon their employer the right to whip the boys, whenever he thought it necessary.

On hearing this he was thunderstruck, and his anger knew no bounds, as he whirled around the room like a top, exclaiming, "them ar pesky rebels put that in, and never read it to me."

This was often done, as I have every reason to believe. The contracts were written by the employers, and such portions as they judged best, omitted in the reading of them, to those expected to sign them. Any one can perceive, that unless there is some sworn official to read these contracts to the freedmen, great abuses must creep in; for but few of the freedmen can read writing, and nothing is easier than for some one to omit certain portions in reading; and then when a dispute arises, which is to be settled by the contract, Lo! and behold! the poor freedman finds no provision for his protection.

This is so often done, that even my own hands have sometimes accused me of not reading all the provisions of the contract, when afterwards found guilty of some violation of its express terms; so that justice to all parties requires the establishment of something akin to the Bureau; and there can be no safety to these poor people, unless some provision of this kind is made. The legislatures of the several states could easily provide a remedy for this state of things, but being mostly Democrats, it is hardly to be expected of them.

It remains therefore for the general government to

throw its ægis of protection over these poor stricken ones, so long the miserable victims of the direst system of oppression the world had ever seen. But I shall dwell longer upon this phase of the subject, when I come to consider the remedy for the wrongs inflicted upon the colored people. At present, I shall confine myself to the practical workings of the Bureau.

When I came to Augusta, Col. Bryant had recently abdicated the post of agent of the Freedmens' Bureau, and loud were the maledictions of the Southerners upon his head. Whoever else among the Northerners might be decent men, even including Gen. Tillson, Bryant was the impersonation of depravity, with them. At length Holmes Parker and myself ventured to pay him a visit, not without many misgivings as to his true character, as we had heard so much said against him; but we thought we would obey the apostolic injunction to "prove all things."

We returned from our visit perfectly satisfied that Col. Bryant's only offence was that of defending the rights of the colored people; and as such, our hearts immediately warmed towards him as to a true defender of the principles of Christianity, as manifested in his self-denying labors for the "least of these, the brethren of Jesus." It is a good rule, in ascertaining the character of an abused man, to enquire concerning that of his traducers. If you find those traducers bad men, you may consider the object of their revilings a tolerably good one. It is so in war. The General most hated by the enemy is the one likely to do his country the most service.

Without a doubt, Col. Bryant had faults, as who is wholly destitute of them? but I am persuaded that the greatest crime he then committed, was in defence of those who had none to plead for their behalf. Certainly there was no excuse for the pusillanimous conduct of Gen. Tillson, the military commander of the district, in refusing to protect the colored people in strewing flowers upon the graves of the Union soldiers, in the Augusta cemetery, after the whites had been allowed to decorate the graves of the Confederate soldiers. For this dastardly conduct, he was rightly denounced with unmitigated severity, by Col. Bryant.

The reason given by Gen. Tillson for his conduct, was, the request of the rebel authorities of Augusta, after arrangements had been made for the festival, by the noble Northern lady teachers, there stationed. The whites were willing the ladies should perform this decoration themselves, with colored servants to carry the flowers, but no procession of "niggers," for this purpose, should desecrate their really beautiful cemetery.

It was the custom of the officers of the Bureau to inspect every contract between the freedmen and their employers, when offered to them for that purpose; and if they approved of its provisions, they promised both parties military protection, in enforcing the contracts. This was a great point gained by the whites, for of what avail was a contract with irresponsible men without means for its enforcements? If a black man failed to do his duty, he was immediately brought before the Bureau, and obliged to conform to his agreement, and many of the rebels gladly availed themselves of this protection. On the contrary, if an employer failed to do justice to his hands, he too, must appear before this august tribunal, and make amends for his conduct. At the time I am writing, neither employers or hands have any adequate protection against each other. If a man chooses to leave his employer he cannot be forced to return. All the employer can do is to forbid others from hiring him, and if he can find the run-away, to imprison him, if it can be proved that he has violated his contract. But this is not the kind of protection the employer wants. If six men abruptly leave him, on a hot July day when his cotton is overrun with grass, it is poor consolation to him to be allowed to leave his cotton, and spend a week in pursuit of these men; even if he succeeds then in having them safely lodged in jail. That will not furnish him with other hands, or kill the grass, that is so rapidly destroying his cotton.

But when the much abused Bureau was in operation, all that he had to do, was to exhibit his contracts to the Bureau, and notify the agent of the elopement of these men; and he could then return to his injured cotton field — while a detachment of soldiers went in pursuit of the missing men, and when taken they were not lodged in jail, but remanded back to the plantation, with perhaps a guard over them, to see that they did not repeat their truancy. I cannot see how any well meaning man, could, possibly object to the operation of this Bureau, except on the ground of expense; but surely money is a small consideration in selecting the instrumentalities, that shall most effectually preserve order in a hitherto rebellious country.

For my part I can safely say, that I relied upon the Freedman's Bureau, fully as much to enable me to govern my hands, as they did to enable them to protect themselves against my rapacity. I do not know as I could have successfully managed my own plantation, if it had not been for this power in reserve; to whom I could appeal if my hands failed to comply with my orders, as I am sorry to say they sometimes did.

But the Freedman's Bureau went down; and with it the last vestige of protection for the colored man, in the late rebellious states. Under its beneficial reign, if a man came to me with a sad story of his wrongs, all I had to do was to write a note to the agent of the Bureau, requesting him to examine into the matter. He would then despatch a lieutenant to the planter's residence, and ascertain the facts; and if he found that there was no cause for complaint, as he sometimes did find, he would dismiss the negro with a reprimand. If he ascertained that the negro had really been abused, he would take the offender to Augusta, for examination; and if found guilty, a trivial punishment would be inflicted upon him. By far the greater portions of the complaints, on the part of the blacks, were dismissed as needless; so that the blacks had fully as much reason to complain as the whites had.

It may be asked, why then did the rebels demand the removal of the Bureau? The only correct answer that can be given is one that savors so much of severity towards our unfortunate white brethren, that I hesitate to give it; but justice nevertheless compels me to do so. The rebels did not wish to be punished for their misdeeds towards the blacks; and did not relish the idea of being called to account for their misdeeds, by a power superior to their own. They were quite willing for the Bureau to punish their refractory hands, but utterly unwilling to be placed in the same category with their former slaves. "Monarchs of all they surveyed," they had so long been, that they could illy brook being criticised for their treatment of their escaped slaves.

And neither did they like to feel the force of *Uncle Sam's* strong arm in restraining them ; they preferring to punish their own hands, and going unpunished themselves when they deserved it, to the operation of even-handed and exact justice.

CHAPTER XI.

THE CHANGE FROM SLAVERY TO FREEDOM.

If that heroic leader of the anti-slavery hosts, during the days of the imperilled existence of that sacred cause, *Wendell Phillips*; or that remarkable man, anointed of God to arouse our guilty nation from its terrible lethargy, on the subject of slavery, *Wm. Lloyd Garrison*, could have visited our plantations during these summer days, their philanthropic souls would have been gratified by the changes apparent in the condition of these men and women.

It is not to be wondered at, that, during the first days of freedom, the exuberant joy of the once dead, but now living human beings, should have led them into the commission of some grave errors. Good luck, on an ordinary scale, frequently unduly elates wiser and better balanced men than the Southern slaves were. We have all heard of the Scotch farmer, who was so overjoyed at being elected deacon of his church, that on his return home, not finding his wife, he embraced his cow, exclaiming, "O, my gude cow, ye is na common cow; ye is a deacon's cow now."

What then must have been the feelings of our fellow-men, at the first dawn upon their benighted souls of the day of emancipation! As the early rays of the sun of freedom glanced across their cabin doors — after grandly illuminating the Eastern sky, and dispelling the darkness of Slavery therefrom; and as a voice from God's glittering throne was heard in their utterly astonished ears, uttering the words, "You are free *men* and free *women*," was there not some excuse for the irregularities usually attendant upon all manifestations of extreme joy?

It must be remembered that from their earliest childhood, the one great yearning of the colored man's soul, had been for freedom; and now that in the providence of God, it had come almost without exertion on his part, how could he help being overcome with joy? Far be it from me, to defend these irregularities; but considering that for the most part, unlike as it was when emancipation was conferred upon the West Indies slaves, there was no friendly hand stretched forth to guide them, it is not surprising that they committed some excesses.

The planters themselves, in many instances, were greatly to blame in this matter. Sitting moodily in their houses, in some instances, they refused to let their former slaves know of their newly acquired rights, and sometimes declared that they should never be free, with their consent. This I learned from the lips of the freedmen themselves, to whom were addressed these fearful words. In no case of which I can learn, was any attention paid to the act of Congress emancipating them. That remained a dead letter, until the surrender of Lee; and its provisions were not universally heeded, until the State conventions of the succeeding fall, passed their acts abolishing Slavery, the slave-holders clinging to the doctrine of State rights, to the last.

In some cases, the black men were informed of their freedom, and asked to remain with their masters, and were whipped, if they refused. In one case, a woman's mistress tore her clothes into strips, because she thus declined the kind offer of a home. They told the freedmen that if they left them, "the Yankees would hitch them to heavy wagons, and make them drag sand all day." But in spite of all this, many of them ran away, hoping that the good news of their freedom might prove true. This was previous to the full acknowledgment on the part of their masters, of the reality of their emancipation.

If wise leaders had been present, and good advice could have been given the freedmen, as soon as they learned of their emancipation, as in the W. I. Islands in 1839, much suffering would have been avoided. As it happened, great numbers of the newly emancipated ones refused to work, judging that freedom consisted in the privilege of not working. They wandered about from place to place, helping themselves to whatever they could find, and according to the story of the whites, large numbers died from starvation; but according to the declarations of the blacks, they were brutally murdered by the whites. Often children ran away from their parents, and parents from their children. The banks of the Savannah river were lined with the living and dead forms of these forlorn creatures.

On our plantation, in the fall succeeding emancipation, and previous to my arrival, the hands utterly refused to work; and were removed by force by the military, as they would not even gather the crops they had raised; on the ground that they had received no pay for their labor during the summer. No Freedman's

Bureau then lifted its kindly voice to cheer them on, or stretched out its helping hand to guide them aright. It was usually hate on the one side, and dogged stubbornness on the other.

It is a remarkable fact, that almost universally, as soon as the slave absolutely knew that he was free, he took up his "line of march" for some other place. No matter how well he had been treated, he could not realize his actual freedom, until he had tasted the sweet privilege of walking away from the plantation unmolested; with no ferocious dogs baying at his heels, or almost as ferocious men pursuing after him. Of the truth of this fact, I am assured by both whites and blacks.

Oftentimes however, he returned to his former master, especially if that master had been a tolerably easy one, and hired himself to him for a year; but no matter how kind he had been to him in the days of slavery, the freedman would not remain with him, until he had seen a little of the world, and known by actual experience that he was really free; so true it is, that all mankind like to be their own masters, and regulate their own affairs. I have yet to learn of the first instance, and I do not believe one can be produced, of one who did not take his freedom when it was conferred upon him. Nor have I yet heard, during my residence here, of the first man or woman who wished to return to slavery. Oftentimes when some of my men would chafe at the strictness of some of my regulations, they would attempt to divert me from my purpose by saying, "I neber in slavery time, hab dat to do." But all murmuring would instantly cease, when I would suggest that they could return to slavery if they chose, that the doors of slavery were still wide open.

But still it must be confessed that the black man has very inadequate ideas of what freedom really requires of him. I am sorry to be obliged to confess that with too many of them, the idea still prevails, that to be free, is to do just as they please. Many laughable incidents were continually occurring, illustrative of this fact. In particular, they objected to being ordered about, and I found during this Summer, that they would generally obey me, if I asked them pleasantly to perform a particular task. At one time, I had ordered some work to be performed, under the direction of Richard, the husband of Margaret. He soon came to me, saying that "Yellow Bobb" would not obey his orders. So I sent for "Yellow Bobb," and asked him why he refused to obey Richard. He replied, "Mr. Stearns, I have never refused to obey you once since I have been here, because you always speak to me pleasantly; but Richard ordered me about like a dog, and I won't mind him."

And why should not the black man be partially susceptible to kindly influences, like the rest of mankind? I generally found the majority of the hands ready and willing to mind *me*, although Mr. Prince constantly assured me that *he* could do nothing with them, without swearing at them roundly. During this summer, I seldom had an unpleasant word with the hands, always excepting Margaret, who seemed to be managed better by frowns than by persuasion. But I cannot conceal the fact, that those who always said, "Yes, sar, yes, sar," very obsequiously to my face, when ordered to do a particular thing, quite often imitated one of the "certain man's" sons in the Scripture, who said to his father, "I go sir," and "went not." But still they seemed as anxious to please me as I could reasonably expect, as the following extract from a letter written to my friends at the North, about this time, will show:

"We all work hard now, for it is in the height of the season, and much cotton will be wasted, if not gathered when ready. Sometimes, these pleasant evenings, we work an hour or two by moonlight; it is so much more comfortable working then, than in the heat of the day. I work with them myself part of the time, as it encourages them to do their best, and my overseer works all the time. He is the best hand on the place. I also stimulate them to extra exertions, by the promise of a reward to the one who will pick the greatest amount of cotton. I encourage them also, by the promise of a holiday by and by, when the present hurry slackens a little. It is wonderful to see how many of these poor fellows will strain every nerve, to merit my approbation. It rejoices my heart, to watch them coming home from the field at night, singing, laughing, and joking; and their children running to meet them. "O," say they, "it feels so good to be treated like a man, and to feel that we have no master."

The desire to learn during this summer was very great. Nearly every noon for some time, quite a class would come to my piazza, and spend an hour in learning to read, and as I have mentioned, Mr. Parker would teach many of them, in their cabins at night. When I told them of Mr. Garrison and Mr. Phillips, their enthusiasm knew no bounds. "Let us see them, send them here, that we may thank them ourselves," they would say in their meetings, after I had related to them what these noble men had done for their race.

There were only two persons on the plantation who did not feel some interest in learning, and they were

Margaret and Richard. The others made commendable progress in learning to read, and completed the first reading book, by learning on Sundays alone. Altogether, I felt well satisfied with the result of my labors, at the close of the first summer. The hands had done well, as far as I could see. They had generally obeyed my orders, had worked tolerably well, and had shown a commendable interest in moral and religious teaching; with one exception to which I shall allude in the next chapter.

Many and dismal were the stories related to me, by these emancipated ones, of the horrible workings of the hateful system of slavery. I had been an advocate of the anti-slavery cause, for many years, and I thought I fully understood the accursed nature of slavery, both from hearing of it from others, and by actual observation myself, during a few years former sojourn in a slave state; but after living here awhile, I was constrained to say "the half has not been told me." I never heard much worse recitals than those I listened to from the overseer's lips. I was pointed to the spot where the blood hounds pounced upon a white woman who was gathering berries; and literally tore her in pieces. I was told of a place where some fugitives lived a long while in concealment; and when a posse of white men discovered them, the fugitives fired at them and killed all but one, and then retreated to some secure place. My overseer related to me an incident that came to his knowledge, of a lot of hands that were kept working all day, and the whole of the succeeding night without food; owing to some mad freak of their owner. Our hands said they were often kept picking cotton on moonlight nights until midnight. And then the terrible whippings described to me, would occupy too much space for me to record in this narrative. Suffice it to say, that some of my own hands related to me as extreme cases of cruelty as ever occurred under "Legrees'" administration. My overseer said he had refused to work for some parties, because they required him to perform more severe whipping than he thought was just; and he made no pretentions to being an uncommonly merciful man.

CHAPTER XII.

THE AUTHOR FOUND HE HAD FALLEN AMONG THIEVES.

As has been already hinted at, there was one exception to the interest of the people in moral improvement. They did not like to hear the sin of stealing spoken against. As it was in the North, during the early days of the agitation of the Anti-Slavery enterprise, there was one sin that neither preacher nor people were expected to include in the category of those crimes, about which they prayed in the words of the church "collect," "Good Lord deliver us." Slavery was a *tabooed* subject everywhere. Says the Rev. Samuel J. May, in his recent deeply interesting work, "Recollections of the Anti-Slavery Conflict: "Dr. Ware, who had charge of the Hollis Street pulpit, in the absence of the pastor, invited me to supply it, if I could do it consistently with my new duties. I engaged for two Sundays. But at the close of the first, one of the chief officers of the church waited on me by the direction of the principal members, and requested me not to enter the pulpit again, assuring me if I should do so, that a dozen or more of the prominent men would leave the house." And this, too, from a Society of those priding themselves upon being paragons of morality, in contradistinction to the "evangelicals," who, as they say, lay too little stress upon works.

At another time, he ventured to invite the congregation at the Summer Street church, where he had officiated that day, to attend a lecture, by Wm. Lloyd Garrison, on the sin of Slavery, and prefaced the invitation by some soul-stirring words, on the subject. At the close of the meeting, the pastor sharply reproved him, and gave him to understand that he would never have another opportunity to violate the propriety of his pulpit. A lady came forward and assured him, with much feeling, that during her whole life, she had never before heard the subject of Slavery dwelt upon in such a manner.

And so it was on our plantation, in reference to stealing. Quite a number at length refused to come out to preaching at all, giving as a reason that they "did not want to hear so much talk about lying and stealing; but we want to hear the gospel. If Mr. Stearns would only preach the gospel, like as we have always heard it, we would be so glad." The pressure of "public opinion" became so great, that at times it seemed as if we should be obliged to abandon our public meetings altogether, as they threatened not to come to meeting at all, unless I would let stealing alone.

Now this seems very strange to Northern ears, so accustomed to hear stealing ranked among the vices utterly inconsistent with the Christian name. But we must remember that latitude and longitude have much to do with peoples' ideas of right and wrong. Some sins are looked upon as virtues, by people in a different locality from ours. And some virtues are regarded as vices in the same locality. I well remember a man in

Kentucky, some thirty years ago, who denounced a favorite preacher of his as no better than a horse-thief, because he had said he should not return to his master a fleeing fugitive.

Slavery had destroyed the moral perceptions of the slaves, leaving them nothing but instinct to guide them; and those instincts were their only criterion by which to judge of right and wrong. Even to-day, it is a mooted question among them, which is the superior light, the Bible, which they cannot read, or their own hearts always open to their cognizance. It is a common remark among them, " whatever my own heart tells me is right, that *is* right." Of course their "own hearts," did not forbid the taking of food and clothing, to render themselves comfortable, and so it was not wrong in their estimation.

When I first went among them, they did not consider it a sin to steal, and for me to denounce it as such, was being harsh and cruel, and depriving them of their privileges. Especially to say that a man could not be a Christian and steal, was a libel on the Holy Ghost; that had "called them into the marvellous light of the gospel." So far from my oft-repeated assertions, and quotations from the Bible, in denunciation of stealing, making much impression upon them, they were only led to doubt my piety; for no one could be a child of God, and doubt *their* religion. To doubt their religious character, was one of the greatest sins a man could commit; for had they not "done got religion years ago in the wilderness?"

Mr. Hancock, a Northern man, who lived eight miles from me, once said to me that on his plantations, "they would keep their meetings up until midnight, and then adjourn to my water-melon patch." No Northern person can fully understand the moral bewilderment of those poor creatures on this subject. They had heard it said, "he that provideth not for his own household, has denied the faith, and is worse than an infidel." They could not provide for their households in the days of slavery, they said, without stealing. If it was such a sin as I said, then they had been committing sin all their lives; and they could not admit such a charge against themselves, and their fathers and mothers, who were now in heaven. I shall treat upon this connection of stealing with their religion at another time.

One day I thought I noticed an unusual decrease in the amount of bacon, I had in reserve for my hands. I weighed a few of the shoulders and then ascertained from the number on hand, that nearly five hundred pounds of meat had vanished. I made diligent search after it, but of course no one knew where it was. The overseer said, some of it was poor and he had thrown it away; but there was no getting rid of the fact, that nearly one half of the hogshead of bacon, I had purchased on my first arrival, was gone, besides what had been given to the hands. There were only two persons who had the key to the meat house, and they were the overseer; and Margaret, the cook. The value of the meat thus abstracted was about one hundred dollars.

Not long after this, I found that the meal was going off rather fast; and on strict inquiry, I was convinced that nearly two bushels of meal a week had been taken, during the whole of the summer. At the time I missed it, the thief had grown bolder than usual, and had taken between four and five bushels. The overseer told me how much corn he had sent to mill every week, and I knew the exact amount given out for rations, and in that way discovered the theft. Who the guilty parties were, could not be divined. When they steal, they always manage to do it at a time when other parties have visited the premises, so that suspicion cannot rest upon them alone. In this case, the thief was either the overseer, the man who went to mill, or the cook; and of course we could not condemn any one of them in particular.

Early one morning in the fall, the overseer came into the house and informed me that our sweet potatoes had been stolen. I rushed to the patch containing them, and found to my dismay that nearly an acre had been ransacked by the thieves, during the preceding night; every hill opened, and all the largest potatoes removed, perhaps thirty or forty bushels in all. Not the least trace of them could be discovered, but two years afterwards, a colored man on the place told me who the thieves were, on condition of my not mentioning his name as my informant. He said the overseer and one of my hands were the thieves. The whole conduct of the overseer looked very suspicious, and the other man turned out to be a notorious thief. So here was property taken to the amount of nearly two hundred and fifty dollars, during the first few months of my sojourn among these people.

And so it has been ever since. Property always walking away, and no trace of it to be found. What the remedy is for this terrible evil, it is hard to say. Converting the blacks does not seem to prevent it, for the converted ones (so called), steal as much as the unconverted ones. I think, however, in proportion as they become land owners, thieving will decrease, as it will then be for their interest to prevent stealing; and at length a public opinion will be created, hostile to the practice. It also seems plain to me that a truly converted person will never steal; but if this is so, then are there but very few Christians among the plantation hands, and at least one half of them call themselves by that name.

CHAPTER XIII.

GOING AFTER SUPPLIES, AND DESCRIPTION OF AUGUSTA.

Living as we did eleven miles from both store and Post-Office, obtaining our supplies was no mean task. We were not blessed with fleet horses, that would carry us over smooth roads, to our trading place, in a short time; but three and sometimes four hours were consumed in travelling the distance each way. Then as soon as I was ready to start, first one and then another of my sable friends would appear with a request for me to procure this or that necessary for them, such as a pound of sugar, a quart of molasses, or a spool of thread. Often I was so overrun with these applications, that a half-hour would be consumed in receiving the numerous messages, when I was already three-fourths of an hour later than my usual time, on account of some neglect in feeding or harnessing the mules; and every moment was precious, owing to the precarious nature of the roads, rendering it desirable that I should reach home if possible before dark, an end but seldom attained, however.

It would have been "taking thought for the morrow," in their estimation, to have entrusted me with their little errands on the previous day; but they nearly all waited until I was ready to drive out of the yard, and then followed me up, until I was nearly out of sight of "the quarters." One of the chief things desired was *tobacco*, which is the never-failing solace of the colored man, in all his trials. Next were soap, soda, needles, thread, homespun, shoes, &c., &c. A very desirable step would be to open a small store on our place, where these little wants of the hands could be easily supplied. As it was, much of my time was consumed in making these purchases, and in delivering them to their pleased recipients, on my return.

The hands were paid one half of their wages, at the end of each month, and it was no uncommon thing, in spite of all my endeavors to prevent it, for them to take up their wages for two or three months in advance. If there were only fifty cents due them, on pay day, they were quite pleased. As has been said, we seldom reached home until after dark, very frequently not before nine o'clock, and sometimes not until much later. Once we broke down in the middle of one of the terrific hills we had to descend, and my wife and I remained two hours on the hill, waiting for the arrival of help for which we had sent, and twelve o'clock at night saw us still on the road. Sometimes, owing to the unusually muddy condition of the roads, we took another and a leveller route, which increased the distance several miles, but we were more than compensated by the fine condition of the roads on that route. This road led us by the U. S. Arsenal on the "Sand-hill," and through the "piney woods" region, a belt of land extending through the State of Georgia, celebrated for the extreme salubrity of its climate and exemption from that scourge of the South and West, malarial fever. This region abounded in sand, but in wet weather the roads were excellent. There was one serious drawback about the road, and that was the multitudinous cross-roads that met us, every mile or two, and rendered it almost impossible for us always to choose the right one, except on very bright moonlight nights. Quite a number of times we were forced to pass a large portion of the night in wandering through these "piney woods;" but perseverance usually brought us to our home, by two or three o'clock in the morning, at least. I used to think of our defenceless condition, while lost in these woods, and would say to myself, "If the rebels only knew that we were here, in this condition, would it not be rare sport for them to try their skill as marksmen, with our carriage as a target?" But He who shut the mouths of Daniel's lions, placed His benevolent hand over the eyes of these our enemies, so that they did not see us, and we were never molested.

Our mules were not of the fleetest kind, and having been well worked during the week, it was no small undertaking, to force them into a brisk trot. It exhausted the whole power of whipping, twitching the reins, and of two or three human voices, to prevail upon them to mend their pace; and when all these resorts failed, a boy would sometimes alight and run by the side of the mules, and whip them as we went. This seemed rather cruel, and contrary to the humane teachings of that little "heavenly monitor," "Our Dumb Animals;" but it had to be done, or Augusta merchants would have been late in the day in supplying our wants; and perhaps daylight of the succeeding day would have found us still on the road.

About one and a half miles of the ordinary route was through deep sand, and no power on earth could possibly force the mules out of a walk, in travelling that portion of the road. Oftentimes, we met upon the road men who looked as if they wanted to shoot us; but we were never attacked, although others residing on the place, once were. We always carried a loaded revolver, and sometimes two of them; and oftentimes involuntarily grasped our weapon as we met the ferocious gaze of some hater of Uncle Sam's domination. Quite a number of these polite gentry would refuse to return the bow we made them, on meeting them, and some would look as if nothing would more intensely gratify them, than the privilege of shooting us through. It certainly seems to me that Almighty God must have sent his angels to watch over me, or I should have been murdered, while passing over these lonely roads, at such unseasonable hours. Going tô and returning from Augusta occupied so much of our time, in previous preparations, and in resting afterwards, that we lessened the frequency of our visits, and afterwards went to town only once in two weeks.

Augusta contains about 15,000 inhabitants, one half of whom are colored, and of the remainder a large portion are of foreign origin, and many of them Germans. It is a neat looking city, and contains many objects of interest to the stranger, among which are one of the most beautiful cemeteries anywhere to be found, luxuriant in flowers and shrubbery; the U. S. arsenal on "Sand hill," an elevation two miles out of Augusta, besprinkled with handsome residences, the abodes of some of the aristocracy; and the Confederate magazine, one and a half miles from Augusta, in another direction.

The arsenal and magazine of course are now U. S. property, as the former always was. Over it constantly waves the U. S. flag. The churches in Augusta are numerous, and many of them quite handsome, and beautifully situated in the midst of groves of majestic trees, and sometimes surrounded with pretty little parks. The Court House is a handsome structure, prettily situated, and the jail and hospital occupy prominent positions.

A deep canal runs through a portion of the city, supplying a large cotton factory, and several large flouring mills with water in abundance; and when it is enlarged, as is now proposed, a vast amount of water power will be furnished to the city. The cotton factory is managed discreetly by Northern agents, or was at one time, if not to-day; and makes a larger dividend than is common at the North. The streets of Augusta are wide, cleanly, and arranged at right angles with each other, and bountifully supplied with trees. Broad street, the principal business street, is very wide, and on it are four large hotels, well-conducted and elegant; at any one of which the rankest republicans from the North can find good accommodation, and gentlemanly treatment.

The stores of Augusta are numerous — capacious, and well-filled with all kinds of desirable merchandise; often at very low rates, and never at prices very much exceeding Northern ones, quite different in this respect from Western stores. The merchants are polite and accommodating, and never hesitate to sell goods for cash, to the most rabid of Northern radicals, the bitterest Southern rebel, and the most ignorant negro.

I can truly say, that I was never more politely treated by any mercantile community, than I have been by Augusta merchants. I should say that they exceed in an urbane spirit and an accommodating disposition, great numbers of Northern merchants. Without aiming at personality, I cannot refrain from testifying to the uniform politeness, accommodating spirit, and perfect honesty of one firm ; with whom I have done the most of my trading in the grocery line, since my sojourn here ; and that is the well-known firm of O'Dowd & Mulherin, near the Planters' hotel. Northern people, who may have occasion to trade in Augusta, cannot do better than to bestow their pratronage upon this eminently deserving firm. Other firms are also well worthy of their patronage, but I speak of this one because I have received unlimited favors at their hands, and wish to show my gratitude to them in return.

There are several banks in Augusta, one of which is the Freedman's Savings Bank ; which is well patronized by the colored people and Northern residents, and under the indefatigable efforts of its present able and worthy cashier, D. A. Ritter, Esq., is fast assuming a high rank among similar institutions. These banks have been the means of great good to the colored people ; having induced them to practise economy, and save their earnings to such a degree, that under their influence, great numbers of the freedmen have become the owners of houses and small farms. This bank occupies a large and handsome building in a prominent position on Broad street, which building was formerly owned by a Southern bank. So far as I can learn, this is one of the few Northern institutions, that has failed to awaken the prejudices of the Southern people.

The colored people in Augusta own four or five churches, principally of the Baptist order ; and on Sundays these churches are well-filled with intelligent and well-dressed hearers. One of these churches was brilliantly lighted with gas, has a nice pulpit, with handsome cushions and a gallery on three sides; and will hold seven or eight hundred persons. Several of these churches were used for schools, and are hung around with maps, large mottoes, and supplied with other school appurtenances.

I am well acquainted with the pastors of two of these churches, the "Springfield" and "Central;" and am glad to be able to bear witness to the truly Christian character and eminently apostolic zeal of both of them. The Northern Methodist church has also a flourishing society under the charge of Rev. Mr. Rogers, a white clergyman from Mass.; whose self-denying labors among the blacks cannot fail to produce remarkable results, seconded as they are by the enlightened counsels of the energetic presiding elder of the district, Rev. Mr. Spillman. Other distinguished Northern clergymen who have labored for a season in Augusta, have been called to different fields, in the great vineyard of the Lord.

For several years there were eight or ten schools for the freedmen in Augusta, under the direction of the Am. Missionary Association; whose labors for the freedmen throughout the South, are deserving of the highest commendation, not only on account of the good resulting to the blacks directly, but also to the whole country, by fitting these emancipated ones for the discharge of the new duties devolving upon them.

The teachers in Augusta, employed by this association, were in the main, self-denying, talented, and accomplished, and eminently fitted for their labors, which were laborious in the extreme. So great was the desire for instruction on the part of the blacks, that these teachers were often compelled to resume their task in the evening, after the labors of the day were over; a practice that I would by no means recommend other teachers among the freedmen to adopt; for the simple reason that no teacher can long pursue it, and retain a tolerable degree of health.

To labor among those thus anxious to learn, is far pleasanter than to attempt to teach those who are not sufficiently advanced to appreciate the benefits of education, as is apt to be the case on the plantations: but when this indifference exists, the necessity for education is still greater than where a readiness to learn is manifested. The intelligence of the blacks in Augusta is so far beyond that of the plantation blacks, that one would hardly suppose that they belonged to the same race of beings.

I am sorry to be obliged to add, that these teachers received but very little sympathy from the native white inhabitants of the place. I am credibly informed that hardly an instance has occurred, of the Southern white ladies visiting them. I saw one respectable Southern lady, who was about leaving for the North, because her friends had all abandoned her, for the simple reason that she had rented part of her house to the lady teachers, and boarded with them for her pay. One lady informed me that in passing through the street one day, she was actually spit upon by a gentleman who met her; but I think this is the only instance of the kind that has ever occurred.

Several of the schools, however, during this summer, (1866,) were interfered with, by the throwing of rocks into the windows, and among the pupils, and the protection of Gen. Tillson had to be sought in several instances. The Southern people look with an evil eye upon all Northern efforts to enlighten the blacks. Their religion fails to inculcate the grand principles of benevolence that distinguished the life of the great founder of Christianity, and are copied by all of his true followers.

The Southern religion seems to lack this great essential of Christianity, or its advocates would not fail to commend the heroic labors of those Northern teachers, who submit to this social ostracism, for the sake of doing good to a despised race. But these teachers have their reward, in the satisfaction of contributing much towards rolling back the mighty waves of ignorance and consequent crime, that threatened to overwhelm our Nation, by the emancipation of the slaves. It will not be many years, before all intelligent Southerners will bless those who have thus endeavored to remove from their midst these heavy burdens of crime and woe.

CHAPTER XIV.

THE AUTHORS' SICKNESS, AND ANIMADVERSIONS OF THE REPUBLICAN PARTY.

On first arriving at our house, we discovered that from eighty to a hundred panes of glass had been broken from the windows, by the slamming of unfastened blinds. My friend and I at length concluded to commence the work of repairing the windows, and I accordingly procured the materials, and we applied ourselves to the task in earnest. The old putty was impervious to the attack of the glazier's knife, and it proved an almost herculean undertaking; but at the end of two weeks in August, we had the satisfaction of seeing the job completed. The sash in many instances were too small for the glass, and an immense amount of cutting and trimming became necessary. All this labor, during those hot days, produced a severe headache on my part, which was heightened about the same time by a reception of a letter from a friend in Colorado, informing me that the enemies of the Union in his vicinity had sent South a number of papers, containing a letter of mine on the disloyalty, and other crimes of the Southern people. I was aware that I had stated only the exact truth, but knowing that our Southern friends did not always relish having the whole truth told respecting them, I did not know what might be the consequences of my animadversions of them.

On the following Sunday, I rode fifteen miles in the hot sun to Mr. Shermans' place, and conducted the exercises of a Sunday school and religious meeting, which lasted several hours, and then sat up quite late at night, conversing with the family. The consequence was, that I slept but little during the night, being troubled with visions of rebel crowds, coming to our retreat to attack me; and I arose in the morning devoid of all appetite for my breakfast. Anxious, however, to return home, I started for Augusta, but on my arrival there, was utterly unable to proceed any farther. Mr. S. called at the Freedmen's hospital to ask the physician there, a personal friend of his, to prescribe for me; but as soon as he laid his eyes upon me, he ordered me brought into the hospital, where I was carried, more dead than alive, and hardly able to remonstrate if I had been disposed, against being carried into such quarters. My physician afterwards informed me, that I was as pale as a sheet at this time, and he thought "good for a six weeks run of fever." But on being laid on a bed in the upper story, in a large room, entirely distinct from the other occupants of the building, and with a fine breeze blowing upon me, I began to revive, and by the next day felt considerably better. I had every care and attention bestowed upon me by the kind physicians of the family, and by the estimable lady, the wife of one of them, who presided over the afflicted ones confined in that establishment; passing like an angel of mercy from one room to another, and even rising sometimes at the hour of midnight to see some of her black proteges. Kind and loving words, and sympathetic attention are quite as necessary for the recovery of a patient, as the best of medicines; and I did not lack either of them, so that my recovery was rapid.

Baths were also given me by the colored attendants, and every means possible were used to hasten my recovery. Other visitors came to see me, and at the expiration of ten days, I was able to return to my plantation, eleven miles distant. Mr. and Mrs. S. were also very kind and attentive, bringing me various articles of comfort from their plantation, and altogether I fared much better than I had any right to expect from my singular position. I did not know how it would seem to others, that I was cared for in a freedman's hospital; but I concluded that as I came South to labor for the negro, that it was fitting I should be thus domiciled with him.

I introduce these incidents of my sickness and confinement in this place, for the purpose of testifying to the noble efforts of our government in behalf of the freedmen, during the first year or two of their emancipation. Here was a large three-story brick building, formerly used as some kind of a manufactory, fitted up and made comfortable for the freedmen; and physicians, medicines and board furnished them gratis. The existence of this hospital prevented a vast amount of suffering among the freedmen, who, when they became sick, had often no place of resort, their meagre wages not sufficing to pay the expenses of their sickness and recovery.

At first, it seemed as if our government could not do too much for its black wards. Afterwards the government changed its tactics, and to-day it seems to be too anxious to avoid trouble and expense on their behalf. Then, in all the exuberance of its gratitude for the part the colored people had performed during the war, the Nation longed to bless this down-trodden race.

To the republican party, under whose auspices all these beneficial acts were performed, may be addressed the words of the Apostle to the Ephesian church, "I have somewhat against thee, because thou hast left thy first love;" and may the concluding part of the divine exhortation be heeded by the members of this party, "Remember therefore, from whence thou art fallen, and repent and do the *first works*, or else I will come quickly and remove the candlestick out of his place, except thou repent."

I do not assert that the great and glorious Republican party, under whose auspices we were saved from destruction in Kansas, and by whose act the greatest event of the nineteenth century took place, is sunken so low, that the country would be benefited by the exchange of its domination for that of the Democratic party, which has always and forever been the ally and bosom friend of Slavery and the slaveholders. Far be it from me to utter such an insane declaration.

I charge the republican party, not with intentional wrong, with unusual corruption, but simply with having "forsaken its first love." Entering into power as the sworn friend of the black man, it should have continued its efforts until he was free indeed, and not have left him at the mercy of his life-long enemies, thinking that time would assuage their enmity towards him.

But it is not entirely too late for this noble party to retrieve its lost reputation, and from this time forward to espouse the cause of the black man so vigorously, as to eclipse all of its former efforts in his behalf. God gave that party life and power, that it might do his chosen work for the elevation of the black race. When it refuses to perform this task any longer, its days will be numbered, it having been "weighed in the balance, and found wanting."

In another portion of this work, I shall endeavor to point out what seems to me the necessary steps for the republican party to take, in order to accomplish this beneficent purpose. I can conceive of no reason why this party having begun so gloriously, and having been so signally rewarded for its wise labors, should not continue them, until the end is attained, which it has desired so earnestly.

It seems to me it is the mission of this party, not to content itself with the emancipation and enfranchisement of the blacks, but to press forward "toward the mark of the prize of its high calling," even the full and complete deliverance of this despised race, from its deprivations and persecutions, and the placing it upon the same pedestal of political rights and pecuniary welfare, now occupied by other portions of the human family; and to do this, not because it is the *black* race, but because the race belongs to the great family of man, and the interests of that whole family must suffer, when the right of any of its members are trampled under foot.

CHAPTER XV.

MORE SICKNESS AND MORE BLESSING.

Hardly had I sufficiently recovered from my sickness, to be able to attend to my numerous duties, when after a severe day's labor in painting portions of my house, I was seized in the night with severe pains, and soon found myself in a burning fever. I was entirely alone in the house, my friend having gone to Mr. Sherman's, to superintend his hands; he and his family being sorely afflicted with that great Southern epidemic, the chills and fever. I was not able to arouse any one, and I lay in that condition until one o'clock of the succeeding day; and how much longer I might have been left thus to lie, I know not, "if Yellow Bob" had not needed some tobacco.

Margaret had called in the morning to ask about the breakfast, but seeing nothing of me, she was waiting for me to come to her, before she stirred in the matter of cooking. As soon as it was known in the quarters, however, that I was sick, the hands began to pour in, and I did not lack attendants any more that day. After a day or two, I was moved down stairs and placed on a lounge in the dining-room, and here I lay, day after day, subject to the tender mercies of my dark colored friends, in the way of companions and food. "Aunt Pheny," who was "a practising physician," and who might often have been seen on the road with an umbrella to shelter her from the rays of the sun, once paid me a visit, and volunteered her services as nurse and physician. I gladly accepted them, and asked her to make up my bed, which request she endeavored to comply with; but she began at the wrong end of everything, putting both of the sheets at the bottom of the bed, and arranging one of the blankets for me to lie upon, and another to cover me up with. I looked on for awhile in wonder, and then gave her leave to desist from the difficult task, and weak as I was, managed to complete it myself. I suppose it was the first time in her life she had seen sheets upon a bed, and was ignorant of the manner in which they were to be used.

It was now the last of October, and quite chilly weather; and one night Margaret left me alone for several hours, while she was delivering a terrific homily to some one, on the subject of lying. At length she concluded that moral teaching would not atone for her lack of faithfulness to the sick, and some time after dark, she came in to see if I wanted anything. "Margaret," said I, as she entered, "do you intend taking care of me or not? I would like to know, so as to get some one else, if you are too busy."

"O yas, to be sure, I'se yer nuss, but dem niggers out dar done called me a liar, and I'se no gwine to stand dat;" and so saying, she swung herself around with all the air of a noble martyr, suffering unrighteously at the hands of the wicked.

I told her I did not see why she should leave me to suffer, because others had called her a liar. "Dem ar blacks," said she, "is so orful provoking, dey's no manners at all, to call me, who am de cook, a liar. Le'm me catch 'em at dat agin, and I'll *kill em*," said she, bring-out the latter words with terrific earnestness, indicating that she meant what she said.

Thus had Margaret left me in the cold and dark, and threatened with a chill, for nearly two hours, while she was engaged in vindicating her character. Perhaps not a solitary instance of a person transgressing one law, to prove himself innocent of violating another.

She at length issued her mandate, that from that time forward her slanderers should be *poisoned*. The reader may not comprehend the meaning here of this term, and I will therefore explain. One day, some time previous to my sickness, I was called upon to visit Lizzie Freeman, a smart young married woman, who had evidently, as some one's house servant, seen better days than those she was now experiencing, as a field hand. She was lying very low, and apparently had not long to live. She lay in a kind of stupor, refusing all nourishment, and hardly noticing any one. As soon as I spoke to her, however, she feebly stretched out her hand, and smiled faintly at me. "I am sorry to see you so badly off, Lizzie," said I; "what is the matter with you?" Turning over in the bed, and uttering a dismal groan, she said, "O, matter enough, Mr. Stearns; Margaret has poisoned me." And she began to shed tears profusely, as she thought of her almost helpless condition, and at length she sank down into her bed, seemingly unable to utter another word. "Poisoned you?" said I, "what has she done that for?" Lizzie aroused herself again sufficiently to reply, "O, she said if I ever came into the yard again, she would poison me; and I went there, and she's done done it, and I must die."

I assured Lizzie that poison could be removed from her stomach, and that she was not necessarily obliged to die. "O, it aint that kind of poison," she gasped; it's worse than that." I asked her explanation, and at length she managed to tell me, that Margaret had poisoned her by *throwing a stick down in the yard*, and she *had walked over it*, and that was the way Margaret poisoned her victims.

Of course I laughed heartily at this delusion, but the overseer said they all believed it, and I could not convince them of the contrary. He said Margaret was supposed to be in league with the devil, and had power to kill any one secretly, who walked over her enchanted stick.

It took days to reason the notion out of Lizzie's head, but after a while she began to believe what I said, and she concluded to take the Dr.'s medicine, and to eat something; and at length she fully recovered, and lives to-day a monument of reason's power over superstition. But she was not perfectly satisfied that Margaret had not done something to her, until I had written to my wife, and received her opinion on the subject.

It was in this way that Margaret enforced her power over her enemies. It was not every one who was thus favored by the evil one. It was only here and there that his Satanic majesty thus highly favored his liege subjects. But the case of the enchanted ones was not perfectly hopeless. On nearly every plantation, there was some one who could conquer Satan; and for a sum of money, his services could be secured in removing the effects of this awful poisoning. This person derives great benefit in a pecuniary point of view, from his remarkable healing powers, as the poor blacks will give all they possess, to be saved from dying.

But to return to my sick-room. After this threat Margaret's character was not so often traduced, and she was able to take better care of her patient. A few extracts from my diary at that time, will show how I relished her peculiar way of taking care of sick people.

"Oct. 29. Sick to-day, but a little easier. Black nurses execrable. Can't understand anything."

"Oct. 30. Did not dare to take medicine, for there was no one to take care of me. Did I not wish for my wife to nurse me? Dismal times."

"Oct 31. Almost every night lie awake. Terrible headache. Out of all patience with the blacks. Horrible nurses. Can't understand anything. Poor creatures, they know no better. Slavery has crushed them clear down to nothing. Must have charity for them."

"Nov. 2. If I had a good nurse I think I should get well in a few days. Wretched condition to be in. No one to see, or to do anything for you, but ignorant, stupid blacks."

"Nov. 3. Woke up crying because I had dreamed my mother was here, and found she was not. Horrible excitement of brain. It is so tedious not sleeping."

"Nov. 4. Composed in my mind some letters and sermons, and felt very happy in dwelling upon the love of God. How fortunate to have one with you all the time, whom you can love when earthly friends are away."

But I was not doomed to remain long in this condition. About ten days from this time, my wife and dear little Bell came to comfort and console me, and it seemed like living again. It is such a relief to behold once more the faces of loved friends, after such a solitary life as I had been leading.

Etta decided at once to have nothing more to do with Margaret, and she exchanged her for Susan, who was somewhat afraid to brave Margaret's wrath, by stepping into her shoes; but finally concluded to do so, and Margaret was dismissed.

Susan was directly the opposite of Margaret, in every particular. She was kind and obliging, and never refused to do the least thing when asked; although she was troubled with a poor memory, the universal failing of the blacks.

Etta brought with her numerous articles of food and for household use, and we began to live like "white folks" again. We had a bountiful supply of Irish potatoes and apples from the North, and a large cooking stove to cook them with. This was placed in the "big house," and there was no more screaming for the cook at the top of your voice, while the cook was nowhere to be found, but was busily engaged elsewhere, in defending her character, or in poisoning her enemies.

This stove was gazed upon with astonishment by the black people. Every one had to come in and take a look at the wonderful object; and Susan's dignity was greatly enhanced by being installed as the presiding genius of this new institution. It was long, however, before she could "get the hang" of the strange affair, as she said, and Etta's patience was severely tasked in initiating her into its mysteries.

CHAPTER XVI.

MR. SHERMAN'S TROUBLES WITH HIS LANDLORD.

Not many days after I was thus blessed, Mr. Sherman came to our house, and related a sad tale of his treatment at the hands of his landlord, a wealthy citizen of Augusta, and a cordial hater of the black race. My indignation was greatly aroused, and although not yet recovered from an attack of the chills and fever, I had on the day of Etta's return, I considered it my duty to go to his assistance, and if possible to rescue him from his pitiable condition.

But I cannot better describe the whole affair, than by copying extracts from a letter I wrote shortly after, to a distinguished Northern politician, detailing the whole affair. I afterwards saw this same gentleman, and on alluding to this matter as a *legal* outrage, he replied, "the South is full of *legal* outrages on the black man."

Would that his warning voice had then been heeded, and his plan adopted, for preserving order at the South. Years of anguish to the loyal people, and vast sums of money to the government would have thus been saved. But to my extracts.

"I have just passed through a scathing fire, out of which I trust I have come without serious injury; though not without the smell of fire upon my garments. It seems to me as if I had just awakened from some hideous dream; and just escaped from the terrible pressure of some severe nightmare. I am sure I would not repeat the experience of the last few days, for quite a sum of money.

On Friday last, in company with my wife and little girl, I passed through town, and proceeded to Mr. S.'s residence. On my arrival there, I learned that Mr. S. had been indeed in the very jaws of the lion, but had escaped alive. It seems that in an unguarded moment, trusting to proof that he had in his possession, he had signed an agreement to pay his landlord at a future time *about* a certain amount of corn; in return for some he had borrowed from him, which had not been measured. Without giving his tenant an opportunity to obtain this corn from his fields, he having been sick with the typhoid fever for some time; the landlord pounced upon him, and demanded the whole amount, leaving out the word *about* or construing it into much more, rather than less than the amount specified. The sick man demurred at paying more than the exact amount received of his landlord; offering to go with him and measure the bin where the cotton had been kept, and also the wagon in which it had been hauled; but 'no,' said the inexorable man, 'I will have such a number of bushels;' naming some two hundred more than Mr. S. felt sure he owed him; which was worth one dollar and a half a bushel. Every one who knew anything of the circumstance, advised him not to pay the extravagant demand.

Suddenly, at about dark, a few nights afterwards, the Sheriff appeared at Mr. S.'s house, and after attaching everything he could lay his hands upon, amounting to much more than the claim of the landlord, he arrested Mr. S., and took him to town, five miles distant, in spite of the tears and entreaties of his wife, who was confined to her bed with sickness. It was considerably after dark when they reached town, and difficult to find business men; but the Sheriff politely informed him that he must lie in jail that night, unless he could give bonds for his appearance at court, the next April; and this, after the debt had been amply secured by the property attached, thus rendering his appearance at court entirely unnecessary. Mr. S. stated to me that he had taken an active part in instructing the blacks on his place, and had often been severely blamed by his landlord, for so doing. The landlord could not conceal his hatred of the Yankees, and frequently said he would "never step inside of a Yankee's house," and never did go inside of Mr. S.'s house, always remaining outside, when he came to do business with him.

At this time, the paramount desire of both landlord and Sheriff seemed to be to get Mr. S. into jail; but the Sheriff at length gave him permission to go and see a few Northern friends, who secured the name of a wealthy colored man as his bondsman, the Sheriff in the mean while advising the colored man not to sign the bond.

The Sheriff refused to take any of the Northern men as bondsmen, alleging their insufficiency of property. Notwithstanding the law exempts from attachment a horse and a cow, the Sheriff attached them also, obliging Mr. S. to return home on foot, sick as he was, at twelve o'clock at night.

You may imagine my feelings, and those of my wife, as he told us this story; and as we looked on the care-worn features of his wife, now almost reduced to a shadow by the sickness of her husband, and the unremitting persecution he had endured, we felt exasperated enough, and Etta almost boiled over with indignation. I tell you, it is difficult preserving one's Christian equanimity, under such circumstances.

But this was not all. I told my friend I would go to town with him the next day, and see if we could not *replevin* his property. But before that could be accomplished, the Sheriff appeared again and re-arrested Mr. S., on another charge. The poor man was thunderstruck, and had no idea what was coming now, and feebly asked what it all meant. "The cotton, man;

have you forgotten the cotton?" exultingly exclaimed the Sheriff. "What cotton?" tremblingly asked Mr. S. "Why the ten bales of cotton you owe for the rent of the land," the Sheriff replied, triumphantly. "I do not owe it, sir," replied Mr. S., with what little strength he had remaining. "Well, you will owe him by-and-by, won't you?" asked the Sheriff. "Not under a month, and the payment is well secured by another man's signature," replied Mr. S.

"Never mind that," responded the Sheriff, "we don't go by Yankee law here, thank God." And you ought to have seen the air of triumph with which he uttered these words. It seemed to me as if I could almost look over his shoulder, and see the shadow of Andrew Johnson standing by, and smiling with grim satisfaction, at this embodiment of "my policy."

Here we were, surrounded with rebels, and what could be done? If a territorial government like that you have advocated, had been in operation, its officers would have been loyal, and this outrage would not have occurred. But there was no power or officer, except rebels, to whom we could apply, and of course we could not expect much mercy from them. It was three o'clock P. M., and something must be done before night. With the assistance of several Northern men, I tried to borrow this money for Mr. S., but unsuccessful in that, I saw that my friend must either lie in jail that night, and his poor wife be brought to death's door, or I must pay the debt myself.

This I could ill afford to do, for I knew that I should need all of my means, to pay my own debts; but friendship triumphed over self-interest, and after urgent solicitation, I prevailed on my cotton-factors to deliver to me an amount of cotton I had left with them on sale, they being very loth to do it, as it deprived them of their commission for selling, amounting to twenty-five or thirty dollars. But their benevolence finally prevailed over their interest, and I returned in triumph to our persecutors, with an order for seven bales of cotton, it being all I had in town, to be delivered to the unjust landlord, the next morning.

At first, these wicked men peremptorily refused to settle, unless they could have the whole ten bales that night, and said Mr. S. should lie in jail, unless it was all produced. Here was a new dilemma. It was now dark, and the stores were many of them closed. But in company with two Northern men, I started again in pursuit of the remaining amount. We were unsuccessful, and returned in two hours, with heavy hearts. But the counsel for Mr. S., who, although a strong Southerner, had worked well for his client, in spite of his being a Yankee, at length prevailed upon the opposing counsel to wait until morning for the sum still due, and we returned in triumph to Mr. S.'s home. This was on a Northern Thanksgiving day, and we found a good turkey dinner in readiness for us on our return, Mr. S. having saved his turkies from the general wreck. This Thanksgiving dinner was devoured with as keen a relish, and as thankful hearts, as often characterizes the eating of such dinners.

The next morning we returned to town, and succeeded in borrowing the requisite amount, and the whole debt of thirteen hundred and fifty dollars was paid by myself. The colored men were of great service in this case. Not only did the one first alluded to, save my friend from going to jail, but at the request of a Northern man, in whom they had confidence, several others came forward and signed the replevin bond; thus enabling Mr. S. to obtain possession of his property and his farming operations without farther molestation. They thus showed themselves capable of gratitude towards their friends."

I have introduced this lengthy narrative to show in the first place the animus of the Southerners towards the Yankees; and secondly, the readiness of the intelligent colored people to do all in their power to protect the latter. This step on my part, rendered it necessary for me to undertake a journey to the North, in the middle of the winter, to obtain the means to replace in part the sum I had used to protect Mr. S., which I obtained from funds I had in Colorado; but I was obliged to hire in Boston, at a high rate of interest, a sum sufficient to liquidate the debt incurred the next morning, after our arrangement of the principal portion of the debt. The whole expense of this journey, including interest I had to pay, and telegrams to Colorado, added to what I had already paid, made a total of fifteen hundred dollars wrung from me by the treachery of others.

This step resulted in a series of privations to my own family, that was wholly unanticipated. As some of my friends may blame me, for what may seem to them a rash act on my part, I will state that in an unfortunate hour I had signed my name as security for the payment of the thirteen hundred and fifty dollars; and if I had not paid it as I did, I should have been obliged to pay it some months later, and I thought I might as well pay it then, and save my friend from all the suffering consequent upon my refusal; little dreaming that I should never receive it back from him. He sacredly promised to give me every bale of cotton raised on his place, if necessary, to liquidate the debt; but I never received a single bale. The season proved a very unfortunate one for both Mr. S. and myself, an early frost destroying the cotton everywhere. His whole crop amounted to only nine bales, all of which was consumed in paying his hands; and mine amounted to only eleven bales. No one could tell the deep disappointment this failure of my crop caused me, as I had relied on the crop to pay the mortgage given on my farm at the time of its purchase. My whole crop fell short forty-seven hundred dollars of the amount we had hoped to obtain, and it left me one thousand dollars behind, in paying the expenses of carrying on the farm. It seemed that the first cotton seed planted was several years old, and failed to come up, rendering it necessary to replant the whole; and this second planting was not accomplished early enough to allow the cotton to mature previous to the early frosts. When I purchased the place, everything looked flourishing, and I was not informed of the fact of the second planting until long afterwards.

It was a melancholy sight to walk through the cotton fields, and see the stalks covered with immature bolls; not more than one fourth of the whole number of bolls having become perfected.

What the result of this failure of my crop would be in reference to the payment of the mortgage, I could not tell; but on stating the case to Mr. Dozier, the gentleman holding it, he very graciously extended the time for payment to another year. Mr. Prince took occasion before he left, to assure me that the cause of the failure of our crops, had been "my spending so much time with the blacks in teaching them to read, and their heads were so full of books that they could not work." I rather wondered that he had not mentioned this to me before, in season to save a portion of my crop. But having full confidence in the all wise power that governs the world, I bowed in humble submission before his chastening rod; feeling fully assured that although

> "He works in a mysterious way
> His wonders to perform,"

yet "all things work together for good to them that

love him;" and although ignorant to-day of the reason of all of our afflictions, to morrow's rising sun shall dispel the dark clouds surrounding us, and show us in resplendent light, the reasonableness of all of God's dealing with us; and that "not a sparrow falls to the ground" without his consent.

"Ye fearful saints fresh courage take;
The clouds ye so much dread,
Are big with mercy, and shall break
In blessings on your head."

CHAPTER XVII.

A RETROSPECT OF THE PAST YEAR, AND COMMENCEMENT OF A NEW ONE; WITH EXTRACTS FROM LETTERS FROM THE SOUTH.

Thus ended my first year's experience as missionary and teacher among the freedmen. If its close found me less enthusiastic in reference to their immediate elevation, it did not find me any less determined to labor faithfully for the accomplishment of that end. I had sounded the depths of their degradation, and ascertained that they were greater than I had previously believed, I had met with great pecuniary loss, but this was of small moment, if my great object in coming here could be promoted. Money, time, efforts, and what little ability I possessed, were all to be used to promote this end, the elevation of the blacks, and through them, that of the entire South. If others looked upon my enterprise as Quixotic, it mattered not to me. If others failed to see in these efforts anything but a money-making scheme, that was still less a concern of mine. It was enough for me to know that God smiled on my labors, and his voice was unmistakably heard, bidding me to "go forward."

I felt that I had "labored and prayed and not fainted;" that I had devoted myself to the deliverance from ignorance and vice, of those who had never before been blessed with teachings of morality, and intellectual life. One year could do but little in such a mighty undertaking; nevertheless great numbers had learned to read fluently. Lessons of industry, neatness, punctuality, obedience, honesty and benevolence, had been given them liberally. A multitude of facts had been made known to their astonished minds; and some intellectual life, had been developed among them.

The great principles of the Christian religion, had been explained to them, in a different way from ever before. The doctrines of Jesus had been taught those hitherto almost ignorant of his name. A desire to be pure and holy, had been partially awakened in their minds; and above all, a yearning after a higher life in every respect had been created in their souls. It was true, the darkness around them could still be felt, but *some* rays of divine light from the orb of celestial glory, had penetrated those dark recesses, and partially scattered the surrounding gloom. It was my duty to buckle on the armor for another year's contest with the powers of darkness; and to gird myself anew for the "irrepressible conflict," still going on between God and the devil, right and wrong, and light and darkness.

In commencing another year's labor, I needed pecuniary assistance, and Mr. Sherman, having some means at his disposal, concluded to unite them with mine, in another attempt to befriend the poor and needy, and to "deliver him that is spoiled, out of the hands of the oppressor." The work before us, was somewhat different from that proposed by others, engaged in labors of love for the freedmen.

They confined themselves almost exclusively, to the

education and moral development of the colored race; we added to these ends, the equally important one, of finding homes for the benighted ones, from whence should diverge rays of pecuniary, moral, intellectual, social and political light, that should thoroughly illuminate the surrounding darkness. I do not say, that our plan was wiser than that of others, only that it was more comprehensive; and perhaps for that very reason may not have been so wise; as we sometimes err in attempting to accomplish more than can be thoroughly performed.

Be that as it may, we still believed that a right physical basis lay at the foundation of the colored man's welfare; that education and religion alone could not elevate him so rapidly, as these combined with efforts to benefit him physically. Consequently, we had a herculean task before us. To develop the black man in all of his habits, and modes of life, is a far greater undertaking than merely to educate his intellect.

Mr. Sherman was unremitted in his efforts to produce a change in their industrial habits. Our plan may have been termed one to establish a model farm, or self-supporting industrial school; where all that related to man's external welfare should be taught and practiced, as well as those things that concerned his moral and intellectual progress.

But we also found the black man the victim of the white man's hate, and as such he needed our protection. We saw a mighty struggle going on between the supremacy of the U. S. Government, and that of those who had sought its overthrow. We found that the spirit of the rebellion, still flourished in the hearts of many of its former supporters; and that without strenuous measures on the part of the government, the great objects of the war would fail of accomplishment. The black man was looked upon as the cause of the defeat of the so-called Confederacy, and as such, was most cordially hated. Of course, those who espoused his cause, were deserving of a like fate with him. I have already detailed the attempts made to break up our Sunday school, but I have not stated that even if we had not taught such a school, our very presence here, as a friend to the Union, was enough to bring upon us the maledictions of all the disloyalists around. This then, was another portion of our task ; to defend our government against the unjust aspersions of its enemies, and to defend its allies, whether white or black.

At this stage of my narrative, may I be pardoned for saying, that our lives were safe, just in proportion to the stringency of the government measures for our protection ? Whenever the government wavered, and under the lead of that traitor, Andrew Johnson, attempted to re-instate the rebels in their former places, then did we tremble from fear ; but when military rule was declared, we felt relieved from a heavy burden, and as if we could breathe freely. It was *not* the severity of the Reconstruction measures, that afterwards endangered us, but their *lack* of severity. Let this fact be well weighed by our Northern friends.

We had not been many months underway in the second year of our enterprise, when we began to reap the benefit of those so-called severe measures. The change was like that from darkness to light, and during the whole of the ensuing summer, life and property were nearly as safe as any where at the North. It was really amazing to witness the marked change in the temper and disposition of those around. Smiles and bows met us, instead of frowns and averted faces; and if the glorious military rule of those days could have been continued, according to the programme of the more radical republicans, high-heaven would not now be bending in sorrow over the accumulation of the woes, of the Union men at the South.*

But in an evil hour, our party took counsel of its enemies, and abated the stringency of its measures, and our enemies at the South began to prepare anew for their work of persecution. As an inhabitant of the South, I may be permitted again to express my conviction, that, "Reconstruction" has been a failure, *not* because of its undue severity, but because it stopped mid-way in its benign work, and left us, with one foot in the mud of pro-slavery hate, and the other struggling to find a firm foundation elsewhere — a most miserable condition of uncertainty.

The true policy should have been not to have re-admitted a single State, without the most ample guarantees for future good behavior, with the condition of immediately remanding each State back to a territorial or provincial government, if the guarantees were not fulfilled. If Georgia failed to allow the black man the fullest liberty in voting as he pleased, then Georgia should have been walked *out* of the Union, as fast as it was trying to walk *in* to that loyal enclosure. And when Tennessee failed to carry out its positive promises, it should have been previously understood, that Tennessee was no longer a member of the Union. These States had severed the Union of their own accord. Its

* The above passage was written before the enforcement of the Ku Klux bill. Since the rigid enforcement of that benevolent and judicious act, comparative "order reigns in Warsaw," at least as far as I am acquainted at the South.

priceless advantages should not have been at the beck and call of those who had so long scouted them, and gloried in their acts, but should have been accorded to humble supplicants only, and to those no longer than they remained humble and submissive.

"Show pity Lord. O Lord forgive;
Let a *repenting* rebel live."

So it should have been with our government, and the Southern rebels. When they had thoroughly repented, they should have been received back into the Union, and should have remained there no longer than they showed their repentance was not to be repented of, but one that brought forth "fruits meet for repentance."

I hope I may be pardoned for thus expressing myself freely in this matter. This narrative would be incomplete, without alluding to the great barrier in the way of the development of the freedmen, afforded by the want of protection on the part of the U. S. Government, against their enemies. As an evidence of my feelings at this time, I will present the reader with some extracts from letters, written to Northern friends, during the first year of my Southern residence, premising that all that time, and during much of the time afterwards, excessive caution was necessary, in thus promulgating my views at the North; and that oftentimes, those letters appeared from some person living at the North, as having been received by him, from a Southern friend, without alluding to the part of the South where that friend resided. With the exception of the times when our good Uncle Samuel extended over us the shadow of his protecting wing, it would have been extremely unsafe for us to have written a true statement of affairs here, and had it published at the North.

Some of the facts contained in the letters given below, have been alluded to before in this narrative; but I thought it no harm to publish them, in the language used at the time of their occurrence, as the reader will thereby be convinced, that in this narrative, I have not trusted to my memory alone, for the facts presented to my readers.

From the Colorado Miner's Journal.

"PLANTATION HOME, GA., JULY 10, 1866.

As I have many friends in Colorado who wish to know what I am doing at the South, and what I think of the country, will you allow me to address them through the columns of your paper? You may wonder why I date my letter so indefinitely; I will tell you. I am here like Daniel in the lion's den; not that I am like Daniel exactly, but that the people about here are considerably like Daniel's lions; that is, they would devour me, if a strong arm did not prevent them. In this case, it is a terrestial and not a celestial power that protects me, viz: the military power of the government. For a long time after leaving Colorado, I hesitated about pitching my tent in this Sodom, so fearful were the statements continually reaching us, concerning the condition of Johnson's friends in the reconstructed South. But at last I got tired of waiting for Congress to do something, and concluded I would run the risk, and go and witness for myself the state of affairs in that rebellious country. Accordingly, on the last day of April, I left Springfield, Mass., where I had been residing since my return from Colorado, and started for the sunny South. I visited various places before coming here, among which were Charleston and Savannah, and found there unmistakable evidences of the need of a restraining hand on the part of our uncle, towards his wayward children. I did not come to the conclusion that it was time to "kill the fatted calf and make merry with our friends," on account of the repentance of our Southern brethren. On the contrary, every step I took in this disloyal country, convinced me of the absolute necessity of making our would-be converted brethren of the South, pass through a period of probation, such as sinners in the Methodist church are very wisely required to pass through, before being admitted to the full privileges of the church; and as they are required to remain in the outer courts six months on trial, so would I have these political sinners kept outside of the Union for six years at least. Nothing can be fraught with greater ruin to the nation, than the present re-admission of these semi-rebel States. No Northern man, except a miserable doughface, can remain here with safety, without the protection of the military, and if Congress re-admits the Southerners unconditionally, according to Johnson's plan, the next step will be the withdrawal of the military from almost the entire South, and the forced abandonment of the South by all loyal Yankees. But as facts are far more important than theories, I will proceed to present you with a few of them. On my arrival at the South, they had begun to lessen their domineering tone a little, in consequence of the passage of the "Civil Rights Bill" over the veto of the President. They had begun to think that the power of the President was not omnipotent, and that they might at last be forced to receive terms from the hated Radicals, and therefore, were less violent in their denunciations. But that measure not being followed by anything radical on the part of Congress, and the prospect being that the "milk and water" amendments of the reconstruction committee would be the only thing demanded of them, they have grown jubilant again, and are as loud-mouthed as ever in their denunciations of the government and its friends.

But to my facts. On the last fourth of July, not far from here, the military commander of the post threw a U. S. flag across the sidewalk. The streets were thronged that day, and nearly every lady refused to walk under the flag, and actually left the sidewalk and trailed her robes in the dirty street, until she had passed the hated emblem, when she resumed the sidewalk. This was told me by the commander himself, who sat in his office and watched this sublime movement. But you may say this was only the spite of the ladies. But you must remember that the Southern ladies are not believers in "Woman's Rights," and would not therefore have taken this step without the sanction of the male portion of the community. Not long since, in this same town, the Mayor of the place refused to allow a procession of colored children to decorate the graves of Union soldiers buried there, because it would be construed into an insult to the Southern people, and the procession was obliged to abandon the project, or there would have been a mob. Every Yankee that comes South is called a d—d Yankee, and people "wonder what they want here." The papers publicly urge the people not to sell their lands to the Yankees, but I am happy to say that love of money is more powerful than political hate, and almost every day I am solicited to send to my Northern friends offers of such and such valuable lands. Yesterday I rode over a splendid plantation of two thousand and seven hundred acres, the owner of which wishes to sell it, on account of losses sustained by the war. A few days ago a couple of men, riding by my house, stopped and enquired of one of my hands, who owned the place; she told them a Yankee, and one of them immediately said: "God d—d him he ought to be shot." Said another man a few days ago, to my overseer, at my gate, "tell that man, God d—him, we are coming to give him hell one of these nights." Said another man, and he a near neighbor, whose plantation joins mine, "God d—n them d—d low-born Yankees, we will make them smell hell one of these nights." The brother of this man last December, killed a colored man for trying to prevent him from abusing his sister:

We do not feel safe any of the time when we ride about the country, or go to town. We carry our revolvers with us, take them to church with us, and sleep with them under our pillows, besides keeping a breech-loaded rifle all ready for action, any time. Frequently we are called up in the night, and get our firearms all ready, supposing the enemy are upon us. This is about as bad, as it used to be in Kansas in border ruffian times, and I feel even more insecure, than I did then, for we have no friends but the blacks, and they are very poorly armed. But I am very sure they will not drive me away alive; if I go, it will be because my dead body is carried away. What is life to any one without freedom, to do what you deem to be your duty! Our offence is that every Sunday afternoon, I collect my hands together in the shade of some of the large old trees, that my yard is partly filled with, and instruct them in the alphabet, and in the first principles of morality and religion, in all of which they are sadly deficient. I am assisted in this work by Mr. A. H. Parker, for four years a member of the first Colorado cavalry. Other hands from the neighboring plantations come in, so that our Sunday school now numbers over one hundred pupils, mostly adults; seventy-five of them have already purchased the National Primer, and all are anxious to learn. We feel amply repaid for all our efforts in their behalf, by their gratitude, and eager wish to improve themselves. Most of them spend their two hours' nooning which I give them, in learning their lessons, and it is a pleasant sight, I assure you, every noon and every night, to see on the door step of every negro cabin, a knot of darkies trying to pry into the mysteries of the spelling book.

But more facts. Said a lady, a few weeks ago, in addressing a neighbor: "I think it a burning shame for you to let your house to a Yankee; it is a grand insult to every Southern lady." A gentleman living near by, said he would never pollute himself so much as to put his foot inside of the house of a Yankee, and he had lost $100,000 by the war, and then had a Yankee living on his plantation, but had never been to his house. Last 4th of July, the colored people marched through the streets, protected by the military, but the remark was made afterwards by the white people, that it was a shame and disgrace to the whole country. I have not a doubt that if there had been no military there, this procession could not have passed through the streets."

July 13th. — Since writing the above, I have seen a Southern Union man, the first native-born Southern Union man I have seen since I came into the State, always excepting the blacks. He lives in an adjoining county, and more than corroborates all that I have written above. He gave me a detailed account of the outrages perpetrated upon the blacks in his neighborhood. A gang of men went from house to house, robbing the inmates of their money and clothes, and violating the persons of the women, and no white person, except himself, had ventured to condemn the outrages, and his life had been threatened repeatedly for so doing, so that he was compelled even to go to his work armed. One darkey took the law into his own hands, and shot one of the ruffians dead, and wounded another, for the doing of which he was lodged in jail, and finally an attempt was made to hang him by a mob, but no attempt was made to arrest the white men. He says that the white men are so angry, that they have lost their slaves, that they wink at every outrage committed upon them, and many of their employers utterly refuse to pay them their wages, after they have fairly earned them. This man opposed the war from the onset, and for so doing was threatened with death. He says they were told at the commencement of the war, that all they had to do was just to take a musket, and show it to a Yankee, and he would be sure to run. It is emphatically a reign of terror in that county, for the poor black man and his friends. This man told me that he had always been opposed to Slavery from a mere boy. These events occurred just about the time I came into this section of the country. The outrages were finally lulled for a season, by the arrival of a small military force, the officers of which threatened to burn the county, unless the robberies were stopped, and the ruffians then left for South Carolina. They all lived in the vicinity of their crimes, and were well known to every one, but no attempt was ever made to punish them.

After such a description of affairs, your readers may be astonished at my inviting them to come here and settle; but this is the only way to stop these proceedings effectually. Every live Yankee who comes and settles here is a pillar of strength to the few who are here, and a terror to the haters of the blacks. The poor blacks seem to crouch under the wings of the Yankees as chickens gather beneath the wings of the mother hen. They will work for a Yankee at much less price than for a "reb," as they term all the Southerners. You can't make them believe anything else, only that the Yankees are their friends and the Southerners their enemies. I am overrun with applications for next year, when the old contracts expire.

No Northern man who is disposed to treat the blacks like human beings, need have the least fear about obtaining laborers, although the Southerners complain much. It tickles the darkies mightily to receive, according to the custom here, at the end of each month, one half of their wages. They turn it over and their eyes glisten while they say, "Dat ar is more money dan I'se ever had afore in my life."

This country must be settled up by Northern people, in order to develop its resources. The farm I am on has never been manured until a very little this year. With a good system of manuring it would produce double what it has. Large fields of tolerable good land lie idle, year after year, when they would produce good crops of cotton by proper cultivation. It is estimated the increase of the crop would doubly pay the cost of applying guano. Then the Southern people, never can manage the blacks as well as Northerners can. Force is the only law they know anything about, and it is utterly impossible to succeed with that now without crushing the blacks.

Yours, truly,

C. STEARNS.

The next extracts are from an article published by a Northern friend, giving my statements as written for private perusal.

SPRINGFIELD, JAN. 21, 1867.

"I am frequently receiving letters from my friends at the South, containing earnest appeals in their behalf, and representing their situation there as anything but pleasant, on account of the spirit and feelings of the people. Many of these letters contain information of value to the Northern people, and with your permission I would like to present a few extracts from them to your readers, premising that the reason my friends do not write directly for your and other Northern papers is, because as they say, it would render their situation more dangerous than it now is, and they dare not do so. And is this the fruit of our long and bloody war, that Union men dare not even give a bare statement of facts that are daily transpiring there? Has not our blood and treasure been wasted for nothing? And what shall we think of our government, that thus allows the fruits of the war to be rendered valueless? Cannot the United States government protect its citizens everywhere in the exercise of free speech?

Says one of my friends, "We do not feel safe any of the time when we ride about the country or go to town. At every unusual noise in the night we start from our beds and seize our fire-arms, thinking that perhaps the enemy is upon us. We never see a white man approaching the house even in the day time, without an instinctive feeling of fear, and we are always relieved when the man approaching proves to be a colored man, for then we know he is a friend. I know not why the whites should feel so towards me, for I certainly entertain no feeling of ill-will towards them, and would not hurt a hair of their heads. My religion teaches me to forgive my enemies, and I would do them all the good in my power, although they hate me and the blacks terribly. But yesterday the enigma was solved. An overseer on another plantation came to see me, and I expressed to him my surprise at the feeling manifested towards me by the whites, telling him as I have you, that I wished them no harm. "O," said he, "I can tell you why they hate you. Are you not in the habit of holding a Sunday school and teaching the negroes to read." "O yes," said I, "I believe intelligent laborers are more profitable to hire than ignorant ones, and for that reason, if for no other, I wish my blacks to learn to read." He laughed heartily, and said, "Well, I respect you for what you are doing, but you can't make one of them slaveholders ever believe that a negro is capable of much improvement. They always despised him, and now they hate him because he is free." "Well," said I, why then are they so mad with me for teaching them, if it will do no good!" He laughed again and said, "How long have you been at the South?" "Not long," said I. "I thought so," said he, "or you would not try to reconcile the language of the Southerners with itself. It is true, they are all the time talking of the stupidity of the negroes, and yet only last week a man told me that if you went on teaching the niggers they soon would know as much as they did." I felt inclined to laugh in my turn now, but reflected that the "birds of the air" might carry it to the rebels, and I desisted.

The fact is, they greatly fear this teaching of the negroes. I have heard no other charge brought against me, only I that I was "a d—d Yankee," and was teaching the negroes.

The teachers from the North are everywhere insulted and abused. No Southern lady invites them to her house, and any one who dares to associate with them is immediately ostracized from the social circle to which she belonged.

Said a Northern lady to me the other day, "I never pass through the streets, without being insulted in some way or other." She was the wife of a physician of a colored hospital I passed a man on the road the other day, and bowed to him, as I usually do. He bowed in return, and after I had passed him, I heard him say, "God d—n your Yankee phiz." Even the children partake more or less of this spirit. A little girl of my acquaintance was one day walking through the street, and she heard some other little girls behind her talking. One of them says, "There goes a Yankee girl; well I am sure I would not speak to her;" and then added, with a great deal of emphasis, "why, I would not speak to my own mother, if she was a Yankee woman."

A gentleman of my acquaintance from the North, who has been longer here than I have, told me the other day that "I could not begin to conceive of the bitter hatred they all felt towards Northerners." Why it should be so I know not, for certainly they have received nothing but leniency at the hands of the North, and what few Northern men there are here, are certainly powerless to do them harm. But a friend who was here at the close of the war, tells me there is a marked difference between their conduct now and at the close of the war. Then they ate liberally of "umble pie," but now they seem to have forgotten their humiliation, and are as proud and restive as ever. I have no doubt it is because "sentence against an evil work is not executed speedily, therefore the heart of the sons of men is fully set in them to do evil." If Johnson had not revived their sunken hopes, I question if their conduct would have been so bad as it has recently been. Yea, more; I verily believe that he is responsible for nine-tenths of the murders and outrages committed here, for he is everywhere quoted, lauded and praised. No man, not even Jeff Davis himself, would be treated with greater respect than Johnson would, if he should come here; but alas! for Sumner or Thad Stevens: *they* had better not set their feet on this "consecrated soil" at present.

And yet, the Southerners are continually crying out at the oppression of the North, in not re-admitting them to the Union. I told a lady the other day, I did not see why they fretted so much about it, when they fought four years to get out of the Union; that I should think they might be contented to stay out a little while. Will you not urge upon all you see the importance of keeping the South out at present? You can't imagine how badly we feel, when we read in the papers of the attempts to admit the South back into the Union. We tremble, lest it should be so. I do not know what I shall do, when that takes place, for then the few soldiers here will be withdrawn, and we shall be at the mercy of the Southerners. Say to all of your friends, 'Do not admit the South at present. Let them stay out until they have repented, if it is for twenty-five years.' All the Northern people here with whom I am acquainted say the same. *We* desire more than anything else the establishment of a territorial government. Not these bogus State governments, under the direction of a few pretended loyalists. They are not what we want. They could afford us *no* protection, and would be a complete farce, if established, for every Southern man would be opposed to them. It would not be just to the South, and in all our dealings with them, we shall aim at exact justice towards them. What we want is a *bona fide* territorial government, like that of Nebraska and Colorado, administered by the United States government, and its laws subject to the revision of Congress, although the legislature is elected by the people — "for this we pray and ever will pray."

Now, says the Northern writer, I have presented you the views of my "Southern friends," and it is for you to say whether you will second them to the public. Coming from the South, from those in the midst of the "burning fiery furnace," they are entitled to much weight, it appears to me. These writers "speak what they do know, and testify that they have seen," and are no uncertain witness. They write almost at the peril of their lives, and certainly can have no other motive than to tell the truth; and shall not their voices be heeded by the Northern public? Some of them have invested their whole fortunes in the South, and they feel that their all is at stake in this matter. Protection for themselves and the blacks is all they ask, and this they feel they can have only by the establishment of a territorial government in each State, backed up by a sufficient military force to sustain it.

Respectfully yours, R. W. S

In corroboration of some of these views, I give an extract from a Southern loyal paper, which I noticed in the Springfield paper containing my friend's article.

WHAT LOYAL SOUTHERNERS WANT.

The Raleigh (N. C.) *Standard* thus speaks of the policy that government should adopt towards the leaders of the rebellion, who are now aspiring also to be first in the work of reconstruction: — "Government must strike them in such a way as to deprive them of all influence. The great body of our people are disposed to submit in good faith to the Government, and to accept the Union on the terms laid down by the majority, and they would do so but for those wicked instigators and leaders. Let Congress deal with them. Let it strike them down, both as a measure of security for the future and of just punishment for their crimes. Let this be done in an act to reorganize our State governments on a loyal basis, and the loyal people of these Southern States, once in possession of supreme power over these traitors, will answer for it that they will no more disturb the public peace or influence the people against the Government. This is all the loyal people of the South ask. Pass Mr. Stevens' bill and they will take care of secessionists, latter-day war men and traitors of all kinds. They will not torture, or shoot, or hang them, or malign, or persecute them, as they did the Unionists during the rebellion, but they will make them know their places, and will see to it that they never have power again over this people, whom they have ruined by their folly, selfishness, and wicked ambition.

But to return to my narrative. Still clinging to my original idea of making the blacks partners in our farm labors, I was overruled by the wishes of my partner, Mr. S., who thought we had better try the plan of wages this year, and then next year adopt the co-operative plan. We determined on cultivating about four hundred and fifty acres, and had twelve animals and twenty-seven hands for our working force. These were placed under the immediate control of Mr. S., while my labors were to be confined to the general supervision of the farm, the providing of means to carry on operations, keeping account with the hands, and attending to the cultivation of our large garden ; besides our Sunday work, in which we both participated. It is unnecessary to dwell upon the events of the year, as they were not materially different from those of the previous one, except that the hands manifested a more restive spirit, and that I was oftener called upon to settle disputes between them and their overseer. These disputes sometimes assumed a tragic form, and in one case, a woman threw a deadly missile at Mr. Shermans' head. At another time, a man named Isaac, threatened to kill Mr. S., because he endeavored to prevent him from whipping his wife, this being a pastime not unfrequently indulged in by the blacks. At this time, Isaac quoted one of our Northern friends as an example of wife-whipping, and said everybody at the South whipped their wives; a statement I am greatly inclined to doubt.

Singing songs while at their work, was another of their pastimes, and they would " drop the shovel and the hoe," in the midst of their labors, and sing a religious song. Then, they claimed the privilege of carrying their guns to the fields, in order to shoot a stray rabbit, or squirrel, that might cross their path. So much time was consumed in this diversion, that it became necessary to prohibit the practice of carrying guns to their work, which they maintained was a great encroachment upon their rights as freemen. Then, whenever in the plentitude of their wisdom they deemed it necessary for their physical welfare that they should enjoy a holiday, they *took* that holiday ; however different might be our opinion on the subject. Once, right in the height of cotton planting, Saturday morning found every hand flatly refusing to labor, for they had "concluded to have a holiday." It was in vain that they were told they might have two holidays, if they would wait until the cotton was planted. They wanted it then, and have it they would ; and as is often the case with the unfortunate planter, we were obliged to submit to their unreasonable demand. On the night of the same day, the larger part of the disobedient crowd might have been found at their prayer meeting, shouting and singing the praises of God.

It has been already mentioned that we had no society except that of the blacks. No one who has not tried it, can imagine the deficiency in one's life thus occasioned, or the absolute solitude of our situation. We saw faces it is true, but they were not those bearing the stamp of a well-trained intellect. We heard voices, but they were not those used in tones calculated to regale the intellectual or moral ears ; but those used in every variety of harsh and discordant sounds.

While in Augusta, a Southern lady of our acquaintance informed my wife that it was not the custom of Southern ladies to call upon Yankee ones, and hoped she would "not take it amiss, or as intended as a slight of her in particular." My wife gravely replied, "I should be glad to see any Southern ladies who wish to see me; but they may rest assured I shall not lament their absence. They can do as they please, and I shall be satisfied." This remark was uttered with firmness, and as indicative of her conscious superiority to these same Southern ladies; but after all, every one craves human society, and if we cannot have that of our equals and superiors, we are sometimes glad of that of our inferiors.

I would remark that this prophetic promise of our friend was almost literally fulfilled, not half a dozen Southern ladies having ever honored us with a call, and the Southern people are proverbially fond of visiting. So that, when we heard that those noble and self-denying ladies, the Augusta teachers, contemplated making us a visit, we were highly delighted. Some six or eight came together at one time, with several gentleman, and we had a nice time, they remaining about two days, and some of them longer. The gentlemen talked to the blacks, and gave them very excellent advice, a large concourse having gathered on Sunday, for the purpose of hearing them. The ladies talked to them in a familiar manner, and sang beautifully to them, and it was a time long to be remembered on our plantation.

A little later in the season, some of them came again, and we had a strawberry festival in honor of them. The tables were spread under the trees, and all "went merry as a marriage bell." After we had partaken of our repast, the blacks were bid welcome, and the tables were quickly filled with our sable friends, for the first time in their lives, probably, allowed to gather around a white man's table. The little ones of course enjoyed it hugely, and *our* little ones no less than the black majority. The bulk of the preparations came upon our wives, as such things always do, and we men had not much to do, except to enjoy the occasion, just as the "cruel men" always enjoy themselves, from the diligent toil of their wives.

Mr. and Mrs. S. were blessed with a charming child, of about eleven years of age, named Lizzie; and she and Mary Bell, my child, never forgot the scenes of that day, so glorious to them. One of the worst evils connected with our kind of life, was the utter absence of all out-of-door amusement for our children, without mixing with the black children. If Lizzie or Bell stepped their feet outside of the house, it was the signal for the arrival of a whole bevy of little black children, whose uncouth ways and manners were of no advantage to our beloved ones.

Children, of course, are creatures of imitation, and it does almost seem as if they had an instinct for the bad, in preference to the good; for it was not long before we found our children undergoing a rapid transformation, from white to black children. Often have I been compelled to say to my little one, "Why, Bell, all you need to make you a perfect black child, is to paint your face black." But play they must, and all we could do was to select a few of the best of the colored children, and limit her associates to those few.

I am sure if evil ever obtained unlimited sway anywhere, it is on a Southern plantation of negro children. Words cannot describe the perverse spirit there is in the hearts and lives of these little imps of darkness, as I am constrained to call them. We look forward to the rising generation of blacks as an agreeable offset to the depravity of their parents; but I must confess, sickening as it is to contemplate, that as far as my observation extends, this "rising generation" does not hold out a very alluring prospect of usefulness. It is true that they will be more intelligent than their parents, but I fear that their morals will be no better. The only hope I can see is in establishing boarding-schools, where the children will be kept from home contamination for a few years, until good principles have taken root in their minds, and then send them out to influence others. If the reader knew all about these homes, he would not wonder at my conclusion.

CHAPTER XVIII.

SOME ITEMS OF FARMING EXPENSE.

It may not be uninteresting to the general reader, to learn some particulars respecting the cost of farming at the South, and the amount of capital necessary for successful farming. I will therefore digress from my narrative, sufficiently to present a few facts upon this subject. I would not advise any Northern man to commence operations here, unless he has the means of defraying all his expenses, until about the middle of August, at which time his corn will be ready to feed to his mules. To be sure, a very large portion of Southern farmers require an advance on their crops, from their cotton factors; but this system is a bad one to follow, as the farmer is hardly ever out of debt. As has been already stated, two men and one mule will cultivate from thirty-five to forty acres of land. If you have the same number of hands and mules that we had, viz, twenty-seven hands and twelve mules, then your expenses, until about the 1st of August, will be for stock $1200, allowing each animal to consume eight quarts of corn, and eight pounds of fodder or hay each day, reckoning the corn at $1.25 a bushel, which is its average price. The rations for your hands will cost you $34 a piece, until Sept. 1st, when the corn will be hard enough to grind; this will make the whole cost until August, for rations and feed of mules, $2,118. But these hands will require extra rations to the amount of $500, for which they will repay you at the end of the year. Then you will have to advance them about seventy-five dollars for tobacco, and one hundred dollars for shoes. Your blacksmithing materials will cost you fifty dollars more, and tools another fifty dollars; and a thousand and one nameless articles, about one hundred dollars more. A few of your hands will need coats and pants, which will amount to another $100, and your seed will cost $100. Then your family expenses for food at the lowest possible rates, without allowing anything for luxuries, will be $200, or a grand total of $3,393, which will be the cash capital you will require, to carry on such a farm as ours, with 200 acres each in corn and cotton, and 50 acres in wheat and oats.

At the end of the year, you will have about $3,000 more to pay, for the feed of the mules, rations from Sept. 1st to the end of the year, and the balance of the wages of the hands, making your expenses for the year, $6,400.

To this amount, you can add whatever sum you choose, for the extravagance of your wife, unless she is one of those rare women, like my own wife, who knows how to accommodate her expenses to her husband's means.

The proceeds of your farm ought to be as follows: from 200 acres of corn, 1500 bushels, worth $1,875; fodder, worth $500, wheat and oats $500. The two hundred acres of cotton should produce seventy-five bales, which, at twenty cents a pound, will be $6,300, allowing four hundred and fifty pounds to a bale, or a total of $9,175, or including sweet potatoes and garden vegetables, and a few hogs, about $9,500; from which deduct expenses, $6,400, and you have left as net proceeds for the year, $3,100. But these returns are subject to several contingencies, such as follows. Your corn may not be planted early enough. The hogs may destroy one-fourth of it, the rains an eighth, and the thieves an eighth; and a drought a large portion of the remaining one half. Your cotton may not come up well, and you may not get a good stand to begin with. It may rain too little, and it may rain too much; and it may be overrun by the grass. Or, the rust may take it, the army worm, and the grasshoppers may commence their ravages: or other worms may strip the stalk of its foliage, and then an early frost may nip it in the bud. But if none of these things occur, you are quite likely to get good crops; and then if none of it is stolen, and your gin house does not burn down, you may be fairly recompensed for your labor. But if any of these things happen, your profits of course will be less.

Now, I do not wish to discourage any one from attempting to farm here. On the contrary, I invite all Northern people, of whatever religious belief, to come here, and try for themselves; but I do not wish to have my great desire for Northern neighbors or even the settled convictions of my mind, that the settlement of the South by Northern laborers, is the great desideratum at the present time, to influence me to mislead people, and induce them to come here with their eyes closed as to the risks they run. I am like an honest merchant who sincerely desires to sell you a piece of goods, but does not on that account cover up the defects of his merchandize. I heartily desire the settlement of this country by my Northern friends. I long for the building up of a better order of things than exists here at present. But I do not intend to persuade persons to come here, who will afterwards curse me for inviting them hither.

Farming everywhere, is subject to contingencies without number. Nevertheless, farmers manage to live more comfortably than any other portion of the laboring population. They are their own masters at least, and not subject to the vicissitudes of trade like mechanics and merchants. Farming at the South, if rightly managed, can be made as productive as elsewhere. But one element of success in all places, is to be prepared for reverses; and to build no more "castles in the air" than is absolutely necessary. "Forewarned, is forearmed," and the husbandman who expects but little, and is fully prepared for failure, will be far more likely to succeed than one who comes here imagining that crops are raised by magic, and without the same sturdy blows bestowed upon the bosom of mother earth, that are necessary elsewhere.

In these remarks I have alluded more particularly to the capitalist. I think the prospect for the working farmer very much better. If Northern farmers, with their sons, will come here, and labor as they do at the North, industry will no more fail of its reward here than at the North and West. Indeed, the same amount, and the same kind of labor that are bestowed in other places, will reap a more abundant reward here, for the plain reason that farming operations here, can be carried on through the whole year. Two crops of most kinds of garden vegetables can be raised almost as well as one, with additional labor of course. Hardly is the finale of the cotton crop marketed, before preparations can be made for another. There are but very few days in the winter when the ground is frozen too hard for ploughing.

I do not wish to encourage rich men to come here and become gentlemen farmers; for that system has prevailed too long already, and its tendency is not to elevate the blacks. I do wish, by all means in my power, to encourage working men of the North to become Southern farmers. In another portion of this work, and at another time, my ideas upon this subject will be more fully expressed.

CHAPTER XIX.

SICKNESS AND DEATH IN THE AUTHOR'S FAMILY.

It now becomes my painful duty to dwell for awhile upon more melancholy scenes, than any yet portrayed in this narrative. The angel of death, always ready to pluck the fairest flowers from terrestrial gardens, beheld the brilliant one in the person of my talented wife, growing in our Southern home, and resolutely determined to carry it from hence, and place it by the side of other beautiful flowers in the paradise of God. Accustomed to a more fertile soil, and to a less tropical heat, this rare plant drooped and pined away, amid the arid, mental and moral scenes of this "land of misery," as she often termed it in dating her letters. Quick and energetic in her temperament, and the pattern of neatness and refinement, she could not endure the slow and slovenly motions of the people around her. A few extracts from one of her letters, will best convey to the reader the state of her feelings, during a portion of her sojourn here. Under date of March 18, 1867, she writes to a female friend, "I'll tell you all about darkey help when I see you. Four weeks ago, some of the teachers from the Augusta colored schools came out on Friday night, and stayed until Sunday after dinner; and four other Northern friends came and visited part of the time while they were here. I should have enjoyed their visit hugely, had I been well, but it was all I could do to keep around the house; and I could not go out on the plantation with them, which you know was rather hard for poor me. They are the only ones of our color, that I have seen at the plantation since I returned last November. * * * * The negroes are the worst thieves that the Lord ever permitted to live. They steal everything they can lay their hands on. An old man, a rebel, said, "show me an honest negro, and I will show you hair in the palm of my hand; and I believe he could, for I do not believe there is one in this cursed land; but enough, I will tell you the rest when I see you, which I hope will be in the early part of summer. I do not feel as though I could live here through the heat."

Her worst fears were realized. During the month of August, we had incessant rains, so that not a cotton blossom made its appearance during the whole of the month; a very rare occurrence, and one hardly ever known before. Then in September the sun appeared, and shone with unusual brilliancy, filling the air with a deadly malaria, owing to the vast amount of water, remaining standing everywhere. On Thursday, the fifth of September, she complained of feeling unwell, and I suggested that we had better obtain help from the negro women, our cook having become incapacitated for labor. Her reply was, "No, it is far more labor to teach them how to do the work, than it is to do it myself."

She continued performing alone all the labors of our household, including those of the regular baking of the family, until the following Monday, when exhausted nature would permit no further violation of its laws; and she was obliged to yield to the necessities of the case, exclaiming as she did so, "I shall never do another day's work like this." Help was then obtained from the quarters, and she was confined to her bed until Saturday morning, when the fever seemed to have left her, and she arose, and dressed herself, and went into the parlor, in her usual good spirits. A physician was on the place that morning, but she declined calling him in, saying, that she felt perfectly well and should soon be about again. But alas! how mysterious are the ways of Providence! That afternoon while she was asleep, the fever was observed to return, and at five o'clock she awoke quite delirious. A messenger was despatched to town, for a physician of her acquaintance, who arrived about Sunday noon, and soon after, another was summoned from the neighborhood.

She had remained delirious from the time of her awaking, Saturday P. M., with occasionally a lucid moment. She seemed unconscious of what was passing around her, and could not speak intelligibly. Every effort was made by the physicians and other energetic assistants, to check the disease; but God had not decreed that these means should be blessed for her recovery, and at seven and a half o'clock on Sunday evening, her spirit took its flight to her everlasting home, leaving her husband and child overwhelmed in misery.

The blow came so utterly unexpected, that for a moment I was completely crushed. The reader will pardon me for quoting a few extracts from my diary at this time, as it will seem to point to others similarly afflicted, the only true source of consolation at such an hour.

"O God, help me to bear this last, this great and terrible affliction. At seven and a half o'clock this morning, the spirit of my wife departed from its earthly tenement, and left me a widower again." * * * "For some time past, she has been remarkably kind and affectionate; and especially during the past week of her sickness. Her feelings towards the colored people have been greatly ameliorated, and she has learned to forgive them, and overlook their multitudinous failings. She has evidently been looking forward toward her heavenly home, for some time, and trying hard to lead a Christian life, as the condition of future glory; and I think she died happy, in the consciousness of our mutual love, and of a joyful re-union of our spirits, beyond the grave. And O, how desolate I should now feel, if it were not for God! But He has drawn near, and enabled me to be comparatively calm and peaceful, amid all the trying scenes connected with the event. God is my hope, and I shall 'not be moved, although the foundations of the earth be shaken.' O God! how dreary my life seems, now that my wife is taken from me! O, how heart-rending, to think that I shall never more on earth hold sweet converse with the one I loved so well! To Thee, O God, do I come for consolation and help, and I feel that thou alone can give it me. O, give it me now, or I sink beneath the blow."

The reader will again pardon me for dwelling upon the manner in which these consolations were imparted unto me. Etta was a firm believer in that everywhere caricatured doctrine of Spiritualism. Many of her most intimate friends, people of extraordinary purity and goodness of life, were also Spiritualists, although neither she nor they endorsed all the "vagaries" connected with the sublime doctrine of "ministering spirits, sent forth to minister to the heirs of salvation."

The reader may doubt the truth of the following recital; but it was as real to me as my own existence; and without the consolation thus imparted, my brain must have reeled beneath the heavy blow, situated as I was at so great a distance from all our friends. As soon as a few words of prayer and consolation had been offered, by a Northern friend, I rushed out of the house, and paced the road in front of it, in indescribable agony. The death was so sudden, and accompanied by no farewell words; no breathing of love towards the survivor's; no expressions of faith in her eternal home; all on account of her unconscious condition, and the effects of her death I knew would fall so heavily on me, in my utterly isolated condition, that my brain was on fire, and all I could do was to cry out in agony, "O God, have mercy on me, and save me from losing my reason."

Hardly was this cry of distress uttered, when, as plain as the light of the stars that calmly shone above me, did the form and features of my beloved one appear before me, and for the space of nearly an hour, did she pour into my stricken heart such words of glorious consolation as she only could impart. All the sorrows of my isolated life, and the deep desolation of my condition were known more fully by her than by any other human being; and she could impart unto my wounded soul such sound philosophical reasons for her removal, as restored my soul to something like serenity, and enabled me to return to the discharge of my duties, to my beloved child, a second time bereft of a mother's care and love. She promised to be with me, and aid me in life's great work, and to labor assiduously for my welfare, and that of my child; a promise, let me say, which she has faithfully and nobly kept.

I know this will seem like folly, to perhaps the great body of my readers; but I could not do justice to the memory of my wife, without recording these events.

The doctrine of the ministration of departed spirits to their friends on earth, is as old as the Scriptures, and as real as the experience of every pure-minded person, whose "conversation is in heaven," like Paul's. It does not destroy the force of this cardinal doctrine of Christianity, the operation of spiritual influences upon men's minds to make them holy, because some, or many, who believe in it, are great errorists, in other respects; any more than it destroys the force of any other good doctrine, that bad men have believed in it. No one can lament more bitterly than myself, the errors and follies of many calling themselves Spiritualists; but is it not the same with Christianity? Has not every conceivable crime been connected with the Christian name? Was not Slavery universally defended by the so-called Christian church? But who ever thought on that account, of rejecting the benign doctrine of our glorious Lord and Saviour, Jesus Christ?

So with the doctrine of ministering spirits. It is a blessed, soul-comforting doctrine to believe, that a mother, a sister, a husband or brother, stands ready to aid you in the divine work of living for God, and not for yourself; and because bad persons believe it, or profess to believe it, shall we throw it from us as unworthy of our notice? No intelligent, pure-minded spiritualist like my wife, and her friends, will for a moment deny that the great "father of our spirits," can save us by and through human instrumentality; and no logical mind among them can possibly deny that he "who spake as never man spake, while on earth," can now be commissioned of God to "bring many sons unto glory." Christ and the holy angels, and "the spirits of just men, made perfect," according to Paul, all unite with God in lifting man from his degradation, and fitting him for a life of purity and perfection beyond the grave. If some of those called Spiritualists, deny the power of Jesus thus to aid in saving man, it is because of their failure to comprehend the genius of Spiritualism. They are mere outside believers in its husks and covering ; and know nothing of the pure spiritual kernels hid from their blinded eyes.

To me, Jesus is "the chief among ten thousand," and "the one altogether lovely," and I expect in heaven, if admitted there, to sing as loudly as any one. "Blessings, and honor, and glory, and power be unto him that sitteth upon the throne and unto the Lamb forever," for thou wast slain, and hast redeemed us to God, by thy blood, out of every kindred and tongue, and people, and nation."

The death of my wife imposed on me, more onerous duties than ever, and so burdensome did they become, that I was at length under the necessity of requesting my sister, then at the North, to come to my relief; which she did in the following December, 1867. About this time, Mr. Sherman, the farm superintendent, abandoned the farm, and became immersed in politics; and his energetic and benevolent lady had some time previously taken up her residence in Augusta, as a practicing physician; and I was left all alone with the cares of the family and of the farm all devolving upon me.

The Constitutional convention to frame a new constitution for our State, was about to assemble; and on my declining to leave my child and participate in its deliberations, it was deemed advisable that Mr. S. should occupy the position. At the election of members for the convention, our party polled about four times as many votes as the rebels; many of the latter refusing to vote from stubbornness.

For many days previous to the election, my yard was thronged with anxious freedmen, eager to learn about their new duties, and desirous to cast their votes in the manner best calculated to promote their own interests. I was surprised and delighted to see the comparative ease with which these new-born politicians comprehended seemingly abstruse political problems.

At first, it seemed nothing but folly to attempt to explain politics to them, but I soon saw, however dull they might be in matters of a moral and religious nature, they were keen-eyed in their political vision, fully justifying the buoyant expectations of those who had conferred upon them these. political privileges. Indeed, they seemed to excel in their political instincts, the great body of Northern copperheads; forcing me to the conclusion, that if political stupidity should debar any persons from the exercise of the elective franchise, this exclusion should no more embrace within its limits these ignorant ones, than the whole body of Northern politicians, who failed to see why the rebellion should be *thoroughly* and *immediately* crushed, instead of experiencing a lingering death, alike cruel to rebels, and to the lovers of freedom. I here insert the following brief account of the election written by a Northerner to friends at home.

"The great election is over, and an exciting time we have had of it. We have won a victory, but it has been by the skin of our teeth. Every effort the spirit of Satan could suggest has been put forth. We have had to take our lives in our hands and go forth to advocate the cause.

Lies, threats, revilings, abuse, and even murder and assassination have been meted out to our party. The poor blacks have been hunted from pillar to post, and every effort made to intimidate them, but to their lasting honor, be it said, they have stood the test nobly. But very few voted the rebel ticket, only about six thousand out of ninety thousand, and some of them through ignorance and fraud, supposing it was "the right ticket." Many stayed away from the polls through fear of the rebels, upon whom they depended for work, but great numbers have boldly, and in the face of death, marched up and deposited their ballots for freedom and republicanism. History furnishes us with but few instances of moral heroism like this. The rebels raved and swore like madmen from the pit. The negroes were obliged to go armed, and in many cases political meetings were broken up, and the negroes driven away. Had it not been for Gen. Meade's soldier's, there would have been no voting at all in many counties, and blood shed in many others. We suppose we have a very small majority perhaps, six or seven thousand."

R. W. S.

Columbia Co., Georgia, Dec., 1867.

CHAPTER XX.

COMMENCEMENT OF THE THIRD YEAR OF THE AUTHOR'S LABORS, WITH A DESCRIPTION OF MRS. LOVING, A "POOR WHITE," AND OUR FIRST DAY SCHOOL.

Christmas duly arrived, and with it, its crowd of dusky expectants, for the amount due them, for their past labors. To satisfy them, when they were wholly ignorant of any arithmetical process, was a formidable task, and consumed a great part of the night. Mr. S. thought it foolish to explain everything to them; but said, "settle with them according to our books, no matter how much they may grumble." But it seemed to me, the better way, to remove all difficulties from their minds and explain to them every knotty point, and help them to reckon as well as they could. The course usually adopted by the rebels is, to add up their accounts and tell them the exact amount due, waving all explanation; they deeming it too much condescension to make out the items of their accounts. But I adopted a different course, and by one or two o'clock in the morning, had the pleasure of seeing them all depart with the smile of satisfaction upon their countenances.

All were anxious to be re-employed, but some of them we did not want at any rate, and others whom we would have gladly retained, we were obliged to dismiss, as it was not my purpose to employ so many hands the coming year, as I had the past. I decided to limit the number to about fifteen, instead of twenty-seven, the former number.

About this time, a tall, lean, lank specimen of humanity made his appearance at our place, and representing himself as a strong Union man, although a Southerner, he begged for employment the coming year. He told sad stories of his persecutions in this county, on account of his Union sentiments, thus awakening my sympathy, and inducing me in an unguarded moment to employ him as overseer. He evidently understood to perfection the Southern art of brag, and boasted loud of his exploits in the Union army in Louisiana, under Gen. Banks, for whom, according to his story, he had acted as a Union scout; and he related many thrilling tales of his hair-breadth escapes from the enemy. He and many others, according to his story, after living in the swamps for weeks, had escaped to Bank's army, and accompanied it on its return North, which partly accounted for his now being in Georgia, his company having been sent to Augusta, just before they were mustered out of service. He professed to understand all about Southern and Northern farming combined; as his father was a Frenchman, and had lived many years at the North, previous to his removal to Louisiana.

His wife was a native of this State, Georgia, and answers so well for a description of a portion of that class, known as "poor whites," that I will endeavor to draw her portrait. She was tolerably good-looking, and of much fairer complexion than many of her compeers; stout, and full in the face, exhibiting no signs of the scanty fare, described by her husband, as having been their portion for some time. She was somewhat acquainted with the art of reading, and vainly imagined herself qualified to impart its mysteries to the illiterate negro children around her.

Her presence at the breakfast table, was enough to considerably lesson the cost of feeding one's family, so uncouth and uncleanly was she in her appearance. I am not quite certain, whether her face was ever washed or not, but her hair was uncombed, and its tangled folds swung loosely around her stained neck, and over her broad shoulders. The way she supplied her year-old baby with necessary aliment, was a caution to all believers in dietetic regulations.

I have read somewhere, that in Strasbourg, geese are fed for the market by holding their necks up, and literally crowding the food down their throats. It was so with this woman. She held her little one upon its back, in her arms, forced open its mouth, and then crammed it full of every variety of food the table was supplied with ; not omitting the greasy pork, which is the delight of every Southerner. How the little one managed to live, under this terrible infliction, I know not; but its screams could be heard at all hours of the day and night, as it were, protesting against this unnatural treatment. The mother by no means stinted herself, in thus administering to the wants of her youngest child. The weekly allowance to a hand is about three pounds of meat, but this woman and her husband, often consumed more than this amount at a single meal.

It fell to her lot, at one time, to deal out the rations to the hands, and her custom was, to visit the smoke-house at an early hour, weigh out each persons' allowance, and then slyly detach from every piece, from twelve to sixteen ounces, of the most fatty part, and carry it to her house under her dirty apron; thus securing a dozen pounds of meat per week, in addition to her and her husband's regular allowance. Her appetite was so insatiable, that she would gorge herself with this greasy mess, thus surreptitiously obtained; and then, as I was credibly informed by those who saw her do it, she would walk behind her house, and through her mouth disgorge her stomach of its contents.

She was so dirty in her household arrangements, that the blacks would refuse to eat food which she had cooked and offered to them. Her habits were too filthy to mention, and her modesty was decidedly below par. Her reputation for honesty was also at a discount. She even encouraged the colored people to steal from one another, and she frequently stole from us when opportunity occurred. Once she bestowed upon her husband quite a flagellation with a heavy strap, because she imagined he had told me of some of her filthy habits, on account of my public reproval of the vice of uncleanliness.

Her capacity for teaching may be inferred from the fact, that she often sent to us to ascertain the meaning of such *hard* words as "tower," "void," and "various," when they occurred in the lessons she was essaying to give to a few of the colored children; and she informed her children that *all* was a thing to peg shoes with. There, she pronounced *thar*,—where, *whar*,—and everything she particularized, was "this yer," and "that ar;" and all her pronunciation and diction were similarly destitute of euphony and lady-like polish.

But I forbear further mention of her failings. I do not forget, that degraded as she was, she was still a sister of the human family, having God for her father, and

all mankind for her brethren; and I only mention her case, that my readers may know, that the colored people are not "sinners above all that dwell in Jerusalem," in the matter of dishonesty and filthiness.

About this time, through the munificence of some of our Northern friends, we were able to add materially to the physical enjoyment of numerous little ones on our place. The stinted and hungry looks of these children of want, had attracted my sister's attention, on her first arrival; and many plans had been discussed by us, for ministering to their necessities. At last, it came to me one sleepless night, while cogitating on this subject, that the New York plan, then in vogue, of feeding the poor with soup, would be a good one for us to imitate. A benevolent Northern lady, whose physical form is now in her grave, had sent us twenty-five dollars, to be used for our Sunday school, and considering the hungry condition of some of the scholars, we concluded it would not be a misappropriation of her bounty, to apply it to their material wants. We first put it to vote, in a meeting of the colored people, which they would prefer: its appropriation to the purchase of books, which were very much needed; the repairing of the school-houses, which was still more necessary; or in procuring food for the children, in the manner that had been suggested to our minds. The people cried out unanimously, "feed the children, and we will repair the school-room for nothing;" which promise, on their part, was measurably kept. We procured a soup bone every week in town, and with the addition of several pounds of rice, half a bushel of turnips, and a few other vegetables, and four quarts of Indian meal, an excellent soup was produced. Some of the colored women prepared the vegetables, and my sister, and Susan, the cook, performed the remainder of the labor. Some thirty-five or forty women and children, were thus furnished with a good meal, three times a week.

They were seated in rows on the floor of our dining-room, and after singing a verse or two, they proceeded to devour the delicious food; it being the first time in their lives they had ever enjoyed a repast of that description. Each one was furnished with a little bowl and spoon, and it was amusing to see how quickly the bowl was emptied in most cases, and, like Oliver Twist, they called aloud for more. Some of them would empty three or four bowls in rapid succession, while others would sit demurely, waiting for more, merely signifying their wishes by an energetic jingling of the bowl and spoon. On the whole, their behavior would have done credit to any children's birth-day party, among more highly civilized little ones.

But their manner of approaching the house was a *sui generis* one, most certainly. At the first tingling of the bell, which notified them that the soup was ready, they almost equalled the feats of renowned circus-riders, in their gyrations and lofty tumbling. They ran, they jumped, they halloed at the top of their voices, and the boys turned summersaults without number, in their eagerness to reach the house, and in their exuberant joy, at the prospect of having their hunger satisfied. My sister said she could never afterwards think of this scene, without shedding tears. They came along, waving their hats and handkerchiefs, crying out, "Hurra for the soup!" and flourishing in the air the tin cups, which most of them brought, in which to carry a few spoonsful to their mothers at home

At first, some of them drank the soup from the bowls, and others dished it out with their hands, not knowing the use of the spoons; but after several weeks, my sister succeeded in inducing every one to eat with spoons, like "white folks," and also to stand around the table. This feeding of the little ones we would gladly have continued longer than we did, but our own scanty funds would not allow the expense.

Afterwards, when the children were not so hungry, they were employed in some trifling job, and at its close were given the choice for their pay, between a biscuit and a child's paper. It was really amusing, to see some of them take a biscuit in one hand and the paper in another, and look alternately at each in a very wistful manner, and then reluctantly choose the paper, in almost every case. One little outcast boy, named Wesley, whose hunger was so great, that he often surreptitiously skimmed the crumbs from the top of our swill-pail, hesitated a long time between the two, and at last the scale turned on the side of the paper, and he surrendered the biscuit, saying, "When I eats dis yer cake, it all be gone; but dis yer paper I can keep allers, and sometime I'll get larning from it, p'raps."

On my first arrival at our place, it seemed the part of wisdom for me to confine my labors in teaching to the adults of our neighborhood, as I saw that their opportunities for learning would soon pass away, while the children could learn at any time, and could be instructed by their parents, after they had themselves learned.

This was in accordance with the desires of the adults, who promised to teach their children, if I would teach them. Consequently, for the first two years, our Sunday labors were confined to the adults, as it was impossible for two or three individuals to instruct both children and adults. Therefore, on my sister's arrival, she found the children had been almost wholly neglected, and almost immediately determined to commence a day school, for their benefit. During the second summer, I also had a night school, for the instruction of adults, but it seemed that none of them had kept their promises, in relation to their children. This fact will account for the ignorance alluded to in the following interesting description of our "first day school," written by the teacher, Miss R. W. Stearns, of Springfield, Mass.

"I proceed to give some account of the first regular day school on the plantation. The honor of starting the first school, really belongs to Lizzie Sherman, who did her best to teach the children, a few months before I came. The pupils, unaccustomed to anything like order or discipline, were entirely beyond her power to control, child as she was, and she soon ceased to try to initiate them into the world of letters, so "funny" and strange to their darkened minds. She then turned her attention to the teaching of singing, and the speaking of pieces, in which she succeeded admirably. The children yet repeat over their pieces and songs, and cherish the memory of dear little Lizzie as a sacred remembrance. It was on the 8th of January, 1868, that I commenced teaching. The school was taught in Mrs. Loving's room, our Sunday school room being quite too cold for me. Three long and rather rough benches were brought in and ranged around the bright glowing fire, in the large open fire-place. They were soon filled by about twenty-five or thirty children and women, each child striving noisily for the place nearest the fire. When some degree of order was restored, I took a survey of my school, and the grotesque and uncouth attitudes, the outlandish dress, the eager stare of the eyes, the half-stupid and half-intelligent look, were all so new to me, that I looked at them again and again, in order to take in the whole scene, and then burst into an almost uncontrollable fit of laughter. The sad and downcast glance of the eager, wistful eyes, soon recalled me to my duties, and made me quite sorry, especially when one little creature timidly remarked, "Don't laugh at us, Miss Stearns; we's dunno any better." Tears filled my eyes, and I began to question them. They were ignorant of the first principles of everything. Baffled in all my preconceived plans for organizing the school on the first day, I exclaimed, 'Well, what do you know?'

'We's dunno noffin; we's come here for you to teach us,' said a bright boy of twelve years. 'But I don't know where to begin,' I said. 'Begin *anywhere;* it will all be new to us,' said the same boy. So I began to teach them a simple prayer, telling them to repeat it after me, sentence by sentence. This they did, with great gusto, screaming at the top of their voices, and stamping their feet to keep time. When we had finished, I told them to repeat it again, just as I did, and be careful not to speak any louder than I did. They obeyed, till we were about half through, when the scream was fairly deaf'ning. I ceased and remonstrated with them, when the little spokesman replied, 'You said, thank God for this school; *we do;* we thank him *mighty heap*, and we thank him out loud, so he can hear.' I assured them he could hear, if they spoke as low as I did. They seemed skeptical, but finally repeated it to my satisfaction. I then questioned them in religious and Scriptural knowledge, but found them as ignorant there as in relation to human sciences. They did not know who Jesus Christ was, they did not know the name of the first man, or of any other man spoken of in the Bible. They did not know the name of the first book, or of any other book in the Bible; they could not count five; they did not many of them know the names of a single letter. In short, they knew *nothing*, as they had said. I had no foundation on which to rear the temple of knowledge. I had to make one, and step by step I taught them, until, at the end of a month, I was astonished myself at the results. They excelled particularly in Bible history, and in repeating verses and lessons in concert.

The outlandish dress I have mentioned, is worthy of more particular description. It was made of a coarse cloth, called Osnaburg, the threads of which are about as coarse as tidy yarn. The dresses of the girls were somewhat like a child's night-gown, with a string run into a hem round the neck; straight sleeves, reaching to a little below the elbow, the whole dress in one piece, with a seam behind, and with a twine string tied around the waist. They were straight about the body as a pillow-case, and nearly touched the ground at the bottom. That of the little boys was made somewhat like a boy's undershirt, reaching half way below the knees. They were not very clean, but at my suggestion, they were washed that night, after the children were in bed, and next day they came bright and clean. They assured me they had no better clothes, and many of them had no change. Their feet were bare, and looked red and cold. I mustered up all the old shoes in the house, during the week, and Sunday morning found me writing to some friends of the cause at the North, respecting their very destitute condition. This appeal met with a response which brings me to the opening of the first barrel. It was a bright, beautiful day in early Spring. My scholars were arranged in three rows, one behind the other, so that all could see, and article after article was displayed to their eager and astonished gaze. None was given out, till all on the place had seen the whole. Not a murmur or complaint of the distribution was heard; no talking or begging, but a spirit of quiet thankfulness seemed to pervade the scene; and I have often wished for the pencil of a painter, to describe it. This first barrel was followed by two others, from the same place, Springfield, Mass. — our home—and by a large box, equal to two barrels, from Boxford, Mass., also one valuable one from New York, containing one hundred and fifty copies of Wilson's First Reader, slates, pencils, and writing-books, and others from other places. This business of collecting clothing and distributing it, has been carried on from year to year, until twenty-four barrels have been received. What those poor creatures would have done without this aid, God only knows. He has put it into the hearts of his children at the North to furnish it from time to time, for which we are very thankful. Every one on the place was provided with a Sunday suit and a hat and shoes.

How very different they looked in their 'North clothes!' oh, how they gazed at each other, and turned round and round, and admired themselves in the glass! and with what contempt they looked at the dirty rags lying on the floor — which they wished they need never use again. But such things will wear out, and there is room for more. If any persons feel disposed to bestow any of their supernumerary articles of clothing upon them, they can obtain necessary information, by corresponding with me on the subject." R. W. S.

CHAPTER XXII.

GREAT POLITICAL CHANGES, AND DEATH OF LIZZY SHERMAN.

Previous to a description of that great change that transformed our adopted state from a rebel to a loyal one; I will briefly allude to a few of the pecuniary trials of this, and the past years, in order to bear my testimony to the ever faithful providence of God, in enabling us to carry on our labors of love for his benighted ones. Many times during the second year of these labors, had our funds become nearly exhausted, and it seemed uncertain in what manner they were to be replenished. By the middle of the summer of 1867, all of my available funds had been expended, I having paid out over $2,000 that season, in providing for the wants of our people, and of our "dumb animals;" and our cash expenses still amounted to some $75 per week.

By the kindness of our Augusta mercantile friends, we had obtained some supplies on credit; but the time approached for the liquidation of these claims, and not a dollar appeared, for that purpose. At this emergency, Mr. and Mrs. S., succeeded in obtaining a considerable loan from two colored men in Augusta, who advanced it solely for the sake of the cause in which we were all engaged; thus refuting, in their case, the foul calumny, that the freedmen would never be able to take care of themselves; and also showing the existence of gratitude in some hearts, at least. This timely aid enabled us to "keep the ship afloat," until a kind Boston friend authorized me to draw on him for $1,000, as a loan. Both of these sums were afterwards repaid, with interest, the former out of my own private funds; so that the kind benefactors of the colord race, lost nothing by their liberality, and conferred great benefits upon God's suffering ones; the lately emancipated slaves.

Shortly after the commencement of the year 1868, whose history we are now writing, pecuniary troubles again stared us in the face. The author had resorted to every shift to obtain the means to carry on the place until September, when the first cotton would be ready for the market; and after selling a number of his mules, most of his cattle, and making other necessary changes, he found himself still minus, about $1,000, of the sum absolutely necessary to carry on operations. He had many doubts as to the manner in which this sum would be provided; although confident that He whom he served, would not allow him to continue this "warfare at his own charges."

One day, while lying on a sick bed, with his mind greatly agitated by the fears naturally arising from his present pecuniary condition, a messenger from town arrived, with a letter from a devoted friend of the freedmen, in Binghampton, N. Y., and an intimate friend of his departed wife. He opened the letter, and, reader, what do you think he saw? He could hardly credit the testimony of his eyes, which were immediately filled with tears, as he dropped the letter, and offered a prayer of thanksgiving, to that God who had been silently at work in his behalf.

The letter contained a *draft* for *nearly* $1000. "Is it possible," said he to himself, "That here is money enough to carry me through to harvest, and I am to have no more weary hours of pain and anxiety as to how all these mouths of man and beast are to be filled? No more medicine was necessary to return "soundness to his limbs," but he was soon able to go about his daily business.

Words cannot express his gratitude to the friend who had shown such a self-sacrificing spirit in behalf of the poor freedmen; for this person had actually *mortgaged* his *farm* to obtain the money so opportunely forwarded; affording another proof that some men are instinctively benevolent, and all are not selfish as is sometimes asserted. Who but God, operating perhaps through the spirit of my departed wife, who had promised to aid me in every way, could have persuaded this man to have performed a deed so entirely uncommon in the annals of benevolence? To be sure, the money would have been paid at some time in the distant future; but my kind benefactor was not under the least obligation to have paid it for a long time.

If I might suggest an opinion as to how he came to do this remarkable deed, I should say, that being a prominent member of the religious body termed Spiritualists, a part of whose faith is to hearken unto mental impressions, he listened to the voice of God addressed to his soul, where other men would not have thus listened, and was thereby induced to do as he did. To God be all the glory. By the reception of this sum, the author was enabled to devote more of his time to the great political change then going on in our beloved, adopted commonwealth. Congress had defined its position, and had offered to the contumacious states, another opportunity to return to their former snug quarters in our immense political fabric. This offer was more difficult to be complied with than the former one; but many of our inhabitants rightly deemed it best to accept it, lest the third offer should be still more stringent in its conditions. Great numbers of the white inhabitants of our mountain regions were friendly to our cause; and systematic efforts were put forth to turn the scale in favor of the cause of freedom and loyalty to the Union. Bitter was the contest. The rebels gnashed their teeth as they beheld the sceptre about to depart from their hands; and especially as it promised to be accomplished through the efforts of their former chattels. Their objections to negro voting vanished like lightning; and Boston and New York could boast of no more diligent efforts to persuade the working men to vote the democratic ticket, than were witnessed here.

"Barbacues" were everywhere held, and the colored people were invited to sit down and eat with the whites, if they would only promise to vote the democratic ticket. Various sums of money were also offered the negroes on the same conditions. Prominent democrats stationed themselves on the highway, and urged their tickets upon the numerous throngs of darkies that were everywhere hastening to the polls. It is a curious fact, that at the identical moment when democrat orators at the North were making the "welkin ring" with their noisy shouts about the danger of negro domination, their Southern allies were equally vociferous in urging these same "nasty niggers," to join their party, and become loving member of their political church. Great inducements were extended to every negro, to induce him to join hands with the party that had always cursed his race, and connived at their enslavement. It was only necessary to remind a crowd of listening negroes, of the fact that the democracy had thus enslaved them, to quickly dispel the illusion thrown around their minds, by the argument and promises of windy democrat declaimers.

The election commenced April 20, 1868, and lasted four days. On Saturday and Sunday, April 4th and 5th, we held a grand political meeting at our house, which was attended by about two hundred persons on Saturday, and about five hundred on Sunday. The only white Southern people present, were the sheriff, to preserve order, and an overseer on a neighboring plantation. Many of our republican friends were present, and took part in the exercises; among whom, were Romulus Moore, a candidate for the Legislature, and Mr. Cobb, both colored men; and Messrs. Sherman, Rice, Somers, and Loving, white men. The meeting continued from ten A. M., to five P. M., with a short intermission; and was enthusiastic beyond description. At one stage of the meeting it was rumored that a colored democrat was on the place, and a rush was immediately made for him by his colored brethren; and it required all the gift of persuasion that several of us possessed to induce, them not to molest him, so great was their indignation at any one of their number, who, for "a mess of pottage," would prove recreant to his and their principles. I cannot better describe the election, than by giving extracts from my diary, at the time:

"Messrs. Sherman, Rice and Loving, left Sunday P. M. for Apling, our county-seat, and Linconton, in Lincoln county; but at night Mr. Loving returned, with the sad news that the creeks were up, and that the men who left here in the morning could not go on, and had lost all the tickets, their revolvers and clothing. This morning it poured down rain again, but finally cleared off, and one hundred men started from here for Apling. We sent seven mules, and two large wagons to carry the lame. At night our men returned with the news. The men had to swim the creek, and wade up to their chins in water, carrying their guns in one hand, over their heads.

Some of them came near drowning, and they had a desperate time, generally. At Apling the rebels were out in strong force, and would have doubtless killed the blacks, if it had not been for the soldiers. They seized Mr. Loving, and threatened his life, for giving the blacks the right kind of votes. They think it is an awful thing for the blacks to have the right to vote; but they try very hard to have them vote their ticket. On Thursday I started for Apling, with two of our hands, and another man, who had been waiting for some days for an opportunity to ride. Reached A. at one o'clock, and found Mr Rice quite wearied and anxious to return; and after making a farewell speech to the rebels, he returned with Mr. Loving, while I remained behind. Just before he left, Mr. Sherman, and George Parks, a colored man, came on from Linconton, bringing dismal accounts from that stronghold of rebeldom. About twenty of the rebels followed them ten miles, insulting and threatening them at every step. They hooted, swore, and did everything but inflict blows upon them. They would have done that, if Mr. S. had replied a word to their insults. I found them very bitter at Apling, but not nearly as bad as at Linconton. One colored man at Apling was knocked down with a rock, and another stabbed, for voting the republican ticket. One rebel turned off a colored man for voting, and the soldiers went after the rebel, but he escaped. They also arrested a man for trying to prevent one of his hands from voting, and put him under bonds; but he brought forward the colored man, and the poor fellow declared that he did not want to vote.

On Thursday night we had a fine meeting in the colored church, and I congratulated them on their courage and manliness, and Messrs. Sherman and Moore, spoke in the same strain."

Our ticket was elected by a vote of sixteen hundred and seventy-five republicans, to four hundred and fifty democrats, but when the returns were made out, the names of about four hundred of our voters were dropped from the list by the managers, for reasons best known to themselves. The ostensible one was, that on the registered list those names were not precisely alike those on the voting list; which would necessarily be the case, for the one who registered Jack Morley's name, for instance, would be quite likely to spell it somewhat different from the one who recorded it, when Jack or John voted. Many of the colored people have several names, and sometimes give one, and sometimes another; which arises from the fact that after freedom, great numbers dropped their old surnames, along with their slavery robes, and adopted new ones that suited their fancy better. So that when they registered their names, it happened that many of them termed themselves Smith, Gray, and Jones, and afterwards called themselves Johnson, Parks, and Hill. With them, the surname is termed the *trimming*, and may at any time be altered, while the given name they always adhere to, so that Levi Reid was called Levi Curtis, or perhaps by some other "trimming."

The following account of this same election was sent by the writer to a Northern friend, who caused it to be published, and I give it as furnishing some additional particulars, hoping the reader will pardon whatever repetition he may perceive.

COLUMBIA, CO., GA. May 1, 1868.

"Dear Friend, — Thinking that a few items of information respecting our recent election would interest you, I will give you a slight sketch of our political life, in this semi-rebellious country. Our friends literally took their lives in their hands, and went forth to engage in this battle. Several of their number were brutually murdered, many more injured, and multitudes insulted almost beyond the power of endurance. My sickness occurred in the midst of the campaign, or I might have been brought home a bloody corpse. I lent my horses and carriage to some friends to go to a meeting, and they came home minus several bolts from the carriage, and some of its ornamental work; and one of the horses was so unfortunate as to lose a portion of his ears, nearly all of his mane, and a large portion of his tail; and this they rejoice over as a great rebel victory. I felt glad the poor creature got home alive, and also those who rode behind him. At another time a blood-thirsty mob pursued a friend of mine ten miles, with threats of vengeance upon him, for his temerity in venturing into the lion's den. They said he was the only white man who had ever dared thus to go through their county. Another friend of mine was repeatedly threatened with assassination, unless he desisted from his attempts to give the right tickets to the colored people, and a plot was actually laid to attack him on the way home. Quite a row was occasioned by about twenty words I uttered to the blacks at one time, and blood might have been shed if the soldiers had not been present. One colored man in this county was knocked down with a rock for voting our ticket, another was stabbed, and many were turned off from their homes. Col. Bryant was repeatedly assailed, and many more of our friends would have been, if they had replied to the insults they received. But in spite of everything, the blacks did nobly. Their enthusiasm knew no bounds. The great mass resisted every attempt to intimidate them, and marched boldly to the polls in the face and eyes of the rebels, and voted the republican ticket. About one hundred, with guns on their shoulders, started from my house on the morning of the election, and walked twelve miles to Apling, the county seat. The streams were up from heavy rains, and they had to swim and wade creeks, with the water up to their chins, and when they got there were as wet as drowned rats. I saw one man, ninety years old, who walked all day alone to get to Alping; and came near getting drowned in crossing a creek; but they pursued their way undaunted alike by the storm and the threats of the rebels. The wrath of the rebels knew no bounds to see their chattels transformed so soon into citizens, when they had fondly hoped to be able to re-enslave them. Out of 1,700 black voters in this county, only about 25 voted the rebel ticket; and out of 90,000 in the State, only about 4,000 or 5,000. We have carried the State by about 15,000 majority. We have about 95,000 votes, and the rebels about 80,000. Not far from 40,000 whites, (the "poor whites," mostly,) voted the republican ticket, and about 20,000 blacks remained at home, intimidated by the rebels. These were those who could not be reached by our efforts, living in sections where it was not safe for a lecturer to go.

Yours truly, C. Stearns:

I am particular in describing the scenes from minutes made at the time, and not from recollection, as the time will come when some of these statements will be denied.

I was so unfortunate as to be elected to the office of "Judge of Ordinary," the duties of which office included those of a Northern judge of probate, and many others, it being an office of a somewhat anomalous character: In the words of the new State Constitution, "The Courts of Ordinary" shall have such power, in relation to roads, bridges, ferries, public buildings, paupers, county officers, county funds, and taxes and other matters, as shall be conferred upon them by law; and the books, papers, and proceedings of the "Inferior Court" shall be transferred to, and remain in the control of the "Ordinary," who shall perform the duties of said Courts, until otherwise provided by law.

Of course, whoever filled this office, possessed almost unlimited power over all County matters. Juries were drawn in part by him, election precincts and managers appointed, public building were at his disposal, and the funds of the county under his control. He was, as it were, "grand mogul" of the county. Is it any wonder, therefore, that a howl of despair went forth from every rebel heart in our county, when they learned the sad news that the control of their county had passed from their hands into that of a terrible Radical, like that "d—d old Stearns," as they pleasantly called me? I almost pitied them myself, and secretly determined that every judicial act of mine should be performed with a single eye to the best interests of these very rebels, who so thoroughly hated me. I determined not to exercise the absolute power entrusted to me; but whenever an important measure was proposed, to call a public meeting, of the white voters of the County, and be guided by the will of the majority, in all of my public acts of a purely business character. But of this resolution, my rebel friends of course knew nothing. They simply saw the stubborn fact, that a "d—d Yankee, elected by niggers," was placed in authority over them, and it was too much for their rebellious natures to endure, and they accordingly adopted strenuous measures, to prevent the occurrence of so sad a catastrophy.

But before I proceed to describe these measures, I must digress, to allude to another sad event, that occurred not far from this time. Little Lizzie Sherman, the idol of her parents, and a general favorite among all her Northern acquaintances, fell a victim to her praiseworthy efforts, to outstrip her rebel mates in scholarship. Before the close of 1867, her parents had placed her in a fashionable school in Augusta, and she was making great proficiency in her studies, when death claimed her as its own, and her lovely spirit was taken possession of by him of whom she loved to sing, "The Lord is my Shepherd, and I shall not want." She was a beautiful girl, and endowed with a fine genius, and a loving and affectionate disposition, although of course not wholly free from the common errors of childhood. Her death created another appalling chasm in the little circle of our Northern acquaintances, of which she was the brightest ornament. It affected my own child so much as to bring on a relapse after a fit of sickness, from which she did not fully recover, until her return to the North in June. Little Lizzie lies at the side of that other precious one, in the Augusta cemetery, whose death preceded hers about six months.

Her earnest efforts in instructing the colored children on our place, have been already alluded to, and some of her teachings will never be forgotten by them. But notwithstanding the amiability of her disposition, she was made the butt of ridicule of her rebel schoolmates, on account of her Northern origin. They would hardly ever speak to her, and in passing her at school, *gathered up the folds of their dresses*, so as not to come in contact with her.

At one time, some of them asked her where her father lived, and she told them on a plantation. They asked if it was owned by a Yankee, and on her replying affirmatively, they sneeringly said, "Well, we wish you would tell us where it is, so that when we go into the country, we may not step our feet upon it, as we do not wish to pollute our feet by treading on a Northern man's land." To all of these taunts, she replied, in accordance with the precepts of Jesus, and sedulously endeavored to return "good for their evil." It is unnecessary to add, that she was at the head of all her classes, although they contained pupils much older than herself.

It was the custom at intervals, for the scholars to repeat before the whole school, some verses from the Scripture; and the next day after one of the most shameful of the above occurrences, it was Lizzie's turn to repeat verses; and she selected the following appropriate ones, and in a distinct tone repeated them before the whole school, some of whom perhaps heard them then for the first time in their lives; learning to forgive one's enemies not being a prominent part of the education of Southern children: "I say unto you, love your enemies, bless them that curse you, do good to them that hate you, and pray for them which despitefully use you and persecute you; that ye may be the children of your Father which is in heaven, for he maketh his svn to rise on the evil and on the good, on the just and the unjust."

The repeating of this passage at such a time, brought tears in the eyes of the teacher, who promised that from that time, Lizzie should be subject to no more insults of that character.

In order to show that all of the Southern people do

not partake of this diabolical disposition towards their enemies, I would state that at her funeral, many of her rebel acquaintances officiated, and in the sad hours preceding it, were profuse in their kind offers of sympathy and aid to the family; and some of those who had so rudely treated her, asked the forgiveness of her friends. The physicians also, who were Southern men, were unremitting in their attendance upon her, and in their efforts for her recovery, often visiting her ten or twelve times a day. The Southern character so conflicts itself, that it is hard to understand it properly. At one moment, breathing out the most intense hatred towards all Northerners; at another, extraordinarily zealous in attempts to benefit either one of these very Northerners, or some of their own acquaintances.

It seems to me that the true Southerner excels as much in devotion to his friends, as in hatred to his enemies, being more like the ancient Jews, who were taught, "Thou shalt love thy neighbor, and hate thine enemy," than like followers of him who says, "love your enemies."

About the middle of June, I was forced to bid adieu to my sister and child, whose health rendered it necessary for them to return to the North. I was thus left alone to buffet with the rebels, having no white friends on my place, except Mr. and Mrs. Loving. For four months, I was entirely alone in our large dwelling, with no companions but those who occasionally came to see me on business. But our Sunday school was very flourishing, and large numbers came out nearly every Sunday; and to crown all, the Spirit of the Lord drew near and blessed our religious efforts, and quite a number of souls professed to find peace with God, and many more became anxious enquirers after the way of salvation.

CHAPTER XXIII.

TERRIFIC MOB AT APLING, AND NARROW ESCAPE OF THE AUTHOR FROM DEATH.

As has been mentioned in the preceding chapter, our rebel friends saw fit to adopt severe measures to prevent my being ensconced in my new office. From the time of the election until the September following, rumors of various kinds were continually reaching my ears, in reference to their designs. The governor was not inaugurated until July 22d, and I did not receive my commission until about a month afterwards. If I had been aware of the settled determination on the part of my involuntary constituency, to prevent me from occupying the position to which I had been elected, by a majority of more than three to one of the votes of the county, I should not have ventured to have taken possession of the office, alone and unprotected. But, accustomed as I was to the Southern art of intimidation by braggadacio, I paid no attention to the mutterings of the distant thunder of rebel wrath.

On the contrary, I laughed at their threats, and regarded them as the blowing of the idle wind, and confined my attention to the duties before me. As soon as I could make the necessary arrangements, I packed up my things, and started on my hazardous journey. A few extracts from my diary, previous to my arrival there, will show the true state of affairs at this time.

On the inauguration of the governor, the miltary power was withdrawn, and we were thrown upon our own resources again; an unwise measure on the part of the United States Government, but one that could not well have been avoided, under the peculiar theory of govermental interference entertained by those in authority. The detestable doctrine of State rights, as interpreted by the haters of the Union, had imperceptibly infused its virus into all portions of the body politic, and even those who stoutly denied the Southern exposition of the doctrine, on an emergency, adopted it as their rule of action. Consequently, as we had become a State, all of. our helpless inhabitants must be thrown at the feet of the rebel Juggernaut, to be crushed beneath the ponderous wheels of its terrific car. But to my extracts. Under date of August, 1866, I wrote as follows:

"Outrages upon the negroes becoming very common. Last Thursday night, one was taken from the jail at Apling, and hung, by a mob. Another came to see me, to show me how he had been brutally stabbed by his overseer. Two other men were threatened with being shot. A negro woman was beaten on her head with a board and hoe, and I am beset by a stream of applicants for aid in some shape. It is worse now than it has been for some time. Last night, a gang of men on horseback broke up a prayer-meeting of the blacks, about two miles from here, and constant threats are made against me, if I attempt to take my office."

About this time, I was aroused at twelve o'clock one night by a crowd of blacks under my bedroom window, who seemed to be in great distress and had come to me for protection. They said if they only had guns, they could take care of themselves, and earnestly desired me to send North and obtain some for them. They said they were entirely at the mercy of the rebels, and had just been driven away from some land they had rented. Their situation seemed pitiable, but what could I do? If I moved hand or foot in their behalf, my own life would have been the penalty of my temerity. I could only therefore recommend them to the mercy of God, and tell them to wait patiently until Gen. Grant was elected president, and then I believed their wrongs would be righted.

Sunday, Sept. 6th, I wrote in my diary as follows: "I never went to any place with such melancholy feeling as I go to Apling with. I know not what will befall me, but I trust in God who has always been with me, and will continue to be. My whole nature shrinks from the contest, that I fear will be my portion there, but God says 'go,' and I must do his will whatever may be the result.

"Sept. 7th, I wrote, "Spent to-day in preparing to go to Apling, packing dishes, cooking utensils, bedding, provision, &c., as I cannot get a place to board there, or even blacks to cook for me, as they are all so afraid of the rebels."

Tuesday, Sept 8th, I wrote as follows, "Started this morning for Apling, with Frank Cummings for driver. Broke down about three miles from home, and had to send back and get another carriage, which occupied two and a half hours. On reaching Waltons', one and half miles further, I requested a cup to get some water in, and he threatened to shoot me if I did not clear out immediately: and refused to allow me to drink from his well, which was at the side of the road. This seems ominous. I told him who I was, and thanked him for

for his civility. Just before we reached Apling, we met a man on horseback, who gazed at me intensely, and then turned and rode to town in a gallop."

This is about the last entry in my diary for nearly two months, during which time the sickness consequent on my Apling treatment, rendered me unable to write. The reader will now pardon me for digressing from my style as a simple narrator of passing events, and describing in my own way, the thrilling scenes through which I passed. When the iron thoroughly "enters a man's soul," he may be pardoned for expressing himself strongly in condemnation of his wrongs. But not one word will be uttered here to the truthfulness of which I would not be willing to be qualified in a court of justice. I copy mainly from a statement of this affair made just after it occurred, premising that no description I can give of it, can accurately describe the fiendish nature of the whole transaction.

I reached Apling about 5 P. M., and hitched my mules a few rods from the Court House. It was court week, and a distinguished Southern politician had been in town, manipulating the grand jury, and counselling them to recommend to the citizens, to allow all the officers on our ticket to take their seats, except myself and a colored man, elected to the office of Coroner. Having arranged everything for the contemplated action of the people, as I have every reason to think, he left the town shortly before my arrival, in company with others, who were equally anxious to avoid all identification with the mob. Perhaps they did not wish to witness the violence, which their common sense must have told them, would follow the excited appeals which they made to the crowd. As I walked up to and passed by the court house, I was greeted with a shower of hisses, from the upper windows of the building, and with exclamations, "There he is; there's Stearns."

This surprised me, but I walked calmly on, until I reached the Post Office, quite a number of rods distant. I entered the building, and obtained my mail matter; and perceiving quite a crowd of men in the room, which was also used as a store, I bowed politely to them and said, "I am glad to see you, gentlemen," to which some of them replied, "Well if you are, we are not glad to see you." I remained here, perusing my letters, until prudence suggested my departure, and I repaired to the office of the Ordinary, on the lower floor of the court house. I was followed by a motley crowd, some of whom hooted at me, and others remained silent. On entering the Ordinary's office, I sat down and commenced reading. Soon the crowd increased, until the hall was pretty full, and I remarked, "Come in, gentlemen, and be seated; I would like to have a talk with you." Quite a number availed themselves of my invitation, and one or two took seats at my side. Those remaining outside, called to their comrades to come on and see me; "it was only twenty-five cents for a sight," they said. This I supposed to be on account of their being unaccustomed to see a Northern republican, with his benevolent principles written on his face, in so striking contrast to the brutal features of their own leaders. The room was soon crowded, it holding from fifty to seventy-five persons. One of the persons who sat at my side was a Northern man, who had resided at the South many years; but he acted the part of a perfect gentleman, during the whole of the fiery ordeal that followed. One old man in the back part of the room, was especially violent, damning and cursing me in the most terrific manner. The remainder of the crowd indulged in conduct between the two extremes.

One man repeatedly aimed blows at my head, but the gentleman sitting near me remonstrated with him, and he did not actually strike me. One of them pulled my nose slightly a few times, but this was the nearest approach to physical injury, I received that afternoon. But of all language it had ever been my lot to listen to previously, this surpassed the whole. I must say that no vulgar fisherwoman in the London market, could equal in Billings-gate oratory these foul-mouthed defenders of Southern rights, on account of whose wrongs so many crocodile tears are shed by dish-water philanthropists at the North. They stormed, they raved, they brow-beated me; they called me a "d—n low-lived Yankee, a thief, a scoundrel," and every other name that could be drawn out of the filthy pool of their Satanic hearts. Talk of politeness and of gentlemanly manners as peculiar to Southerners! Truly, if this was a specimen of their qualifications in this respect, then the greatest boor that ever disgraced the barn-yard of a Mexican "bull-whacker" is a perfect gentleman; yea, more, if this conduct was gentlemanly, then might a company of Bedouin Arabs, wandering across the desert, in pursuit of their human prey, be deemed model gentlemen, and perfect Chesterfield's of politeness!

To all of this terrific abuse, I replied in the mildest manner possible. While they raved, I tried to reason. While they cursed, I strove to pray inwardly. While they sought to irritate me, I endeavored to soothe their excited feelings. May I be pardoned for saying,—that in my opinion, no power in the universe, but that of the spirit of the Living God, could have enabled me to bear patiently all that abuse. I was not conscious of one angry feeling towards them, during the whole of this conflict with these Ephesian "wild beasts." I felt sorry for them, knowing that they were misguided, and ignorant of the "glorious gospel of the blessed God," through whose power alone was I able to "possess my soul in patience." If I had uttered one irritating word, I have no doubt I should have been torn in pieces immediately. I tried to tell them of Jesus, but they hooted at his sacred name, and laughed immoderately.

The reader will excuse me, for pointing out the means used by myself, in this emergency, to preserve my feelings unruffled; as it may be of use to some other soul, subjected to like temptations. First, before I went to Apling, I gave myself up to God, to obey him perfectly in every respect. I promised to follow the leading of his Spirit, implicitly. Then, when the "fiery trial" came upon me, I trusted in Him to show me my duty, and to lead me to say and do exactly what was right; and the consequence was, that my soul was filled with calmness and heavenly love, which enabled me to pity them, and to bear all their cruel taunts, with patience. This experience proves conclusively to my mind, that God is a prayer-hearing God, and able to preserve us from wrong in the midst of the greatest temptations.

They accused me of causing the blacks to commit outrages upon them, and made me responsible for every act of violence lately committed by a black man in Georgia. They told me, positively, I could not live, and hold the office to which I had been elected; for, as they said, "the white people of the county are determined you shall not, at all hazards, because you were elected by the niggers; and we will be d——d if the niggers are going to rule over us. We built this court house with our money, and we are going to occupy it." They said, "this is so important an office, and places our property at your disposal, and we know you will steal it."

Some of them would then ask, "Are you going to take this office?" to which I would reply, that I did not know. "Well," said they, "by G——d, *we* know, and we are determined that you shall not." Some who were milder than the rest, reasoned with me, and asked me why I did not resign, seeing there was such a state of feeling towards me? Others said, "before you came here we could do as we pleased with the blacks, but now they are all turning against us."

I observed, that so long as I continued to talk to them, they made no attempt to strike me; but when, from sheer exhaustion, my words failed, then they would rush upon me, until met by a fresh volley of words, furnished by that Spirit, as it seemed to me, who has promised to speak in us when brought before our adversaries; and give us "a mouth and a wisdom that they shall not be able to gainsay or resist." When thus met, these ferocious men would fall back again, as if repulsed with some physical weapon.

How long this contest between truth and brute force would have continued, I know not, had not the sheriff of the county made his appearance, and informed the crowd that they were disturbing the court, then in session, up stairs. But soon the court adjourned, and I apprehended a resumption of hostilities on their part; but, strange to say, not long after, one by one, they left the room, until it was entirely empty. I then felt a sense of relief, and went to the window to obtain a breath of fresh air. I was then invited out of doors by one of the crowd, with the humane assurance, that if I ventured out, "I will beat you into such a jelly, that your own wife will not know you." This polite invitation he repeated several times, when a bystander whispered something in his ear, and he immediately took off his hat, and said, "I ask your pardon, Mr. Stearns. I did not know your wife was dead. Excuse me, sir." This affected me so much, that I burst into tears. I was unmanned, at the sight of such a demon-like nature, changed so suddenly into a humane man, by the transforming power of domestic affection; for if he had not loved his own wife, he could not have felt so deeply for another's affliction. Does not this little incident afford convincing proof, that the worst of men have a spark of humane feeling left within them? Is there not some good in even a demon? After they had all left me, I sought the sheriff, and claimed his protection for the following night; but he blandly informed me that he was under the necessity of leaving town very soon. The next move was to decide on my quarters for the night. Neither of the hotel keepers seemed desirous of having me for a guest, on account of the danger to them; so I concluded to pass the night in the barn-yard, containing my carriage. A friendly black man came secretly to us, and told us that the rebels intended attacking us during the night, and carrying off all our "traps" that were in the carriage. We determined, therefore, to guard our property; and with revolver in hand, I paced that barn-yard, the greater part of the night, changing guard occasionally, with Frank, my faithful black defender.

It was a fearful night, truly; surrounded as I was, with blood-thirsty enemies, and almost entirely destitute of friends. Much of the time I spent in silent prayer; and I can assure my readers, that waiting throngs of invisible beings, seemed hovering over me; and either they, or the "God and father of our spirits," whispered joyful words of consolation and courage to my fearful heart. If God willed that I should then and there fall a victim to the violence of my enemies, I was willing to be thus sacrificed. But I besought God to show me my duty, and to direct my steps. The stars sent down a brilliant and cheering light upon me, and though forsaken of man, I felt that holy angels, and glorified spirits were still "hovering around," although unseen by mortal eyes.

I watched closely the gate that led into the enclosure, determined to repulse, if possible, any one who should enter the yard that night; but morning dawned, at length, and nothing had occurred, except a great variety of unearthly noises, that I could hear in the distance, sounding like the summoning of men, for some important conflict. And so the result proved. At about twelve o'clock, the next forenoon, while sitting in the court-room, up stairs, the court having adjourned, I beheld a motley crowd rush up stairs, and after gazing at me, with a subdued ferocity, mingled with a curious air, they took their seats around the room. I viewed them closely, and was convinced that this crowd could not be influenced by reason, even as much as the one of the previous afternoon. At first, my knees trembled a little, as I beheld their fierce and besotted features; but I prayed for strength, and instantly all fear left me, and I could look upon my would-be murderers with comparative calmness.

At length a stout, red-faced and brutish looking man

walked up to me, and after questioning me a little as to my intentions, cried out, "Come on, boys, let's pitch him out the window;" but the "boys" did not respond to his murderous intentions, and he contented himself with cursing me to his heart's content. I asked him in what way I had ever injured him, that he should be so full of rage against me. His only response was, that "We own the Court-house, and it shall not be occupied by niggers or the friends of niggers."

In a few moments, a mild and pleasant looking gentleman, a lawyer from Berzilia, in a polite manner, said to me, "Why do you persist in holding this office against the will of the people? Why are you not willing to resign seeing they feel so about it? I told him I would tell them all, if they would give me five minutes to speak in without interruption. To this request, they all assented, and I spoke as follows, the kind gentleman holding the watch, to see that I was allowed the whole of the time agreed upon.

"Did you not engage in war against the Northern people?" They replied affirmatively. "Were you not beaten in that war?" They nodded assent. "And after you were beaten, did you not agree to submit to the United States government?" They replied as before. "Then," said I, "the Congress of the United States gave these negroes the right to vote, on account of their services in the Union army; and as well-meaning and sincere men, ought you not to submit to its will, until the Supreme Court has decided its acts are unconstitutional." To this proposition they quickly replied, "*No*, we will be d—d if we will. It is only a rump Congress and had no right to let niggers vote, and we don't care a d—n for it." My time was now out, and I desisted from farther talking.

Soon after, a portion of the crowd left the room, and as I was afterwards informed by a bystander, they replenished the stock of whiskey in their stomachs, reloaded their revolvers, doffed their coats, and they soon re-entered the room. They rushed upon me immediately, crying out, "G — n d — n you, get out of this court-house, it was built with our money, and you shall not stay in it any longer." They then seized me and dragged me to the top of the stairs, and hurried my departure from the hall of justice, by pushing and kicking me until I had reached the bottom of the long flight of stairs, some of them crying out, "Let's put him into the creek."

As soon as I reached the outer door, I hesitated a moment whither to direct my steps, but seeing a crowd on the steps of the post-office building, which was across a lawn, in front of the court-house, I turned my face thitherward, when I was met with a fiendish shout, "Don't come here, G — d d — n you, we have no use for you." I was at a loss then what to do. I looked above and saw the hot September sun pouring down unwonted rays of burning heat. I looked upon the ground and that did not open to afford me a hiding place. I cast my eyes behind me, and there was a crowd of infuriated savages, maddened with whiskey. I gazed before me, and I saw only another company of enraged human beings ready to destroy me. I turned my eyes to the right hand, and then to the left, and no friend appeared. I thought of the judge of the Superior Court, with whom I was acquainted, and who was of our party; but then I reflected that he could do but little for me, and by flying to him his life might be endangered also, and I determined to fight my own battles, with the Lord alone for a helper.

I had in my side coat-pocket a loaded revolver, which I resolved to use at the last extremity, and to sell my life as dearly as possible. At length, one of the crowd cried out, "Go that way," pointing to the road leading from the town; but I well understood what that meant, so I firmly refused, saying, decidedly, "I shall *not* go there, or anywhere else, until my carriage is brought to me." "Where is your carriage?" said they. I told them, and they then agreed to send a man for it, and ordered me to remain standing under the hot sun, until it came, which command I was forced to obey. And there I stood for an hour, at midday, with the fierce rays of the sun falling on my unsheltered head, and receiving such insults as they felt disposed to heap upon me. One man threw at me a rock as big as a man's head, but two other men caught his arms quickly, and the rock fell harmless at my feet, the disappointed villain boiling over with impotent rage.

The crowd continued to urge me to resign my office, and they would not molest me. Some of them said I must agree to three things; viz: "to resign the office of Ordinary, to refuse to take any other office to which I might be elected by the negroes, and never to come to Apling again." My kind defender in the court room was indefatigable in his efforts to protect me, not because he sympathized with me, as he said, but because he was opposed to mob law. Two others were equally valiant, and apparently for similar reasons. One of them was the old man who was the most excited of the crowd the day before. After a while, my carriage hove in sight, the mules being driven by the ever faithful Frank, who had stood by me to the last, although previous to this, he had been repeatedly urged to flee for his life.

As he alighted from the carriage, a miserable ruffian asked him whether he was a democrat or a radical. He replied "a radical," when the brute attacked him, beating him on his head severely, and kicking him several times. Frank did not recover from the effects of these blows for several weeks. My kind defender now said, "Well, if you will not promise to resign this office, I can do nothing more for you;" and he left me, and walked toward the crowd, on the steps of the Post-Office building. I then saw that but a step remained between me and certain death, and that my colored comrade would share the same fate, and I wished to know my duty. Previous to this, I had come to the conclusion, and it was impressed on my mind, that it was of no use to try to hold the office, unless I could have soldiers to protect me; but I did not wish to resign in reality, only to hold its duties in abeyance for a season, hoping that there might be a change in affairs ere long.

I then said in my heart, "O Lord, what shall I do now? Shall I resign or not?" Instantly the answer came to me, "It is useless to hold out any longer. They will kill you and Frank too, and there will be none left to tell the story. If you die here, it will only add another to the long list of victims already sacrificed on the bloody altar of Southern hate, and your death will soon be forgotten. If you live, you can testify of these atrocities, and do much good." I hesitated no longer, but calling my protector to me, I made known to him my terms of capitulation, viz: that if they would allow me to retire with "the honors of war," carrying my arms and all of my property with me, and would agree not to molest either of us on our return home, then I would promise not to occupy the office in question. He repeated my terms to the crowd, who immediately cried out, "That's right; bully for him," although a few demanded the first terms spoken of; but others said, "No, that's enough;" and turning to me, said, "You have done right. You may come to Apling whenever you wish, and we will protect you." I stepped into my carriage, and Frank applied the lash to the mules vigorously, and we rode off, accompanied by a deafening shout of triumph, on the part of the victorious contemners of the United States Government.

I must confess that I was happily disappointed in being permitted to ride away unmolested, as I expected to be followed by a volley of rifle balls from the cowardly mob.

Was I right in resigning this office? If I had been required to renounce my principles, or to vote the democratic ticket, I feel sure that all hell could not have prevailed upon me to comply; but as the question was simply as to holding a particular office in form, which I was satisfied I could not hold in reality, I think I did right in compromising with this bloody crowd. If I had not yielded, I should never have lived to write these pages. Still I felt a little ashamed at having succumbed to them, and I afterwards told my protector so. But he replied, "You could have done no different if you had been Napoleon Bonaparte." He then said, "If you will go home and mind your own business, and not attempt to make political capital out of this affair, by and by you'll have lots of friends all around you."

I saw the sheriff shortly afterwards, and asked him why he was not on hand to protect me. "O," said he, "I could do nothing in such a crowd. They would have killed me if I had interfered." The Judge to whom I have alluded, afterwards assured me that the sheriff would have been killed if he had tried to protect me, and that the mob told him so at the commencement of their operations. Thus were "law and order" trampled under foot by those in whose behalf so many vociferous calls are being made, as eminently worthy of pardon for all their past political offences.

CHAPTER XXIII.

THE VALLEY OF THE SHADOW OF DEATH, AND DETESTABLE CONDUCT OF THE REBELS, WITH MR. LOVING'S "SUI GENERIS" EPISTLE.

Without wishing to introduce any strictly personal matters into this narrative, still I cannot continue the "thread of my tale," without briefly alluding to the consequences to myself, of the rough treatment portrayed in the preceding chapter. Hardly had I reached my home, and described to my excited colored friends the scenes that had occurred at Apling, and furnished a brief statement thereof, for the Northern press; when I was prostrated on a bed of sickness, from which I did not arise so as to be able to perform any labor for two months. Death nearly claimed me for his own, but God had other work for me to do; and the grim messenger, always ready to contend with the Almighty for the physical forms of his servants, ceased his pleadings, and stood one side while God asserted his authority. I do not mean that God worked a miracle to save me, but I have no doubt that he acted through me, to induce me to do the things that he saw would prolong my life.

I was first attacked with the chills and fever, sweating so profusely that hardly a dry thread was left in my clothing, I having being obliged to prostrate myself upon my bed so suddenly, that I had neither time nor strength to remove my garments. The next day I was removed up stairs, and there I remained for more than three weeks, enduring the alternate misery of shaking cold and of burning heat, succeeded by copious sweats. I had no attendants except my ignorant black friends, who were anxious to aid me, but lacked ability in that line, as the reader will remember in the case of a former sickness.

Our faithful cook, Susan, understood what to do tolerably well; but hardly two weeks had elapsed before she succumbed to her arduous labors, and was able to do no more for me. "Aunt Matilda" next undertook the work, and was faithful according to her knowledge; but her strength soon gave out, and there were no others that could be obtained, except at intervals; and for two weeks I was left to the mercy of those who could be spared from the labors of the farm. Mr. Loving spent a few moments with me every day, and occasionally gave me a bath; but he was busy about other things, and could not spare much time to be at my bedside.

At the end of three weeks I was much better, having "missed the chill" several times in succession; and I was able to crawl down stairs, and superintend the cooking of some light food for myself; occasionally eating a squirrel, which the hands brought me. I was also able, after the chills and fever had left me for the day, to spend a little time in writing to friends, for help against the rebels. But as soon as I thus began to improve, providence sent another terrible affliction upon me; and the excitement caused thereby, again prostrated me, and for more than a week I lay very near death's door.

This affliction was the sudden departure of my white

overseer, Mr. Loving, who took with him several hundreds of dollars' worth of cotton; and with his interesting family, left for parts unknown. When I first learned of this occurrence, the most melancholy forebodings filled my mind, as there I was prostrate, and nearly all of my crops remaining ungathered. I could see to nothing myself, and according to the letter sent me by my *kind* friend, I could not depend on the blacks for anything. The rebels, in the meantime, were howling around me like so many demons from the bottomless pit; disproving my friends assertion, that if I "minded my own business, I should have lots of friends."

For a while it seemed as if I could realize fully, the force of our Saviour's dying cry; "My God, my God! why hast thou forsaken me?" Swiftly passed through my mind, as I lay helpless on my sick bed, all the horrors of my situation; and for a moment, I thought, "well, God must be angry with me, for coming down here; and he is punishing me severely for my fool-hardyness." But I struggled with this "fiery dart of the wicked one," and called on God for help; and soon, bright angels appeared around me, and whispered in my ears the following comforting words: "Of one thing you may rest assured; whatever befalls you, God is still your *father* and your *friend*, however dark seems the prospect now around you. He never will forsake those who love and obey him." Reassured by these soothing words, I again "trusted in Him," and soon saw through the angry clouds above me, rays of golden light, betokening a brighter and better day. "When did any ever trust in the Lord, and were confounded?"

Soon a physician and a Northern friend arrived from town, travelling in the night, to avoid danger, and by great efforts on their part, I was enabled to pass the crisis, my pulse, on their arrival, being up to 127 ; and I was utterly unconscious of what was passing around me, except that it seemed to me that the rebels were assaulting the place, and the house was full of defenders, whom I was urging to fight valiantly. I was afterwards informed of this, by the physician.

During the whole of these trying scenes, the boasted Southern chivalry did their best to annoy and disturb me. As long as I was able, every night before composing my eyes in slumber, I re-loaded my rifle, and placed it at the head of my bed, and put my revolver under my pillow, resolved to protect myself as long as I had a particle of strength remaining. I wish I could portray these dark and terrible hours before my readers, in order to show them the character of the foe I had to deal with; but words would fail me, to correctly describe them.

What made the case still worse was, that the madness of our friends in the Legislature had resulted in the ousting from their seats the colored members thereof; and the rebels, emboldened by the result of their villainy, like a wolf who has tasted a little of the blood of its victim, thirsted for a full draught of the life-element of their innocent foes.

To crown all, the horrible doctrines of Frank Blair and Co. were being sedulously inculcated throughout the land, and with the insane ravings of Ben Hill, and others of his elk, sounding aloud, the very atmosphere seemed burning with oaths, imprecations and horrid hate. The red sun emitted no more fiery rays of terrestrial heat, than did these maddened men send forth of rancorous hate, from the unfathomable abyss of their sin-polluted souls.

The rebels themselves were sanguine of victory, and vainly imagined that the ticket headed "Seymour and Blair" was destined to succeed and place them in power again. If the political horoscope of our moral planetary system had truly indicated such a change in our country's future destiny, my situation would have been still worse; but as far as I could read the signs in the heavens, no such a change was there indicated, and this conviction allayed many of my fears, and aided in my recovery. I felt sure that our noble soldiers, who on the field of battle had conquered the myrmidons of secession, would as effectually vanquish them in the great political fight then approaching. I was certain that the great heart of the Northern people could not be so suddenly seized with madness, as to thrust from them the one whom God had so recently selected, to lead them on to victory, and imitate the Jews of old, in preferring "Barabbas to Christ." I was certain in my own mind that General Grant was to be our next president, and so expressed my feelings to all the rebels who asked my opinion.

If such had not been the case, I am sure I should not have been writing these pages. It was well understood that if "Seymour and Blair" had been elected, almost every Union man would have been driven from the South, or welcomed to the "hospitable graves," so much talked of by our Southern brethren.

I cannot depict all the occurrences of that "reign of terror," that lasted several months. Murders were occurring elsewhere, and for a season, it verily seemed as if "hell was let loose" upon the devoted heads of the Union men. My rebel friends being fully aware of my utterly helpless condition, waxed surpassingly bold.

Not a night passed for some time, without a bevy of them exhibiting the manly feelings of their deluded souls, by firing off deadly weapons all around my house. In one instance they rode into my front yard, and valiantly discharged their revolvers right in front of my house, thus entitling them to the praise of all lovers of true bravery. To be sure, if I had been able to return their fire, they would have hardly ventured so far; but dear creatures! they evidently enjoyed the Christian-like employment of frightening a person lying at the point of death, simply because his sentiments differed so much from their treasonable and diabolical notions. God forbid that I should indulge in any uncharitable feelings towards the poor creatures who thus retarded my recovery, and aided in plunging me into the depths of the physical misery that I endured.

The souls of such men carry with them sufficient punishment for their horrible crimes. I would not lift a finger to increase the severity thereof, only, I would like our government to enact such laws as will prevent the possibility of the recurrence of such scenes.

A few days after the departure of Mr. Loving, I received from him the following letter, which I publish, "verbatim, et literatim," in order to show the true condition of affairs at the time; premising that I did not then, and do not now, believe his statements respecting the colored people, for their future conduct refuted his calumnies. But I have no reason to doubt his assertions respecting his own danger, for I had long noticed that he was terribly frightened, and I knew that the rebels hated him, if possible, more than they did me. The reader can imagine the effect upon me, of the reception of such a letter at such a time.

Sep 27 1865

Mr Stearns dear Sir you will be somewhat Suprized to recive this letter from one that has given you so much trouble. Mr Stearns I would not have done as I have if my life had not been at stake I am threatend on evry side by boath white and black and you are too but I am in mor dangar than yer are I have sold the 3 bails of coton & gon to Louissianna where my property is and when I git there if I have luck to do so I intend selling my land and send you all the money I have got for the Coton you must imploy some purson to cary on the buisiness you will do well to imploy George parks as I think he will do you justiss you can depend on frank and Jarat and John Robenson but you must have some one that is not interested to devid the crops and that is not all if you dont have a disinterested man ther all the time or yer stuff will all go not as I got it but in a more secrete maner I have mad a good crop for you but it will not all be saved for there has been at least 25 bush corn stolen all ready out of the field you will find my acount Book in my. house on the side board you had better git it amediatly for the men may git it and distroy it Isaac warren has got the key Mr Stearns you have no idier the danger you are in if you did you would not stay there for all your crop and place is worth

Mr Stearns you know not the danger you are in even with the black people the men on your place would kill you for little of nothing they say you have preached to them so much about Elivation and Education till they are tired of it and they say the yankeys have not done right by them. They come down here and set them free and give them nothing to go upon, and when these yankeys come down here to farmit they are not willing to give a cent more wages than a rebil and you have caused them more trouble than the rebils has, you made them belive your way was right and they voted your way and now the North wont give them any protection your own men say this and they say all so that if they dont make any thing this year they will murder you and me boath and all the other yankeys that comes in their way. I have caught several colord men on your place stealing and threatend to tell you of it and they sayd they would kill me if I did and all the men on the place joind them and sayd they would help to do the work they sayd that I was there to tend to your buisiness and not to theirs and if I did tell they would all help to kill me I will tell you of some instances one is when Bansfield hog was killed, our own men was in the scrape they took it to the swamp but he pushed them so clost they had to leave it behind, and one of yer men was blody and had to change his clothes and I caught him striping and told him of it and sayd I was going to have him arested for it but I changed my notion when every man on the place got round me in the field and sayd they would kill me on the spot if I did not promise them I would not tell you nor any one else so I promisd and one of them sayd they ought to kill me anyhow for a dead man never would tell any thing, and at one time I was going to town and there was a bag of old irons in the wagon and I asked the driver whose they ware but he did not tell me and on examining it I found the step of yor Cariage in it and a grate many other irons that was valuable I sayd I was going to tell you and he sayd if I did I would be killed by all the hands on the place he sayd they had all agreed to stick togeather in a case of that kind he sayd they were poor, and they had to have a living and the people did not give them enough to live off of and they intended to have it in that way I sccceeded in proswaeding him to let me bring the irons back by promising I would not tell you on examining when I got back home I found that they had took nearly all the old irons on the place I then gathered the remainder up and put them in an old tub in the wood house, now you know these women dont go to town so often for nothing now I will tell you they have been stealing corn and old irons and one thing and then an nother all the time and I have been afraid to tell it to you for my life was in danger all the time they would kill me the very instant I did report one of them you will say I am a grand thief but you are mistaken for if I had been wanting to make a profit out of you I would have waited for a beter time for if I had waited till we had gined out 6 or 8 bails of coton I could have made 6 or 8 hundred dolars insted of 332.60 but no it was for no gain of property or money or friends or good will of any one, but it was for the very time to save life I am shure if my life had not been in danger and I had not had souch short notice and so short time to git away in I would not don it for nothing in this world no Mr Stearns I would not do as I have don for a milion of dolars so far as love of wealth is conserned. My heart is bursting now at the very idier of having to do what I have to save my life but you know life is sweet and espesialy to one that has got a family and a heples one at that like mine. If you git killed you have got something to suport your child with but my family would come to starvation so fare as character is consurned poor people has got non in these days for I have experiansed this fact myself. I was once in good circumstance and now I am poor and I am no more respected than a dog even by my pretended friends

Now you may think my wife had a hand in this affair but she is as clear as the noon days sun She opposed it from the beging but I knew that my time was near out and this was my only chance Just see what a poor man has got to do to live I had to take sids with you when you and your sister acused my wife of being a thief to keep a home if I had not been in the fix I was in I would not stayd a day after you acused her of stealing when I knew she was inocent

I can not finish this as the cars are bobing so I cant write I am yours as ever If you wish to push the Law you Can do so, if do not you will git pay for all the damage I have don to you, and that unexpected, I will send it to your sister as I think you will not stay there long.

yours respectfuly

J. W. Loving.

You will hear from me again soon

P. S. I am a shamd to ask your pardon, for I do not think their is any for me but I hope their is.

But relief at length came. A telegram was despatched to my sister at the North, and with all possible despatch she hastened to my bedside, where she arrived just in season to snatch my person from the insatiable monster death, into whose distended arms I was momentarily expecting to fall. She received the telegram at ten o'clock at night, and was in the cars at noon of the following day. At my request the colored people on the place had come in, and bade their final adieu to me; they had sang and prayed with me, and on leaving the room all had shaken hands with me. I had offered to them a few words of farewell advice, and addressed a short petition to heaven in their behalf.

The sands of life were nearly wasted. A cold sweat stood on my brow. Beckoning angels seemed to stand at my bedside to welcome me into the eternal world. I succeeded in placing on paper, a few words for my sister to read, on her arrival, and committing my soul into the hands of an ever faithful God, I folded my hands in quietness and calmly awaited the result. If my sister's arrival had been delayed one day longer, I am confident no words of welcome would have dropped from my cold and compressed lips. Nothing would have remained but my lifeless form stretched on a bed of death.

But she reached me, and in the good providence of God I was also permitted to see my darling child, on whose account I had told the insane crew at Apling, that I preferred life to death; and they had replied that "*they* would take care of her."

Her presence was entirely unexpected, but as soon as

she understood that her aunt was coming to Georgia to see her sick papa, she clung to her with such tenacity, that it was impossible to leave her behind. It may sound strange to some ears to hear, that she had insisted upon it that her papa was very sick and needed her presence, for some days before the remainder of the family had received any intimation of such a fact. When asked how she knew, her reply was, "God told me so, and I must go and see my dear papa." May I be permitted to state that this is not the only instance of this spiritual clairvoyance that has occurred among the author's children.

It is needless to mention that the presence and joyous prattle of this child, aided effectually in the recovery of her fond parent. She was then about six and a half years old, and one of the most affectionate of children.

The following is an extract from a letter of my sister to her mother, written soon after her arrival.

"I found all here in a state of the wildest excitement. Had my brother died, I do not think all Heaven and Earth could have prevented the shedding the blood of his murderers. Stalwart men crowded our back door in the middle of the day, exclaiming, "we cannot work, the fight is in us, just let us go, we will lay Columbia County in ashes." "Just you say the word, and we will level that Court House to the ground." "We have all been insulted long enough, we will bear it no longer." &c. &c. &c.

I entreated, I expostulated, I told them Mr. S. would perhaps live, and that the best way to save his life, was to go to work and try to save his crops, at that moment wasting in the fields. I told them that such an excitement as what they proposed would occasion, would be certain to cause his death; that the doctor said he must be kept very quiet, and if they had any real true regard for him or me, to keep calm and try to attend to their work, as the only right course and the only safe way.

All the first week I thus entreated in private, but the excited state of feeling still continued. I then called a public meeting which was attended by many from the neighboring plantations. I then laid before them the direful consequences for themselves and to us of thus taking vengeance in their own way. I told them to leave it to the Lord who has said, "Vengeance is mine, I will repay." I explained to them that by the course they proposed they would be arming themselves against the United States government, were they called upon to do it they would be protected; but by thus taking the work into their own hands, they would become *the mob*, and the government would be bound to put them down with all its troops.

I appealed to them by every motive I could command, self-preservation, love to us, obedience to God, &c. &c. And when they saw that their well-meant efforts would only result in greater evils to themselves and to us, and felt how powerless they were to contend with the foe, so much their superior in skill, in knowledge, and in power, they sadly "laid down their fight," as they expressed it, and slowly and reluctantly went to their homes, and the next day to their respective tasks, but their hearts were not in it, and much of the crop was wasted in consequence.

The neighboring physician who had refused to take charge of his case, told me he would have taken it, had he been tolerably sure of a favorable result, but if Mr. S. had died under his care, the negroes would have perhaps burned his house and barn, and perhaps have killed him and his family, supposing him to blame for his death."

R. W. S.

CHAPTER XXIV.

EXCLUSION OF THE COLORED MEMBERS FROM THE GEORGIA LEGISLATURE.

While this dark cloud was overhanging my own abode, events were transpiring in other places foreboding still more evil to all the friends of the Union in the state of Georgia. I allude to the expulsion from our House of Representatives of twenty-five "persons of color" simply on account of their being "guilty of a skin not colored like our own; and the admission of an equal mumber of democrats to fill their places, thus lessening the republican majority by fifty votes. Of course all legislation after this was carried on in the interests of the democratic party, as the republican majority at the outset had been quite small, the republican candidate for speaker having been elected by a majority of only one vote. But the majority in the Senate was greater, so that on joint ballot the republicans had a respectable majority.

It was some draw back to the nefarious schemes of these insane disorganizers, that none of their corrupt legislation could receive the sanction of the governor, as he remained true to the party that had elected him, amid this, and all the other changes that came over the "body politic," in our state. If it had not been for this well known fact, our situation would have been fearful indeed. The protection of the military had been withdrawn, and our representatives had been admitted to Congress, thus creating the impression that Georgia was a loyal state in the Union. But the triumph of these wretched men was short, for by the action of Congress, the entire admission of Georgia was delayed, and the seats of its senators declared vacated, until the rights of these ejected ones could be fully ascertained.

Far be it from me to criticise in a captious manner the action of Congress in this respect, but I cannot help feeling that it did wrong in afterwards admitting to their seats, the senators elected before the proper organization of the Legislature ; in accordance with the provisions of the Reconstruction act, under which they were elected. This act declared that no "person prohibited from holding office under the United States, or under any state, by section third of the proposed amendment to the Constitution of the United States, known as article fourteen, shall be deemed eligible to any office in either of said states, unless relieved from disability, as provided by said amendmeut," This section is as follows :

"No person shall be a senator or representative in Congress, or elector of President or Vice President, or hold any office, civil or military, under the United States, or under any state, who having previously taken an oath, as a member of Congress or as an officer of the United States, or as a member of any State Legislature, or as an executive or judicial officers of any State to support the Constitution of the United States, shall have engaged in insurrection or rebellion against the same, or given aid and comfort to the enemies thereof. But Congress may by a vote of two thirds of each House remove such disability.

A supplementary act passed by Congress July 19,

1867, declared that "the words executive or judicial office in any State, shall be construed to include all civil offices created by law, for the administration of any general law, or the administration of justice."

In accordance with these provisions, and with his duty as military commander of the district, four days after the organization of the Legislature, General Meade sent a letter to Governor Bullock, calling his attention to the matter, and declaring that he could not recognize the Legislature, until satisfied that these Reconstruction acts had been complied with. Gov. Bullock forwarded these documents to the Legislature, endorsing the position of Gen. Meade, and recommending to the Legislature an appointment of a committee, to ascertain the eligibility of its members. This committee was duly appointed, after various propositions to modify its powers, and an attempt on the part of Mr. Tumlin, of Randolph, to defy the power of Congress in reference to the matter, by introducing a resolution declaring that Congress had no right to "define the terms upon which the members of the Legislature might hold their office." The names of the committee appointed were as follows: "O'Neal, of Lowndes, Shumate, of Whitfield, Harper, of Tirrell, Lee, of Newton, and Bryant, of Richmond," three of whom were republicans, and two democrats.

The chairman of the committee reported that two of the members were ineligible, a minority of republicans reported that one person was ineligible, and a minority of democrats that none were ineligible. The house by a vote of 95 to 53, adopted the minority report of the democrats, and declared that all the members were eligible.

But behind all this, legislative scenes were enacted, which, to say the least, failed to do credit to the logical acumen or straightforward character of those concerned in this examination. It was a matter of common notoriety, that quite a large number of the members of the Legislature had participated in the rebellion, and by the wording of the Reconstruction acts, which asserted the ineligibility of *all* engaged in the rebellion, after having sworn to support the Const. of the United States, they were not entitled to their seats. Doubtless the members of Congress who voted for the Reconstruction acts, were aware of the omission of the word voluntary, in reference to those who rendered "aid and comfort" to the rebellion. But even if they did not intend to omit that word, the strict letter of the law must be complied with; and it was not proper for the Georgia Legislature to apply an interpretation of its own, to these acts, unless the language was susceptible of a variety of interpretations.

In this case, the language is so plain, that "he who runneth may read." "No person who has supported the rebellion, after having sworn to support the Cnstitution of the United States, shall be eligible to office.

But honesty and common sense were eschewed; darker counsels prevailed, and the whole committee, and a large majority of the House, endorsed the character of nearly all of the members, and the direst consequences ensued. About two months afterwards, according to the prophecy of those who opposed this unwise conduct, all the colored members of the Legislature, numbering some twenty-eight or thirty, I think, were excluded from their seats, and their places filled by good democrats.

It is very much to the discredit of the colored members of the Legislature, as far as perspicuity of vision is concerned, that they favored the reception of those ineligible members — except the three declared so by the committee. But it is accounted for, on the score of the known magnanimity of the colored race, towards their former oppressors; and should, therefore, be looked upon with leniency; especially as prominent republicans, and those to whom they had been accustomed to look for political guidance, urged them to this course.

What shall be said of such measures, on the part of sworn friends of the Union cause, and of the colored race? A more unfortunate movement could hardly have been made. By it, the balance of power was thrown into the hands of the vanquished party; and the fruits of our hotly contested election, were partially lost. It is true, that these mistaken men, solmnly assert their honesty and conscientiousness, in this matter; that, believing the Reconstruction act meant to say, "voluntary aid," when it did not, and being satisfied that none of these men had rendered "voluntary aid," they were bound by their consciences, to support them as entitled to their seats.

But honesty and conscientiousness, do not always prove safe guides, in political, any more than in moral matters. The result of all this conscientiousness, was as disastrous to the cause of freedom, as if there had been no "conscience" in the matter. When men's minds are made up to pursue a particular course, it is not always easy to detach firmness from conscientiousness. Doubtless the Puritan fathers imagined they were conscientious, in the hanging of Quaker women; but it is difficult for us to believe, to-day, that no other than conscientious feelings, influenced them in such cruel acts. Conscientiousness includes the exercise of our judgement, as to the facts in the case, and diligent attention to all the means of light, in the case under consideration. I cannot but believe, that if those republicans, who decided that these members were eligible, under the Reconstruction acts, had exercised their common sense a little more fully, they would have come to a far different conclusion.

And I am the more inclined to this opinion, from the fact that the judgment of the great body of the republican party of the State, outside of the Legislature, led them to deny the eligibility of these members, and the report of the committee was received with astonishment, by many of the members of the Legislature itself. I am free to confess, however, that some of those who favored the retention of these ineligible democrats, sincerely believed, with their great New York compeers, that amnesty and kind measures were better adapted to pacifying the lion of rebellion, than the severity and awe, usually practiced by professional lion-tamers. Patting a mad dog on the head, may ward off the danger of hydrophobia from his bite, but it requires considerable faith in a mad dog's divinity, to adopt such precautionary measures, and no others.

But notwithstanding the unfavorable aspect of the case at this time, "the wise were caught in their own craftiness," for this action of the Legislature, led to the exclusion of Georgia from the Union, for nearly two years, until the country had become ready for the adoption of other measures of protection, and Andrew Johnson had been shorn of his power to do harm, by the inauguration of his successor.

CHAPTER XXV.

THE PRESIDENTIAL ELECTION IN GEORGIA, WITH AUTHENTIC DOCUMENTS RESPECTING ITS OUTRAGES.

So great was the pressure brought to bear upon the colored voters of this region, that not a solitary one ventured to deposit his vote, for General Grant, in our County. The republican vote dwindled from about 1700 votes in the Spring, to one solitary vote in November.

There was no change in the political opinions of the blacks. On the contrary, they were more firmly rooted than ever, in the republican faith; but who of the members of any party at the North, would march to the polls, and vote according to their political faith, if loaded revolvers were held to their heads, while so doing? The negroes have always been cowed down by the whites, and how can they be expected to run this terrible gauntlet? Some few of our prominent colored republicans went over to the enemy, for "a mess of pottage," but great numbers of the "rank and file" utterly refused to do so mean an act. Many declared that they would be cut in pieces first, and others said they would go into the woods, and live by themselves, rather than deny their principles. In Lincoln County, however, the pressure was so tremendous, that to escape certain death, nearly all of the colored, and some of the white republicans, voted the democratic ticket. I have seen some of each class, black and white, who have assured me that they were just as strong republicans as ever, but they voted the democratic ticket, to save their lives. Strange as it may seem, our "tyrannical" government never, in a solitary instance, used its power to intimidate a single democrat from voting as he pleased. I challenge our enemies to produce a single instance where United States soldiers intimidated in the least degree, democratic or other voters, from voting as they pleased; but innumerable were the instances where no republican could vote as he pleased, without protection from Uncle Sam's friendly arm. Whoever asserts that the suspension of the habeas corpus, provided for in the Ku-Klux bill, facilitated the encroachment upon the rights of the Southern people to vote as they pleased, either betrays his utter ignorance of what he is writing or talking about, or asserts an *unblushing* and *unmitigated falsehood.*

About two hundred men from this vicinity went to Augusta, and voted the republican ticket. A large number started from near my house, at a little past midnight, so as to reach Augusta by daylight. The rebels had arranged their plans for assaulting this party on their way; but by the early starting of the blacks, they were thwarted in their nefarious design. They followed them, however, on their return from town, and attacked them at Rea's creek, about two miles from town, firing at them one or two times, but soon *desisting*, when they found the black people *prepared* to *defend themselves.*

The men who attacked the party were well known to the assailed, two of their leaders being our neighbors, and of highly respectable character, in other respects. Foiled in their attempts upon these well armed blacks, and deeming it necessary to show their devotion to the "lost cause," by mobbing some friend of the Union, they attacked a gentleman by the name of Skinner, living a few miles distant, firing at him, beating him, and in other ways insulting him, and also insulting his wife; a noble instance of the manly courage of the rebel crew, that were shouting aloud for Seymour and Blair. In Augusta, fire arms were used quite freely, and the republican sheriff was *shot dead*, and two republican negroes were reported to have been shot, beside many being wounded. In order to prevent further disturbance, the polls were closed at about two o'clock. The Hon. Foster. Blodgett, republican mayor of the city, was assaulted with revolvers, and only saved his life by taking refuge in his own house. How hard it is for the Southern democracy to carry on an election, without summoning to their aid "the dogs of War."

It may not be uninteresting to my readers, to peruse the following accounts of this election in other places, which I will publish, leaving the reader to make his own comments. From their character, it can be easily perceived why Georgia, with a former republican majority of 17,000, gave Seymour and Blair some 30,000 majority.

BUREAU R. F. AND A. L.
Headquarters, Sub. Dist. Savannah,
SAVANNAH, GA., Nov. 9, 1868.

Brevet Col. J. R. Lewis, U. S. A., Assistant Commissioner, etc. State of Georgia.

Colonel, — I have the honor to report the killing of James Parsons and Peter Hopkins at the polls on the morning of the 3d inst. I knew nothing of the affray till after it was over, but from the testimony of many present, and opposed in principle, I am satisfied that the following statement is correct: — In their eagerness to vote, the freedmen, on said day, assembled early at the polls, where order reigned until about eight o'clock, A. M., when the employees of the Central Railroad appeared in a body, and claimed, as a right, that they should be allowed to vote immediately, and return to their work. The freedmen, as was their right, claimed the privilege of voting in the order of precedence, being first at the polls. The authorities volunteered to make way to the polls for said employees, which resulted in the killing of the above named men, and the seriously wounding of Sam Norman, —— Green, —— July, —— Gay, and Edward Graham. Two policemen have died from wounds received on said occasion. It is impossible to state who fired the first shot. The following conclusions are obvious and indisputable: Not one in fifty were armed, while the democracy had one or more revolvers. Not one in ten of the freedmen carried sticks or canes. Immediately after the affray, the freedmen adjourned to New Street Church, and unanimously resolved to retire to their respective homes, rather than risk their lives or bring on a riot, as they unquestionably would had they again went to vote. This conduct proved conclusively their desire to avoid all disturbance, while, from minging with the *masses* at the polls, it was evident that *they* desired nothing more than a repetition of the morning's scenes.

The crowning point of their chivalrous conduct, was at dark. When a man, with a cart, was removing from the Square in front of the Court House a campaign banner, bearing the portraits of Grant and Colfax, a crowd of men and boys charged after this man, captured and tore up the banner, which was then taken up by mounted men, and displayed through the streets as trophies of their gallantry.

I would add, in conclusion, that to deceive the ignorant freedmen, the democratic ticket, headed with pictures of Grant and Colfax, were freely used.

I am, etc., very respectfully,

Your obedient servant,

J. MURRY HOAG,

Brevet Capt. U. S. Army, and S. A. Com'r.

A true copy,—M. FRANK GALLAGHER,

Brevet Capt. U. S. A., A. A. A. G.

We next give the democratic idea of a free election, as illustrated by the conduct of the members of the party at Americus. This statement is official and may be relied on.

BUREAU R. F. AND A. L.,
OFFICE AGENT DIV. OF AMERICUS,
AMERICUS, GA., NOV. 9, 1868.

Brevet Captain M. Frank Gallagher, A. A. A. General, Atalanta, Ga.

Captain,—I have the honor to state, that on the morning of the 3d inst., there seemed to be a preconcerted action with the whites that there should be no election. No officers were present to open the polls, and no movement made until 10 o'clock, when I went to the Court House, at the request of three freeholders who had in my office previously qualified, and requested the Ordinary that a place be furnished to open the polls, and that three freeholders had taken the necessary oaths, and were ready to commence the voting in accordance with law. The Ordinary replied that he had given the necessary instructions to citizens who had announced their intention to open the polls.

At that time Captain Shiver, and one Foster, Special Police, wanted to know if niggers were going to open the polls. I replied, that was there intention, when they swore that the freedmen should not, Foster saying that if they attempted it, they would get the contents of this, opening his coat and touching a calvary pistol.

At this time others came up and said it should not be done, and if I wanted trouble, that was the way to begin it. In the meantime citizens began to crowd around, and the most moderate told me they would see that polls were opened, and I desisted from any farther attempt. After this, there seemed to be some attempt to open a voting place, and at quarter past twelve the voting commenced, the whites at one window, and the freedmen at another. It would be useless for me to attempt to describe the voting. Every freedman was asked by the managers, questions not pertinent to the case—such as, "where do you live ?" where did you work last year ?" then hold a consultation ; then ask if he had paid his taxes, and if not, was immediately rejected, and not allowed to vote.

Out of *fifteen hundred freedmen* that were here to vote, only *one hundred and thirty-seven* could vote, except those they could bribe to vote the democratic ticket, who voted without a challenge, or tax paid, or any other delay ; so that the vote stood nine hundred and sixty-seven majority for the democrats. The whole affair was such a farce, and everything connected with it so illegal, I do not see how it is possible it could stand as a legal vote, or showing the sentiment of this county.

Very respectfully your obedient servant,

(Signed,) W. C. MORRILL,
Agent, etc.

A true copy,—M. FRANK GALLAGHER,
Bvt. Capt. U. S. A., A. A. A. G.

In Muscogee county, matters were carried with a high hand, as will be seen by the following:

OFFICE S. A. COM. BUREAU, R. F. & A. L.
Columbus, Ga., November 29th, 1868.

Brevet Colonel J. R. Lewis, Assistant Commissioner, Atlanta, Ga.

COLONEL—I have the honor to forward herewith, the reports of agents Chapmen and Pokorny, in reference to the election held on the 3d, instant. You will perceive from their statements that the Governor's proclamation about the payment of taxes, was entirely ignored in some counties; and the vote of colored men refused, who had failed to pay their taxes for 1867.

With the exception of this county, I have heard of but one ballot box being opened at the several county seats in my sub-district, notwithstanding that orders were given to have three at each court house. In Talbot county the polls were not opened until nine o'clock. The managers of election who were first appointed were set aside, and others took their place who *refused to take the votes of colored men unless they were for Seymour and Blair.* In Marion and Chattahoochee counties, but few colored men voted, their taxes being unpaid, and the managers refusing to receive their votes *unless they were for democratic candidates, in which case no questions were asked.* In Muscogee county the proclamation of the Governor was complied with, and all permitted to deposit their votes, who were entitled to do so. The republicans charge that the votes of non-residents and minors were received by the managers, and that many voted twice, and even three times, at the different ballot boxes. Intimidation was used to prevent the freedmen from voting for the republican candidates, threats being made that, unless they voted as directed by their employers, they would be discharged and driven off. In many instances, violence was used to compel them to vote for democratic Electors, if they voted at all.

I am, respectfully, your ob't servant,

(Signed,) JOHN LEONARD.
Bt. Maj. U. A., S. A. Com'r.

A true copy: — M. FRANK GALLAGHER,
Brev. Col. U. S. A., A. A. A. G.

OFFICE AGENT BUREAU R. F. & A. L.,
Columbus, Ga , Nov. 9, 1868.

Brevet Major John Leonard, S. A. Commander, Columbus, Ga.;

In regard to circumstances connected with the recent

election in my district, so far as the facts have come to my knowledge, I have the honor to report, that in Muscogee county, there was much unfairness, and violation of law at the ballot boxes.

It may be out of place to remark here, that the Ordinary of our county so arranged the Managers of the election, as to give almost the entire control of the polls to the democrats, and of eighteen Managers, the republicans had but three. Many persons who were clearly entitled to vote, were refused permission to do so by the Managers. A large proportion of the republican voters were challenged, and compelled to swear in their votes. At two of the polls in the city of Columbus, persons from other counties in this State, were not permitted to vote for Presidential Electors; but at the third poll *all persons* were allowed to vote, provided they voted the democratic ticket. It is believed that many persons in Alabama, voted in this city. Minors were permitted to vote, and they and others repeated their votes, no questions being asked when a democratic ticket was presented. Money was freely used for the purchase of votes. The democratic candidate for sheriff, made open and public proclamation to the voters, inviting them to come up and get their money in one hand, and votes.

Muscogee county has about three thousand voters. The republicans polled less than in April last, when they carried the county by four hundred majority. About three thousand six hundred votes were polled at the election November 3d, about eight hundred more than in April.

In Chattahoochee county, but *three Republican votes* were cast. There are *seven hundred Republican voters* in that county. Persons report that they were not permitted to vote, unless they had previously paid their taxes. It has been stated that there were no votes sent to this county, except a few from this city. Chattahoochee county has about fourteen hundred registered voters, a majority of them being Republican. The returns show a vote of about six hundred at the late election. Many of the colored men walked from ten to twenty-five miles, to vote in this place, but were *refused on their arrival here, unless they voted the Democratic ticket.*

Citizens of Marion County report that all colored persons were refused the right to vote, unless they had paid their taxes. One individual estimates that three hundred persons were excluded on that account. There are about eleven hundred in Marion county.

None of the statements in this communication have been verified by affidavits, but they are thought to be substantially correct.

Very respectfully,
Your obedient servant,
(signed) C. W. CHAPMAN.

A true copy — M. FRANK GALLAGHER,
Bvt. Capt. U. S. A., A. A. A. G.

We close the testimony for to-day, by showing the disgraceful manner in which the Taylor Democracy acted.

OFFICE AG'T. BUREAU R. F. AND A. L.,
BUTLER, Ga., Nov. 4, 1868.

Brevet Captain M. F. Gallagher, A. A. A. General, Bureau R. F. and A. L., State of Georgia.

Sir,—I have the honor to report, that yesterday morning, at half-past nine o'clock, the election polls were opened at Butler, Taylor County, Ga. It seemed to me that the cause of this delay was, that nobody here had the experience or the right knowledge in such case. The colored people appeared in strong force, and even at day-break many of them gathered before the Court House. A few minutes after the commencement of the election, a great excitement prevailed between the freedmen, on the ground that votes were refused on account that the voters (colored) had not paid their poll tax. I have done what I could to secure the peace, and to calm those who were touched by this unjust proceeding or mode of action. Quiet was restored, although the freedmen, through the continuance of the election, bitterly complained about unjust and unfair treatment. Many of them agreed, or had the promise from their employers, that their poll tax should be paid from their wages, but had no receipts in their hands, and many votes were refused, notwithstanding the voters were ready to take the oath to the above facts. Confidentially I was informed that between 175 and 200 votes of colored voters were refused.

The whole crowd inside of the election room, the canvassers, challengers, or what their name may be, were composed of real Southern democrats, and their action a mere farce. In consideration that the result of this election at Butler, Ga., is any how of no influence at all, I will not molest you with further particulars. The political *terrorism*, oppressed on the people during the time between the last election and this, was so far successful, that only *two votes were given by white republican voters.*

I am respectfully, your obedient servant,

A. Pokorny,
Agent B. R., F. and A. L.

A true copy,—M. Frank Gallagher,
Brevet Capt'n U. S. A., A. A. A. G.

To show the excitement attending this election, I will close this chapter with a short extract from a letter from my sister to Northern friends, written after the election.

"And here let me add an amusing incident that occurred on the day of the election. A neighboring physician was seen riding up the yard, and on reaching the house, he asked for a radical ticket, as some one wished to vote on that side, and they had only one kind of a ticket. The ignorant blacks understood him to ask for a *radical*, and exclaimed, 'What for would he want a radical, but to kill him?' and twenty-five or thirty men, women and children rushed into the house, in order to prevent his seizing my brother, as they verily believed was his intention; but as he only wanted an Augusta republican paper, out of which to cut the radical ticket, for a vote, he was allowed to leave unmolested. We could not help but feel grateful to them for their well-meant zeal in our behalf; but we were glad to find it quite unnecessary at this time."

R. W. S.

CHAPTER XXVI.

INTERVIEW WITH THE AUTHOR'S CREDITOR, AND GREAT PERPLEXITY AS TO DUTY. GOOD SIDE AND DARK SIDE OF REBEL CONDUCT.

But while political events of so trying a nature were occurring, the author's pecuniary affairs were also approaching a fearful crisis. Mr. D. ——, to whom his farm was mortgaged for several thousand dollars, grew impatient as the end of the year approached, and at length demanded immediate payment. For two years he had acted the part of a humane gentleman, and showed no disposition to crowd his unfortunate debtor. But being a strong rebel, although a man of urbanity and generosity, he could not brook the author's "meddling with politics," and determined to show him no more leniency. I cannot better describe my feelings at this emergency, than by quoting again from my diary.

Monday, Dec. 21st, 1868, I wrote as follows:

"Mr. D. —— did not call to see me, and so I went to see him. He said he was surprised at my letter, and that I should claim the homestead, and abused me much at first, calling me a d — n rascal; but he afterwards became quite civil, and referred me to his lawyer. He abused me much for my efforts with the blacks, and said I was encouraging them to be lazy, to steal, and to hate the whites; that I had told them to shoot those of their number who joined the democrats. He said I could never make any thing from the farm, because I did not know how to manage the blacks. They would not work for me, because they did not fear me, and took advantage of me." Dec. 25th, I wrote, "I am not able to give an answer to those who want to hire land. I was never so perplexed in my life as to my duty. Cannot see any light hardly, and know not what to do. In a few days it will be too late to lease the land, and I cannot do it until I hear from D——. Returned home very much depressed."

Dec. 29th. "My lawyers assured me there was no risk in renting the land, as the crops would be secure from seizure, and at length I decided to go on and rent out the land; but on my return, a new trouble awaited me. The blacks who wanted to hire the land had got tired of waiting, and had hired land elsewhere."

So here I was, unable to go on, and obliged to do something to extricate myself from the hands of an inexorable landlord. In my distress, as usual, I called upon God, and in an entirely unexpected manner, relief appeared.

On the first day of January, 1869, Mr. S——, a white man living a few miles from here, rode up to my house, and on entering, said he had accidently heard I wished to rent my farm; and if we could agree on the terms, he would like to hire it for the ensuing year. This was joyful news, as it would enable me to go to the North, and endeavor to obtain a loan of the sum needed to satisfy my creditor. I would do nothing, however, without consulting those of my hands who had agreed to work for me on shares another year.

At night, I called them all in, and found them unwilling to hearken at all to the idea of being turned away. I then told them of my situation, that it was necessary for me to go to the North, to obtain the money; but still if they were unwilling, I would not go, but would stay and do the best I could. At last, some of them proposed that I should let Mr. S. a part of the farm, and allow them to work the remainder, and I could go to the North, and they could stay and work. This seemed so reasonable, that I at once assented, and on a second visit from Mr. S., concluded a bargain to that effect. So here was manifested the wisdom of God, and my former perplexity was accounted for. If I had become satisfied sooner of the propriety of letting the land to the blacks, and had leased it to them, I could not have gone to the North, as it would not have been safe to have left all of my possessions in their hands.

I now begân to make preparations for the North. Some of my friends suggested the idea of my trying to borrow the money temporarily in Augusta; but at first I scouted the thought, until some unseen influence seemed to urge it so powerfully upon my mind, that I resolved to make the attempt, although I felt certain that it would be unsuccessful. But I thought I could then say to my Northern friends, "I have tried in Augusta, and cannot get the money." We did not wish to *be obliged* to sell the property, to pay the debt, as in such a case it would not have brought one half of its real value; and besides, all of our labors in behalf of the blacks would have come to an inglorious termination.

On enquiry, I ascertained that there was only one man in the whole community, of whom there was the least possible chance of my obtaining the money; and he was a hard character to deal with. In the mean time, two of my neighbors had positively agreed to buy land, to the amount of nearly one half of my debt; but on my applying to them to close the bargain, one of them flatly refused to pay the amount he had so positively promised, giving as a reason for his refusal, that Congress was about to pass the "Butler bill," and Grant had agreed to sign it; "and," he said, "if that does pass, I want all my money to leave the country with, as the niggers will get land, and I do not wish to live near them." This was a severe blow to me, for I had applied to the money-lender for only one half of the amount of the debt.

But my faith was still strong in an overruling Providence. I knew I was engaged in the work of God, and Jesus, the inspired exponent of his character, had positively declared that if we sought only to build up his kingdom, he would certainly provide for our real wants. I carried my case to my Father, believing that he cared for his cause, and for me, because I was trying to promote it, and I was influenced how to act.

Through a chain of fortunate circumstances, and by my strictly following the lead of God's Spirit, Mr. R. was induced to loan me the whole amount I needed, which was over $5000, although nearly every one had said it was no use to apply to him; and it was some time before I could even ascertain where he lived, some seven miles from town. He himself stated that he had repeatedly refused to loan any more money on real estate security; but somehow he felt inclined to accommodate me, of whom he had never heard, except as a "stirrer up of sedition." I suppose some of onr modern philosophers will rail at the idea, but I feel it my duty to state for the encouragement of the sensible believers in God's power and goodness; that this man could not have been persuaded to this act, by other than divine or heavenly influences. At least so it seems to me, for he had not the least particle of sympathy for my work, and could do better with his money elsewhere. I passed one or two nights at his house, before this desirable result was obtained.

My joy was so great that I could sleep but little on the following night; but spent much of it in thanking my Heavenly Father for his goodness, and in seeking further directions from him.

In the meantime, my hands on the farm, with the exception of four, as soon as they saw I had leased the place, made a rush for new homes, and a general stampede ensued. It was amusing to see the road filled with flying men and women, in the morning after my final arrangement with Mr. S. They found no fault with him, but they said they were free, and they did not wish to be rented out with the land; a thing which I had never thought of doing, only that I had recommened to them to work for Mr. S. But he succeeded in obtaining other hands, and some time after we all started for the North, my sister and child, a little in advance of myself. The following account of a little colored creature we took with us, is from the pen of my sister.

"It was thought best to take with us to the North a little heathen child from a neighboring plantation, who had never attended our Sunday school. Her name was Sarah, and she was a perfect Topsy, smart and energetic, but wicked and very ignorant. She did not know her age, neither did any of the family, but by comparing ages with those we did know, we found her to be about ten years old. She did not know how to do any kind of work, never had done anything except to run after a child, and pick up chips and dig a little in the garden.

She had never seen a silver spoon or fork, and the look of wonder and interest wich which she examined Bell's little fork was curious to behold, turning it this way and that way, holding it in the sun and then rubbing her fingers over it, then holding it to her face, casting side glances at us to see if we would forbid her touching it. At last she threw it down as if afraid of it, exclaiming, "What is that ere thing good for any how? what do you do with it?

She was ignorant of the names and uses of the most common articles of housekeeping. She could not count three. She had never heard of Jesus Christ; she did not think she was a sinner, for she said she could "sing a heap of sweet himes;" but yet she would steal and lie without the least compunction. Her whole religious knowledge consisted in the belief that God made her, and that the Virgin Mary died for the world. When asked what she knew *about* God, she replied, "I dunno nuffin 'bout him, reckon he mighty big man, make me and many oder folks — but he gone way off. I never seed him I didn't." She said she had no name but Sarah, was born "down yonder in the piny woods," had "allers lived in Georgy, came norf wid Missis Tunus." She had never seen any dishes washed, or rooms swept, or beds made, and she did not like to work — she liked play better, she said. She stared with astonishment at a handsome Northern parlor, as she stood at its door in a neighbor's house and said, "Well, well, I'se got to heaven. I ain't so bad girl after all. I got here." But she was afraid to enter the room, and no persuasion could induce her to sit down upon one of the velvet chairs, or to remain in the room but a few minutes. When asked afterwards why she did not remain any longer in the room, she replied, "I afraid God came pretty soon, and he say, "go back, Sarah, you can't stay here."

This was after being at the North some four months. Her whole nature was a mystery to me. I could do nothing with her. I could not teach her a letter, or a word to spell; and yet, when first given a book, she kissed it all over, and crawled into a corner, as if fearful it would be taken away from her. But my dear mother, ever hopeful and courageous, undertook the task of teaching her, and in about a year, she had learned to read in the Bible. We have left her at her father's, feeling that we had done all we could for her. She was very unwilling to go back to her home, saying she could never live again as they did at her father's; but my dear sainted mother, who always had patience with, and forgiveness for the worst of sinners, was gone from me, and I could not bear that burden without her.

Sarah looked very disconsolate, when she bade us good bye, as we left Georgia for the last time, exclaiming, while the big tears streamed down her dusky cheeks, 'I don't like it one bit, you goin Norf widout me.' But we felt compelled to leave her, trusting that the seed sown in hard labor, and watered with many tears, may yet spring up, and 'bring forth fruit to the honor and glory of God.'" R. W. S.

Mr. S., our tenant, was a kind-hearted and accommodating man, and during the time I sojourned under the same roof, which was several months, proved as good a neighbor as I had ever had in my life; but he could not brook the idea of the negroes learning to read, and he urged me much to desist from my efforts to instruct them. He said, "It will have a bad influence over my children, to see little nigger children dressed up and going to Sunday school." But finding it useless, he at length desisted from farther remonstrance, and left me to indoctrinate my negro youngsters, with whatever heresies I chose.

About this time, it was no uncommon thing for a party of rebels to ride by my house, hooting and yelling, and then stopping to discharge their pistols at the house. Fortunately none of these shots ever hit the house, but some of them did not lack much of so doing. But when these loving gentry ascertained that a true Southern gentleman resided here, they quite urbanely informed him that they would deny themselves the pleasant pastime of insulting and abusing an unoffending man, as long as he remained here; and after my absence, I do not think another shot was fired. Mr. S. and myself seldom discussed politics, but we lived as pleasant under the same roof as two brothers, thus showing that there is necessarily no "irrepressible conflict" between Southern and Northern men. The female members of our respective families, also lived in harmony with each other, a condition not always realized, even when the neighbors are members of the same church.

CHAPTER XXVII.

TRIALS AT THE NORTH, WITH NEW INSTANCES OF GOD'S GUIDING HAND.

It was a perilous undertaking. Several thousand dollars were to be borrowed, on security in one of the most notoriously bad States in the Union. I was placed between two fires. — First, I must exhibit the character of these Southern outrages, in order to induce the President and Congress, to do something for our protection; and then, after portraying this sad state of affairs, I must ask for a loan, to be invested in such a God-defying country.

As General Butler well said, when I wrote to him on the subject; "I fully agree with you, in all you say of the South, and admit the great necessity of your section being protected; but how then, can you ask us to invest our funds where property is so notoriously insecure?" Other Northern men reasoned in the same way, and it seemed almost madness to press the matter.

But I resolved to do my duty, and leave the rest with God. As I walked through the streets of Boston, and listened to the rumbling of some of the immense truck wagons, that seemed created for the very purpose of mocking my puny efforts to obtain relief, and saw the mighty throng impelled forward by some irresistible influence, I said to myself, and to my Father in Heaven; "Well, let the universe roll on, and accomplish its own behests; and if I am crushed beneath the mighty juggernaut, let God's will be done; the interests of the world will still be looked after, by Him who 'never slumbereth, or sleepeth.'"

For full two weeks did I pace those streets, alternating between hope and despair, but still determined to do my duty. On my way to the North, I had been invited to visit Gen. Grant, and state to him our grievances; I did so, and was agreeably impressed with his sincerity and honesty; and was quite delighted, in parting, with his positive assurance, "You shall be *protected*;" which promise was fulfilled by his sending Gen. Terry to our relief. But it was expedient that Georgia should be kept out of the Union, until the colored members of the Legislature were restored to their seats; and it was necessary to influence the public mind upon this subject.

Accordingly I lost no opportunity to urge upon all with whom I came in contact, the absolute necessity of something being done by Congress, for our protection. I wrote to this effect in in the newspapers, and addressed public assemblies; but I seemed "pulling down with one hand, what I built up with the other." How could I succeed in this matter of obtaining funds, when I prefaced every appeal for them with a long dissertation upon the turbulent condition of affairs in our State. But I seemed directed to pursue this course, however unreasonable it might seem to others. I felt determined to secure protection for our people, even at the risk of losing my property.

Many prominent republicans, so-called, absolutely refused to listen to my plans for the elevation of the blacks; others of whom I hoped better things, evaded my written requests for an interview; and others, equally prominent, listened to my tales, and seemed deeply interested in our affairs.

The editor of the "Workman," evinced the greatest interest in the condition of the Southern laboring classes; and was so gentlemanly and cordial in his treatment of the subject, that I felt much encouraged to go on in my important undertaking. The editors of some other papers, also showed a commendable interest in the matter, and especially the editor of the "Journal." But on my first stating my views to Wendell Phillips, that noble philanthropist immediately sanctioned all of my plans, and promised me all the assistance in his power. This was the first ray of hope that had lit up my disconsolate soul, and I departed from my interview with him, strengthened, refreshed, and exalted. All through that arduous summer, when ready to falter in these efforts, did he drop sympathetic words into my ear; and when my physical strength was nearly exhausted, from being obliged to live in an *un*-aldermanic style, did he drop into my collapsed purse, the means so needed to furnish me with strength for my enterprise.

In other portions of my work, having alluded to the habit I had formed of calling upon God for assistance, and believing by his Spirit he *would enlighten my mind*, and show me the steps necessary to take, to insure success, I may be permitted here to relate the particulars of what seemed to me strange guidings of his Spirit, but I suppose others will say, "strange hallucinations." But lest my readers should misunderstand me, I must say, that these leadings are usually based on the propriety of the direction given. In ordinary circumstances it is not safe to follow an impression, unless the thing suggested commends itself to your reason. But I cannot deny that in rare instances, God, either by his own Spirit, or some other celestial being, influences us to do an act; which we can see no reason for performing. In one instance, some years ago, my life was saved, by following a direction that I could see no reason for at the time. I do not wish to be understood as claiming any especial guidance on the part of heaven. I experienced nothing but what may be experienced by all, if they will hearken to the "light within." In this case I was simply told what to do, and no reason was given to me for doing it, and yet I obeyed. I had written to an anti-slavery friend, living near Boston, and was about to mail the letter, when something said to me, "carry it to Mr. ——'s store, (which was one and a half miles distant,) and ask him to give it to this man who lives in the same town with him." I did so. The gentleman to whom I gave it, cheerfully agreed to deliver it as I requested, and then said to me, "well, Mr. S., how do you get along in your mission ?" I had previously presented its claims to him, and showed him the absolute necessity of the blacks having land of their own, and he had seemed deeply interested in the plan, and regretted his inability to aid in its furtherance. I replied to his enquiry, "Very poorly indeed. I am almost discouraged." "Well," said he, "have you seen Mr. S. ?" As he mentioned his name, I at once recollected him as one of Boston's most reliable philanthropists, with whom I had formerly been acquainted, and I wondered I had not thought of him before. I told him I had not seen the gentleman in question. "Well," said he, "you had better see him by all means. He is just the man to help your cause, for he has the charge of a fund, to be used for the purpose of benefiting the blacks.

Here, then, was the reason for my curious direction. In that way, I heard of the one who afterwards became deeply interested in our movement. I returned to my room, prepared a statement of the case, and with a beating heart called upon the gentleman. He received me with great politeness, listened with interest to my story, then dropped the ominous words, that sent a thrill of pleasure through my all but despairing heart,—"I think the blacks ought to have land of their own." How wise and humane seemed this declaration, in comparison to the unfeeling one made by other "renowned" friends of the cause! "O, we have done all we can for the blacks. We have emancipated them, given them schools, and the elective franchise. Now let them shift for themselves."

Mr. S. examined my papers, and promised to give me an answer if I would call on him on the following Monday. Imagine my feelings, as on that day I called upon him, and received the encouraging response, "I will loan $500, and if necessary, $1000, to the enterprise, if others will make up the amount to $6000."

No fond mother ever experienced greater joy, at the sudden turn of the complaint of a darling child, than I did at this sudden change from the sickness of despair, to the more favorable symptoms of health, in reference to my enterprise. I almost danced for joy, and I could not keep the tears from my eyes.

Those only can fully appreciate my feelings, who have been engaged in similar undertakings, and watched the life of some darling project, from the first moments of its struggling infancy, as hatched in the throes of his heated brain, it sought to breathe the air of a new existence; to the moment when, after inhaling the invigorating air of heaven, and being fed upon proper spiritual aliment, it stands before him, a promising youth, bidding fair to enlighten and bless mankind, by its future rapid growth, and vivifying presence.

It is unnecessary to mention other incidents of a like nature, during my five months' sojourn in Boston, that Summer and Fall. In many other instances were my steps seemingly directed by my faithful Lord and Master. And why should they not have been? Was I not engaged in a heavenly mission, and one receiving the sympathy of my Heavenly father? Did he not know the sad necessities of the colored man, and did he not feel interested in all efforts for his redemption?

May I remark, that among those who labor in God's cause, there is far too little faith manifested in his ability and willingness to aid that cause. We imagine that we are better than God, and have started a cause that he is not interested in, when the great fact of the Universe is, that not a sparrow of moral effort falls to the ground, or essays to fly, without God's knowledge.

God is at the bottom of every enterprise for the good of man, and if we are doing God's work, he will give us success in that enterprise. If it is not God's work, then we ought not to wish for success. But we must trust him implicitly, for "without faith, it is impossible to please him." Our want of trust, sometimes proceeds from the want of an entire willingness to have God's will done, whatever it may be. If he does not will our success, than *we* must not will it. We must be absolutely submissive to the will of God in the matter, and then fully believe that *he will do* whatever he sees best in the premises.

In the month of September, the same year, I was summoned from my labors, to perform the last sad office of consanguinity, to a beloved and only brother. The victim of disease for several years, he at length received the cheering summons to him, to "come up higher," and joyfully he obeyed the call; and we confidently hope he is now where God has "wiped all tears from all eyes," at peace in the bosom of his Maker and God. This event stripped from my mother almost her only prop, and increased the great and earnest desire to visit the South, which she had so long cherished.

After a multitude of ups and downs, of encouragements and discouragements, through the almost miraculous providence of God, and after innumerable delays; the $5500 necessary to prevent the farm from falling into the hands of the rebels, which would have frustrated our project of dividing it among the blacks, were actually obtained, and were paid to the sheriff in Georgia, just *one hour* before the sale was to take place. There were delays in getting to the cars, further delays by taking the wrong route, on the part of the Boston lawyer, who came to Georgia to see that the papers were made out right. He did not reach Augusta, until Saturday night, and the sale was to come off at Apling, twenty-four miles distant, at ten o'clock Tuesday morning. Monday saw still more delays, of a provoking nature, partly in getting so large a draft cashed, and partly by the unaccountably mean conduct of the man who had loaned me the money; he, at the last moment, when there was no time to contest the matter, demanding $200 interest, in addition to the $650, paid him in advance, at the rate of two per ct. a month; which demand was the amount of the legal interest at seven per ct. per annum.

But in justice to our Southern friends, I must state that this man was originally a Yankee, although a strong Southern man in his principles.

As we had not expected such conduct on his part, we were almost wholly unprepared to meet this demand, but we were at last able to do so, through the generosity of the Boston lawyer, all of whose services in this cause were wholly gratuitous, and performed at a great sacrifice of his pecuniary interests elsewhere.

Mrs. B——, a lady of great philanthropic renown, accompanied the party to Georgia, promising to return to Boston, and take measures to establish an "Industrial School," on our plantation; but for some unknown reason, failed to keep her promise. Rev. Dr. F—— generously advanced a large portion of the amount necessary, for immediate use, on the supposition that Mrs. B. would raise sufficient funds to repay him, her ability to do which, she had constantly and unequivocally asserted. This gentleman afterwards demanded the refunding of the money, which caused great trouble and distress on our plantation; and if it had not been for that noble and Christ-like philanthropist, Mr. S., who again came to the rescue, the cause would have failed at last, in spite of all the hair-breadth escapes from defeat which it had experienced.

After the payment of this money, and the consequent disappointment of many of my rebel friends, who had confidently believed that they were to be delivered from my hateful presence, a large and enthusiastic meeting of the colored people in our neighborhood was held, and all were anxious to obtain a slice of the land thus wonderfully saved for them. Every rod of the land was almost immediately subscribed for, and the most of those who agreed to take it, professed to have means to provide for its cultivation.

Thus encouraged, I returned immediately to Boston, hoping to obtain means to help all who had taken land, and not anticipating the least difficulty in so doing, as Mrs. B. had declared that she had $20,000 subscribed, and ready to be paid in by the first of January.

But it seemed that it was not the will of God that I should succeed in this matter, and future occurrences have proved that it was not for the best to have Mrs. B's. plans carried out, for a still more comprehensive undertaking has. been commenced on our place, under better auspices and promising infinitely greater results. But the disappointment at the time was very great, and I returned South with a heavy heart, knowing how keenly those of the blacks who had no means, would feel their inability to go on with their land, and would not be able to comprehend my failure to help them.

After procuring tickets for our party, which consisted of my aged mother, my sister and child, and myself, my means were again exhausted, although I had more means at my disposal on my arrival in Georgia.

But some time previous to this, being highly elated with the magnificent prospects exhibited before me by the sanguine but eccentric Mrs. B., and beholding in imagination my desolate plantation turned into a busy working hive, the hum of whose industrial pursuits should sound like pleasant music in all our ears, it seemed to me that without a new mistress my home would be only a one-sided affair. Accordingly, I again plunged into what many term the stormy sea of matrimonial life, and I bore from its depths a trophy, well calculated as it seemed to me, to invest my Southern home with new charms both for myself and the numerous blacks around; who insisted upon it, previous to to my departure in the spring, that I should thus confer happiness upon them as well as myself. This lady was the daughter of an old anti-slavery acquaintance, and was herself deeply imbued with sympathy for the suffering freedmen, and anxious to contribute her mite for their elevation. But it was not convenient for her to go to her new home in connexion with us, and she and her son, a lad of twelve years, remained until the following April, at which time they joined our isolated family circle.

CHAPTER XXVIII.

RETURN TO THE SOUTH ACCOMPANIED BY THE AUTHOR'S MOTHER—GREAT TRIALS DURING THE SUMMER, AND THE GIN HOUSE ON FIRE.

After my return to my Southern home, eighteen or twenty colored men were supplied with land; this number being all, out of the fifty or sixty who had subscribed, who found they had means to carry on their land with; and thus we failed to accomplish *all* that we had fondly hoped. Many of this latter number also, needed assistance before the year was out. But this was a good beginning for our new enterprise, and I felt joyful at even these diminished fruits of our labors. A number of other colored persons engaged with me in cultivating land on shares, expecting at the end of the year to obtain land of their own. Having suffered so much at the hands of my last overseer, I determined to dispense with the services of one this year. We cleared about twenty-five acres of new ground, and proceeded to do the best we could in the way of farming; it being the first year I had undertaken to manage a farm myself. We also resumed our moral and intellectual efforts in behalf of the blacks, in which labor of love we were now joined by our venerable mother, who had long wished to be engaged in a work of this kind. Although eighty-four years old, yet she entered into the spirit of all our movements with alacrity and delight. A class of children came to her room daily, and she instructed them in the mysteries of reading and spelling.

She was always in her place in the Sunday school and meeting, and she took a lively interest in the temporal affairs of our forlorn friends. My labors were arduous in the extreme during this summer. Besides the care of the farm, my boy of twelve and I, performed all the labor in our large garden, and all the numerous "chores" connected with such a farm. Emerson acted as runner between me and the blacks, and many were the rebuffs he received from them for his faithfulness, as they did not relish the idea of being watched, especially by a boy. But he was not daunted in the discharge of his duties by their uncivil treatment, and finding it useless, they ceased their persecution and became quite friendly.

It becomes my pleasant duty to bear testimony to the worth of one colored family, whose intelligence caused them to appreciate our labors more fully than did the more degraded ones. The uniform kindness and symphathy of Robert and Mary Lee, experienced no diminution, from our first acquaintance with them, until we left the country. If a large portion of our flock had been like them, we should have been abundantly recompensed for our efforts in their behalf. They, with all the family, were seldom absent from our Sunday services, although residing five miles distant. There were seven children in this family, all of whom took the deepest interest in learning to read ; and the eldest girls became good scholars in Geography and Arithmetic, and could write very pretty letters. Mr. Lee was deeply interested in politics, and afterwards became the republican candidate for the Legislature from our county. Mrs. Lee would perform severe labor for her old mistress, sometimes without remuneration; and when asked how she could afford to do it for nothing, her only reply was, "You have told us to be benevolent, and I thought it my duty to help her all I could, for she is mighty poor." To assist such a family is a pleasure; and if any kind friend, on reading these pages, should feel moved to aid them in any way, I know of no colored family at the South upon whom their gifts could be more worthily bestowed.

In July of this year, we were restored to our former condition as a state in the Union, and deprived of military protection. "The dogs of war were then let slip again," and the firing around our premises was resumed, accompanied by the same unearthly yells that indicated fully their origin, as none but rebels could so well imitate the savage cry of the Indian. Even my boy, when alone upon the highway, was not exempt from their insults, they being equally destitute of decency and manly courage. At one time, a rebel presented his revolver to him, when he told him whose boy he was, but he quickly withdrew it, on Emerson's drawing up his gun in self-defence.

At another time, they fired at one of my men, while standing in front of my house, and at another time at three colored girls, in the road very near my house. They also fired into the yard, and came very near hitting my boy, the ball striking the ground in front of him.

We had other great trials during this Summer, first, from that direst of all terrestrial curses, poverty; secondly, from the wrongs done to our property by the colored people, and thirdly from an increasing indisposi-

tion on their part to learn. The prospect also seemed fair for a complete triumph of the democratic party in our state, in which case we judged it would not be safe for us to remain in our isolated condition. All of these things conspired to produce in the minds of our family, a conviction that God had other work for me to do, in some more highly favored portion of his vineyard. This conviction increased, until in August we all came to the conclusion that it was our duty to leave Georgia, as soon as the way was providentially opened. In my diary under date of August 8th, 1870, I wrote as follows:

"At last the path of duty seems to be made plain to all of us, and it is as follows: I am to write a book, giving an account of my life here, and describing the black people, and as soon as the way is opened, go to the North, and get it printed, and then devote myself to public labors in behalf of the colored people. As soon as the plan was mentioned to our family, it met with their approval, and I have prayed that if it was God's will, I might feel more and more sure of it. I am certain I can never cultivate a farm successfully with the blacks as laborers. Nothing can be done without incessant and minute supervision of them, such as I am not able to give."

I insert this extract, that our friends can see that our removal from our field of labor was on account of no hasty resolve, but a plan that had been long maturing. In June, a member of our family was taken sick, and the blacks being such poor nurses, it devolved upon me to attend to that duty myself; and consequently I could not superintend the labors of the farm, which, as a matter of course, were shamefully neglected, for my poor darky friends will seldom work for others, without constant supervision. The more intelligent blacks acknowledge that this is the case.

But it seems the time had not quite arrived, for the complete carrying out of this plan. Sometimes, in the depth of my agony, I would cry out, in the words of the immortal Casabianca,—

> "Speak, father, speak,
> If I may yet be gone;
> And but the *booming shots* replied,
> And fast the flames rolled on."

It is through suffering only, and that of the intensest nature, that souls are thoroughly subdued into a condition of perfect submission to God, where they can joyfully say at all times, "not my will, but thine be done, O God." As has been already mentioned, our sufferings from poverty were great during this Summer, sometimes our funds being reduced to a solitary dollar; but kind friends at the North, hearing of our needs, came to our relief, and our wants were from time to time provided for. "They that wait on the Lord shall not want any good thing." If God did not furnish us with an abundance of the necessaries of life, it was doubtless because he saw that it would not be for the real good of the Universe that we should have them. "Jeshuren waxed fat and kicked."

During the Fall, a scene occurred on our plantation, which, on account of its unusual nature, it may be best for me to describe here. This was an apparently terrible fight between two of my hands. David R. had sold to me a small quantity of hay, of his own raising, and I had sent Willis J. after it, with a wagon. David saw Willis coming down the gin-house road, with the hay, and fancied that Willis had taken a little more than he had a right to, and ordered him to stop his wagon, which Willis refused to do. David then took a rail, and attempted to stop the mules, when Willis sprang from the wagon, and attempted to strike David. The latter was defended by some of his relations, who heard the loud talking, and ran to see the cause of the dispute. It was not long before every man, woman and nearly every child on the place was at the battle ground, which was some forty rods from "the quarters." Willis was prevented from striking David, when he broke away from all restraint, and ran to his house, and returned with a formidable butcher knife in his hands, with which he swore he would "cut David open." The man was so infuriated that it was with extreme difficulty he could be prevented from executing his bloody purpose, and a general fight ensued. Guns and clubs were freely displayed, and it seemed impossible to prevent the shedding of considerable blood. After a great effort, however, the combatants were separated, and all parties at length returned to their homes, uninjured. Both of these combatants were members of the colored church, and one was a preacher to his colored flock. David, the preacher, was clearly in the wrong, for if he was dissatisfied with the amount of hay in Willis' possession, he was to bring more on the following day, and to deduct from it all that Willis had brought that night. But Willis was manifestly as wrong in wishing to kill his antagonist for so trifling an offence. To the credit of the colored people, let it be said that was the first occurrence of the kind on our place, since my arrival here.

Another scene was witnessed about this time, which

reflected great credit upon the colored people. One day, while my wife and I were absent, the inmates of the house were alarmed by the cry of fire. A white preacher passing, discovered it, and rode on to the quarters, crying out, "your gin-house is on fire!" He was followed by a squad of rebels, who uttered a different cry. They came by, clapping their hands, and shouting, "joy! joy!" and afterwards some of the same loving brethren joined in the chorus, exclaiming, "we spose Stearns' d——n gin-house is burned."

As soon as the colored people heard the alarm, they rushed from the quarters, forty or fifty rods distant from the fire, some with buckets, and some with pans and dishes of water on their heads and in their hands. My sister heard the alarm, and rushing up stairs, exclaimed, "O, mother, we are ruined; the gin-house is on fire!" to which excited remark, the placid old lady replied, "Can't *you* put it out?" My sister then ran to the gin-house, and saw some of the men wringing their hands and looking on with affrighted and despairing looks, and exclaiming, "It's no use to do anything; the gin-house can't be saved." But others had commenced operations in earnest; and even the little children "toted" water until they could hardly stand. One faithful old woman drew water from the well, until her sturdy limbs gave away, and she fell prostrate upon the ground. Three little girls especially exerted themselves until they could do no more.

Fortunately my sister was well enough to superintend the affair, and under her direction they all worked and did wonders. She said she never saw a fire at the North so quickly subdued, and where the necessary orders were so well obeyed. One of the laziest men on

the place, ran like lightning to our house, and with the speed of an antelope rushed up stairs, and sprang through the garret scuttle, and seized a ladder kept on the roof, for a like emergency at the house, and in less than no time, with the assistance of two others, he had it on the ground, (the house was two stories high,) and in a second more it was on its way to the gin house, and stout men were mounting it, and clambering upon the gin-house roof. A colored man, named Dred Keith, who had purchased land of me, was ginning his own cotton, at the time the fire broke out, and he also worked like a Trojan, and quickly quenched the flames directly over the gin, and then forced his way through the roof, and threw the water upon it, that was passed up the ladder by the excited crowd below. Dred lost quite an amount of his own cotton, but he said, "never mind my cotton; let it go, and save Mr. Stearns' property."

Thanks to a merciful providence, and the alacrity of the men and women, the fire was finally subdued, without destroying hardly any cotton but Dred's. The gin and the roof of the house were damaged considerably, but the hands took hold the next day and repaired the damages as well as they could. We had a large amount of cotton in the building, and direful would have been the result to me, in my embarrassed circumstances, if all this property had been destroyed. Stephen, the lazy one, suddenly transformed into a Diana of speed, after the fire was quenched, made the following speech to the crowd, from the top of the gin-house: "See what the Lord has done for us all! If this gin-house had belonged to a rebel, it would have been burned to the ground by this time;" to which his sable auditory responded, "Amen!" He also exclaimed, in the fervor of his religious zeal, " See how the Lord scriminates between saint and 'sinner-man!' Dred's cotton is burned, and Mr. Stearns' and John's is saved." Stephen was " a professor," and exhorter, in spite of his inherent laziness, and Dred was a " sinner-man." I suppose his meaning was, aside from the general superintendence of God, that if the house had belonged to the rebels, the colored people would not have worked so hard to put out the fire, which was probably the case.

The fire caught from matches dropped among the cotton, by thoughtless children at play, some of which had been found and taken from the cotton. It is by no means an unusual occurrence for a gin-house to burn down, sometime from improper friction of the machinery, and sometimes from bits of stone getting into the cotton, and striking the iron ribs of the gin.

CHAPTER XXIX.

ANOTHER ELECTION — DETAILS OF ITS OUTRAGES, AS GIVEN BY SWORN WITNESSES.

In the plenitude of its political wisdom, Congress had decided that our Legislature must be re-modelled, although distinguished republicans in our State, with the governor at their head, argued that the time of the old members had not legally expired; but timid friends of our cause at Washington, feared the establishment of a precedent that might work harm at some future time, and so a new election was ordered, and we were promised military protection. One night, two of our white friends stopped at our house, on their way from Apling to Augusta. One of them had addressed a democratic crowd at Apling, at their especial request, and had been rewarded for his temerity, with severe blows on his head, as the only argument they felt capable of using, in reply to the forcible ones used by him. It seems to be the way of the rebel democrats, to "prove" their "political" doctrine orthodox, by "*un*-apostolic blows and knocks." Wo be to the man who calls into question their political orthodoxy, in presence of overpowering numbers of these "elect" ones. He will be quite apt to retire from the field in a "hors de combat" condition, if not intellectually vanquished.

Shortly after the election was held, with the following results. The republicans were everwhere routed,—"horse, foot and dragoon;" and rebels were every where elected. Petroleum V. Nasby, I believe was not present, but his favorite "modus operandi," as described in his account of his presidential campaign in Kentucky, was every where adopted. The "knock down and drag out" principle, was found the most effectual in "pulling down the strongholds" of republicanism, and consequently obtained great favor among our fair-minded and chivalrous friends of the rebel democracy, in whose behalf so many tears have been shed by false-hearted republicans, on account of their subjection to greater disabilities than they deserve.

The war has ceased, and where is the traitor who has received merited punishment, for the part he has taken in deluging our fair land with the blood of so many of its citizens? What respect can the Southern rebels possibly have for the United States Government? How would it have been, if the South had conquered? The life of Robert Lee, our colored friend, was threatened for the part he took in the election, and he was obliged to abandon his home, and take refuge with a neighbor, and at length leave the county entirely. Here is a small portion of the sworn testimony respecting these outrages, the whole forming a large pamphlet. Thus much for "free speech" in Georgia. I am sorry to be obliged to add that the rebel members were allowed to take their seats in Congress, in the face and eyes of all the testimony given, the reason whereof I am not able to affirm.

LETTER OF THOMAS P. BREAD,

CLAIMING

His seat as Member of the House from fifth congressional district of Georgia, and Testimony taken by him before proper tribunals.

WASHINGTON, DISTRICT OF COLUMBIA,
January 17, 1871.

TO STEPHEN A. CORKER:—

SIR: You are hereby notified that it is my intention to contest your right to a seat as a member of the House of Representatives of the forty-first Congress of the United States, from the fifth congressional district of the State of Georgia, upon the following grounds particularly specified, to wit:—

1. That at the general election held in the counties of Washington, Jefferson, Burke, Columbia, Warren, Glascock, Hancock, Taliaferro, Oglethorpe, Elbert, Lincoln, Wilkes, and McDuffee, on the 20th, 21st and 22d days of December, 1870, intimidation, violence, and a reign of terror existed to such an extent that republican voters, in such numbers as to determine the result of the election, were compelled to vote against their will for you and Dudley M. Dubose, Esq , the democratic candidate for the forty-second Congress, or were prevented from voting for any one when it was their desire and intention to vote for me for the forty-first Congress, and for Isham S. Fannin, Esq., for the forty-second Congress.

2. That, previous to the election, in several of the counties aforesaid, republican voters who intended to vote for me, were shot, beat, and otherwise maltreated, with a view of intimidating them so that they would not vote for me at the election aforesaid, and they were thus prevented from voting for me, as they intended to do; that organized bands of desperadoes were known to exist in several of said counties, acting in the interest of the democratic party and against the republican party; that colored men and Union men, on account of the threats and acts of violence of these desperate men, were afraid to vote for me, and did not vote at the election aforesaid, as they desired, and intended to do; that in each and all of the counties aforesaid fraud was practised and intimidation used by democrats toward republicans, so as to destroy the freedom of the ballot-box and prevent many thousand republicans who desired and intended to vote for me, from

doing so, and that the number of voters so prevented from voting was enough to determine the result of the election.

3. That republican voters who desired and intended to vote for me for the forty-first Congress, and for Isham S. Fannin for the forty-second Congress, were, contrary to law, prevented from doing so, because they had not paid the poll-tax assessed against them, which tax had been remitted by the legislature of the State.

4. That in the county of Hancock, aforesaid, the managers of election were wrongfully and illegally arrested and confined in jail, with a view of preventing republican voters who desired and intended to vote for me, from doing so, and that the election in said county was held by persons who had no legal right to act as managers of election.

5. That a few days prior to the election aforesaid, when the cars arrived at Washington, Wilkes County, upon which republican speakers were expected to arrive, who were to address a republican meeting in my interest and in the interest of the republican party, a band of armed men entered the cars with the avowed purpose of murdering said speakers, and that not finding them this band did shoot at three of the leading republicans of the county, friends of mine, killing one, mortally wounding another, and seriously wounding a third; that on account of this shooting, which occurred but a few days prior to the election, many voters were intimidated and thus prevented from voting for me as they intended to do.

6. That in Burke and other of said counties the ballot-box was opened and votes cast for me abstracted, and ballots with your name upon them put in place of them.

7. That the illegality of your election is further shown by the fact that at the election held in the spring of 1868, for governor and other State officers and members of Congress, the republican candidates received seventeen thousand four hundred and forty-seven (17,447) votes, in this congressional district while the democratic candidates received but nine thousand six hundred (9,600) votes, although at the late election above mentioned you and other democratic candidates received fifteen thousand seven hundred and fifty-nine (15,759) votes, while I and other republican candidates received nine thousand four hundred and eighty-two (9,482) votes, and that this change was effected by the illegal and revolutionary means above mentioned.

8. That the election in said counties was null and void, and the votes cast should be thrown out; that in a fair election I should have had a large majority of the votes cast in said counties; and therefore you are not by law or right entitled to a seat in the forty-first Congress; that in fact I did receive a majority of the legal votes freely cast in said district, in counties where the election was not controlled by unlawful influences.

THOS. P. BEARD.

STATE OF GEORGIA, *Morgan County:*

Personally came M. A. Woods before me, who, being duly sworn, deposes and says: I reside in the county of Wilkinson and above-named State; that I am deputy United States marshal; that I was at Sandersville, in the county of Washington and State above named, during the late election for Representatives in Congress, on the 20th, 21st, and 22d days of December, 1870; that I saw many persons in the vicinity of the polls wearing badges, upon which was printed "police;" that said persons did commandingly order many voters to exhibit their ballots before offering to vote, and that the said persons did substitute other ballots, or change the names on ballots, without consent of said voters; and that voters were ordered by said persons to vote the ballot so substituted or changed; that many persons were publicly denounced, and abusive language used toward them for voting for the candidates of their choice, in a manner calculated to deter many from voting as they preferred; that this affiant did protest against such illegal conduct upon the part of said persons, and for such protest was threatened with violence and forced to leave the above-named county for safety.

M. A. WOODS.

Sworn to and subscribed before me this 9th day of January, A. D. 1871.

[SEAL.] W. WOODS,
Ordinary.

Before me, a duly appointed commissioner for the southern district of Georgia, came Robert Battey, of the city of Augusta, Richmond County, Georgia, who, being sworn, deposeth and saith, he was present at the polls on the first day of election, December 20, 1870, at Louisville, Jefferson County, Georgia, and on offering to vote for members of Congress, the managers of said polls refused to receive his vote, on the ground of his not having paid his taxes; but on telling them he would telegraph for higher authority, they, on consulting some of the democratic leaders, said he might vote, according to the law, which he accordingly did. He talked with and saw several republicans who were not allowed to vote because they had not paid their taxes for 1869. The democrats were threatening and intimidating the colored men, and taking down the names and descriptions of voters, for the purpose of Ku-Kluxing them after election, especially his, the said Battey's, and they swore "they would get him at night," etc., and they did hunt for him after he had voted, and at night, in bands armed with pistols. They, the desperate democrats, who were thus intimidating the colored voters, were openly armed at the polls. He furthermore saith that he is confident from what he saw and heard of what was done there, that several hundred republican colored voters were kept from the polls during the election there.

ROBERT BATTEY.

Sworn to and signed this 2d day of January, 1871.

THOMAS ROBINSON,
United States Commissioner.

Before me, Thomas Robinson, a commissioner duly appointed by the circuit court of the United States of America for the southern district of Georgia, personally came Aaron W. Gilbert, of Waynesboro', Burke County, Georgia, who, being duly sworn, deposeth and saith that he was present at the election held in Waynesboro'; that on the first day, December 20, 1870, the polls were not opened till after ten o'clock; that they were closed at twelve, and not again opened till about three in the afternoon; that at least four hundred republicans were challenged by H. H. Perry, manager, for non-payment of taxes for 1869, and at least three hundred of these were kept from voting during the entire election That on the second day of the election, December 21, 1870, the democrats drove all the leading republicans, white and colored, from the vicinity of the polls, and, in fact, from out the village, by force, threats, and cries of "The Ku-Klux are coming," etc.; and that they openly bribed the colored men to vote the democratic ticket, who heretofore had been recognized as republicans. That on the third day of the election, December 22, 1870, he, Aaron W. Gilbert, above mentioned, was again, with others, driven from the polls, out of the village, and into the woods, by armed democrats, with threats and force, who were led on by Thomas C. Belt. That the before-mentioned Gilbert then went to the polls held at Sylvania Court-house, Scriver County, Georgia, where he arrived at about 4 P. M., and found that no man who was at all suspected of being a republican was allowed to vote, unless he could show a certificate of having paid his taxes for 1869; and that at least two hundred and fifty republicans were kept from voting at that polling-place by the democrats, by reason of not having paid their taxes for 1869; and that during the election held in Burke County, Georgia, at least three times as many republican votes were cast as were cast for the democrats, to the best of his knowledge and belief, but that he has every reason to know the ballot-box was trifled with by the democrats. Also, that he is now compelled to remain away from Waynesboro' to save his life, as the democrats threaten to kill him if he returns there.

AARON G. GILBERT.

H. H. Perry, democrat, kept ballot-box at his home each night. Krump Wimberly, democrat, kept key each night.

AARON W. GILBERT.

Subscribed and sworn to before me this 29th December, 1870.

THOS. ROBINSON,
United States Commissioner.

UNITED STATES OF AMERICA, *southern district of Georgia:*

Before me, Thomas Robinson, one of the commissioners duly appointed by the United States circuit court for the southern district of Georgia, personally came William D. Seigfried, who, being duly affirmed, deposes and says, that on or about the 16th day of December, 1870, while making purchases in one of the principal grocery stores in Augusta, said district and State, a white man, professing to be a resident of the county of Columbia, said district and State, entered the store and addressing the proprietor, proclaimed the prospects of the coming election as bright for the democrats; declaring "Old Columbia will be all right. We intend to carry the election against the radicals if we have to do it by blood," or words to that effect. A significant shake of the head by the said proprietor brought the conversation to a sudden close.

W. D. SEIGFRIED,
Teacher "National Theological Institute."

Affirmed to and subscribed before me, at Augusta, Georgia, the 13th day of January, 1871.

THOMAS ROBERSON,
United States Commissioner.

Robert Sullivan; lives in Columbia County, Georgia, and was at Appling December 20. Jim Blanchard, a white man, struck me with his fist twice on the side of my head, and cocked his pistol at me, and attempted to strike me over the head with it, all because I said I was a radical. I saw Moses Malord struck over his eyes with a big stick by a white man, because he said he was a radical. I also saw a great many colored people prevented from voting, unless they would vote the democratic ticket. I should think three-fourths of those who were there were thus prevented from voting. The language of the whites was, "Stand back, stand back, G—d d—n you," and then they would offer them a democratic ticket, and tell them they could vote that. I saw a man standing near the polls with bottles of whiskey, offering to treat all who would vote the democratic ticket. A great many negroes voted the democratic ticket, but nearly all of them did so for fear of the whites, who threatened them in various ways if they did not. If left to themselves, hardly any negroes would have voted the democratic ticket. Nearly all refused thus to vote, until they were threatened so severely. All of this I solemnly swear to be true, according to the best of my belief and knowledge.

ROBERT SULLIVAN.

COLUMBIA COUNTY, GEORGIA, *January* 1, 1871.

Sworn to and subscribed before me.

C. STEARNS,
Notary Public and ex-officio Justice of the Peace.

William Townsley; reside in Columbia County, Georgia; was at Apling December 20 and 21. On the first day I did not vote, because the democrats would not let any vote but democrats, if they could help it. They crowded around the place of voting, and kept away all they could. On the second day I tried again to vote, but it was worse than on the first, and I came away without voting. A great many colored men voted the democratic ticket because the whites threatened them so much unless they did. More than one-half of the colored people were kept from voting the radical ticket from fear. The whites have threatened Robert Lee, who was on the radical ticket for the legislature, and he has been obliged to leave his home and go to Augusta to live. All of which I solemnly swear to be true, according to the best of my belief and knowledge.

his
WILLIAM × TOWNSLEY.
mark.

COLUMBIA COUNTY, GEORGIA, *January* 1, 1871.

Sworn to and subscribed before me.

C. STEARNS,
Notary Public and ex-officio Justice of the Peace.

Much more testimony of the same kind could be easily obtained, if it were not for the fear on the part of witnesses that violence would be used towards them on account of their testimony. Some have related to me what they saw, but declined to have their names go before the public, and several of the above witnesses particularly request that their names shall not be published.

C. STEARNS,
Sewallville, Columbia County, Georgia.

Edmund Green; lives on the Hick's place, Columbia County, Georgia; was at the election at Apling, Columbia County, on December 20, 1870, and wished to vote the republican ticket, but could not, on account of my life being threatened by the white people present. A good many others were prevented from voting in the same way. Charles Harding, a colored blacksmith, was struck on the head and covered with blood because he was a radical. In my opinion over five hundred colored people were, on that day, prevented from voting the republican ticket at Apling. In Lincoln County all the colored people, nearly, were forced to vote the democratic ticket, by threats of death, and of being driven from their places.

All this I solemnly swear to be true to the best of my belief and knowledge.

his
EDMUND × GREEN.
mark.

COLUMBIA COUNTY, GEORGIA, *December* 25.

The foregoing statement was made before me, and sworn to as above stated.

CHARLES STEARNS,
Notary Public and ex-officio Justice of the Peace.

Willis Jackson; lives on C. Stearns's place, Columbia County, Georgia; was at the election at Apling, December 20, and saw a white man strike Charles Harding over the head with a hickory stick of the size of a common broom-handle, because Harding said he had voted the radical ticket. About the same time another white man kicked my father, Eli Jackson, because he said he had voted the radical ticket. In my opinion over five hundred colored people were, on that day, prevented from voting. The white people were going about, drawing their pistols, and cutting at the colored people who attempted to vote the radical ticket, and threatening to kill them if they thus voted.

All this I solemnly swear to be true.

his
WILLIS × JACKSON,
mark.

Before me —

C. STEARNS,
Notary Public and ex-officio Justice of the Peace.

COLUMBIA COUNTY, *December* 25, 1870.

George Parks; I am a carpenter in Columbia County; was at Apling December 20; attempted to vote several times, but did not, because whenever I attempted to vote a rush would be made by the white people, who would cry out, "Stand back; stand back," and flourish slung-shots in the faces of the colored people; they would then seize hold of the arm of a colored democrat and drag him up to the polls, crying out, "Here comes a big democrat; let him vote." In all cases, every colored man who would vote the democratic ticket was allowed to do so; but, I think, five hundred or six hundred colored radicals were prevented from voting.

All of which I solemnly swear to be true, according to my best belief and knowledge.

his
GEORGE × PARKS.
mark.

Sworn to and subscribed before me.

C. STEARNS,
Notary Public and ex-officio Justice of the Peace.

COLUMBIA COUNTY, GEORGIA, *December* 25, 1870.

Eli Jackson; lives on C. Stearns's place, Columbia County, Georgia; was at Apling December 20, and saw Charles Harding struck over the head, because he said he voted the radical ticket. A white man kicked me with all his power, because I said I had voted the radical ticket. I believe a good many hundred colored people were prevented that day, by force, from voting the republican ticket; but every colored man who wished was allowed to vote the democratic ticket.

All of which I solemnly swear to be true according to the best of my belief and knowledge.

his
ELI × JACKSON.
mark.

Sworn and subscribed to before me.

C. STEARNS,
Notary Public and ex-officio Justice of the Peace.

COLUMBIA COUNTY, *December* 25, 1870.

William Mitchell; lives on C. Stearns's place; was at Apling December 20; and I believe three-quartors of the colored people present were prevented from voting the republican ticket by the threats and blows of the white people. I heard one white man threaten to kill a colored man if he voted the radical ticket.

I solemnly swear this statement to be true according to the best of my belief and knowledge.

his
WM. × MITCHELL.
mark.

Sworn to and subscribed before me.

C. STEARNS,
Notary Public and ex-officio Justice of the Peace.

COLUMBIA COUNTY, *December* 25, 1870.

Colbert Hitt; lives on C. Stearns's place; was at Apling December 20; saw Charles Harding after he was struck; and also Lewis Whittaker, and heard him say he was struck in the middle of his forehead with the muzzle of a pistol, because he said he was a radical. I did not vote as I intended to, because I was afraid I should be struck by the white people, who surrounded the polls and watched every man to see what kind of a ticket he had; heard them threaten to kill men if they did not vote the democratic ticket; think that five hundred colored men at least were prevented that day from voting the republican ticket. The second day a colored man who attempted to vote the republican ticket was driven some distance from the polls, and very few voted on that day.

All of which I solemnly swear to be true, according to the best of my belief and knowledge.

his
COLBERT × HITT.
mark.

Sworn to and subscribed before me.

C. STEARNS,
Notary Public and ex-officio Justice of the Peace.

COLUMBIA COUNTY, *December* 25, 1870.

Jim Jackson; lives on C. Stearns's place; was at Apling, December 20. A white democrat told me to stand back, and if I did not he would cut me with his knife if I voted; but I voted in spite of him. Many others were afraid to vote and did not. I should think several hundred.

All of which I swear to be true, according to the best of my belief and knowledge.

his
JIM × JACKSON.
mark.

Sworn to and subscribed before me.

C. STEARNS,
Notary Public and ex-officio Justice of the Peace.

COLUMBIA COUNTY, *December* 25, 1870.

Charles Johnson; lives on C. Stearns's place; was at Apling, December 20, and saw a man draw a pistol on Allen Porter, a colored man, for trying to vote the republican ticket: heard a white man say to another, "If we can't vote it out, we will fight it out;" heard a great many colored people say they were not allowed to vote, and did not for fear of the whites; heard the white people threaten to shoot Mr. Sherman for being a friend to the colored people.

All this I solemnly swear to be true, according to the best of my belief and knowledge.

his
CHARLES × JOHNSON.
mark.

Sworn to and subscribed before me.

C. STEARNS,
Notary Public and ex-officio Justice of the Peace.

COLUMBIA COUNTY, *December* 25, 1870.

On the morning of the 20th of December, 1870, the first day of election, I arrived at Apling, the county seat of Columbia County, Georgia, at about quarter past 10 o'clock, A. M., where probably over one thousand people had assembled, three-fourths or more of whom were colored. I drove up very near the court-house and asked for the military commander, when Lieutenant C. B. Hinton appeared, saying he was in command of twelve men. I said I came to attend the election, and felt obliged to put myself under his protection, knowing that I would not be safe without it; then told him who I was; that I had represented the twenty-ninth district in the legislature for the past two years, and now I held the appointment of deputy marshal, showing him my commission, but I preferred that he would say nothing about my appointment, only treat and protect me as a citizen. The lieutenant pledged his utmost for my safety. I then appeared in front of the court-house window, where two of the commissioners were taking votes, and passing them to a colored young man appearing to be seventeen or eighteen years of age, who put them into the box.

I spoke to the commissioners or managers, asking them if the board was properly organized; they said it was. I then asked for James M. Anthony. Mr. Gray, one of the managers, said Mr. Anthony was not here. I remarked that Mr. Stearns's family was very sick, and he could not be here. Robert Lee is the next man. "Yes," said one of the managers, "Robert Lee is here." I said, "Not Robert Lee, proper." "Yes," said one of the managers, "Robert Lee, and the only Robert Lee we know in the county." I remarked that Robert Lee, proper, was on the ground. I then asked for an interview with them. They asked me inside. I took Robert Lee with me and introduced him to the other managers saying, "This is the man whose name I introduced to the governor for manager, and the same man the governor appointed and the senate confirmed."

The managers then asked me if they should not empty the box and vote over again. To this I said I had nothing to do with it; I was no manager of elections; my object was only to state facts; they had them, and they must act as they thought proper. They then asked Lee where he lived. Lee told them where, and that he had been in the county four years. They asked him his full name, to which he replied that it was Robert Lee, but about five years ago he put R. in his name. This was not known by myself nor his friends at the time his name was given to the governor; but, nevertheless, said I, this is the man. At this time Dr. Casy came into the room, and I was asked to leave. Very soon Robert Lee, proper, was told to go out; young Robert Lee, as I have called him, was permitted to remain. Here I will remark, that in the evening the acting ordinary came to tent to see me. Among other things I asked him if he knew this young Robert Lee. He said, no. "Where does he live?" "I believe he is a clerk or runner down to the store." "Where did he come from?" "I think," said he, "that he came from Sawdust, on the railroad somewhere." "When did he come here?" He replied that he came the evening the commissioners came in for the manager. "Who is he, anyhow?" "I don't know." I then asked very many colored men who he was. None knew him. So I called him a man of straw, having no right to the position as manager. He, however, was made manager. I then took my place in frontof the window again, by the side of the rope, fifteen feet from the window, where the voting was done, and took my pencil and paper, and began or prepared to keep tally, — to write down the names as they were spoken by one of the managers.

But before voting commenced (the second time), a man standing upon the steps said all the democrats will vote over again, white and colored. All the democrats come up and vote over; and so they did. For an hour or more voting went off briskly without any apparent trouble or intimidation to speak of, until, to appearance, the democrats had mostly voted. And when the republicans, or those who carried their vote in their pocket, preferring not to show their ticket, made an effort to get to the ballot box, then threats began in good earnest — swearing, showing and swinging sling-shots, exhibiting the bowie knife, so said the lieutenant, and using other methods of intimidations. Closing up the passage-way with white men that had voted, twenty, thirty, and perhaps fifty men at a time, so placed before the passage-way that it was almost impossible for a man who did not show a democratic vote to get through, and if one did, a cry would start up, "Mark him, d—n him, mark him!" And in two instances I saw the sheriff put a colored man who had succeeded in getting through, back over the rope, obliging them to get through again if they could. Then again, intimidation was caused by the use of such awful oaths that no God-fearing man could help fear. And that if any one voted the radical ticket, the Ku-Klux would visit him in less than two weeks And the man who swung the sling-shot over the heads of the colored men, said "G—d d—n the nigger who votes the radical ticket, he will not get home," and various other threats were made. I think I heard enough threats to fill two sheets like this, yet no remonstrance or orders to stop it while I was permitted to remain in hearing and seeing.

And still these threats and intimidations were allowed; no real effort was made to prevent or bring to justice the law-breaker (but the colored man must submit to all this, not allowed to say one word). I spoke to the lieutenant to have that sling-shot put away. He went to the man and said to him he had better put it up. He said he spoke to the sheriff about it, and said the sheriff ordered it put away, but the order was not regarded, for I saw him swing it over the heads of the colored men, and heard the language that would accompany such a weapon for more than two hours. I will give the managers credit of once saying to the sheriff that he must keep order, or voting would stop. The sheriff repeated the order or demand, and that was all it amounted to, for the disorder increased until I was taken off the ground, which was between three and four o'clock, P. M. This disorder might have been stopped easily. The lieutenant was on the ground; his men were near by, and it only wanted an order from the managers or sheriff to have brought the soldiers and made order at once.

In the fore part of the day I was found at my post, front of the window seated by the rope, tallying and taking notes of what was going on, when Dr. Casy came up in front of me and said, "Who is manipulating affairs in Augusta, that he should send a clerk up here to manage our affairs?" To this and other similar remarks I made no reply, but took notes, etc. Whereupon the doctor turned to the lieutenant and said (so said the lieutenant), "If Sherman don't put up that pencil and paper I will take it away from him and slap his chops." The lieutenant said that would not do for the colored men regarded him their friend, and if you undertake that there will be a row. The doctor then made other threats (so said the lieutenant), until the lieutenant said he would try and get Sherman to put his paper up, and so he did. He came and asked me to put it up. After making this request three times, and saying he could not prevent trouble if I did not, I consented to lower my manhood, suffer my freedom to be directed and dictated by the mob. I put my paper up, containing about 200 names. I still kept my pencil in hand, counted, and occasionally marked my count on the margin of a newspaper. To this the doctor made objections and tried to prohibit it. About this time, or soon after, a cry started up that the niggers had guns. The cry was loud; trouble was indicated, and, in fact, seemed to be at hand. A tremendous stampede took place at once; nearly all was on the run in the direction of the guns which was over the river. The colored men had guns stacked half or three-quarters of a mile from the court-house, and twenty or twenty-five men left to guard them until they could be relieved by others who had gone forward to vote.

Here the doctor appears again, and proved to be the moving spirit in this gun excitement, as he acknowledged in his letter to the Chronicle and Sentinel of Augusta, "that he commanded a force that took possession of the bridge and would not let the belligerents cross."

It was also found that the doctor, as those in his command, had double-barrel guns, revolvers, and other weapons in abundance, but the colored men could not even be allowed to stack their guns three-quarters of a mile from the court-house. The doctor, by threats and show of weapons, prevented the colored men crossing the bridge until the lieutenant came with his men, crossed the bridge, and took possession of the guns, placed a guard over them, relieving some twenty or twenty-five colored men from their charge. This done, order was restored and quietude for the time being, as it had been at the polls in the absence of these leading spirits; but when the doctor with his force returned something must be done with Sherman. About this time bell rang for dinner and the polls closed for an hour. After dinner voting commenced again, and for half an hour or more it went off quietly, I keeping count until the doctor came, when he again appeared inside the rope before me with insults and riotous remarks, and looking around I saw groups in threes, and fives, and more, making Sherman their object of insults. Finally, a man walked in front of the rope, and stepped over it on my right. Soon after another man walked in front of the rope and stepped over the rope on my left; others pushed their way through the colored crowd to my back. The first man on my right took off his hat, and throwing his head down and partly in front of me looked me in the face. The one on my left took off his hat, placed himself in like position, looked me in the face, both making mouths, etc., unbecoming any human being. In this condition I remained for some time, until these men began to feel under my cloak, and, as I was told, showed weapons, when the lieutenant saw my danger, spoke to the managers, and asked if he should not ask me over the rope. He at once came and said, "Sherman, walk over the rope and stand by the building." I did so. The sheriff then took those five or six ill-designed persons back near the doorsteps of the court-house from whence they came, only to give them another starting point, which was at once improved by backing around the corner of the court-house (inside the rope) to get at my side. This was done. And *the above all in plain sight of the managers and the sheriff*, but nothing said to them. Here, again, their insults were lavished on me, and in a way that is not easily described. After fifteen or twenty minutes in this uncomfortable position the lieutenant was spoken to by the managers, so he said, and was requested by them to take me off. The lieutenant at once communicated this to me.

I said to him, "I have a right here." He left and in a few moments returned, and made his second request, and then the third, and at the same time said I was in danger, for he could not control the mob, which would soon make an attack on me. I then stepped up to the window, and said, "Messrs. Managers, is it your request that I should leave the ground?" When one of the managers (Mr. Hicks) said, "Yes; leave." Then one of the clerks (Mr. Hudson) said, "Yes; d—n you, leave! Your presence creates disturbance, and you better leave. G—d d—d you, leave!" I then said, "Mr. Gray (another manager), is it your request that I should leave?" He replied that he did not want to say anything about it. "Have I not a right here?" I asked. He replied that, as far as he had seen of me, he did not see why I could not remain. At this time I was standing with my back toward the crowd. The lieutenant stepped up and took me by the arm and walked me off, saying, "I do this for your safety. I have seen what you have not." As we walked off, probably two hundred of those white fiends followed quite a distance with yells and shrieks never heard anywhere in the civilized world except in Georgia. When this crowd returned to their voting place they found the ground made vacant by the running of at least eight hundred colored persons. On seeing many of these frightened persons at a distance, the whites took after them and ran them to the woods and hills, firing guns or revolvers, yelling, shrieking, etc., like so many wild men.

Here the election seemed to be broken up, so much so that one of the managers said to the lieutenant, "This makes this election illegal; and if I report this as it is, this county will be thrown out." After this there was but little, if any, voting done the first day. I judge from appearance, as I was in a tent near by where I could see. After the colored men left for home, taking their guns, the sergeant who guarded them said he counted 263 guns. It was said by some of them that but very few of these two hundred and sixty-three men voted. Some of them did, and others gave me their names. and where they lived, and the reason they did not vote. In every instance the reason given was fear, caused by threats of being Ku-kluxed, by being turned out of a home; others caused by the threat that they would not live to get home if they voted a radical ticket. I took about one hundred names, and in many instances the names of the men that was said to have made the threats. I have the names of several of the men who carried revolvers, sling-shots, and who caused such intimidation, but I have not the names of the men who gave me so many insults except Dr. Casy; others seemed to be strangers. I could not find a colored man that knew them.

I did not go near the voting place on the second day. I kept tent, not even going out for dinner, it not being considered safe, but I saw and heard what I never saw before at an election. Liquor seemed to be very plenty, running horses, firing of revolvers by the dozens at a time, etc. I forgot to mention that liquor was plenty on the ground the first day. It was carried around in glass bottles, even inside the rope. The managers made no mention of it, or gave orders concerning it.

I went to tent Tuesday, A.M., and left for home Thursday morning, escorted by the soldiers.

Thus went election in Columbia County, Georgia, December 20 and 21, 1870.

JOSIAH SHERMAN,
Deputy Marshal Columbia County.

Signed before me this 7th January, 1871.

[SEAL.] H. I. G. WILLIAMS,
Notary Public, F. C.

Before me, Thomas Robinson, a commissioner duly appointed by the circuit court for the southern district of Georgia, personally came Judson DeLyons, who, being sworn, deposeth and saith, that he was present at the polls at Apling Court-house, Columbia County, Georgia, on the first day of the election, Tuesday, 20th December, 1870; and that no colored republican was allowed to vote so long as a democrat could be found, the colored men being crowded away from the polls, and intimidated by armed democrats, who, in addition to pistols openly carried in their belts, had knives, sling-shots, sticks, etc., to "punch" at the colored men, and scare them back. The democrats, though armed themselves, hearing that the colored men had left their guns about half or three-quarters of a mile from the polls, commenced whooping, cursing, and swearing, and firing pistols, and started to secure the guns and destroy them. The United States soldiers, under Lieutenant ——, however, kept the crowd from the guns and took charge of them. They, the democrats, next questioned said DeLyons' right to be present at the polls, and because he was distributing republican tickets, not only threatened him with violence, but did set a number of dogs on him; and he fled for protection to the soldiers who were stationed about four or five hundred yards away from the polls. After dinner, about four o'clock, he, the said DeLyons, came again to the polls, but after a half hour or so, the democrats "made it so hot" for him, that he was again compelled to go away from the polls — the democrats following them, whooping, cursing and yelling. On the second day, December 21, 1870, as soon as the polls were opened, he, DeLyons, saw three colored men chased and hunted by dogs, set on them by the democrats because they wanted to vote a republican ticket. And about noon or dinner time, when a number of colored men were seen coming to the polls, the democrats commenced firing their pistols, yelling, and whooping, thus scaring them away from coming and voting. And that in the afternoon, he, the said DeLyons, was compelled to leave the voting place entirely, as his life was in constant jeopardy. He also adds, further, that on the first day of the election he saw a colored republican, who had been badly cut about the head, and was bleeding profusely, who said he had been attacked by a white democrat on account of his being a republican; and that, to the best of his knowledge and belief, at least five hundred republicans were intimidated from voting at said polls by reason of the unlawful and violent conduct of the democrats.

JUDSON DeLYONS.

Subscribed and sworn to before me this 3d day of January, 1871.

THOMAS ROBINSON,

United States Commissioner for the Southern District of Georgia.

UNITED STATES OF AMERICA,
Southern District of Georgia:

Before me, Thomas Robinson, a commissioner duly appointed by the circuit court of the United States for the southern district of Georgia, personally came William S. Mayfield, of Clay Hill, Lincoln County, who, being duly sworn, deposes and says, that he was present at the election held in and for Lincoln County, in said State, on the 20th, 21st, and 22d days of December, 1870; that he was one of the managers of the election, having been so appointed by Governor Bullock; that two other managers acted, who were nominated by the ordinary and confirmed by the senate; and that two others who had been appointed by the governor could not be found in the county; that six hundred votes were cast during the three days, of which the democratic candidates received five hundred and ninety-three, and the republican candidates only seven; that according to the last census, there are about ten hundred and fifty votes in said county, there being about six hundred colored, of which number about five hundred and fifty would have voted, under a free election, the republican ticket, and at least seventy-five or one hundred of the white voters would have cast their ballots for the republican nominees, giving to the republican party, at the very least, a majority of two hundred and fifty; whereas the late election returns show a democratic majority of five hundred and eighty-six, making a difference against the republican party of eight hundred and thirty-six. According to the records of the previous congressional election, some eight hundred votes were polled, of which the republican candidates received six hundred or more. One of the managers of that election stated to this deponent that he was willing to swear that it was a free and fair election. This deponent further states that in order to show the intimidation used, he deposes as follows: That he attended a colored meeting held at Salem Baptist Church, in the county of Lincoln, on or about the sixth day of November, 1870, at which time he, after having talked to them on political matters, told them that he would be there again on the fourth day of December, 1870, that being their regular meeting day; that business at that time took him to another part of the State, so that he was prevented attending as he had promised; but that a band of desperadoes, dressed in disguise as United States soldiers, being armed with revolvers and bowie-knives, rode up to the church during the meeting, some going inside, the others staying outside, and asking, "Where is that damned radical, Mayfield," saying "if he was here blood would be shed." Finding that this deponent was not there, they rode off, leaving the colored people very much excited and frightened. Excitements of this nature were systematically carried on up to the time of the election, which were so successful in intimidating the colored men that many of them did not attend the election at all; others who did attend on the first day with the intention of voting, were met some distance from the polls by these desperadoes, who told them that they must vote the democratic ticket, or have a row; in consequence of which many men returned to their homes without voting, while others through fear of being visited by midnight assassins, took the democratic ticket of them and voted the same, afterward saying they would advise all their friends not to come to the polls, which accounts for the small number of republican votes polled.

W. S. MAYFIELD,
Assistant Assessor Third District Georgia.

Sworn to and subscribed before me this 6th day of January, 1871, at Augusta, Georgia.

THOMAS ROBINSON,
United States Commissioner.

DECEMBER 26, 1870.

MESSRS. EDITORS: If you will bear with me, and allow me a small space in your columns, I will inform you how the late election was managed in the portion of this congressional district in which I reside. Of course the Chronicle and Sentinel, Constitution, and other violent democratic papers will call it a glorious victory and a free and fair election. If by having a crowd of ruffians forming and moving in every section near the polls, insisting that every one shall take their ticket or have what they call a row; and what do these parties wish to be understood by a row? Simply this, a knock-down, a few pistol shots; the results similar to the example we had placed before us a few days ago at Washington, Wilkes County. The coloring would be in the above-named papers a negro-riot, of course, etc. If by the above simple illustration "which can be enlarged a thousand fold without being exaggerated one iota," is a free and fair election, then we certainly have had an exceedingly free, fair, and an honest one. I can obtain at least twenty affidavits from citizens of this county who were deterred in the above manner from voting; they would not take the tickets offered by these men; rather than have a disturbance and bloodshed they returned to their homes without having cast their vote; others, for fear of being visited by *midnight visitors*, took the tickets so offered and voted them, thus aiding against their will in electing those who have been elected on the democratic ticket in this section of this congressional district.

JUSTICE,
By W. S. MAYFIELD.

MAXEYS, GEORGIA, *December* 30, 1870.

DEAR SIR: Your favor of the 29th instant is before me, and contents noticed. And, in reply, I have to say that the election in this county was carried by intimidation. To illustrate: The colored people were told publicly that to vote without having paid their taxes for 1869 would be to vote illegally, and that the punishment was confinement in the penitentiary, and that several of their number was then under arrest and in jail, and would be prosecuted with all the rigor of the law. This can be substantiated by any number of witnesses of either party. And further, parties told a voter who was willing to swear that he had paid his taxes in an adjoining county, that if he did vote under his oath, they would prosecute him, and the penalty would be the penitentiary. The result of these intimidating measures was that not one-half the voters of this county polled their votes.

The election was held on the first day at this precinct, under the election bill of 1870, and at the court-house, from first to last, under the old election law. Some part, therefore, must be illegal, independently of the intimidating measures used. It is the commonly received opinion of all intelligent and thinking men that there has been no election held in this county, but that a farce has been enacted.

I am, very respectfully, your obedient servant,

J. H. BRIGHTWELL.

Mr. W. J. WHITE, *Chairman*.

LEXINGTON, *January*, 1871.

SIR: According to your request I will give you a true statement of the election in Oglethorpe County, held on 20th, 21st, and 22d days of December, 1870. I will state nothing but what I would swear to and can prove. First, the commissioners took the oath laid down in the late election bill, but then three of the commissioners said they would not allow any voter to vote who had not paid his poll-tax the year previous, and so conducted the election the first day with a great deal of dissatisfaction and contention with the colored voters and their friends, the democrats telling the colored men if they did vote that it was contrary to the law and the Constitution, and they would prosecute them and put them in the penitentiary, and that they were better friends to them than we were; and by that means scared them out of their vote. The second day the commissioners, or a majority of them, agreed that if they would take the oath that they had not paid the tax, nor had not had an opportunity of paying they would allow them to vote. Under that head, then, with hard persuasion, we got a few of them to vote; but the lawyers and a number of other men threatened them so hard with the old law and the penitentiary that we could not do much with them; but after the turn of the day we got to voting them so heavy they had some four or five arrested for illegal voting, which, we believe, was done to intimidate; for this reason, there were a good many more that took the same oath and were not arrested. They held a commitment trial, and committed them to jail, and kept them there until the election closed. We believe this was all to intimidate, as well as the threatening to the penitentiary. The names of those arrested and put in jail are, Jim Eberhart, Randle Jones, Adam Smith, Miles Dozier, Lewis Stevens, and one other, I do not recollect the name. The third day passed off quietly, on account of these being in jail, only every day there were several colored men that had paid their taxes and did not have their receipts with them and were not allowed to swear to it, and were not allowed to vote unless some white man would vouch for them that they knew that their taxes were paid. This the commissioners done. Several cases under my own knowledge, and I heard several others say so. All these are facts under my own knowledge, and they can be proven by a host of witnesses.

J. F. CUNNINGHAM,
Deputy Sheriff of Oglethorpe County.

Mr. William J. White.

P. S. — There are a great many reports, of which I cannot state as facts, but other reliable men will, that there was a great deal of threatening of different kinds, and hiring them with different kinds of pay. I heard some men say they saw a colored man have some money that was given to him to vote a democratic ticket; showed the money, and was trying to get more. All such doings as this: telling them that the republicans were not their friends — that they were; that the republicans were just ruining them; telling them that they owned all the land and stock, the republicans none, and how could we be their friends?

J. F. CUNNINGHAM.

I wish you to let me know whether you get this or not. We have some doubts about our letters ever reaching their destinations on some occasions.

J. F. C.

No comments of mine can add anything to the overwhelming force of this testimony. Read and ponder it, ye craven ones, who for a mess of miserable pottage, far inferior to Esau's savory dish, will inaugurate measures for the reinstation in office, of the despicable villains whose exploits are here recorded. Shame on any man, calling himself a Union man, who can apologize for such men; and talk of their sorrow for their crimes, and our duty to kill the fatted calf in their behalf.

We can all see, as in a glass, the reflection of the deeds that will everywhere obtain, when the South is allowed to manage its own affairs, without any interference on the part of the National goverment. Here is the delightful state of affairs for which we are preparing. Who can say that another war will not be the sure and certain result of that policy, that thus proposes binding the Union men of the South into bundles, and casting them into the heated furnace of Southern hate, whose fires are so devotedly tended by Northern supporters of the rebel democracy?

CHAPTER XXX.

AFFLICTING DISPENSATIONS, AND DEATH OF MY AGED MOTHER.

Thus ended 1870, the fifth year of my Southern sojourn. By the good providence of God, and after herculean efforts on my part, the whole of Rev. Dr. F.'s claim was adjusted, and my poor sainted mother was spared the terrible infliction that at one time seemingly awaited her, of seeing our property torn from our hands, and re-consigned to the rebels, from whose grasp it had so remarkably been rescued. If our ever kind and sympathetic friend, S. C. S., had not again come to the rescue of our colored friends, I see not how this sad catastrophe could have been averted.

My mother's health had been failing for some time, and a few days after the commencement of the new year, her holy and perfect soul took its flight to its everlasting home, from which it now looks down in joyful satisfaction, at the final result of our Southern mission. Her disease was the slow typhoid fever, and was short in duration. Before her eyes were closed in death, we were able to impart to her the joyful intelligence, that the claim of Dr. F. was adjusted, and the black people would be allowed to retain their land and homes, from all of which, they would have been ejected, if F., and his unfeeling advisers, could have had their own way.

A little previous to this event, she, with her own hand, signed a mortgage of her Northern property, in order to do her part towards preserving this place, inviolate, for the sacred purposes for which it had been reserved by the God of Israel. Words cannot describe the seraphic smile, that played upon her features, as she became conscious that her self-denying act, had accomplished its purpose. How often had she said to me; "O, Charles, don't turn these poor colored people out of doors. The Lord will provide a way to prevent it, I am certain." Her friends at the North, severely blame us, for allowing her to commit this rash act, as they termed it; but "the secret of the Lord is with them who fear Him," and she knew what her Lord and Master wished her to do, in the premises, and hesitated not to obey his commands. Happy will it be for all, when they are as willing to obey God's commands, without regard to consequences. My mother was also a woman, not easily turned from a purpose once formed, to do a good act, and our puny efforts to thwart her benevolent wishes, we well knew, would be useless.

I must here beg my reader's pardon for introducing the following testimonies to my mother's worth, from those who knew her well. I do this, because she has numerous friends who will peruse this book, and would be pleased to read these particulars respecting my mother, who came as near being a perfect woman as any one with whom I have ever been acquainted. If the reader is not interested in these particulars, he can turn over these pages, until he reaches another chapter.

"At the request of my brother, I here subjoin a brief account of my dear mother's life and death. She was in many respects a remarkable woman. Left a widow at the age of thirty-five, she never married again, but endeavored to train up her four children in the fear of God, and lived to see them all professedly walking in the truth. The promise given her as she said, when first left a widow, that, "great shall be the peace of thy children, and they shall be all taught of the Lord," she oft repeated to us children, and strong and unwavering was the faith with which she rested on this promise, even when its fulfillment was delayed. Those who only saw the sweet gentleness of disposition she manifested, supposed her *easily influenced;* but we who knew her more intimately, were aware that this was an erroneous idea. She was strong in her convictions of right, and very positive in her adherence to them, especially upon points of religious faith. Though a champion of the Anti-Slavery cause, from her first knowledge of it, and ever warmly defending the so-called Garrison party, yet she retained her own religious opinions, unshaken by the views of those she revered for "their work's sake."

Her many Springfield friends can recall many interesting incidents in her Anti-Slavery life. She was one of the first in S. to extend a welcome hand to "Sojourner Truth," and always remained her firm friend. The Temperance cause always found in her an earnest and zealous advocate, and she carefully trained her children to walk in her steps, in this respect. She was also a firm and unwavering advocate of the "Moral Reform" cause, which she espoused in its infancy. She was a life member of that Society for thirty years, and active in promoting its objects. No annual Thanksgiving day ever passed, without contributing her mite for the "Friendless Widow's" funds. Though always limited in her means, yet she was "rich in faith, and in good works very abundant." She was very active in visiting the sick and poor in our town, and *never did a needy one call upon her for aid in vain.* Her house was the home of the wayfaring one, and never was a meal so scanty, that it could not be shared with those more needy.

During the last two years of her residence in Springfield, she was actively engaged in collecting clothing for the poor freedmen on my brother's plantation in Georgia, and in the neighborhood around him, and many an article was contributed from sheer personal regard for her, by those indifferent to the cause in which she was engaged. She joined our Georgia mission at the age of eighty-four, and threw her whole soul into the work, according to her custom in other enterprises, regarding nothing as too valuable to be cheerfully contributed to the work, so that it was necessary for me to restrain her liberality in this respect. One of her first acts was to deprive herself of necessary clothing, for the benefit of still greater sufferers than herself; and one of the last was to dictate a letter to a friend in Vermont, which was responded to, by sending her a valuable barrel of clothing for the freedmen.

Through her long life, she had loved and labored for the poor slave, and now she desired to see them herself, and to witness the practical workings of freedom, and though she was in some respects disappointed in them, yet we well may say her life there, was a fitting close to her whole suffering and laborious career. Though her refined and cultivated nature shrank from too close contact with objects so degraded as some of them were, yet she spent her strength to the last, in teaching these poor forlorn children, nearly twenty of whom were under her instruction. One of them was a tall boy, seventeen or eighteen years of age, whose loud voice grated harshly on the ear, when mingled with those of the smaller children, and him she undertook to teach alone, and actually taught him to read and spell, and something of arithmetic. She was always in the day-school, at its opening in the morning, and sometimes spent the whole day there, either taking classes of four or five, or teaching the pupils individually. One of them was a beautiful girl of seventeen, who was almost white, to whom she had taught history and grammar, and who apparently loved her with the affection one would feel for a mother, and now cherishes her memory among that of her dearest friends.

Upon her death-bed, my mother was asked if she was not sorry she came to Georgia? She replied, "No, I am very glad." Hers was not a spirit to take back any thing she had given to God. Her frequent exclamation, during her last sickness was, "Tell me, Oh, tell me, what is the will of God concerning me, and I will do it." It was the will of God to usher her well-trained soul into that brilliant abode, every crevice of which is penetrated with the celestial light, that is poured forth from the resplendant form of Him who is "the light thereof," and whose glory fills the whole heavens; there, not so much to bask in the luxurious and softened light, as to gather so many of its golden rays about her person, as would form a spiritual halo, for the attraction of the many less developed ones, among whom she wished to labor. She believed that our labors of love on earth, only fitted us for more perfect ones hereafter. "For as one star differeth from another star in glory, so also is the resurrection of the dead." Great as is the loss to us, we are therefore constrained to say, to her, and to the world of mankind, it is *great gain*.

Her affectionate and loving child, R. W. S."

"SPRINGFIELD, MASS., JAN., 1872.

My Dear Friend, — As I understand you intend alluding to the purity and excellence of your dear mother's life, in the book you are writing on Southern society, I have thought this little fragment from my recollections of her, might form an agreeable contrast to the dark shades of life your history will compel you to draw, and perhaps serve to arouse within some of those darkened minds at the South, some aspirations after a higher and divine life than is usually exhibited around them. If you agree with me, you are welcome to publish this extract, furnished by myself, for the eloquent eulogy pronounced on the occasion of her death, by the elder of the church to which she formerly belonged.

"Mrs. Stearns was my dearest friend outside my own family. She did more to improve my character, and cultivate my faith in God than all the rest of my acquaintances. She exemplified her christian character more by deeds than words. I will speak of a circumstance that occurred several years ago, the first summer of my intimacy with her. I had returned to rest early one night, when a boy came after me to go over to Mrs. S.'s house. I immediately arose and went. "Come in," said she, as I knocked at the door, "you are younger than I, and it is now nine o'clock, but you must go to our neighbors and get some food for the breakfast of a poor family whom I have taken in, as I have not enough to supply them all, they are so hungry." I looked at her smiling face, pale but resolute, and wondered if I had better obey. I could not resist the sweet pleadings of heavenly love written there, and I obeyed not without reluctance.. Others were alike moved with myself, and the result was a bountiful supply of provisions, not only for the breakfast of the poor travellers, but to cheer them on their tiresome journey. After they had thrown their weary forms upon the soft couches so kindly prepared for them, I said,

"Grandma, how could you do this thing? A woman at your age with no man in the house to call on, to let such a family in, there's no knowing what terrible event might follow such rashness!" She replied in tones never to be forgotten,

> "Give to the winds thy fears,
> My Father is at the helm.

I have experienced too much of the loving kindness of my merciful father, and his tender mercy has been too freely given me, for me to refuse any of the human family the accommodations of my home for one night. I have a prayer-hearing God, an ever present help in time of need." I being obliged to return home left her with her numerous guests, whom she had chanced to meet, on her return from one of her favorite moonlight walks which she enjoyed so much. They had walked all the way from Canada, and were on their way to Hartford, Conn., penniless and wearied out. As she was never known to pass an object of distress even in the street without dropping a word of sympathy, she stopped to question them a little, and learned their condition, and immediately took them to her home, although she was seventy years of age, and was that night alone. She provided them with water and towels, and made them take a good bath, and then furnished them with supper and made beds for them. There were nine persons in this wayfaring family. In the morning I went over and found them all right, and refreshed by their food and rest, and she was in the act of praying for them, and such a prayer as I shall ever remember. Years afterwards, the man came to see her, and stated that up to that time, he had led a wicked life, but the unusual nature of his treatment, together with the prayer offered up, had so impressed his mind, that from that day forward he began in earnest to try to lead a new life, and had come to God for that purification of his nature those words of prayer had pointed out, as possible through faith in God's holy Son. He also wished her to receive a small sum of money from his wife, which she finally did and applied it to the carrying out of some cherished plan of benevolence.

"I well remember how beautifully your mother talked to us that morning, she thought she had become blind, while confined to her bed, from the effects of that terrible fall. She looked up at me, as I hurried into her room, and said; 'I can see you; I am so thankful I can see you once more; but I had a most distressing experience last night. I awoke about one in the morning, and as I could not see, I concluded the shock to my system had caused total blindness.' 'O! what did you do? Did you call no one?' said I. 'No;' said she, 'at first, I prayed to God that I might become willing; desiring to remember, that I had been most wonderfully blessed, in having my sight so many long years; that I had read my Bible many times over, I trust understandingly; had committed to memory, many and many a hymn, that will comfort me the rest of my days; and I almost concluded it was a kind Providence, enabling me to cast all care, for the future, on my God. Perhaps, thought I, it will be easier so to live, at my time of life; to rest under the shadow of 'the Rock that is higher than I.' May I say from my heart, though he slay me, yet will I trust him.'

"She often said to me, 'The Lord will do much better for you, than you ask for yourself;' and she always tried to cultivate in her friends, a childlike, and trusting spirit. How many such instances of her rare faith in God, could I narrate, if space permitted? I desire, humbly to thank God, that it was given to me to know her; and may I ever reflect on, and try to imitate, her pure example, and most beautiful faith. As to her future, I doubt not, she will be 'a shining seraph, in the day of the Lord Jesus,' as was beautifully remarked at the funeral sermon in S., by one who knew her well.

Yours sincerely and truly, M. G. D."

May I be excused for adding to this testimony, the simple remark, that religion, when allied to benevolence as in my mother's case, is surely undeserving of the maledictions heaped upon it by those reformers at the North, who can see no beauty in a well developed character, simply because the symmetry of such a character, is produced partly by a rational faith in the name of the "despised Nazarene."

CHAPTER XXXI.

PECUNIARY DIFFICULTIES, AND DELIVERANCE FROM THEM; WITH ARRIVAL OF NORTHERN EMIGRANTS.

Sad were our feelings, as we entered upon the trials of another year, bereft of the wise counsels, and the earnest sympathy of our sainted mother. But her death was not the only dark shadow that crossed our path; poverty, dire, unflinching, soul-crushing poverty, again pressed its heavy heel upon our devoted heads. Every member of our lessened family-circle, felt its cruel touch; but the most worthy one of all, was where "the wicked cease from troubling, and the weary are at rest," in the bosom of her Father, God. We rejoiced that however much the remainder of us might suffer from pinching hunger, she was where the saints of God "hunger no more, nor thirst any more."

But other troubles followed closely in the wake of this one so great. God, for wise purposes, saw fit to allow our income from every source to cease, and we met besides with heavy losses on our farm, among which was that of the remnant of our once bountiful dairy and a valuable horse. Our land remained in our possession, but we had no means for its cultivation, and it was therefore valueless for present needs, unless parties appeared to hire or purchase, and then we should have received no immediate income. We had used all our

available funds, in discharging the debt due our Boston creditors, and were literally penniless. No colored man appeared who could pay anything down on his land, although many wished for it, without paying anything until the end of the year. We could have indeed sold out to our rebel neighbors on advantageous terms, but that we had refused to do, when sorely pressed for means to pay the Boston creditor, and now that his claim had been satisfied, it did not appear at all right for us to distrust God, so much as thus to cut off our colored friends from the opportunity to own land, we were able to offer them. Previous to my mother's death, a rich rebel had urged us to sell to him, and we felt somewhat inclined to do so; but my mother so strongly urged me, that I forebore, and the result proved that her faith was not ill-founded.

Perhaps the reader may not perceive the connexion of my own pecuniary affairs, with either the black man or the rebels, and certainly cannot see how they were owing to the "outrages" of the latter. But even if they were not, it would be inexcusable in me, after having been delivered safely from the hands of these rebels, and having survived the losses consequent upon some of the "characteristics" of the blacks, not to render "honor to whom honor is due," for the unmistakable protection afforded me in all of my trials and dangers, by Him "who never slumbereth nor sleepeth," or allows the faintest cries of any of his obedient children to go unheeded. I am writing this book for the purpose of enlisting the sympathies of others in behalf of the colored people, and of inducing them to do as I have done at the South, by laboring for these poor and imbruted ones. If I could not recount to them some of my deliverances from these trials, I should fail to encourage them; and if I created the impression that no pecuniary sacrifice was required of laborers in this unpromising vineyard, they might afterwards curse me for persuading them to embark in such an undertaking. I wish the reader therefore to understand distinctly, that losses are likely to follow all who engage in this mighty enterprise, but that in the midst of them all, the right arm of the eternal Jehovah will always and forever be extended in their behalf.

We met with severe losses in our Northern property also, and it became absolutely necessary for some one of our family to hasten thither, to repair those losses. But we were wholly destitute of the means with which to defray our expenses. Nevertheless, my sister commenced packing her trunk, as something seemed to urge her to this course, and to say, "the means will be provided as soon as you are ready."

We sent to those at the North whom we supposed would be ready to help us, but were flatly refused, on the ground that helping us would be helping the blacks, and the parties refusing did not wish to aid *them* in any way. In this our distress, we again cried unto the Lord, fully believing that we should be heard, and then a voice said, "write to such and such persons." We obeyed, and the answers came in a few days from both of them, complying with our request. This was the more remarkable, as we had not before thought of writing to either of these persons. I again beg the reader's pardon for so often alluding to these "heavenly suggestions." I do it for the sake of aiding others, who are alike needy and know not which way to turn. It is my firm and unwavering belief that when a soul enters into a solemn covenant with God, to do his bidding always and at all times, and keeps this covenant, that soul will always be furnished with means to enable him thus to obey God; for it would be singular enough for God to command one for instance, to publish a book, and then fail to provide him with the means for so doing. I therefore believe that on my arrival at the North, a way will be opened for the publication of this book, although at the time of writing these lines I have only a small portion of the necessary means on hand; and when I commenced the task not one single cent that could be used for that purpose.

God has created man for a beneficent purpose. It cannot be his desire that man should really and permanently suffer. He must therefore have so arranged the laws of the Universe that obedience to them will prevent permanent suffering. Of course non-obedience to them, being a disturbance of the beautiful harmony of the Universe, must cause misery, as an injury to one of the strings of a musical instrument, must mar the musical enjoyment of its player, and of the listener to its sounds. As man's nature is diversified, so are the laws of that nature, answering to the different strings of a guitar or violin, each one of which is necessary to produce perfection of sound. The spiritual laws of the Universe are as essential as the material, and ploughing and hoeing are no more essential to material results, than are hearkening and believing to spiritual ones. Honesty is one of the laws of our moral nature, obedience to which will produce moral pleasure, but it may be obeyed, and yet the body suffer from a broken limb. So, believing in divine or spiritual influence will not preclude pain from non-obedience to physical law; neither will obedience to all the moral and physical laws of the Universe, produce perfect bliss, while the spiritual laws of our being are neglected, But obedience to all physical, moral, intellectual and spiritual laws, will produce the highest happiness humanity is capable of enjoying.

An elegant house is a good thing. Superb furniture delights the eye. Music and statuary add to these other enjoyments. Comfortable clothing detracts not therefrom. A well furnished library is above all price, and a quiet conscience added thereto is better than all. But far beneath all these factitious advantages lies the substratum of the human soul—the ever present *Me*—of the philosophical school, never satisfied with the attainments of the *not* me of the outward world. The wants of this imperative ruler of the human being must be met, which they cannot be without fellowship with an eternal *me*, fully capable of satisfying all of its loudest demands. No human *me* is thus capable, but a divine one can meet all of the wants of this clamoring spirit, the principal ones of which are, light and love. "God is *light* and in him, is no darkness at all." "God is *love*." Light to know the truth, love to obey it. There need be, and there *is* no miracle necessary, to bestow this light and love upon the insatiable *me* of the human soul. It is simply receiving spiritual influence, as the needy earth receives the welcome rain, by baring its bosom to the heavenly outpouring. So we shall receive innumerable spiritual blessings by imitating Nature, and gladly throwing ourselves open to this divine power, which always envelops us, and seeks to pour its innumerable gifts upon all who sincerely court them.

The air that we breathe, the flowers whose perfume we inhale, the stalwart trees, beneath whose shade we regale our weary limbs, the wide-spreading and universal grassy verdure around us, all are overflowing with the redolence of the breath of the Almighty, imparting a health-giving power to these inanimate things. "Why should it seem incredible" that the same being should seek to impart spiritual life, to that higher workmanship of his Almighty hand, the human soul? Shall he who "stretcheth out the North over the empty place, and hangeth the earth upon nothing," be thwarted in his endeavors to enlighten and purify the human mind? Is there not "a spirit in man?" and does not the "inspiration of the Almighty give understanding?" Will not God "guide the meek in judgment, and *teach* the meek his way?" Is it not true that "I will *instruct thee*, and *teach thee* in the way which thou shalt go; I will guide thee with mine eye?"

There seems to me not the slightest tincture of fanaticism in thus crediting the assertions of Infinite Wisdom, and taking him at his word. But even if there was too much credulity manifested in this practice, if the results are good, why should we not reap the benefit to be derived therefrom? *Too much* faith may produce extra hazardous efforts, resulting in narrow escapes from destruction. But who shall measure the terrible depths of that knawing, mental disquiet; who shall describe the melancholy echo of that "sounding line" which we almost despairingly drop into the tumultuous waters of doubt around us; who shall estimate the amount of that paralysis of soul, all produced by a *lack* of rational faith? Verily, if a superabundance of faith "has slain its thousands," a *deficiency* of this life-giving element has "slain its tens of thousands." But I am wandering far from my narrative. Excuse me, patient reader.

Our other wants were at length relieved, and before the close of the Summer, we knew what it was to sit down to a table, and eat sufficiently to satisfy our hunger, which had not been the case for many months previously. "The young lions do lack and suffer hunger; but they that wait on the Lord shall not lack any good thing." They may lack what seems to them good things; but in such cases, it is manifestly *best* for them that they should thus temporarily suffer.

Many things of an unpleasant nature occurred this summer and fall; but as so much of this character has been already alluded to, I will omit in this narrative any farther reference to the faults of my sable friends, and will hasten to the close of the narrative. In the spring of this year, (1871,) I resolved to defer no longer the commencement of the task to prepare for publication, a narrative of my Southern experience. But as the weather increased in warmth, I was obliged to desist from it for a season, but was able again to resume it in the fall. This interim of labor allowed me to think still more earnestly upon the grand remedy for the unfortunate condition of the colored people, which, at the commencement of my task, I judged to be the furnishing them with land according to my adopted plan; but after praying earnestly and repeatedly for light upon this subject, my mind was suddenly influenced to see that another remedy was to be added to those already partially adopted: *the introduction, into the midst of this class, of a body of Northern laborers, whose example of neatness, order, sobriety, intelligence and industry*, should serve as a standing rebuke to the poor colored man for his deficiences in these respects. Accordingly, before I knew of the plans of others, I prepared the chapter on

Northern emigration, and resolved to present it to my Northern friends as the grand desideratum in the negro's case. It is true, that the attention of Northern philanthropists has long been drawn to the necessity of Northern emigration, in order to benefit the South, and I had myself labored for the accomplishment of this purpose, but the *new light* on this subject was, that these emigrants should be *working men* and *women*, in lieu of capitalists and politicians. Not necessarily carpet-baggers, (as the rebels facetiously term Northern adventurers,) but genuine settlers, who should *themselves* till the soil, and establish the various mechanical arts that have made New England the glory of all nations. My plan is more fully developed in Chapt. VI., of the second part of this work, and I will add no more upon the subject at present, except to briefly allude to the realization of these ideas, as far as this county is concerned, by the arrival of quite a number of the right stamp of men and women, who seem disposed to carry out the very idea, that my mind had been led to dwell upon as so necessary in the negro's case. I am not sure as they will approve of this publicity of their philanthropic purpose, but I am sure they will pardon me when they consider that the knowledge of their example will perhaps influence many others to "go and do likewise."

About the close of a bright sunny day, near the middle of October, 1871, my heart was made glad, by seeing a horse and buggy drive into our yard, with two men, one of whom proved to be the Rev. Joseph T. Curry, of Boston. He had sent word of his intention to be here about this time, and notice had been given of it to the colored people, all around. They seemed much pleased at the news, and flocked in great numbers to hear him preach his first sermon, which was on Sunday, the 22d of October. It is difficult to divest the colored man of the idea, that in some way or other, the arrival of a Northern man will result in his benefit; and in this case he had promised to send them some teachers, if they ardently desired a week-day school. In his sermon, Mr. C. dwelt upon the blessings deemed by him to be in store for the colored race, and it was amusing to see with what complacency they drank down his favorite doctrine, that their race was destined to be particularly favored of God, in the introduction of that "new dispensation" he believed was about to dawn upon the earth. I could not deny that numerous passages of Scripture seemed to favor this idea, and was myself quite pleased to hear it so ably and eloquently advocated. It mattered not to me, or to the blacks, how singular his religious faith might be in other respects, he had come ostensibly to lift the degraded from their unfortunate condition, by imparting unto them the blessings of a thorough education; and it was no consequence whether he labored under the auspices of the great denominations of the day, or pursued his course solitary and alone, without being the organ of any particular denomination, as he declared was his position. They seemed highly delighted as he explained to them his educational plans, in their behalf. About a week after this he returned to the North, to engage his teachers, after having been received with the utmost enthusiasm by the colored people in Augusta, who flocked in great numbers to hear him whom one of their pastors termed this "wonderful man."

On the 9th day of December, he again entered my yard, with the pleasing intelligence that an accomplished

Northern teacher would soon be upon the ground, and also a family to superintend the affairs of the mission. Thus seemed to be answered our long continued requests to God, to furnish us with teachers, for the permanent establishment of a day school upon our place. Ever since my first arrival here, this object had lain very near my heart; and Mrs. Sherman, whose daughter Lizzie taught the first *week day school* established on our place, had often asserted that no progress could be made in civilizing these people, until we established a day school. I had corresponded with Northern societies on this subject, and at one time the Quakers in Pennsylvania had partly concluded to send a teacher here. I had applied to Baptists, Methodists, Congregationalists, and Unitarians, to establish a day school on my plantation; but while they all admitted the necessity of the work, their funds would not allow them to send teachers, unless I would contribute more to their support than I felt able to do; but here, in the providence of God, were men and women ready and willing to come and do what others had refused to do, wholly at their own expense. While I do not blame other societies for their inability to comply with my urgent requests, I respectfully ask them not to condemn me for accepting the offer of those whose religious tenets they so highly disapprove, as they do those of Mr. Curry and his associates. It is unnecessary for me to state that I do not endorse these opinions, although I cannot help regarding their advocates as honest and self-denying men and women, as it has often fallen my lot to behold. Their deep piety is unquestioned, and the fervor of their religious zeal knows no bounds. In proof of my assertion that I do not endorse their peculiar faith, I may be allowed to

state, that just before I left Georgia, my own religious opinions, as expressed in another portion of this work, were severely denounced by Mr. Curry, and I was assigned to those regions of the "*dead*," so thickly peopled with the souls of unbelievers, according to his honest opinion and peculiar faith.

On the 16th day of January, 1872, my hopes were realized in the arrival of seven persons from the North, who were destined to form the nucleus of the colony Mr. Curry was intending to form, among whom was the accomplished and intelligent lady above alluded to, who had been a teacher in one of the Boston public schools. A beautiful site for a village was selected, which commanded an extensive view of the surrounding country, and a portion of South Carolina; and as soon as necessary arrangements could be made, the school was put in successful operation.

A second installment of these "pilgrims of hope," soon followed, and at the time of this writing, early in March, nearly fifty persons, principally from Massachusetts, have become residents on our plantation, on portions of land contracted for, by their leaders. These new comers went immediately to work, with an energy that showed them to be of true Yankee grit, remodelling the place, and making arrangements for the accommodations of others. The rebels all around seemed pleased with the idea of Northern working-men coming here, and not depending upon the blacks for labor; and numerous offers have been made by them of land, and the necessaries of life, for the accommodation of the pilgrims. They say all they want is, that "the emigrants should not meddle with the negroes. We can put up with anything else."

And now as the way is open for my retiring from the scene of my nearly six years labors among an oppressed and ignorant race, I gladly bring this narrative to a close, hoping that I have not by its length entirely wearied the patience of my readers, and bespeaking from them their candid attention to other and more important parts of this work. Previous to this however, I wish to express our gratitude and that of the blacks, for the numerous gifts to our mission of clothing and books from various friends of the freedmen at the North. Our little enterprise has been sustained mostly by faith, having no organization pledged to its support; but He who approves of every sincere effort to advance his course, no matter by whom undertaken, has not withheld his smiles from our work, and has not entirely forgotten our necessities.

In particular we would mention the reception at one time of four barrels of clothing with the freight prepaid, from the Sanford St. Colored Church, Springfield, Mass., through Mrs. Harriet Thomas and her mother-in-law Mrs. Sophia Thomas; as well as three barrels at a later date, from the society worshipping under Elder Curry's auspices in Springfield, with the freight also prepaid. Also numerous donations from members of other churches in Springfield, very valuable boxes from Rev. Mr. Coggins' Society, in Boxford, Mass., and an exceedingly liberal donation of new school books from Rev. Mr. Van Normans' school of N. Y. city; and at sundry times various donations from other societies and individuals; all of which have been applied according to the expressed wishes of the donors, to the relief of those suffering ones connected with our Sabbath school and mission.

I will only add, that on the 6th of March, 1872, we bid adieu to our long cherished colored friends, and started on our mission to the North in behalf of the entire colored race at the South; holding several interesting farewell meetings with the objects of our sympathy here and in Augusta, and "Commending all to God and the word of his grace which is able to build them up, and to give them an inheritance, among all which are sanctified."

Augusta, Ga., March 10th, 1872.

CHAPTER XXXII.

LEADING CHARACTERISTICS OF THE FREEDMEN, SUCH AS SELF-ESTEEM, UNWILLINGNESS TO OBEY ORDERS, WASTEFULNESS, LYING AND STEALING.

It is my purpose now to introduce a few of the *prominent characteristics* of the colored race, as far as my observation at the South has extended. I will commence with that of *self-esteem.*

It will hardly be credited by those not familiar with them, that *self-esteem* is one of the most prominent traits of character of the freedmen. It is well known that their white neighbors possess this quality to perfection, but that a race sunken so low as the blacks are, should also abound in this quality seems a marvel indeed. But so it is, from the smallest child that tottles across the yard, to the gray-haired veteran, soon to enter upon such scenes as will produce humility in the wisest of men — all seem to possess the most unlimited confidence in their own abilities. It is seldom you can find a man who will own his ignorance, or inability to perform a specified task. Said a man to me one day as he was attempting to gin cotton, but failed to do it well, "I know all about ginning." A young man from the North at length discovered the cause of the trouble, which though slight, had entirely escaped the notice of this expert ginner. And so it is with all kinds of labor. Valuable property is often seriously injured, because these men will pretend to knowledge they do not possess.

In one instance a carriage needed repairing, and one of these men was asked if he could take it to pieces, so as to perform the required task. "O yes," said he, "I have worked on carriages all of my life;" but after fumbling over it for a long time, he was forced to own that the task was too great for his genius, and yet it was a comparatively simple one.

We have found this trait the most formidable obstacle in the way of their improvement. They cannot be made to realize that they are spiritually "poor and blind and naked," but they believe they are "rich in goods and have need of nothing" spiritually. Said one of the most ignorant ones, to whom I was endeavoring to explain some simple problem of morality, "It may be as you say, for I suppose you know a *little more* than I do; you can read at least, and I cannot." To convince them of the unbounded treasures of wisdom and knowledge, hid from them by their ignorance, is an almost herculean task. Every man as soon as converted religiously, enters at once upon the work of preaching to others, without the least possible feeling of embarrassment or show of diffidence, An ignorant boy of eighteen or twenty, just emerged from the slough of sin, as he believes, will talk as flippantly as the oldest saint on religious matters; and I do not believe would at all hesitate to address an audience of learned divines, if so invited. On some accounts it is well for them that they are so conceited, for no possible amount of reproof will ever disturb their equanimity of soul. They do not like to be reproved, it is true, but reproof never wilts them down, and discourages them as it does other mortals. The winds and waves of rebuke may blow and beat high around their heads, but their imperturbable souls are as placid and calm as under the influence of a gentle summer zephyr. "God knows my heart, and he will save me," is their inevitable reply to religious reproof.

Closely allied to this sublime self-conceit, is an *utter unwillingness to obey implicitly* any order given them. I can hardly recollect a single instance, of perfect obedience to an order, during my sojourn among them. It matters not what the direction is, it is utterly and entirely impossible to induce one to obey it entirely. The smallest child is guilty of this disobedience, as well as the wisest man among them. It is often extremely ludicrous to witness the mistakes they will make, in their efforts to evade your command. I suppose the reason of this is, that under the reign of Slavery, this implicit obedience was required of them, and they cannot comprehend the idea that freedom is consistent with such obedience; but it seems derogatory to their present condition, thus to obey. A large portion of the difficulties between them and the whites, are traceable to this cause. It is extremely annoying to a Northern man, and doubly so to one always accustomed to receive implicit obedience from them. An acquaintance of mine, once while sick, called in his head man, and gave him minute directions as to the disposal of several of the crops, then being gathered. The corn, fodder, and hay, were to be put in separate apartments, each one of which was particularly designated by my friend. To make sure that his orders were understood, he required the man to repeat them over to him, which he did correctly; but on his recovery, on entering his barn, he found the crops disposed of in an *entirely opposite* manner from his directions. I once directed a man to drive to a certain house on Broad Street, Augusta. He had nothing to do but to obey my orders. I looked for him for a long time, without perceiving him, and at length went in quest of him, when I found him slowly approaching the house from a street at right angles with the one he was upon, and which would have led him directly to the desired point. His only excuse was that he "thought he would try the other street." At another time, my overseer and I both directed a man where to go and wait for us, when he reached Augusta; but on our arrival there, we looked in vain for him, but at last found him, after several hours' fruitless search, quietly waiting on a back street, entirely away from the specified spot. In both cases, no excuse was offered for this disobedience. Every one claims the privilege of deciding for himself as to the propriety of your commands. This might be tolerated, if they would dispute your orders at the time, for then you would know what to expect; but they invariably respond to your orders, "Yes, sar, yes, sar," and sometimes with a low bow. If you tell a house servant to place a chair in a particular part of the room, it is sure to be placed a few feet distant at least. If you wish a window opened, it will probably be the door that will be thrown wide open. We had a house servant who was as kindly disposed as one could be, and in most respects a very desirable servant, (and this was not Margaret,) who for years would never use the exact proportion of acid and soda, in mixing bread; so that her bread was usually unfit to be eaten, unless you measured out those articles yourself. At last she became convinced that our directions were necessary, and she was much pleased with the result of following them, saying, "I never could see afore why you was so 'ticular about these things." Others would abuse us for requiring such obedience, and say it was good enough for them, and they guessed it was for us. A Southern lady informed me, that sometimes they directed a thing to be done precisely the opposite of their wishes, and then it would be done as they really wished.

How to account for this obstinacy I know not, but I know that it is a real and tremendous grievance, and I doubt not caused many of the cruel whippings inflicted upon the blacks while slaves, although the evil was not nearly so great then as since freedom. It is not by any means true that the Southern blacks are *willingly* an obedient race. They easily succumb to violence, but unless that is used or threatened, it is not a part of their nature to obey orders. And there is no doubt that they derive this trait, as well as its corresponding one of inordinate self-esteem, from their white neighbors. They do not like to obey much better than the blacks, as will be perceived by the lack of perfect discipline in their soldiers. The whole Southern people fancy they were "born to rule," and not to obey. It is sometimes amusing to see how even the blacks, will tyrannize over those subject to their orders. I once appointed a black man temporary overseer on my plantation, and his overbearing way of ordering the men about, soon produced mutiny among them. Indeed, during the days of Slavery, a black driver was always considered worse than a white one.

Even the little children will "lord it over" each other with a vengeance, whenever opportunity offers. I am inclined to think that if the blacks should obtain power in this country, they would prove more tyrannical than the whites, and for that reason I believe power should be partly withheld from them until they become enlightened. Parents tyrannize over their children, and husbands over their wives. The men all claim the right to *whip* their wives, for non-obedience to their commands, but the wives do not quietly submit to these whippings, and terrific commotion sometimes ensues.

But the black race is not naturally a cruel race. *Vindictiveness* is not one of their characteristics. On the contrary, I think they are naturally disposed to be quiet and live peaceably with all men. It is true they are obstinate in their dispositions, but they are not *fighters* by nature, nor of a quarrelsome disposition. In our little community, comparatively few fights occurred. In this respect they excel the belligerent portion of the people of the North. The children are cruel to animals, but this arises more from an innate love of fun, than from a cruel disposition, and also from the absence of benevolence.

Mirthfulness is a very prominent trait in their character. This is manifested on every occasion however trivial. They are disposed to "look on the bright side of things," and seldom appear to be cast down by misfortunes that will well nigh crush their white neighbors. This native exuberance of disposition was often mistaken, during the days of slavery, for contentment with their lot, and we were often told of the "happy and contented slaves." This apparent contentment arose from a happy disposition to make the best of everything, and not from any love of the yoke of slavery. It is the same now. If a crop in which they are pecuniarily interested, happens to fail, they bear the loss with far more equanimity than the whites, who are equal sufferers with themselves. Their organs of *hope* and *mirthfulness* are both extremely large. Nothing is more common in seasons of heavy business depression, and when great losses stare them in the face, than to hear their merry laughter ringing through the quarters, and the surrounding woods. Almost every one of them knows how to sing, and singing is one of their constant employments. They sing at their work, sing in coming from it, sing in their night schools, and sing eternally in their religious meetings. Even their burials are conducted principally by singing, and it is a pretty as well as a melancholy sight to witness one of their funeral processions, the whole company keeping up a continued singing from the time they leave the house, to the moment of placing the body in the grave.

Another of their prominent traits is *approbativeness.* There is always hope for a race or for an individual, who can be influenced by public opinion, but in their case this love of approbation operates in a singular manner. While they are extremely sensitive to reproof, they are not influenced for good by praise. If you praise one of them, he will immediately relax his efforts to please you, he having obtained the object he had in view in being good, viz. your approbation. This was so common that it became proverbial at length, that if you wished Jim or Maria to do well, you must studiously avoid praising them when they did well. While ordinary mortals will reach an almost Atlantean moral height under the powerful pressure of commendation, these people will sink into a corresponding depth of moral delinquency, from the effects of praise for the past. We once had a gar-

dener named Anthony who was at first a model of excellence in his department. The appearance of the garden pleased us so well, and his alacrity in obeying every order, so highly delighted us, that in an unguarded moment we took occasion to commend his excellencies in public, but from that moment his whole character seemed to undergo a complete metamorphosis ; the garden was neglected, and he became as unpromising a hand as the place afforded.

But still they covet praise. They seek for it in their actions, but do not in their minds connect its continuance with their good behavior. At one time, we hired a new hand to cut and bring to the house our fire wood, a job which was by no means a sinecure — as three fires had to be supplied, and the rooms were not constructed on the air-tight principle. The one formerly employed, had tormented us by his neglect of duty, and we had discharged him. The new man worked magnificently for awhile, and blazing fires greeted us, where before, only a few embers served to drive away the chills of our winter atmosphere. We were delighted, and expressed our delight to the industrious worker, when lo ! and behold ! he too, consigned us to the same fate as his predecessor had done, and we were again found shivering over a few coals or half burned brands of soggy wood.

It is often amusing to behold their rage at one another, when accused of some act of delinquency. Such cases as Margaret's were by no means peculiar. To be accused of lying or stealing, aroused their anger, although not considered particularly sinful. In hoeing cotton the planters profit by this approbativeness. They select the best hoer and place him at the beginning of a cotton row, and then say, " boys, see now how many of you can keep up with Bob." It is astonishing to see the sudden change from inertness to alacrity under the influence of this emulation. In cotton picking time it is turned to very great account, each hand having his cotton weighed as he deposits it on the gin-house platform; and the excitement is great to see who has picked the largest amount. The one who falls far behind the others, is made a butt of their ridicule as a "no-account fellow."

Drunkenness is *not* a prominent vice among them. On the contrary, during my six years residence on our plantation, I do not recollect of witnessing more than two or three cases of intoxication, and one of them was on the part of a non-resident, and this among a total population of over two hundred different persons. But neither is total abstinence one of their virtues. Nearly all will drink when it is *given* them, but they do not like to spend their money for it, when they need other things so much.

Another trait of the freedmen is *wastefulness* and *carelessness*. It seems incredible that a class so destitute, should be so destructive of the little they do possess. I was one day speaking of this fault to a colored man, comparatively well off, and expressing my surprise at its existence, when they were so poor, and he replied, "Why, that's the very reason they are so poor; they take no care of what they have got." I can describe their conduct no better than by calling it a perfect *carnival* of waste. Often the things given them, which with proper care would last months, are torn into shreds in a few weeks, so that latterly we have been obliged to confine our gifts to those whom we knew would take care of them. Often a nice little Sunday suit will be put on a small boy, to wear every day, when an every-day suit had also been given him. Hats and caps are thrown around wherever the wearers find it the most convenient, and coats are often found lying near the spot where the owner last worked. The place for Glenn's hat was always in the wood-box. It is a difficult task to teach them to take care of their own clothing; but some of them have learned it to great perfection.

Bits of cloth, buttons, refuse food, and every other nameable article with which they have had any thing to do, are strewn about their premises, with the utmost profusion. Often when viewing this scene of waste, have I been forcibly reminded of the passage of Scripture, "Destruction and waste are in all their borders."

Want of punctuality is another of their distinguishing traits. Procrastination, that great "thief of time," holds universal sway over them, and paralyzes much of their labor. On our plantation were 750 acres of woods, a large portion of which were not one-eighth of a mile from our dwelling; and yet it was only by the most unwearied efforts that our family was kept supplied with fuel. If we had lived in the city of Boston, and wood had been $100 a cord, we could not have been reduced to greater straits for fuel, than we have been for much of the time of our Southern residence. Every white woman on the place had rendered herself hoarse, in screaming to the hands for wood, and every man had nearly broken the third commandment, in his efforts to secure the needed fuel. In the first place, no one could see why we burned so much wood, and in the next place, why was it necessary to cut it a particular length;

and then no one could divine why we wished for an armful in advance of our immediate necessities. They did not wish to see us suffer from cold, as they felt that suffering keenly themselves; but "why go after it, until it was needed to burn?" they said, all of which obtuseness of mind, was in consequence of this everlasting want of punctuality in all their labors. They of course meant to get us wood, but it was a thing that could be put off, and therefore was. It may be asked, why, having exclusive control of these hands, we did not force them to haul us wood in season for our wants; but to answer this question would to be to open a long chapter, in reference to the means necessary to produce perfect obedience among them. I can only say that it required more power of persuasion than I possessed, ever to get a negro to do anything, the reasonableness of which was not clear to his obfuscated vision. As we could not convince him of the propriety of the Northern custom of providing fuel before hand, so all heaven and earth could not induce him to act so preposterously, unless we used absolute force. When we first went there, Margaret never had a wood-pile at her door, but whenever she needed fuel, she went into the adjoining woods, and gathered an armful.

Once I conceived the preposterous idea of having my wood-house filled with wood during the Fall. I called W. to see me, and to talk the matter over with me. I laid down before him the advantages of such a course, and succeeded in convincing him that it would be for his interest to adopt my plan. He was to haul and cut my wood for a certain sum per week, and to use a mule he was working, in helping to haul the wood. I told him I would give him the use of a yoke of oxen, if he would haul the wood then, and convinced him that two weeks labor would complete the job, and he would not then be interrupted in his farm labors during the next season. He was at work for himself, and of course would be much benefited by this arrangement. But the first day of April arrived, and saw my wood-shed as destitute of wood as on the day we made the agreement. He always granted that it was a first-rate plan, and always meant to carry it out; but the oxen were obliged then to go elsewhere, and the wood remained unhauled. If there is any better school in which to practice the glorious lesson of patience, than a Southern plantation, I should like to know of its whereabouts.

It was so in the matter of an erection of a partition we once needed, a job requiring about three days labor, but which we were not blessed to see the completion of, until the expiration of five months. We also waited patiently about three months for the repairing of the roof of our kitchen, enduring many miniature deluges while the slow-moving mechanic was getting ready to do the job.

At whatever hour a meeting is appointed, the audience fails to assemble till about an hour afterwards, and it is usually nine o'clock at night before their own prayer-meetings get well under weigh. If a wagon needs repairing, it is deferred until the last possible moment, and perhaps until the very moment it is needed. In our house, if we were like to need an article of food, the cook would never tell us until it was entirely exhausted, which was slightly inconvenient to persons having to go eleven miles after their supplies. Once it took eight weeks to overhaul and repair a wagon, all the labor on which could have been performed in one or two weeks at the farthest. When the mules were not at work, they sometimes failed to get their breakfast until ten o'clock in the forenoon. If hay of their own needed cutting, it would be left standing until nearly dried up; and if we found fault with all this dilatoriness, we would be denounced as "worse than the rebels." There were times when their anxiety to go to town, would spur them up to "take time by the forelock," and they would manage to start by daylight. It is for this reason, among others, that I cannot conscientiously advise Northern men to come South, and depend on negro labor. In another portion of this work will be found a description of the kind of Northern emigrants needed, as an offset to all this shiftlessness and procrastination.

Want of *perseverance* is another trait in the character of the freedmen. Great numbers would begin to learn, and after a few spasmodic efforts would abandon the task. They must sadly lack the organ of continuity, for it seems almost impossible to get them to fix their minds upon any one subject, for a great length of time. They get tired of listening, even to their own florid preachers, and frequently fall asleep in the midst of the most glowing descriptions of the torments of the damned. Although they often continue their meetings until the break of day, it is not because of their powers of concentration, but simply from a lack of energy to break away from the religious spell, so strangely affecting them. This listlessness of mind is one of the natural consequences of slavery, but is none the less a tremendous obstacle in the way of their mental improvement. I should say that mental laziness was far oftener a fault with them, than the physical malady of that sort, to which Andrew Johnson so often alluded. They are ready enough to work physically, but to persuade them to throw off this mental inertia, is a task of no mean magnitude. I have yet learned of but one motive sufficiently powerful to break this spell, and that is the *desire to own land*. That will arouse all that is dormant in their natures, far more than any other consideration I have seen presented to them.

Another trait of theirs, is the the last one we should suppose they would possess, and that is *conservatism*. Although they have endured so much at its hands in the form of slavery, they still cling to its antiquated form, and prefer its rusty appendages to the bright accoutrements of the chariot of reform. Old ideas, old customs, old ways of performing labor, and especially old sins, seem almost sacred in their estimation. It is on this account they are not so enthusiastic in favor of voting as they ought to be. The new ways must be made fashionable, and then their approbativeness may lead to their adoption. I do not think there is any natural element of reform, or earnest yearning after perfection, in the natures of a majority of them. I think their organ of ideality is very little developed, and they are consequently disposed to be content with things as they are.

I have already so frequently alluded to *stealing*, that it will not be necessary to add much under this head. Both lying and stealing are extremely common among them. Their ideas of stealing are sometimes of a comical nature. At one time, three of our men stole and killed a hog belonging to a brother black, on the next plantation, and they were detected in the theft. One of my best scholars, by the name of Greene Johnson, was connected with the theft. I sent for him to come and see me, and when he made his appearance, I said to him,

"Greene, I am extremely sorry to hear of your being caught in such a scrape. I should not have thought it of you, Greene." Looking up, with some degree of surprise, he replied, "what scrape, Mr. S.? I han't been in no scrape." "Did you not aid Nelson in stealing Allen's hog?" said I. "No, sir," he replied. "I had nothing to do with stealing that ar hog." "What did you do about it then?" I enquired. "O, I only held the hog still while Nelson cut his throat. I did not steal him, sure and sartain, Mr. S." "And did you not help Nelson carry the hog away?" I asked. "O, yes," said he; "I toted him on my shoulders part of the way, because Nelson said if I didn't, he wouldn't give me any of the meat; but I certainly had nothing to do with killing or stealing the hog." And he then asked, with an air of amazement, "Why, Mr. Stearns, you don't suppose I would steal a hog, does you, after what you have told us in the Sunday school about stealing?"

"Greene," said I, "what do you mean by talking so? You surely knew you was doing wrong in what you did?" "No, indeed, I did not," said he, looking completely puzzled, as well as sorry, that I should so wrongly accuse him. I then tried to explain to his besotted intellect, the nature of the transaction in which he had been engaged, and he listened with deep attention, swallowing every word, and at the close of my remarks, he said, with a brightened countenance, "Well, I see now, I'se done wrong; but, Mr. Stearns, I sartain didn't think I was doing wrong at the time of it." He afterwards went to see the owner of the hog, and agreed to pay him, at the end of the year, for his share in the villainy. He said if a man should steal a piece of pork from my cellar, and give him a part of it for carrying away the remainder, he should not consider it stealing; but if a man should steal a dollar therefrom, and give him a part of it for hiding the rest, he should think it was stealing. Perhaps, in God's sight, the moral obfuscation in this case, was no greater than in that of a learned divine, who could sell one of Christ's little ones, and with the proceeds purchase a new theological library.

Nelson's excuse was, that everybody, black, and white stole; and that stealing, was one of those sins no man could live without committing. He was quite indignant because I refused to protect him, against the officer of justice, who was in pursuit of him, saying; "I thought you pretended to be the colored man's friend." I am told by some Northern people, that the blacks are excusable for stealing from their old masters. However this may be, they certainly cannot be excused for stealing, from those whom they regard as their best friends, and I have yet to learn of any difference in this respect, in their conduct. I am pained to be obliged to allude to this crime, so pointedly; but as my object is, to tell the whole truth, I cannot pass over this common practice of theirs. Nothing that we possessed, was safe from their pilfering hands. Watches, clothing of all kinds, household utensils, all kinds of tools, and provisions without limit, were the objects of their indiscriminate plunder. It could not be said that hunger always drove them to the commission of these thefts, for at the moment of their commission, we were supplying some of them with food, gratuitously. They also stole from each other, whenever opportunity afforded, so that every one of their tenements was kept locked, in the absence of its occupants. I think it is safe to say, that property to the amount of fifteen hundred dollars, has been pilfered from me during my sojourn here; although I cannot say that all the thieves were blacks, yet there is no doubt they were, in a large majority of cases. Some of these cases were so aggravating, that I cannot forbear mentioning them.

Some of the inmates of our family had been extremely ill, and while thus unable to watch the household property, these thieves actually ascended the chamber stairs, passed directly by the door of the sick room, and ascending another pair of stairs, proceeded to help themselves to clothing of all kinds, amounting to about fifty dollars in value. At another time, when an aged member of our household, who all her life had been a laborious friend of their race, lay at the point of death, these fiendish thieves, penetrated to her apartment, and actually rifled her trunk of the clothes deposited there to be in readiness for any especial occasion. At still another time, a watch, presented to my sister by her brother on his death bed, and therefore highly valued as a keepsake, was taken from her private room, by one employed as a house-servant, and who had received many favors at our hands. And once, while holding a meeting in our house, for the express purpose of enabling others to right some of the wrongs of these poor creatures, the door of a store-room was accidentally left open a few moments, when some one entered and stole a quantity of meat therefrom. With too many of them, their regard for us and our interest, seemed to depend upon the amount of stealing it would enable them to accomplish. Very near the house we had an half-acre patch of water-melons, and through one whole season we never obtained six ripe melons from the field, although it produced bountifully. But it is useless to multiply these instances; enough has been already said, here, and elsewhere, to show that the propensity to steal, is one of the freedman's most prominent traits of character; and this propensity seldom involves them in injurious consequences. Of all the innumerable thefts committed on our place, we have never been able to detect the perpetrator, except in a very few instances. Perfect adepts in this art, their cunning is beyond conception, and almost always screens them from punishment.

No earthly motive will ever induce them to betray one another, always defending their brethren, as much as the free-masons are wrongly accused of doing. They *dare* not tell of each other, even if so disposed. Soon after my arrival, I was so little acquainted with this trait in their character, that on missing some valuable article, I told my overseer to offer a dollar to whoever would betray the thief. "I can tell them," said he, "but if you should offer them one hundred dollars, it would make no difference; they would never tell on each other."

I am happy to be able to state, that there are one or two limits to this propensity. They will never molest tools left on a newly made grave, where they are usually allowed to remain several weeks after a burial. And they will not steal sassafras wood, believing that burning it ensures ill-luck to the consumer. But Bibles, hymn-books and school-books of every description, they will steal as quickly as food or clothing. We have had at least 200 dollars worth of carpenter's tools stolen from our place, since I came here.

But let it not be supposed that every black man is a thief. There are some who will not steal. We have sufficiently tested them, and feel confident of this fact, although all of the Southern people constantly assert, that there are no negroes who will not steal. At one time a coat was given to one of our hands, who, after carrying it home, found a pair of old gloves in one of the pockets, which he immediately returned to us, asking if we knew they were there; but these cases are so extremely rare, that they form the exception and not the rule.

Perhaps some colored man will feel aggrieved at these statements; but let me ask you, my friend, how can I correctly describe the diseases of your brethren at the South, and leave out this important one? You know the truth of its existence as well as I do. If I call on a physician to visit a patient dangerously ill, what should I gain by varnishing over the ugly-appearing symptoms of his case? I want physicians to rush to the South, and aid in curing the sin-sick souls there so numerous; and it is only by correctly describing the extremely dangerous condition of the patients, that I can expect to arouse the sympathies of these benevolent doctors. "They that are *whole* need not a physician, but they that are sick."

CHAPTER XXXIII.

THE RELIGION OF THE BLACKS, WITH ANECDOTES ILLUSTRATING THE SAME.

I now come to the religion of the blacks, and truth will require of me great "plainness of speech." A more melancholy misnomer than that of the Christian religion, as applied to the heathenish observances of the plantation blacks, cannot be conceived. Volumes might be written upon this subject; but my space admonishes me to be brief. The subject is too peculiarly awful to me to dwell upon it at length. To see a race so thoroughly demented, as to call insane yellings, and violent contortions of body, totally disconnected from any kind of an idea, the Christian religion, is melancholy indeed. I am constrained to say, "if the light that is in them be darkness, how great is that darkness." It is hard to say, that their false religion is the greatest obstacle in the way of their improvement, and yet honesty compels me to make the assertion. The so-called "saints" on my plantation were invariably the worst people I had; more dishonest, disobedient, lazy, less interested in education, and in every other good thing, than those they facetiously termed "sinner men." I can think of no vice that was not practiced by those calling themselves Christians, to as great an extent as by sinners, and some vices to a greater extent. I tried to be charitable towards their religion, permitting them to hold their meetings at the close of ours, and I often remained to witness their unhallowed performances. But a regard for consistency, led me at length to withdraw all support from their religious mummery, for such, and nothing else, are these so-called religious services on the plantations. The name of Christ at first was seldom heard, except in some shocking misrepresentation of his nature and work. When I first came here, he was literally unknown to the most of them. Said a comparatively intelligent woman to me one day, "Mr. Stearns, I have been wanting to see you for some time, and find out about this Jesus you tell off. Will you come in and hear me tell what my ole massa used to tell me about him, and tell me whether it is true or not." Of course I complied with her request, and seating myself on one of her little wooden benches, I listened to her story. "He told me," said she, "that Jesus Christ once *got drunk*, and that one of his sons insulted him while he was drunk, but the other was good to him. After he came to his senses, he found out what had been done to him, and he cursed his bad son, and said his children should always be the slaves of his brother. He said we all came from the bad son, and they all from the good one, and that was the reason why we were their slaves. Now, Mr. Stearns, you know whedder this is true or not: please tell me." Of course I denounced it all as a lie, and she was highly delighted to learn "that Jesus was no such man as ole massa said he was."

The original of this story will be at once perceived. How could they reverence such a Jesus? Nearly all with whom I conversed, expressed great aversion to the

Bible, and were not at all disposed to learn to read its contents. They would appear quite interested while I read some story from a child's paper, and would answer questions respecting it, afterwards; but it was hard to gain their attention while reading the most interesting portions of the Bible. At length I ascertained the reason for this conduct, and found that they considered the Bible a slave-holding document, and therefore did not believe in its divinity. It became my duty, therefore, to dispel this illusion from their minds, and show them that the Bible did not uphold slavery. But to this day the impression remains among the ignorant ones, that "the book," as they term it, is in favor of human slavery. Is it any wonder that they reject a religion founded on such a book? Perhaps our "free religious" friends at the North, might see in this a favorable omen that they had a religion, which, ignoring Jesus and the Bible, was founded on three things: first, their own experience; second, the Spirit of God within them; and thirdly, various visions and revelations; but as the fruits of such a religion were so far removed from the lofty morality always advocated by our skeptical friends, they might not, after all, endorse these men as true disciples of the new school in religion. Said an old aunt, when remonstrated with for not attending our Sunday school, and learning to read the Bible, "I don't want any of your book-religion. I got my religion from God in de wilderness," This same aunt, and all her family, were the veriest thieves upon our place, and she herself was once detected in the act of feloniously abstracting a quantity of sweet potato plants from our garden.

Their common method of expressing contempt for Christ's teachings, was to call them "book religion."

Even the very children would tell my little girl, that the Bible was only an old package of papers tied up together, and of "no account." Sometimes, after we had been here a good while, an animated discussion would arise on the comparative merits of the Bible and "the Spirit within;" a portion contending that the Bible was superior to the Spirit, while others as stoutly asserted, that their "own hearts" were mostly to be relied upon. In proportion to the ignorance of the disputant, he would contend for the superiority of "the spirit within," to the written word. It was in vain they were told, that there could be no conflict between the teachings of the Spirit now, and those recorded in the Bible. The former they knew about, while of the latter they had no knowledge. Their overweening self-esteem, is never more apparent than in their religious faith. What they had experienced they knew to be true, and no power on earth could possibly shake this faith.

Quite an animated discussion on this point once arose, between several of the blacks, in one of our meetings. The disputants were equally matched as to numbers, there being two on each side. The point in debate was, "whether the Bible came from God or not." Two of the disputants were prominent church members, one of them named David, being the spiritual shepherd of the black flock on my plantation. The other two were those denominated by the religious ones, "sinner-men." The two religious ones were wholly uneducated, while the "sinner-men" were among our very best scholars, and were models of good behavior in other respects. Now, reader, on which side of this important question do you suppose these conflicting parties were arrayed? "Tell it not in Gath, publish it not in the streets of Askelon," that the "sinner-men" were eloquent in the defence of the Bible, while the "saints" were as loud in its condemnation. The eloquence of the sinners seemed likely, however, to carry the day, when David arose and denied their right to speak at all on the subject, saying, "dem ar sinner-men, Mr. Stearns, hab no rights at all in dis yer concussion. I protesh agin dem sinners being 'lowed to teach we who are de saints of de living God." Whatever might be said of the truth of David's theology, he had evidently learned from some source, the power of the modern gag-law, and failing to reply to his opponents logic, he resorted to the almost universal weapon of errorists, and attempted to *crush* out the truth. But as I had learned from the Bible itself, that "where the Spirit of the Lord is, there is *liberty*," I objected to his course, and declared that my meetings should always be free to all classes. David, foiled in this attempt to gag his adversaries, all at once arose, as if under the influence of some powerful inspiration of the Spirit, and advancing to the table, on which were lying the Bible and two hymn-books, he seized them in his hands, and holding them up before the excited audience, he exclaimed, at the top of his by no means diminutive voice, "Now here is tree books, all de wich ye say comes from de Almighty;" and growing warm with the brilliancy of the idea, he dashed them down with tremendous force upon the quivering table, and yelled out, "and yet ebery one ob dem is 'tirely different from de ober. Can de holy God write all dese tree books, and dey all so different from de obers?" Saying this, he dropped into his seat, the perspiration standing in big drops upon his dusky forehead, for it was on a warm Summer day. His opponents, not having advocated the divinity of the hymn-books, of course failed to be convinced by his extraordinary eloquence. David himself felt quite crest-fallen, when he was quietly informed that his formidable argument was based on an entirely wrong premise, no one advocating such an idea. I am not able to state the effect of this array of words upon the minds of the auditors; but all could see that David had the worst end of the dispute.

An intelligent Southern gentleman told me not long since, that he thought that nine-tenths of the plantation hands were disbelievers in the Bible. Some of them, however, are now quite anxious to be able to read the Bible, and even David, not long since, applied to me for a copy of the Bible. Thus has the pro-slavery portion of the church of America, in its endeavors to uphold Slavery by the Bible, destroyed the faith of millions of poor creatures in its divinity, while it accused of "infidelity" those who strove to defend the Bible against the worst possible of accusations. It is hard to account for the astonishing ignorance of these people, in reference to Jesus, for many of them had been in constant attendance upon the preaching of their white brethren. Can it be that in these Southern churches, Jesus was as effectually ignored in name, as his precepts were in practice? At one time, in quite a large audience, I asked, "Who was Jesus Christ?" Not one could tell except a preacher, named Brannon, who hesitatingly enquired if he "was not the king of the Jews?" No other one seemed to have the least idea of him, notwithstanding his name had been often mentioned in their hearing, we of course taking it for granted that they were familiar with the whole story of his life and death. But they did not know anything about him, only that he once lived, and in some way was the benefactor of their masters. If I might hazard an opinion upon the subject, it would be that they supposed he was some sort of an adjunct to their masters, in holding them in Slavery, and that therefore the less they had to do with him, the better. How dreadful that the glorious moral light of the Universe, should be so cruelly misrepresented to them! And how could they be righteous, when the main sinews of the world's spiritual strength, were thus ruthlessly cut away from their diseased souls? As well might we expect a star-gazer to behold the rings of Saturn without a powerful telescope, as these imbruted ones to "see God," and become true men and women, without "the light of the knowledge of the glory of God in the face of Jesus Christ." If God has chosen to reveal himself through his Son, can these freedmen know God, except through him who, when praying for his disciples, so pathetically declares, "O righteous Father, the *world* hath not known thee, but *I* have known thee, and I have declared unto them *thy* name, and the glory which thou gavest me, I have *given them*." But it is not my purpose now to describe my own theology, but that of these poor benighted and ignorant religionists.

While I endeavored to describe the life of Christ, and his death on the cross, they listened as to an entirely new story. None of them knew whether he lived fifty or a hundred years ago, or in what country he lived, or what became of him after his death. Of the manner of his death upon the cross, they were totally ignorant. They were alike ignorant of all biblical knowledge. They had never heard of Adam, Eve, Cain or Abel, Abraham, Moses, Joshua, Samuel, or any of the Bible worthies, except Daniel, of whose dwelling in the lion's den they had an indistinct idea. Some of them had heard of the Virgin Mary, even of those who had never heard of Jesus. I once questioned a girl whose father was a religious exhortor, about Jesus, and she replied, "I never hearn tell on him afore. Did he live in Gorgy?" She would sing a song, however, having these words in it, "May I die like the Virgin Mary." I asked her what she meant by that, and she said, "Why, she died for de world, didn't she?" and on again being questioned as to her meaning, she replied, with great animation. "Why, de Virgin Mary did die for de sins of de world, didn't she?" On the whole, I think the Virgin Mary had made more sincere believers in her power than Christ had, and yet there were no Catholics in the neighborhood.

One little boy said "he had hearn tell of Jesus, but he did not know who or what he was." Others of the children were confident they knew who Jesus was, and on being asked to tell who he was, they replied, with great confidence, "He is the brother of Washington." One day a lad about fourteen years old, from an adjoining county, came to my house, to see if I had any clothing for him. He seemed the very embodiment of shyness and fear, and if I attempted to look him in the face, he would at once thrust his head away, and hide it behind the form of some other person, and then cast a sidelong glance out of one corner of his eyes, to see if I was noticing him. After asking him various questions about the people where he lived, and his replying "Some said dat Slavery be done gone, but some say we be still slaves," I ventured to say to him, "Well, my little lad, can you tell me who Jesus Christ is?" If I had asked a Northern Sunday school scholar who

"Vertumnurs" was, they would have been no more surprised than he was. "Wat you say, massa? what be his name?" said he. "*Jesus Christ*," I replied, as distinctly as possible. He scratched his head, looked puzzled, but at length replied, "Dunno, massa; neber hearn ob him." "Don't you know who Jesus Christ, who died for you, is?' said I. Then, as if some new light had burst upon his mind, but still he was not quite certain about it, he exclaimed, with brightened eyes, "O yes, hese *old Mose*, ant he?" accompanying the remark with an inquiring look. I at first supposed that by "old Mose" he meant the Moses of the Bible; but on sounding the depths of his theological knowledge still further, I was somewhat surprised to learn that "old Mose" was a colored preacher of some celebrity, who died not many years ago.

I once asked a little boy, who said he attended a Sunday school in town, and "learned the catechism," who was the first man? "God," he replied; and "who the first woman?" I enquired, "Adam," said he; and so I concluded our negroes were not the only ignorant ones in the world. At other times grown up girls, living within a few miles of us, could not tell who made the world. We found on our place two old women, who did not know there was a God, but both of them have since that time, professed to become followers of Jesus.

But the absence of religious knowledge would not seem so tremendous an evil, if their religion produced any good fruits whatever. It is here that its baneful character is most apparent. With the most high-sounding professions of religion on their part, open immorality is unblushingly practiced. Stealing, a vice not considered elsewhere consistent with a respectable standing in society, among them, is no barrier to the highest religious life. Said a woman, who was remonstrated with for stealing a goose, and told she could not be a Christian and steal, "La me! dus yer think I'se gwine to gib up my Jesus for an old goose?" and she held on to her religion, as if she had done nothing inconsistent with its claims.

Once on visiting a friend's plantation I enquired for a man by the name of Jim, who was a preacher, but usually absented himself from the religious services we occasionally held on the place; because I said so much about lying and stealing as he said. I was told he was in jail. "In jail!" said I with great surprise. "Jim the preacher in jail, what can that be for?" "O nothing," said Thomas, my informer, "he only jus stole a few turkies, and den he sell 'em, and got cotched," and he added, "I went to see him de other day, and he tells me "you jus tell dem darkies as blongs to my church, not to be down-hearted, for de Lord will bring me one day to be wid um agin, an dey must not forgit to pray for me." It never seemed to occur to him, that he had committed an offense inconsistent with *his* religion, and I do not know as he had; as I have never known of a thief being disciplined in this region by his colored brethren. I am sure that when I came here, they did not regard stealing as a sin, certainly not as a "mortal one." And even now, I cannot positively say that they look upon it as a sin, which a christian will never commit. I am in hopes that they feel now that they *ought not* to steal, just as all church members own that they should never get angry; but I hardly think that they will admit that the sin of stealing will exclude them from heaven. Indeed some of them will own that under certain circumstances they *would* steal. I have known whole platoons to arise, and leave their seats and not return to the place of worship, when stealing was touched upon in the mildest manner. And it is a common remark among them, "we would go and hear Mr. S. preach much oftener, if he would leave off preaching against lying and stealing, and preach the gospel." Many laughable scenes have occurred in connection with this strange hallucination of theirs, respecting this vice.

At one time, I gave notice that on the following Sunday, I would deliver an address especially on stealing, and show them why it was wrong. When Sunday came, a goodly number assembled from other plantations, they not knowing the subject of the discourse; but not a soul of the adults on my place, numbering about forty, made their appearance, until very near the close of the sermon, and remarks were being made about God, and the pain it caused him for his creatures to steal. They were always ready to hear about God, and living with him in heaven, but seldom wished to hear of their duties to each other. After the close of the meeting, I was waited upon at my house by a deputation of the brethren, who gravely informed me that my sermon had given great offense, and the people were determined to abandon the Sunday school and meeting, if I persisted in talking about such worldly matters. When I informed them that I could not desist from denouncing the sins they were guilty of, one of them persuasively said, "Now Mr. S., if you must talk about stealing, why not call us together on Monday and tell us about it, and let us have a good heavenly time on Sunday, in worshipping the God we all love so much." At these words I could hardly keep from bursting into a loud laugh, the whole thing seemed so supremely ridiculous, and withal it so forcibly reminded me of similar deputations waiting upon Northern ministers, in the good old days of slavery; and threatening to desert them if they continued to preach against slavery on Sunday. I have now in my mind, the pastor of one of the finest churches in one of New England's most beautiful towns, who at one time preached a tremendous sermon against slavery, when he was waited upon the next day by one of the wealthiest of his flock, who informed him, that he would withdraw from the church, unless he would promise to preach no more Anti-Slavery sermons. The residents of that town will remember, whether the pastor complied with such solicitation, or manfully refused to sell his soul for a "mess of pottage."

While writing these lines, one of my men, and a member of the colored peoples' church, is lying in jail for stealing from a neighboring plantation, he having been in the habit of stealing from me very frequently. Only a few nights before this last theft, he came to me for the key of the meeting-house, so that they could hold a prayer-meeting. Sunday is a favorite day for their indulgence in this unhallowed pastime, as it affords a grand opportunity for the worst ones to leave the house of worship, and prowl around the premises in quest of booty, while the bulk of the worshippers are engaged in a far more ennobling employment. This the blacks acknowledge themselves to be true, saying, they dare not all leave their houses on such occasions, but some one must stay at home to guard against thieves.

But stealing is by no means the only crime committed by the brethren. It would be far easier to enumerate the crimes of which they are not guilty, than those of which they are, for the number of the former, would be very small indeed. But this whole subject is so exceedingly distasteful to me, that I am almost inclined to pursue it no farther. It is not pleasant to record these things; I had much rather tell of the good deeds of my proteges, than of their evil ones; and it would reflect far more credit on my own labors, to be able to say, that these depraved ones were patterns of morality; but would it be right to conceal the truth, in a book professing entire impartiality in its details? Hereafter it will fall to my lot to tell of the "outrages of the whites," shall I not also tell of those of the blacks?

Lying is a vice so inherent in their nature, that it is questionable with me, whether they know the difference between a lie and the truth. I do not think they consider it at all sinful to lie, whenever a lie would be beneficial to them; and such lies as they will tell, none but "the father of lies" can equal them! An instance of this unblushing falsehood, has lately occurred; a gentleman had made a written contract with one of his former hands, to let him have a parcel of land, the use of a dwelling house, and a mule, for which, this mendacious fellow, was to pay him one hundred and seventy-five dollars, out of his first cotton; and in order to render himself secure, he had taken a lien on the man's crop, according to the common custom here. What was his astonishment, when pay-day came around, and the cotton was sent to market, to hear the black man swear that he had never signed the lien, that the man read another paper to him, and then got him to sign this one instead. But this lying was too transparent to succeed, for several persons had seen him sign it, after it had been read to him twice, and minutely explained, and he afterwards owned that such was the case; and he was one of the most *flaming professors of religion in this vicinity.*

Their chief fault of an immoral nature, is an utter, and perfectly reckless *disregard of their word and promise*, in all of the relations of life. No promise that they may make, is considered sacred by them. Said a man once to me, when I remonstrated with him, on the sinfulness of violating an agreement he had made to hire some land of another person, "O, Mr. So-and-so, offered me some land cheaper;" and this seemed sufficient justification for a violation of a positive contract. A man will agree to do a piece of work for you, at a stipulated price, and for a stipulated kind of pay; perhaps after a few days, he will come and tell you he has changed his mind, and concluded not to do as he agreed, and this with all the "sang-froid" imaginable; or, what is altogether more likely, he will not come to you for a long time, and perhaps never again, leaving you in utter ignorauce, as to his intention about doing the work at all.

One of the worst instances of this violation of an agreement has recently occurred, and as illustrative of what I have stated, I will give the particulars of the case. It will be borne in mind, that I am now describing the religious condition of these people. We have on our place, a stout, full-blooded negro, named Willis Jackson. He is of medium height, and about twenty-two years of age. Like most of the blacks on my place, he is a Christian; that is, in his own opinion. Previous to his supposed conversion, he was extremely eager to learn to read, and was a constant attendant upon our Sunday School. After he had "done, *got through* in religion, (their term for conversion,) he grew quite remiss for a while in his studies; but as the novelty of his religion wore away, he again became constant at our exercises; and sometimes severely reprimanded the children, for their inattention, and want of interest in their lessons. He seemed cut out for a reformer, and was always "hauling over the coals" some one for his or her neglect of duty. He was extremely loud in his professions of devotion to my interests, and often entertained me with serious tales of the depredations committed by every one else on my property; always winding up his story, by saying, in a very pathetic manner, "O, Mr. Stearns, it's a perfect shame these niggers treat you as they do. If it want for me, you'd have nothing left; but I allers stands up for you, because you's a Yankee, and has done so much for my race." He seemed so honest in these professions, that we all looked upon him as our best friend among the colored people, and one on whom we could rely in any emergency. It is true, that many little things on his part often occurred, that looked rather shaky, but some how or other, we always managed to find an excuse for him, "because it was Willis." If we wanted any little chores done, that belonged to no one in particular, we instinctively called upon Willis, who was generally very good natured, and quite ready to oblige us. He and his family, however, were always taxing our limited means, by begging and borrowing trifling articles of food and medicine, and implements of labor; but no matter how great our hurry, it was for Willis, and we always left off our work, and waited on him. In short, Willis was the pet negro of our plantation, and in consequence looked upon with disfavor and jealousy by others. Sometimes an open fight took place between them, which Willis always assured us, was on account of his zeal for our interests. Like the rest of his race, Willis was possessed of an an over-powering self-esteem, which was augmented by our confidence in him. He also seemed to regard himself as a special favorite with the Almighty. It was his custom, in every trivial circumstance, to allude to God, and to express his deep devotion to his as well as to our interests. In short, he was pre-eminently the pious one on our place. Once, when he had neglected an important trust confided to him, in reference to the other hands, and in consequence it was dangerous drawing water from our well; I asked him how he expected to get water for his own family, and he replied, "O, I trust in God that he will supply us." At another time, when my boy remonstrated with him for neglecting to feed a mule in his charge, he said, "You shouldn't be so anxious about that mule, you should trust it all in God's hand, and have more faith in him." I have said that he was the very embodiment of self-esteem. It was laughable to see him strutting across our yard, with his head thrown back, so that its top would be on a straight line with his heels. His blue military coat, with its brilliant brass buttons, would then be buttoned to his chin. I do not know that he had ever heard of Alexander Selkirk, but I often imagined I could hear him complacently utter the memorable words that fell from Crusoe's lips, "I am monarch of all I survey." And this was the more apparent, after I rented him a choice piece of land, adjacent to my dwelling, in addition to his own selected plat elsewhere. And now comes the *denouement* of all this pretence on his part. Just a week ago to-day, it accidently came to my knowledge that in spite of all his professions of piety, and of superior regard to my interests, he was intending to take his cotton into town, and sell it, and appropriate the money to his own purposes. The year before, he and some others had failed to keep their agreement, in reference to paying a certain sum on their land, and I had been subjected to great inconvenience and expense, in consequence; and I early in the season determined to guard against a similar catastrophe this year. Accordingly I made them give me a written lien on all their crops, for the payment of a specified sum, which lien rendered it obligatory on their part, to carry their cotton to a particular ware-house in Augusta, as soon as it was ginned, and there leave it until its proceeds were sufficient to liquidate my claim upon them. This lien was read to him twice, and particularly explained, and then signed by him, in the presence of several witnesses. He was told at the time, that if he sold it, after having signed this lien, he rendered himself liable to imprisonment, for so doing. During the whole of the Summer, he had expressed his determination to pay me the whole sum, even if he had no cotton left afterwards; and, considering his great professions, he was the very last man on my place whom I could have suspected of trying to forfeit his word.

Having ascertained his purpose, I was on hand early on the morning of the day on which he was to start; and when he saw that I was about to interfere in his nefarious design, he threw off all disguise, and boldly declared with oaths, that he would never take his cotton as he had agreed. Of course I was obliged to prohibit the cotton from leaving, under such circumstances. A day or two afterwards, it was again placed on our wagon, by his orders, and suddenly I appeared and took my seat on the wagon, when he again swore it should not go to town, unless he could go with it, alone. But, weary with the fatiguing contest, I at length consented to his carrying it to town alone, and on the preceding night, sent my boy into town, to inform the cotton-factors of the state of affairs. He carried the cotton to the place agreed upon, contrary to his solemn oaths, but succeeded in inducing the dealers to pay him one half of the value of the cotton, he representing to them that even then, he would have enough more cotton to pay the whole of my demand. With the fifty dollars thus received, he supplied himself and family with a great variety of necessaries and luxuries, among the latter of which, were forty-five sticks of candy. This was a severe blow to me, as the example, if followed, would jeopardize all my arrangements for supplying the blacks with land; and in order to prevent others from following his bad example, with the advice of a lawyer employed by my Boston friends, to look after their interests in these matters, I despatched a messenger for the sheriff of the county; who soon adjusted matters so that Willis could sequester no more of the funds he had agreed to put in my possession. To the credit of the remainder of the colored people, I will add, that Willis found no justifiers of his course, except in his own family, and happily for us, no imitators of his dangerous example. I must also add, that his brethren in the church, actually "set him back," as they termed it, one of the most encouraging signs I have seen, of a reformation in their religious ideas. This "setting back" in the church is considered an everlasting disgrace, and poor Willis, when he afterwards walked across the yard, held his head at quite a different angle from his heels, from the former one. But the effect of this delinquency upon all of us, was terrible. It kept us in a continual state of anxiety, during the remainder of the cotton season, for if Willis, our "well-beloved disciple," had served us so, there was no telling what the others might feel justified in doing.

But a violation of their agreements is not the only sin they "roll as a sweet morsel under their tongues." In every department of life they fail to apply the sublime principles of the christian religion to their conduct. Indeed, they do not seem to comprehend the idea that religion imposes upon them any duties in reference to others, and especially towards their employers. At the beginning of each year, our hands were required to sign a contract, agreeing to perform certain specified duties, in return for which we agree to pay them a certain sum of money. But it was almost impossible to make even the most pious ones realize that after having signed this contract, they were bound to keep it sacredly, only so far as it suited them so to do; and any attempt on our part to enforce its provisions, was pronounced by them the acme of oppression, as worse than the "rebs" served them. In lieu of other penalties, we relied on fines for non-performance of duties, all of which were specified beforehand in the contract, so that there could be no misunderstanding in the matter. These fines were trivial, and some of them were as follows, "for profane swearing, twenty-five cents," "abuse of animals in their charge, twenty-five cents;" "beating one's wife, fifty cents;" "refusal to work, fifty cents;" stealing, 5,00;" and so on; but not one of them was ever paid without a solemn protest at its injustice. If they had agreed to obey *all* of our orders with alacrity, and never to be saucy or impudent to their employers; still they could not comprehend why they should obey an order they did not like, or why refrain from insulting us when so prompted. It was all oppression on our part, whenever we attempted to enforce obedience, and God knows we were lenient enough towards them. One year the colored preacher, in other respects a noble fellow, was the worst person on the place to obey our orders. He paid no attention whatever to our wishes, expressed or implied, unless the notion suited him. His idea was that he was to be the judge of the propriety of every order, and if it did not seem to him a reasonable one, he would disregard it entirely. Of course, a planter's life must be a very delightful one under such circumstances.

But if half a dozen of them refused to obey us, we were powerless and had to submit. We could only discharge them, and that would leave us without hands. It was this terrific state of affairs that induced all the planters at first to hail with delight the formation of the Ku-Klux order, promising as it did, to rectify all these abuses, as well as to promote the political welfare of the country. Of course all of this was only a pretext on the part of the Ku-Klux, but it was by *pretending* to aid the planters in the laudable object of raising good crops and thus benefiting the whole country, that this nefarious "order" obtained so strong a foothold in the South, that it could not be rooted out; except by the military power of the United States government.

But the point now under consideration is, the failure of the black peoples' religion to make them obedient laborers. It must be continually borne in mind, in this portion of our work, that the object aimed at is simply to show the utter falsity of the pretentions of the blacks to be in possession of the religion taught by our Lord and Saviour Jesus Christ. Of course they were religious, as the Jews, Mohammedans and Pagans were religious, but in no particular was their religion a counterpart of that religion whose fruits of holiness are declared by its founder to be the only test of its genuineness. The question may be asked, why am I so anxious to prove this point? If the religion of the blacks *is* a spurious one, why not leave them in the enjoyment of it so long as it suits their capacity. My answer is, that first and foremost in the regeneration of any nation or people, must their religious institutions be moulded into the forms of morality, or else it is in vain to preach morality to the *people*. If the saints of a nation can be immoral, of course its sinners will be doubly so, or at least they will never be any better than the sanctified ones are. In proof of this assertion you have only to look at the character of all nations where an immoral religion prevails. Therefore, if you would reform the freedmen of the South, you must commence with their religion, and no efforts corresponding with the mighty interests at stake, will ever be put forth to accomplish this task, until the Northern people are made fully acquainted with the hideous evil here exposed. Northern teachers and laborers have an immense task before them; and it is my solemn conviction, that unless it is resolutely undertaken, twenty-five years from to-day will find the schools and all Northern appliances for the regeneration of the freedmen, swamped and swept entirely out of sight, by the fearful waves of social vice engendered and taught by the *religion* of the *Southern negroes*. Perhaps I am alone in uttering this warning voice. If so, it cannot be helped, the necessity is all the greater for others to arouse themselves to the task of coping with this mighty engine of immorality, and sweeping it from existence.

At one time we had a stout young girl to work for us named Priscilla. Among other of her shortcomings, was the inconvenient one to us, of staying about an hour, whenever she went to the quarters on an errand. One day, Aunt Rinah, a great saint among us, and quite an intelligent woman, came in and said to me, "Bless the Lord, brother Stearns, the Lord has given us another soul." "Who is that?" said I, in an incredulous tone, for I was beginning to look with suspicion on all new converts to their religion. "O, it's Priscilla!" said she; "she's done got-through, praise the Lord." I expressed my doubts of Priscilla's piety, when Annt Rinah exclaimed sorrowfully, "You mustn't doubt her, Mr. Stearns, as she has told us her *experience*, and we were bound to receive her." We called Priscilla, and she related her experience as follows: "I saw de old ship Zion, with my name written on it in great big letters, and Jesus Christ hanging on de cross just over de ship. He said, 'Priscilla, get aboard.' I asked him how to do that? He said, 'go to Aunt Rinah, and Aunt Susan, and they will tell you.' I did as he said, and got aboard, and den the old ship began to sail, and sailed on, till it got right over hell, and then it went straight on from dere, to de heavenly land, and I found mesel in heaven." I asked how the inhabitants of hell looked, and she replied, "They were barefoot, had dirty faces, dirty and ragged clothes, and hair hanging about their ears, just like some of the people in de quarters, only ten times worser." She was silent as to the flames of hell, and I did not question her any more as to her vision. But I said to her, "Priscilla, did you know that your religion, if it is genuine, will make you a better girl, and cause you to do your work more faithfully?" "No, sir; will it?" said she, in a tone of surprise. "Did no one ever tell you," said I, "that religion will make you do more as we require of you?" "No, indeed," said she; "Mammy told me if I did not do as you wanted me, you would not keep me; but I never knew that religion had any thing to do with my work."

And this was no doubt the exact truth. Until we came there, no one had ever told them that Christianity would regulate their daily lives. With them, religion was, and is now, to a great extent, merely to pray, dance and sing, in their meetings. It may be added, that after Priscilla learned what was expected of her as a Christian, there was a change for the better in her deportment, until one day she had a quarrel with some one, and she was found "toting" about a big knife, with which she said she was going to stab the one who had quarrelled with her. But it is not in reference to conscientiousness alone, that their religion is at fault. It is equally so as far as benevolence is concerned. It seems as if they could not be made to comprehend the nature of benevolence. While they are tolerably kind towards their own "kin-folks," who are needy, no argument can convince them of their duty to aid those who are not their relatives. When appealed to, to do certain things for the sake of their race, such an appeal seldom moves them at all. One of their deacons, who in the main was quite a conscientious man, and I do not think a thief, was asked to contribute a small sum to establish a free school, but he declined to do any more than to pay for his own children; and he could not to be convinced that those who had money, ought to do something towards establishing a school, that should be free to all. Those who had learned to read a little, were very unwilling to spend the time on Sunday, in teaching those who could not read at all; but after spending a few moments in that way, would abruptly leave their class, and take a book and go to studying themselves. On this account it was exceedingly difficult to find teachers, for all who came to our Sunday school, and each one would complain if he did not receive his share of attention from the Superintendent. As there were but few white teachers, many of the scholars, on account of this lack of benevolence, had to go untaught. There was only one really benevolent black person on our place, and she was nearly worn out with calls from her neighbors. It was always extremely difficult to get assistance from them, when any of our own family was sick, unless they were certain of being rewarded for their services. If I was in danger from the rebels, they would rush to my protection, but that was because it was for their interest that I should live. I am sorry to say that instead of being ready to aid us in sickness, as has been already stated, they took that occasion to increase their depredations on our property. In one instance, a watcher drank the contents of a small bottle of French brandy, and replaced them with camphor from another bottle. There was one woman who was usually ready to watch with the sick, but when she was taken sick herself not a soul would come and watch with her, and her own son, after a hard day's labor, was compelled to sit up all night with his aged mother. As far as my observation extends, selfishness, thorough and entire, is one of their ruling traits. The great majority of them seem almost, if not quite insensible to the claims of gratitude. They seemed to receive all of our favors as a matter of course, and to consider that for some reason or other they merited them. I speak of course only of those who came under my observation, and of those there were but few exceptions to this rule.

But I do not think they are naturally as grateful for favors as the Northern Irish are, at least, they fall far behind that class in their expressions of gratitude. Neither do they express much gratitude for the precious boon of freedom, although they profess to prize it so highly. But perhaps this is owing to the fact, that except in the matter of their religion, they are not a demonstrative race in any respect. Under the influence of their religion, they become excited, but seldom under any other influence.

Their religious exercises are of a novel character, and I will endeavor to describe them briefly. At about nine o'clock in the evening, they collect together, and generally sing a few hymns worn threadbare by oft repetition while the tardy ones are entering. Their singing is limited to a very small number of hymns, which are generally of a solemn nature, quite frequently funeral ones; and these are usually sung to a melancholy tune. It is seldom you hear in their meetings, (I am speaking now of those I have attended only) the notes of joy and rejoicing so common in Northern Methodist prayer-meetings.* After all have assembled, the preacher in charge, a man if possible more ignorant than the remainder,

---

* Perhaps I ought to state that the blacks on our place, and in our neighborhood were nearly all Baptists, and the whites also.

arises and gives out another "hime," as it is termed by them, which is sung in a like melancholy manner with the former ones. He then attempts to talk to them, but in these plantation meetings, it would puzzle a spectator to comprehend the meaning of a single sentence uttered, although doubtless they all have a meaning to the initiated. Often the preacher, who is usually one of the plantation hands, becomes very much excited, foams at the mouth, and stamps furiously on the floor, frequently striking the floor vehemently with the legs of the chair, behind which he attempts to stand, so that your anxiety is aroused for the safety of both floor and chair. Some of them make somewhat sensible remarks founded on what they have heard others say, but I have heard them speak, when nôt one intelligent sentence was uttered through the whole of the discourse.

After the exhortation, the same brother gives out another "hime," which is sung with a little more animation, and then he leads in prayer; and such praying I am sure was never heard elsewhere than in a negro prayer-meeting. The prayer is generally of great length, and full of grandiloquent expressions, borrowed from some white brother, or more talented colored one, strung together, utterly regardless of their meaning, and repeated over and over again, an innumerable number of times, and the whole uttered in a tone designed doubtless to imitate Gabriel, in the sounding of his resurrection trumpet, and which is quite sure to arouse every tired sleeper on the plantation. This prayer, loud as it is, is sometimes half drowned by the utterances and groanings of others, so that sometimes it is almost impossible to tell who, in reality, is praying. Their meetings are usually continued until midnight, and quite

often until *the break of day*, for each brother having a "call to preach," is obliged to "clear his skirts of the blood of his hearers," at every meeting he attends, and as nearly every brother has this call, it is impossible for their meetings to be of much less duration. Just before they break up, when "the spirit is upon them," as they term it, they engage in a kind of Shaker dance, which they term singularly enough, *shouting*. They seldom shout aloud, "glory to God," as we often hear in religious meetings elsewhere. I do not know as I can describe this dance so as to be intelligent to my readers, but I will do my best. A ring of singers is formed in an open space in the room, and they, without holding on to each others' hands, walk slowly around and around in a circle, the back of the foremost one coming close to the front side of the succeeding brother or sister. They then utter a kind of melodious chant, which gradually increases in strength, and in noise, until it fairly shakes the house, and it can be heard for a long distance. This chant is responded to at intervals, by a grand chorus, composed of all the audience, for they are all singers, which response is almost invariably the same. The dancers usually bend their bodies into an angle of about forty-five degrees, and thus bent, march around, accompanying their steps, every second or so, with a quick, jerking motion, or jump, which I can compare to nothing else than the brisk jumping of a frog, only this is very regular, and the motion is designed to keep time with their voices, which it comes as near doing as the firing of the cannon came near keeping time with the notes of the grand organ in that glorious carnival of music, the monster jubilee of 1869, in Boston, Mass. The performers also accompany the jerking of their bodies with a corresponding clapping of their hands, and motion of their arms. The songs are mere repetitions of some meaningless sentences, not to be found in any hymn-book in creation, but handed down by tradition from their ancestors, of whose ceremonies in their native lands, these gyrations are supposed to be an imitation. Occasionally, one of the most zealous of the sisters, throws herself up so as to nearly touch the ceiling over their heads, and then falls down helplessly into the eager arms of some stout brother, who springs forward with alacrity to receive her. I know of nothing similar to this dancing or shouting, in the religious exercises of any other class of people. It is entirely unknown among the white Christians here. One of the leading members of a white church near here, told me the other day, that he had never witnessed it until recently, and he was so shocked with its seeming indecorousness, that he had refused to aid the blacks in building a church, unless they would agree to dispense with these performances. Many of the intelligent blacks here, and in Augusta, are also opposed to them, as they are to this whole system of "all night" meetings. A Northern gentleman, who has spent two years upon the coast of Africa, after witnessing these exercises, told me they were almost precisely like those of the heathen blacks in Africa, only that the latter did not allude to the one God of the Christians. Another Northern gentleman, who had visited the Fejee Islands, told me that these services resembled, very nearly, those of the cannibal-worshippers on those ill-fated Islands, only that ours were not followed by a feast on human flesh, as he had witnessed in the case of the islands mentioned.

I have often heard the blacks relate their religious experience, and seldom have noticed a detail of such mental exercises, as are common at the North, with converted persons. There is seldom even a conviction of sin, or deep sense of having wronged a holy God, and kind and loving Father, or heartfelt sorrow for such acts; and especially is there but seldom an account of an entire consecration of the whole being to God, and perfect submission to his will; and as for faith in Christ, that is reduced merely to some vision of Jesus, hanging on the cross, or otherwise, and seldom has any thing to do with that trust in him to purify the soul from sin, that was the burden of the preaching of the apostles. I once heard a woman testify, that she saw Jesus on the cross, and felt his blood trickle down her person, from her head to her feet. This was considered a remarkable *experience*, and the sister was received into the church by acclamation. Many of them insist upon it that Jesus is still hanging on the cross, giving as a reason for this belief, that they have thus seen him in their visions of him.

But in spite of this absence of a genuine religious experience, no people on earth believe more fully in the old-fashioned Methodist doctrine of "*full assurance*," although their faith, unlike that of the early Methodists, is totally disconnected with its correlative of works. It matters not what sin they may be guilty of, their confidence in their acceptance with God is unshaken. With most people, being a Christian includes so much, that the purest of beings sometimes fear that they are not wholly right; but with these blacks, "not a wave of trouble rolls across their peaceful breasts." I have never seen one yet, professing to be a Christian, who was troubled with any doubts upon the subject of his acceptance with

God. On some accounts, such a state of mind seems desirable. On others, it cannot be considered so great a blessing. But it presents a somewhat ludicrous aspect, to one who believes in the apostolic injunction, to "give all diligence to make your calling and election sure," and "let him that *thinketh* he standeth, take heed lest he fall."

I have already stated, that some of the religious ones manifested far less interest in education, than the unconverted ones. Brannon, one of the preachers, was an exception to this rule, he always being in his place in the Sunday school, and using all of his pastoral influence in favor of education; but David, his successor, exercised all of his powers in exactly the opposite direction, seldom attending school himself, and seizing every opportunity to oppose our efforts in that direction, declaring that *he* knew enough already, and did not want to learn any more. I am informed by others, in other localities, that they often meet with the same kind of opposition. If the teachers would inculcate the religion of the blacks, perhaps this opposition would cease; but as education almost invariably tends to lessen the number of their hearers, their opposition to it, is not so surprising. I have known other instances than that of Willis, where persons recently converted lost all their interest in education, and where they did not like him, ever regain that interest; which I account for, on the ground of their dwarfed intellects, not being able to drink in but one idea at a time.

Before closing this long dissertation upon the religion of the blacks, I ought in justice to state, that in one particular they do seem to have imbibed a portion of the teachings of Jesus. Said I once to a large congregation, to whom I had endeavored to depict the intimate connection of those two great truths of Christianity, viz., love to God, and love to man, "how do you feel towards your masters who have injured you so much?" Instantly a whole row of aged women, seated just before me, responded, "we forgive them, we love them;" and in this respect, it is but fair to say they greatly excel their white brethren, from whose hearts the spirit of love seems to have entirely fled. I have also occasionally listened, to as genuine and affecting religious experiences, as ever a mortal man could give, involving great perception of the holiest acts of a christian's life, and including obedience to the most exalted christian precepts, but this was in a church in Augusta, where a vast amount of intelligent preaching had been listened to by the converts; and where the church was presided over by such excellent men, as the Rev. Messrs. Watts and Jackson, the only colored pastors of Augusta, with whom I am acquainted. I have no reason to doubt that the same results have been witnessed elsewhere, from the preaching of educated and truly pious men; but these results are not witnessed where the preachers are as ignorant as the great mass of the plantation preachers.

It may be asked how could the ignorant blacks have these visions of Jesus, when so many of them had never heard of him? Of course those so utterly ignorant of him, could not have these visions. It was only the more advanced ones who had "heard of him by the hearing of the ear," that were so remarkably blessed as to be favored with these heavenly *visions*. Those who insisted that he was *now* hanging on the cross, were not the heathen ones we found on our first arrival; but those in whose ears had since been sounded the gospel trumpet "long and loud," calling on them to believe in Jesus, and flee to him for salvation.

A few remarks upon the white peoples' religion, and this almost interminable chapter will be brought to a close. I have said that the spirit of love to their enemies, seems to have entirely flown from the hearts of our white brethren. It is said, that during the war, a Methodist minister not many miles from here, prayed in church, that "they might ride in the blood of the Yankees up to their horses' bridles." In no one particular is the contrast between the Southern religion and that of Jesus Christ more striking, than in the universal spirit of hatred sanctioned by the former. On the occasion of the terrible Chicago fire, involving the loss of so many valuable ·lives, and the untold misery of so many multitudes of people, one of the churches of A—— was at one time nearly deprived of its female audience, because the clergyman was intending to lecture upon this great calamity. I am told by those who reside near there, that many expressions of joy were heard in that city, at this appalling disaster, which elsewhere awakened the most unbounded spmpathy, even in hearts of stone. One kind-hearted gentleman, undertook to raise money in behalf of the sufferers, and he had already obtained one princely donation of $1000 and several smaller ones, when he was informed that he would be *driven from the city*, unless he would abandon his heavenly task. Comment on such a satanic spirit is unnecessary.

Said a gentleman to me at one time, "O how I do *hate* the Northern people! I hate them with a perfect hatred; I detest them from the bottom of my soul."

"Not so fast, my good friend," said I to him; "the Southern people have many warm friends at the North.

Only a few years ago an attempt was made to burn a colored asylum with two hundred and forty inmates, by friends of the South in N. Y. city."

"O yes," said he, "I forgot that; yes there are some good people in the North, but the great majority, all the republicans at any rate, I hate with a perfect hatred."

"Well," said I, "then you do not believe in Christianity?"

"O yes," replied he with a smile, "I believe in Christianity. I *profess to be a Christian myself*, and I think I am one."

"What then do you do with that precept of Jesus to love your enemies," said I.

"O," said he quickly, "we have nothing to do with that command, *that was not given to us*."

Another gentlemen who assured me that he was as good a Christian as any about, said that if any one accused him of cowardice, he would *mash his head into a jelly*. Another pious professor refused to send medicine to a neighbor who was a republican, saying he would "see him and all the rest of the radicals in the bottom of hell first." Southern white christians, evidently no more think it a sin to hate their enemies, than the black christians think it is to steal. I will not say which of these two systems is the remotest from the teachings of Jesus, but I think neither of them is in very close proximity to that blessed code.

And now that I have alluded to the Southern white religion, I must be permitted to bear my unequivocal testimony against any attempt, on the part of Northern Christians, to unite the two systems, the Southern religion, and that of Jesus Christ. I am astounded at the remarks of a leading religious periodical of Boston, in 1867, addressed to the Southern churches of its peculiar faith: "We believe in your Christianity, and would gladly receive you to our embrace." If our religion countenances a religion of hellish hate, and one whose advocates do not pretend to have repented of the sin of holding men and women in bondage; but on the contrary, if it were possible would again enslave their fellow-men; can it be the religion of Him who came to "break every yoke, and let the oppressed go free?" Can Northen men and women, who come South ostensibly to teach Christianity, do anything for the furtherance of their noble mission, while they thus strike hands with murderers, and dealers in the "the bodies and souls of men?" Without wishing to be uncharitable, I cannot forbear adding, in the words of Holy writ: "Come out of her, my people, that ye be not partakers of her sins, and that ye receive not of her plagues." "My son, walk not thou in the way with them, refrain thy foot from their path," for "her house inclineth unto death, and her paths unto the dead; none that go unto return again, neither *take they hold of the paths of life.*"

CHAPTER XXXIV.

DOCTRINES PREACHED TO THE BLACKS BY THE AUTHOR.

It may be interesing to some of my readers to know what kind of doctrines I have preached to the blacks, in lieu of that false religion which I have so emphatically comdemned; so that they can judge whether my system is an improvement upon theirs. Perhaps if a different system had been proclaimed to them, better results would have followed. Let me then briefly state, the sum and substance of my preaching to them during my sojourn among them.

First, I have not dwelt upon the doctrine of eternal torment, choosing if possible to draw them to Christ by the cords of love, rather than to frighten them into a forced submission to his claims. As has been already hinted at, their own preachers dwelt upon this point *ad nauseam*. From the beginning to the end of their discourses, the flames of hell are pictured before their hearers, without much regard to commonly received ideas on that subject either. They hesitate not to adopt any version of this doctrine, that may seem to them calculated to influence their stolid flock; oftentimes minutely describing the operations of the devils, who, as they say, are sometimes engaged in pitching back into the flaming gulf, those who have been so fortunate as to partially escape therefrom ; and at others, busy with rakes in hauling coals over the prostrate forms of the damned. On the contrary, I have dwelt much upon the love of God, and have striven to represent God to them as a *father* and *friend* who loved them far more than the kindest parent loved his children, and was grieved beyond measure at their sinfulness. At first this seemed to touch a new chord in their dull hearts, but when it came to urging upon them an abandonment of all sin, because it was displeasing to him, another phase of the question was presented to them. It tickled their fancy to know that God loved them, but it did not seem to them to follow, that they ought to love him so fervently as not to sin against him. On the contrary they said, "If God loves us he will not deal harshly with us, if we do sin a little," thus "trampling under foot the blood of the son of God." Perceiving the tendency of their minds in this respect, I was forced to turn their attention to the consequences of sin, and to show them that, "the wages of sin is death," and that although God loved them, he would not and could not look with favor upon their evil conduct. I tried to point out the unchangeable nature of God's moral law, and to show that he could no more lessen the demands of that law to suit their sinful inclinations, than he could *change* the *laws of gravitation and cohesion*, to prevent injury to their violators. I endeavored to show them that God wished for their holiness because it would promote their highest happiness, and to point out that great law of the universe that sin always and forever produces misery, and that no sinner can ever be truly happy, in the very nature of the case. That on the contrary, holiness always and forever produces bliss, and that a holy person would inevitably be happy, let his outward condition be what it might. I showed them that it was not in the power of God to introduce them into heaven, unless they were holy, and that if he should do so, "heaven would be the severest part of hell" to them. Also, that in the very nature of the case, God *could not* smile upon them approvingly, only as their conduct was a close imitation of his own perfect example. This doctrine was exceedingly distasteful to them. Why sin should thus injure them they could not see. They relished the idea of *sinners* being burned in a fiery hell, for in some unexplained way they fancied they would themselves avoid this dreadful fate. But when the broad doctrine was proclaimed that *all* sinners would be punished, that tribulation and anguish "were to be visited" upon *every* soul of man that doeth evil, for there is no respect of persons with God; "that the wrath of God is revealed against *all* unrighteousness," and that there was no escape from this inevitable consequence of sin, except by an utter abandonment of all wrong doing, they neither could nor would receive any such severe doctrine. They said, "God is not like man, and he is not going to punish us for every little sin." I could not tell on what ground they expected exemption from hell, while those around them were doomed to roll in its flames. It was not on account of their superior exemption from sinful conduct, for they did not pretend to that; and it was not on account of Christ's atonement, for of that they knew nothing, and were entirely silent respecting it in their preaching; their religious faith being a curious compound of infidelity, orthodoxy and superstition, entirely unlike that of any other religious body, it has been my lot to be acquainted with. They rejected the Bible, yet believed in a literal heaven and hell. They knew but little of Jesus, and never dreamed that he was God, and yet they were great sticklers for "having the Spirit of God within them." They knew nothing of the orthodox doctrine of the atonement, and yet evidently relied on something besides their "good works" to save them; and as has been shown, they had some confidence in the Virgin Mary, and yet had never heard of the Catholics. They eschewed common dancing as a great sin, and yet practiced what they called the "holy dance for Jesus' sake."

How to proceed to thread my way through such a heterogeneous compound of contradictory doctrine, was not at first evident to me, and if the conclusion I came to, as to the best way to extricate them from this labyrinth of error, does not commend itself to the reader as the best one, may I ask him to suppress his judgment in my case, until he has been placed in similar circumstances. I realized the responsibility of my situation, and earnestly prayed to the "Father of light," for guidance in my difficult task of removing error, and enforcing truth. Perhaps I erred; but if so, I pursued the course my reason, enlightened as I trust by God's spirit, led me to adopt. My first duty was, respecting Jesus, of whom as I have stated, they were wholly ignorant. I knew of no better course to pursue, than to confine myself to the written declarations of Scripture upon this point, avoiding the language of the schoolmen, on both sides of this great controversy respecting the name of Jesus. It was plain, and could not be denied by any one, that the New Testament declared that Jesus was *the Son of God*, whatever doctrine respecting his divinity might be concealed beneath this comprehensive term. Then, if I told them this fact, I could not possibly err, for no follower of Jesus has ever denied this to be the truth. Then, in reference to the atonement. To "the law and the testimony" I must again refer; and that unequivocally stated, that Jesus was a Saviour of some sort. I then turned eagerly to the various passages of the New Testament, where this glorious doctrine is taught, and found it stated in so many words, that he was "the Lamb of God that taketh away the sin of the world," that Jesus himself hath said, "that God sent his Son that the world through him might be *saved*," and that "whoever believeth on the Son, hath everlasting life." Now here were two things that the blacks could comprehend; first, that Jesus was God's well-beloved Son, and second, that Jesus was in some sense, a *Saviour*. I then searched anxiously for the plainest declarations, as to the character of this salvation. What was salvation? and how did Jesus save mankind? Happily the Scriptures left me in no doubt on this point. The angel, who appeared to Mary, had declared, "Thou shalt call his name Jesus, for he shall save his people *from their sins*." The Holy Ghost, through Zacharias, had declared, that God "hath raised up a horn of salvation," * * * "that we, being delivered out of the hands of our enemies, might serve him without fear, in *holiness* and *righteousness* all the days of our life." Jesus himself had said, "Come unto me all ye that labor and are heavy laden, and I will *give you* rest;" and Peter very early declared to the Jews, "Unto you first, God having raised up his Son Jesus, sent him to bless you, *in turning every one of you from his iniquities*." Peter, Paul and John, often dwelt upon the great purpose of the life and death of Jesus, being to "*redeem* unto himself a peculiar people, zealous of good works;" and John had waxed bold, and declared no man was a Christian, unless he had been delivered from the power of sin, by faith in the blood of Jesus.

With these, and a multitude of kindred passages before me, could I err, in declaring that "Him hath *God* exalted with his right hand to be a prince and a Saviour, for to give repentance to Israel, and remission of sins." And this view of the case seemed to be wonderfully adapted to the condition of their sin-scarred, and morally weakened souls. Slavery had pressed its iron foot so heavily upon their moral natures, that their moral powers had practically become utterly inadequate to the task of keeping God's commandments. Said a colored man once to me, with tears in his eyes, "O, me so thankful for what you done told me about Jesus. Oders has said, obey God or you'll be damned; but 'fore you come, we never hern how us poor souls could 'bey God. Pears like we try, and we like a man trying to 'scend a high hill with a heavy load on his back. He try and den he fall down, and den he try again; but *now* poor me say, 'Massa Jesus help me be good. You say you will. I believe you good man, and you keep yer word,' and now it be so easy to do, as de Almighty say, which we could never do afore," and springing from the ground with unutterable joy depicted on his dusky face, he cried out, "Glory be to God for ginning us dis glorus Jesus, who does help us be good."

The experience of this poor soul accorded somewhat with my own. This view of Jesus had always filled my own soul with light and love and peace, and in proclaiming it to these benighted ones, its power seemed greatly enhanced in my own soul. Stalwart men, in possession of prodigious moral powers, having from their infancy been surrounded with favorable moral circumstances, and being of a lovely disposition, might keep the commandments of God, without relying on Jesus, or any divine influence; but surrounded as I was with bitter enemies, thirsting for my blood, and with friends no less anxious after my purse, I, no more than the darkies, could "love my enemies, and do good to them that hate me," without some unseen hand was stretched out for my moral guidance. With a very low estimate of God's law, I might possibly obey it without help from above; but when "righteousness was laid to the line, and judgment to the plummet," I felt myself inadequate to the task. If there are moral heroes, who can live a perfect life, by and through their own force of character alone, I thank God for their existence. Not many such souls existed in the days of Christ and his apostles; but the world has advanced mightily, since the day when Paul declared, "I know that in me (that is in my flesh) develleth no good thing," and when Christ asserted, "Without me ye can do nothing." If any tried and tempest tossed soul, like those of the majority of mankind, who essays to "do good, and finds evil present with him," should read these pages, allow me to recommend to such a soul, this panacea for his moral ills. Passion, pride, anger, envy, worldly-mindedness, impatience, and a thousand other sins, seem to wish to drag your soul down to perdition. You look at the immaculate law of God, requiring perfect love to Him and to *all men*, and you despairingly exclaim, how shall I ascend these Alpine heights, with this banner, on which is inscribed "Excelsior," in my hands? What good monk shall place beneath me his powerful arms, as my weary limbs begin to fail, under the combined influence of this moral snow, and these fearful blasts, of the tempestuous moral winter around me? Happy will it be for you, before your strength entirely fails, and you are engulphed in the snowy depths through which you are almost hopelessly floundering, if the silvery light, gleaming from some friendly lantern, affixed to the castle of refuge far above you, shall cast its hopeful rays upon your sinking form, and enable you to discover, emblazoned on those celestial walls, the memorable words of an elder traveller in the same dangerous path, "I thank God there is deliverance through Jesus Christ our Lord."

This was, then, the way by which my friends were to be delivered from that labyrinthian theological maze, in whose intricate depths I found them. I was to declare unto them, first, the immaculate purity of God's law; secondly, that by disobedience to its requirements, they had acquired a habit of sinning, that actually rendered them unable to obey it; thirdly, that without obedience to its spirit, there was no Heaven for the soul, either here or hereafter; and fourthly, that there was hope for them, in the fact that God had "laid help on one mighty to save," "who of God was made unto us, wisdom, righteousness, and sanctification and redemption," and that he was "able to save to the *uttermost* those who come *unto God by him*;" and that this gospel "is the power of God unto salvation, to every one that *believeth*." I said to them, "He comes to us as a friend and elder brother, and offers to our souls the glories of Heaven. Beholding us poor and disconsolate, he imparts new life into our souls, and so inflames us with the love of God, that we desire nothing only to glorify and honor God. The world is nothing but a glittering bauble, of no especial value, in comparison with Him, who, once crucified for us, now seeks to be the matchless Saviour of our souls."

But did these darkened beings understand these doctrines; or, comprehending them, did they fall in love with such a Saviour? Truth compels me to admit, that a desire to "perfect holiness in the fear of God," is not an overmastering principle in the African mind, any more than in its more robust counterpart, the Anglo-Saxon one. Indeed, in justice to all parties, I must say, that while some of the freedmen evince a desire to do right, and do aspire after excellence, the great mass of those who came under my observation, manifested no such desire; and many of them seemed to be only thinking animals, whose highest aspirations were to eat, drink, sleep, and play; and in whose souls there was no response to the most fervid appeals to the nobler sentiments of mankind. But I do not on this account despair of their elevation, for I believe Ged has not "left Himself without a witness," in every human soul, and that the most unpromising soil is susceptible of cultivation; but I believe this redemption will require a great multiplication of the means now in use for that purpose, which means, will be alluded to hereafter. In the meantime, let us all labor and pray for the fulfillment of that prophecy, which declares that, "Ethopia shall soon stretch out her hands unto God."

CHAPTER XXXV.

THE MARRIAGE SYSTEM OF THE BLACKS. AMUSING MARRIAGE CEREMONY IN A WHITE CHURCH.

This description of the "black man at the South" would be incomplete, without a few words in reference to the system of marriage prevailing there, which like many other of their customs, differs essentially from that prevailing in other parts of our "highly favored" land. As is well known under the influence of slavery, marriage was virtually annulled, and instead of their present freedom in this respect, being a matter of surprise, it is a wonder that they are not ten times worse than they are. I know not what our modern "free lovers" would say of their mode of life in this respect; but certainly those in favor of "free divorce," would be in raptures at the practical freedom prevailing among them on this subject. The words husband and wife with them, simply mean a man and woman, who feel inclined to live with each other for the time being. Of course they do not advocate any particular theory on this point, for they have never heard of the wise discussions of our modern philosphers upon this mysterious subject. While slaves, all the marriage allowed them, was to live with the one "massa" was pleased with. Now they claim the right to live with the one *they* are pleased with, and no amount of arguing can convince them of the impropriety of following their inclinations in this matter. In this respect, as in many others, they are "a law unto themselves," and "do that which is right in their own eyes."

After emancipation, a rebel Legislàture of Ga. passed an act legalizing the relation existing between those who were living together in March, 1866, and at that time had no other husband or wife. If either party had another "affinity," they must be legally married to some one, or they were to be considered as living in adultery. Consequently, by far the greater portion of plantation hands, are to-day living without any marriage ceremony having been performed over them. Occasionally we hear of a couple who have lived together for many years seeking to be united by law, "after the manner of white folks;" but the number is quite small of those whose consciences urge them to this step. Many of them are too poor to afford a marriage license, but the bulk are too much wedded to things as they were, to wish for any innovation in this respect. We were often considerably puzzled to understand the degree of consanguinity existing between certain parties; they having married so often, and having so many sets of children, who in like manner had married and mixed together, until it would have required the genius of a "Philadelphia lawyer," to have made a plain story out the complicated snarl of their family arrangements. One man named Peter, while living with us had a wife named Lizzy, but various other children than hers claimed their paternity of him, all of whom he endeavored to protect, as far as his limited means allowed. At length, one of the former children created dissatisfaction between Peter and Lizzy and they parted ; both remaining however on the plantation. Peter not believing it "good for man to be alone," soon rushed again into the *jaws* of connubial bliss after his fashion, and introduced to his home another woman ; while Lizzy being of like mind, soon solaced her grief-stricken soul by giving herself to another man, he also having griefs of a like character to assuage, in marrying Lizzy. But Lizzy and her new chaperon having both had some experience in matrimonial broils, soon repeated some of the lessons so easily learned, and a rupture of their very slight matrimonial bond again occurred. Nothing daunted, Lizzy made a third trial for a husband, with whom she managed to "jog along" in the matrimonial course, until this her last lover "flew the track," and again was she left comfortless and alone. But as good fortune would have it, Peter who had experienced some of Lizzy's luck in his matrimonial ventures, was by this time convinced that his old spouse was, to say the least, no worse than some of his new ones, and so one day the two after comparing notes upon their respective matrimonial journeys, and finding them so very similar, concluded to hitch horses together again, and make another grand effort for that earthly bliss, supposed to be found only in the matrimonial heaven. But harmony still eluded their grasp, and they again separated, but the goddess of love a third time bound them together, and Discordia again separated them, and this time she drove one of them into Carolina and the other into Augusta. But let not the reader suppose that a public party, or form of any kind signalizes these oft repeated matrimonial events. The public are not supposed to know or care about these things, leaving every one to regulate his hymenial matters according to his own notion.

Justice compels me to state however that while thus inhabiting the inner ring of the matrimonial course, each party is usually satisfied with one partner, and we seldom hear of their having a lover outside of this course, perhaps for the reason that it is so easy to change a companion when their "affinities" lead them that way. Great numbers of them in the meantime do not change their companions, and as far as I could see, are as faultless in their adherence to the laws of matrimony, as the masses are where no such freedom exists. Some of the men acknowledge that although none of them were faithful while slaves, yet now that they are free, it is their intention to be thus faithful. Young persons quite often obtain a license, and are married legally, but the white clergyman who marries them is not always particular, as to whether the law has been complied with or not. I have known several instances of parties having been thus united without the legal forms being complied with. In this state, a marriage license must be issued by the "Ordinary" of the county where the bride elect resides, but clergymen and others will marry the black people, when the license has been issued by officials in another county, contrary to the plain letter of the law. An amusing instance of these lax ideas has just come to my knowledge. A colored man residing near my place, by his arbitary conduct had estranged the affections of his wife from him, and she had left for distant parts. About six months afterwards he prevailed upon another woman to live with him, on the following liberal terms.

They were to be legally married, but when the truant wife returned, the wife of convenience was to absent herself and return to Savannah, her husband paying all her expenses, and also a moderate sum for her labor as housekeeper during the term of her wife-ship. Under these conditions the twain were actually married by a colored clergymen in Augusta, he, and the officer who issued the license, according to the story of the man himself, approving of the arrangement; but it is my opinion, that they could not have understood the matter thoroughly. The bridegroom had not been divorced from his absconding wife, to whom he was legally married according to the laws of the State.

The following account of a marriage ceremony at a white church not far from here, I received from a white person present on the occasion. "Some five or six couples were to be married, some, if not all of whom, obtained their licenses in another county. At the close of the church services, the minister called upon those who wished to be married, to stand up together in the aisle fronting the pulpit. Previous to going there, some of them had arranged for "grooms and maids" to accompany them to the altar, after the manner of the whites, and of course were slow to obey this summons, which obliged them to leave their "waiters" behind. The minister repeated the direction, ordering all who wished to be married to stand up, the men on one side, and the women on the other. They reluctantly obeyed the summons, when the minister directed them to join hands, eaeh man taking the hand of the woman whom he had selected for his wife. This they did, also, very reluctantly. He then repeated once the words of the marriage ceremony to the whole ten persons, and called for their responses in the usual manner. The men, after delay, replied with the usual affirmative response, but the women persistently refused; when the minister said, "Well, it will make no difference, I suppose. You agree to it, of course, and I pronounce you all men and wives." The colored people were greatly offended, but there was no redress, and they left the church, each one wondering, as one of the men afterwards said to me, who was his wife, and who was her husband. I remember, when surrounded by that blood-thirsty mob at Apling, that one of the charges brought against me was, that I was in favor of a law, compelling the colored people to be legally married; those bringing this charge, seeming to regard it as an act of oppression to pass such an enactment.

CHAPTER XXXVI.

INTELLECTUAL TRAITS OF THE BLACKS, AND COMPARISON OF SAME WITH THOSE OF THE WHITES.

Having said so much upon the moral and social traits of the blacks, my space will allow of but a brief mention of their *mental* characteristics. It will doubtless surprise the readers, as much as it has myself, to learn that in their *reflective* faculties, they are not so deficient as in the *perceptive* ones. Size, weight, number, order, color, eventuality and individuality, are quite small, while causality and comparison are of ordinary size, and language is uncommonly large. They are especially deficient in *number*, or calculation; and to teach them arithmetic, seems an almost hopeless task. I have had them repeat over the multiplication table, with and without the assistance of a numeral frame, probably one hundred and fifty times, and I question whether there is a single individual to day in our neighborhood, who can say it alone. It seems well nigh an impossibility to teach arithmetic even to excellent scholars in other respects, although it can be, and has been done by persistent effort. As has already been stated, they are also exceedingly deficient in memory; the most so of any other class of people with whom I have been acquainted. But in composing sentences that shall contain a specified word, they excel greatly, and even very young children are quite proficient in it; and as I have elsewhere stated, they seem to be natural orators. They use the most words, however, in describing the simplest acts, that I ever heard among any other class. I once told a girl at work for us, to go to Mr. S.'s room, and see if he was going to Augusta that day, and would take a letter for me. She soon returned, and stationing herself in the middle of the floor, she delivered herself as follows:

"Mr. Stearns, I done as yer told me, and I goes into Mr. S.'s room and Mr. S. done gone out to de lot, but I axed his wife, and she say as how Mr. S. done gone to de lot, and when he come in, she says as how she will ax him if he goin' to town to-day, and if he say he be goin', she says as how she'll den ax him if he be willing to carry de letter, and if he say he will, den she send de little boy upstairs, and he tell you, and de little boy can take de letter down stairs, and gin it to him."

Now this is no exaggeration, but the strict literal truth. In all their addresses, both public and private, they abound in comparisons, which often are very appropriate. They reason from cause to effect, quite well also, and are especially good in adapting means to the accomplishment of the end in view. Indeed, they often evince a shrewdness and knowledge of human nature quite surprising. Since their freedom it has been with them emphatically, "root hog or die," and although compelled to root with dismembered snouts, very few of them have died from neglect of rooting, except directly after emancipation. In the great struggle for life, I apprehend with a little assistance in the way of furnishing them land, and the means of its cultivation, they will out distance many of their white competitors. In making this remark, I by no means forget what has been said concerning their degradation. It is one thing to labor expertly for a mere subsistence, being impelled thereto by an over-weening love of life, for which they are distinguished ; and quite another thing to be lifted out of the scale of animal life, and "labor for the meat that perisheth," only as a means to the attainment of a higher and nobler end. Most animals and all savage tribes will exhibit a certain skill in obtaining food and shelter, which often proves the existence of a marvellous degree of animal instinct; witness the bee, the beaver, the ant, and the savage tribes of Africa and America. It is on this lower plane, that the intellect of the plantation blacks is at present principally manifested. I do not doubt its capability of being used, in the higher sphere of moral and religious culture. Although I have been conversant with some pretty low specimens of the African race, yet I fail to see any *native deficiency of intellect*, on the part of the black man. I have watched even these lower forms of life with intense interest, during my Southern residence, and I give it as my settled opinion that the *only mental* and *moral* difference between the two races, is *that* of *education*. Give me an equal number of white and black children, and let them be under my exclusive control for a certain number of years, and I will engage that the average mental product of one color, shall be as nearly like that of the other, as if all the pupils were of the same color. I am not prejudiced, either for or against the colored race. I regard them as my brethren, just as I do the most degraded of the white race, and as susceptible to the genial influences of cultivation, as are their white brethren. "God hath made of *one blood* all the nations of men for to dwell on all the face of the earth." There is a remarkable degree of similarity between the Southern whites, and the blacks in very many particulars. The reader has already perceived this resemblance in some of the distinguishing traits of the blacks. The whites are also noted for *their* self-esteem, unwillingness to be ruled over, approbativeness, mirthfulness, hope, carelessness, want of perseverance, conservatism, unreliability, and false ideas of religion. They both excel in adhesiveness, and I think the reflective organs of the whites, are larger than their perceptive ones. The whites have also large language, and like the blacks are particularly fond of singing. There is no question that the blacks are essentially and thoroughly human. As one of their teachers has well remarked, "They possess the failings of our common humanity to a sufficient extent, to entitle them to a high rank among those intelligences known as *human* beings."

CHAPTER XXXVII.

REBEL ATROCITIES, COLD-BLOODED MURDERS IN LINCOLN COUNTY, AND LYNCH LAW IN COLUMBIA COUNTY.

Having thus attempted to do justice to the character of the freedmen, we will now present the reader with a few instances in which these "bones of their bones, and flesh of their flesh," have been "taken care" of by the rebels, premising that in thus doing, we are only aiming at the presentation of the whole truth, respecting both black and white. We have no ends to compass, in writing this book, but those of justice. We believe the country needs reliable information concerning that class of its wards that it has undertaken to bless; and in all of our animadversions of the colored race, we have aimed at their good only; believing that a knowledge of their true condition is absolutely necessary, to induce the Northern people to put forth efforts for their redemption, commensurate with the greatness of the task to be accomplished. I repeat this remark, already made elsewhere, that it may be deeply impressed upon the minds of my readers, for it seems to me that but very few persons are sufficiently awake upon this subject. It also seems reasonable that my testimony should be added to that of the "thousand witnesses," who have already testified against rebel atrocities. Not because the crimes I shall depict are more startling than those which the public is already familiar with; but simply because this portraiture of the Southern people, would be incomplete, if it did not describe the wrongs done *to* the colored people, as well as the wrongs done *by* them. As some of my democratic friends, have quietly perused the one recital, may I not expect from them an equal degree of attention to the other description. I am aware of the great risks I run in giving publicity to these occurrences, for in so doing, I am exposing my property here to the depredations of my rebel friends; but when the word of the Almighty comes to one and says, "Son of man, go get thee unto the house of Israel, and speak *my words* unto them, that one thus addressed cannot refuse obedience, and still be a 'Son of God.'" I have been called upon to testify against the misconduct of the blacks, I feel equally called upon to "cry out" against the crimes of the whites, but in both cases I trust my motive is the same, viz., love to those I rebuke.

During the time I have resided at the South, I have kept no record of these crimes for several reasons. First, they were a matter of such constant occurrence, that amid the multiplicity of my other duties, I really had no time to record them. Secondly, I did not expect for several years of my Southern residence, ever to be called upon to portray these untoward events. I expected to live and die at the South, and I did not wish to frighten Northern people, so as to prevent them from joining me in my Southern home. Thirdly, not expecting to be called upon for these details, I tried to banish from my mind their harrowing memory, as speedily as possible, and therefore while I listened attentively to these sad recitals, being aware of my inability to remedy the evils complained of, I did not treasure them in my memory. I also considered them temporary evils, which the good sense of the Southerners themselves would eventually rectify.

Therefore my statements will be meagre, and divested of the interesting details, more likely to be connected with freshly narrated events. But they will possess the advantage of not having been perused previously, by the great majority of my readers. The reader will please bear in mind the impropriety of my mentioning the names of the actors in these dramas, and will therefore excuse me for omitting them. If any of them are inclined to doubt my assertions, I am willing to furnish the names of the parties concerned, if they will call on me in private. The events that occurred at Apling during "the reign of terror," of course need no repetition. Nor will it be best for me to dwell upon election atrocities merely, but I will rather present matters that occur in connection with the daily life of the employer and the laborer.

I cannot commence this task better, than by presenting a few of the narratives of the blacks, related to an officer of the Freedman's Bureau, at my house, a short time previous to the closing of their office in Augusta, premising that the facts stated are only samples of what has occurred since. I quote from the record of the Secretary of the meeting:

"R. J. testified, that A., a colored man, was killed in the fall of 1867, at a plantation near ours, by the white overseer on the plantation. A. was in his own house when the overseer told him to open the door, which he did, when the overseer said, 'I thought I told you not to burn pieces of rail.' A. replied that he had no wood, and that he was obliged to burn something. The overseer then ordered him out of the house, and on A.'s obeying, he took a piece of rail and knocked him down twice. A. started for town the next day, and was met by the owner of the plantation, who persuaded him to return, which he did; and not long after he died from the effects of the blows he had received. The overseer kicked him several times after his return."

"W. J. testified, that where he lived last summer, a woman was assaulted by the son of the owner of the plantation, who struck her on her head with a piece of plank three feet long, and the owner of the plantation also struck her on her limbs with a large pine stick, and nothing was ever done about it."

"L. J. testified, that where he lived last summer, a fellow servant was shot through the head by a young white man, a member of the family, who accused the woman named Dinah, of stealing clothes from the house, which theft she denied. She was dangerously sick a long time, but finally recovered, and her husband was paid to let the case alone."

"W. W. testified, that his employer set his dog on to his boy for going to the Sunday school, to 'hear that d——n old hypocrite, Stearns;' and because he interfered to protect his son, he beat him on his head severely."

One day "Aunt Suky," a colored woman seventy-five years old, and bent nearly double from weakness and hard usage, called upon me, and after looking around cautiously to see if any other white person was present, told me she had been beaten on her head by her employer, with a large hickory stick, until she was covered with blood, because she did not bring him some salt, immediately, when he called for it. Her head was then bound up from the effect of the blows, and she came to ask me, if there was no redress for her; but said, I must not tell any one she had been to see me, as they had threatened her life if she informed on them. I was obliged to tell her there was no remedy in her case.

In March, 1869, I learned of the killing of a colored man named Israel, not far from Apling, by a white man, who also cut Israel's father badly. The cause was, that the colored man had informed of a theft of cotton, committed by the white man. As usual, no notice was taken of the event. About the same time, Sam Buck, a colored man, was killed by a white man, not far from here, cause unknown, but no notice was taken of the occurrence.

In the same spring, a colored woman, sixty years old, named Sally, was brutally beaten on her head with a pair of tongs by her mistress, for refusing to leave her child and take care of a white woman's child. She lay for a long time in a very dangerous condition.

About the same time, some colored men stopped at my house, and reported the recent killing of three of their comrades by the Ku-Klux, in Lincoln county, adjoining ours.

The summer before, a colored man was attacked in the woods, by a party of white men, against whom he defended himself, and killed one of his assailants in so doing. He was immediately taken and hung by the remainder of the party.

About the same time, J. D., a colored man, living a few miles from here, was met in the road by three men, a horse-back, one of whom dismounted, and went up to him, and stabbed him terribly in different parts of his body. I am well acquainted with the assailant and with the colored man, and received from the lips of the colored man, the particulars of the case.

In 1867, three white men in front of my house,

boasted of the crimes they had committed against the colored people; one of them laughing heartily while he described the appearance of the woman whom he had beaten; saying, "she was the bloodiest looking beast you ever saw." Another of them said, he made it a point to whip one or more negroes soundly every year, as an example to the others. Another owned that he had fired at a negro for disobeying an order, and "should have shot him, but he dodged behind a tree." Neither of these men were rowdies in the common acceptation of the term, but *well-to-do* farmers, living very near my place, and I do not suppose they imagined they had done wrong.

The first year of my residence here, a white and black man had some altercation on a plantation a few miles from here. The next day, a gang of armed white men rode up to the place, seized the black man's wife, and threatened to kill her, unless she would point out the hiding place of her husband, Overhearing this threat, with true connubial affection, he sprang from his concealment, when he was immediately fired upon by the whole crowd, as if he had been a dog or stray hog, and his body was literally riddled with bullets. Several of the white men were arrested for the cold-blooded murder, but of course were soon discharged.

Previous to this a white man undertook to do violence to the person of a negro girl *at a public place.* She was defended by her brother, when the white man took his revolver and shot him dead instantly. In this case the white man left the county, fearing the rage of the negroes, and also the interference of the Freedmen's Bureau, which was then in operation. Quite a number of colored persons have been taken from the officers of justice in this county, by a mob of white men and *put to death.* In two cases they were taken from the jail in Apling, and in one while on their way to the prison. I learned the particulars of one of these cases from the jailer himself, who was called out of his house at midnight, and forced to deliver up the keys of the jail to the mob, who took the prisoner, and hung him from a bridge near the town. This was the same Apling where the author came so near sharing the same fate.

I give the particulars of the other case, as given me by Aunt Rinah Hill, who has lived on my place several years, and is a woman of veracity. She says, that in the summer of 1869, a little child belonging to R. R., ten or twelve miles from here, bit off the finger of a colored child on the place, whose mother was named Minty. She ran after the white child, without reflecting upon the criminality of a black person pursuing a white one, and meant as she said, "merely to slap it on its ear." The child's father, seeing the black woman pursuing his child, rushed upon her and beat her tremendously with a large white oak stick. This of course roused the ire of Berry, the colored woman's husband, and he attempted to interfere, when the oppressed victim of "imperalism" and "centralization," exercised his natural right" to shoot a black man, and fired at Berry, wounding him in the thigh. Berry fled to Augusta, and on his way passed by our place, and Aunt Rinah gave him a drink of water. The next day he returned guarded by two men in a buggy before him, and the same behind him, and with another at his side a horseback. The next news from this party was, that Berry and his wife, after having been lodged in jail at Apling, were taken out by *a mob and hung*; and it was reported that the heart of the man was cut out and given to the dogs. So great is the horror of the colored people of Apling jail, that some of them declare they never will be taken there alive, and one of them not long since, when on his way for an alleged theft, undertook to escape from the constable, who shot him through his body, without the least compunction.

I cannot begin to recall the instances, of maimed and wounded men, who have come to me with the story of their wrongs. Some with great gashes cut in their heads, some with wounds in their bodies, and others with mangled and shattered arms; to all of which, I have been under the sad necessity of saying, "I can do nothing for you, except to call upon the United States government to protect you;" which seemed to them, almost a mockery of their woes.

It is not for me to say who is to blame, for this failure of the government to protect its citizens. It is, perhaps, inherent in the nature of the goverment itself, and can only be remedied by a radical change in our govermental theory. No true man can cry out against "centralization," when without it, there never *can* be, any safety for "the black man of the South," from "the outrages of the rebels." We have entreated long and loud for protection; petitions have been forwarded to Congress, entreating its interference; and Gov. Bullock has exerted himself nobly, in behalf of his colored constituents; but Congress has chosen to hear the cries of the enemies of the Union, rather than those of its defenders. Some of the blame rests upon those betrayers of our cause, who, in connection with rebel democrats, have visited Washington, and poured into the ears of Congress, and of the President, such misstatements of our condition, as have led them to doubt the necessity of their interference. In the meantime, the craven, false-hearted cry of "universal amnesty," has uttered its fearful notes, all over the land; sounding in the ears of the terror-stricken Southern Unionist, as dismally as the yells of rejoicing, that went up from ten thousand rebel throats, when McDowell's panic-stricken squadrons, fled from the furious hosts precipitated upon them, at the unfortunate Bull Run rout. While we have been surrounded by implacable foes, thirsting for the blood of all true Union men, and have imploringly cast our eyes Northward for assistance, as the dying soldier on the battle-field, lifts his head occasionally, to see if no friendly hand can be found to wet his parched lips; those to whom we fondly looked as the embodiment of all our hopes, have sternly covered their eyes, and looked away from our imploring gaze, being dazzled by visions of future political glory; and instead of responding, "You shall be protected," have uttered honeyed words, in dulcimer strains, that have electrified the hearts of our enemies; but have sent a mournful sound, like that of retreating squadrons, into our ears, filling us with blank dismay, and awaking in our pierced hearts, the most melancholly forebodings for the future.

But to return to my narrative of rebel atrocities. Lincoln county, adjoining this county, is emphatically, "the valley of the shadow of death," for the poor colored man. Ever since I commenced residing here, have terrific stories of his abuse, in that county, reached my ears. Among the many tales of violence perpetrated there, I will simply give publicity to the following, as it is in every one's mouth. In the summer of 1868, when political excitement ran high, there were two colored men, father and son, named Roundtrees, and another colored man named Billy Tully, who were quite prominent republicans, and it therefore became necessary to sacrifice them. Accordingly, one night they were aroused from their slumbers, taken from their beds, and carried to a neighboring mill-dam. They were then offered their choice, to join the democratic club, or to walk out on that mill-dam and *be shot.* With true Spartan courage, they chose the latter fate, when they were immediately placed on the mill-dam, and given the poor privilege of jumping into the water, to escape the rebel bullets, as the Indians often allow a prisoner a chance to run for his life, while they are firing at him. They all three jumped into the water, at a given signal from these "well-disposed" and "repentant" rebel democrats, to deprive whom of political power is considered so very oppressive, and for whom we are so constantly exhorted to "kill the fatted calf." One of the Roundtrees and Tully were shot dead, the other managed to escape by dodging in and out of the water, amid the shower of rebel bullets aimed at his devoted head. He was severely wounded, but fled to Augusta, and was for some time cared for at the "Freedmen's hospital" in that city.

If any one is disposed to doubt this story, I would state that the widow of the murdered Roundtrees is now (at the time of this writing) living at Hon. J. M. Rices' place, two and a half miles from Augusta, and can be enquired of respecting the facts as above stated. Not long since an intelligent white man, from Lincoln county, repeated to me these facts, which I had often heard before, and said some of his family knew the names of the murderers. I have been repeatedly informed by both white and colored men, that during the same summer, it was no uncommon thing to find eight or ten bodies of murdered colored men, lying on the public road. All I would ask of any doubter of these statements, is to go to Lincoln county himself, and ascertain their truth or falsity. But be sure, and not let it be known that you are from the North, otherwise you might not escape to tell the result of your investigations. Col. O. Rourke, agent of the Freedmen's Bureau, once undertook to travel *incognito* through that region. I saw him on his return, and enquired as to his success, and he replied, "Yes, you don't catch me in Lincoln county again, I assure you. I would not take another trip there of this kind for a million of dollars. I saw enough and heard enough to satisfy me, that if they had dreamed who I was, they would have shot me dead instantly."

A Southern lady residing in Lincoln county, stopped at our house and took breakfast one morning, and told me she was fleeing for her life, because she had boarded awhile, Mr. Madison, the republican member of the Legislature from that county, who of course owed his election to the negroes. She stated, that rocks were thrown at her little boy while sitting in her wagon, in front of a store in Linconton, and when a mother's love led her to remonstrate with the ferocious villains who threw them, they said, "well, s'posing we do kill him, there will be one radical less to grow up." Mr. Madison has never deemed it safe to return to Lincoln county since his election to the Legislature in 1868; and the three members from our county all testify, that it is not safe for them to attempt to live in this county.

The public are familiar with the murder of the Hon. Mr. Adkins, an aged gentleman, of unblemished character, and an accredited minister of the Methodist Church North, who was killed by a bullet fired from a copse of woods through which he was passing, on his return to Warren County from the Legislature. He had been repeatedly threatened with death if he attempted to return home; but finally ventured the experiment, and lost his life while riding in a buggy, driven by a negro, who was also killed a few days after. This occurred in the senatorial district adjoining ours.

Not long since a colored man, named Wm. Bowns, fled from the Ku-Klux, in Lincoln County, who, as he said, had attempted to kill him three times. He said, "when a man would not do just as they wanted, they would try to kill him." Some of the blacks say, they would not live in Lincoln County for five dollars a day. A young white man informed me the other day, of quite a number of Ku-Klux outrages in this and neighboring counties, all of which he was inclined to justify on the ground of necessity. He said, that not long since, the Ku-Klux visited a plantation in this county, and whipped seventy-five negroes, because their employer was too lenient towards them. He also said, that in Burke Co., last spring, they burned three colored men, and three white women, alive, because they lived together. His name can be given to any one who doubts the truth of this statement. He also gave me the details of another Ku-Klux outrage, by far too indecent to mention in public. It was his opinion, that there were now nearly as many whippings as in the days of slavery, although the whippings were much less severe than in olden times. The victims were not so often tied and whipped as in the days of yore, but were beaten with whatever implement came handy on the spur of the moment; and were often pelted with rocks, or stones as they would be called at the North. He, himself, used a large raw hide for that purpose. A former neighbor of his, tied them up, and whipped them in the good old-fashioned way of slavery. All of these things he told of his own accord, and attempted to justify them.

A little incident once occurred on my own plantation, which finely illustrates the nature of this treatment of the slaves. I had rented some of my land to a southern gentleman of good habits, and as civil and obliging in all of his intercourse with me, as any man I ever met, and he was also a church member. But his feelings towards the blacks were different. One day, a boy of about fourteen years of age, "sauced him," as he said, and he drew out his knife, and cut the boy's arm severely. He then came to me immediately, and told me what he had done, evidently feeling justified in performing the rash act. The same man came near shooting a colored man who had talked very insultingly to him, and was only prevented by so doing, by the interference of a third person, who peremptorily ordered the colored man away from the place. Now, northern men, if so excited, will refrain from these acts from a wholesome regard for the law; but here, there is no law for the negro, and of course, nothing to restrain passionate men from wreaking their vengeance on those who provoke them. Imagine how it would be in New England, even, if there was no punishment for assault and battery, and then consider the extreme excitability of the southern character, and also they having been accustomed to nothing but deference from the blacks; and the enigma of their acts is easily solved. It is not because the Southern people, in their every day intercourse with the world, are any worse than other people, but it is the peculiar circumstances in which they are placed, that leads them to act so savagely. I make these remarks, because those who have seen the Southerners when not excited, cannot believe that such urbane gentlemen can conduct themselves so unseemly towards the blacks. The reader must never forget, that while many outrages are committed at the North, their perpetrators are almost always punished by law, but here this is seldom the case; and this fact constitutes the great difference between Southern and Northern society on this point. What the friends of the blacks are laboring for, is the establishment of law for their protection.

Let the broad ægis of law be lifted up in behalf of the colored man, and the ample folds of the mantle of justice be thrown around the white man, and these evils will nearly cease. When it cannot be done by our civil law, we ask for the establishment of military authority, as absolutely necessary to protect both black and white.

CHAPTER XXXVIII.

THE REBEL SIDE OF THE STORY. "LET EVERY MAN SPEAK FOR HIMSELF."

I cannot thus arraign before the public bar, the Southern white man without allowing him, like every other accused person to testify in his own behalf. As one of old said to a supposed culprit arraigned before him, "Thou art permitted to speak for thyself." Said a very intelligent Southern gentlemen to me one day, after I had described to him my wishes respecting the blacks, "The difference between you and us, Mr. S., is this. You agree with us that the colored man is degraded, but you *believe* he can be elevated, (and we do not doubt your sincerity) while we *know* that he cannot. "Another" gentleman when told of the plans of others to reform and christianize the blacks, replied, "We have been trying our whole lives to evangelize them, in our churches, in our families, and in every other way, and we have not succeeded, and I don't believe Mr. C. will ever be able to do it." Very many of the Southern people really wish to see the negro different from what he is, but know not how to bring about his redemption. Others despise him, and do not wish for his elevation. But those who would gladly raise him from his moral degradation, cannot conceive of the right way to accomplish so desirable a task. When Northern men and women come down here, and boldly proclaim their faith in the elevation of the negro, Southern approbativeness is touched, and they feel as if "thus saying, thou condemneth *us* also," for have we not tried our best to bring about such a result? Such persons cannot bear to have it said that they are not the friends of the negroes, for they feel in their hearts that they are, and they consider the Northern people guilty of great injustice in denying it; and unconsciously their feelings towards the new comers become embittered.

Among some of the whites, there is a feeling towards the blacks, not possessed by even the Northerners. I have known many instances of great favors being shown the freedmen by rebel whites; sometimes by those who were once their masters, and often by those who were merely acquaintances formerly. Indeed I do not think that the worst rebels hate a negro as badly as a Northern copperhead does. When the negroes are willing to vote the democratic ticket, there is no lack of affection towards them on the part of the whites; and when the negro does his whole duty towards his employer, I am constrained to say that in a majority of instances, I believe his employer feels friendly towards him. But these conflicting interests so constantly arise, that in self-defence the employer feels constrained to use severe measures. The negro often fails to perceive his true relations to his former master; he does not comprehend the binding nature of a contract, and frequently uses his freedom in a latitudinarian way, alike unjustifiable by reason or expediency. In a great multitude of instances, the blame is almost wholly on the side of the negro. And why should it not be so? Emancipation was conferred on him *instanter*, with no instruction as to its duties, and how could his darkened mind understand its true nature? Designing men also, both white and black, in a few instances, took advantage of the negroe's ignorance, and filled his mind with false ideas of liberty, in order to ingratiate themselves with the blacks.

The officers of the Freedmen's Bureau, often found that the black man was the aggressor, in many cases brought before them for adjudication. As is well known, I am not a rebel, although a white man; but still in my intercourse with the blacks, I have often found them disposed to take advantage of me unduly, it being impossible for them to divest themselves wholly of the idea, that no white man can be their true friend; and yet they professed to regard me as their greatest friend. Now if they have been disposed to treat me unjustly, knowing that I was their friend, and not a rebel, is it unreasonable to suppose, that they do treat their rebel employers, with still greater injustice? Do not understand me as justifying the rebels, in their outrages upon the blacks; as far as the heaven is from the earth, so far am I from intending to do that. These outrages ring in the ears of the "Lord of Sabaoth," and he will yet "make inquisition" for the blood of the injured ones, and this, not only of the misguided rebels, but of their *more guilty* Northern compeers, who so steadfastly oppose the adoption of all measures for the protection of the blacks. But in writing this book, I wish to deal out, even and exact justice to all parties. There was a palliation for the crimes of Napoleon, and of other great conquerors. Seldom is an act of villainy committed from sheer love of crime. Men almost always think they are justified, in all their villainous transactions. Doubtless the "Tammany Ring," did that which was "right in their own eyes;" and the loathsome debauchee, finds excuse for his suicidal course, in the strength of his own ungovernable passions. But this mantle of charity, thrown broadly over the whole whirlpool of tempestuous acts, should never be held so firmly down, as to preclude all efforts to cleanse the noisome locality, of its pestiferous elements. The small-pox is indeed a loathsome disease, in spite of all the efforts of friends to mitigate its terrible severity. The great Eastern simoon sweeps over vast tracts of country, carrying destruction in its path, even if the unfortunate travellers are able to escape from its terrible power, by humbly prostrating themselves upon the ground; and so, the acts of the rebels, towards the colored people, are none the less outrageous, because there is some mitigation of their severity, in the kindly relations mentioned; and still less are these acts virtuous, because some extenuation of them can be found. I deeply regret that the blacks should ever place themselves in the attitude of aggressors, but I am compelled to say, that they are sometimes thus guilty; and I know not why I, as their friend, should cover up their iniquities; besides, by admitting the whole truth, will not reasonable people, be more willing to unite in bringing these outrages to a close, than if I had written a partisan book merely, and sought only to denounce the rebels, and praise the blacks? But it is not my nature to misstate facts, for the purpose of sustaining a theory. I am therefore obliged to admit, that the blacks are, *oftentimes*, most *exceedingly and aggravatingly provoking*; and that taking into consideration the irascible nature of the whites, and other circumstances, I am not at all surprised at their insane treatment of these laborers.

But having been an eye witness of these scenes for so many years, can I sit calmly still and behold the immense black cloud of angry elements, sweeping across the sky, and threatening momentarily to burst in unwonted fury on all classes below, and utter no warning voice to those who might escape from the angry deluge? I see elements of discord, and of terrific hate, brewing and gathering strength all over this ill-fated Southern country, which elements are being fanned into a perfect storm, by Northern winds of mistaken generosity; and shall I not cry out to those soon to receive the peltings of the pitiless storm, "beware of your danger, and flee to some 'ark of safety' for protection?" That "ark of safety" is merely the erection of such halls of justice, as will gather within their righteous walls, all perpetrators of villainy, of whatever creed, race or party, there to dispense to them that even-handed, and exact judicial treatment, that the Almighty declares is the crowning glory of his august character. "For my mouth shall speak truth, and wickedness is an abomination to my lips."

Not long since, I had a long conversation with a Southern young man, and I will give his testimony on this subject. He was not a Ku-Klux himself, he said, but if I should have him put in jail, he would be rescued in two days by the Ku-Klux, who were his friends. He had a cousin who was a Ku-Klux, and during his career had killed fifteen men, white and black, and was finally killed himself. It may be well enough to state his ideas of the Ku-Klux, although not essential to his defence of the whites. He said they were generally wealthy men, and not the poorer classes, as some supposed. The whole people approved of the Ku-Klux, considering them necessary to the preservation of order among the blacks. He thought that in this county, there were two hundred and fifty more of the Ku-Klux, then there were men who went into the rebel army. He believed there would have been no Ku-Klux, if the blacks had behaved as they ought. He said the Ku-Klux was not a political organization, but simply a "vigilance committee," to keep all classes straight. In support of this view, he adduced several cases, where they had punished whites as well as blacks. His great idea seemed to be, that kind treatment was thrown away upon the blacks, and that it was impossible to get along with them without whipping them. He said, a gentleman of this county adopted the kind method, and his hands literally laughed at all of his orders. If he wanted a mule saddled, he was obliged to go to the stable, and saddle it himself, and so with nearly every thing else. At last one day, in perfect despair, he called upon a resolute man of his acquaintance, named T., and offered him $200, if he would come down to his place, and relieve him from his troubles. T. came, and in a few days order reigned, where anarchy had previously held sway. If a mule was wanted, half a dozen men stood ready to saddle him. Previous to his arrival, there was no such thing as getting the hands out early in the morning, but after T. had been there two days, all were at their work by sunrise. The method he adopted, was an indiscriminate use of blows, belaboring the recreant ones with whatever implement was at hand, until no one thought of disobeying his orders. He mentioned other similar cases, and cited his own. He said he was naturally a very passionate man, and he had a brother who was still more irascible. This brother hated the very sight of a negro, but his father was very indulgent towards them, and was consequently run over by them, as all were, who did not resort to blows in their treatment of them. He said the blacks would not obey *him*, without the use of blows on his part, and he was so hasty, that he was afraid he should kill some of them; and he should have killed one not long ago, if his wife had not prevented him. For this reason, he was determined to abandon farming, and engage in some other business. He said the people in this county were "very spunky," and would never submit to being *obliged* to treat the negroes kindly. He believed they would fight, rather than alter their course in this respect. His old grandfather, who is over ninety years old, told him the other day, that he was ready at any time to go to war again, to subdue the negroes. He thought this war would come on in less than three years. He and many others were in favor of sending the blacks to some other place, and he thought the Southern people would gladly pay the expense of all that would go away.

This testimony I introduce, for the sake of allowing all parties to be heard. I know nothing of either the truth or the falsity of his statements, but he seemed to be a fair and honest man, and to deprecate what he considered the sad necessity of the present treatment of the negroes. It will be observed that he admits fully the charges made against the whites, and justifies their cruel conduct.

Only a few days ago, a wealthy planter near me said, "The only way of managing the negroes, is to beat them with a ten foot pole." Now this is the usual defence of the Southeners, when they talk on this subject, that the negroes behave so badly, that force is necessary to compel their obedience. I must also add, that one of their reasons for hating the Northerner is, their supposition that the Northerners are the cause of much of this disobedience on the part of the negroes. But in this idea they are evidently mistaken. I have never seen or heard of a Northener, who did not earnestly strive to induce the negroes to obey their employers, and be honest and true towards them.

I have done with this defence of the whites. It is short, but comprehensive on their part. It is the sum total of their defence, for all the outrages committed since I camė to this region. As I have said, it is too true in many instances, but instead of affording any real justification for the whites, it is only a strong additional reason, why the poor, erring black man should be protected by the strong arm of rigid and impartial justice.

Colored voters swimming the Creek on election day. p. 205.

CHAPTER XXXIX.

WHO ARE THE KU-KLUX? WHAT ARE THEIR AIMS? AND HOW SHALL THEY BE OVERTHROWN?

I have purposely omitted nearly all reference to this body of villains, until the close of the first part of this work, so that the main portion of my book may partake as little as possible of a partisan character; but I cannot reconcile it to my conscience, to let this occasion pass without an attempt to enlighten the public mind in reference to a subject seemingly so shrouded in mystery.

Good men seem to differ widely in their opinions, respecting this nefarious organization. On the one hand, we hear it asserted that the "Ku-Klux" are made up to a great extent of the irresponsible element of the South, young men who graduated in the rebel army, and at the close of the war, found themselves without means, and never having been accustomed to labor, were incapable of adapting themselves to the new order of things. Then it is said, that the Ku-Klux are chivalrous gentlemen, with their bosoms burning with indignation at the wrongs of the comparatively small number of Southern gentry, still deprived of political rights; and if "a generous measure of amnesty could be passed, it might prove the solution of the difficult problem."

Others assure us that the Ku-Klux are the disfranchised ones themselves, anxious to prove their repentance of their former acts of rebellion, by a continued series of still more rebellious acts. Then, it is gravely asserted by some who ought to know better, that the supposed acts of a few men in robbing the treasury of Georgia, of a large sum of money, are the excuses of the Ku-Klux, for their hellish outrages; although they began to be committed, at least a year and a half before these so-called robbers had access to the Georgia treasury; the one beginning as early as June or July, 1868, while these "peculators" were not placed within reach of the Georgia pie, from whose luxurious contents they were supposed to have abstracted so many sweetmeats, until December, 1869. But all of these suppositions exhibit a great degree of ignorance, as to the whole matter of Southern Ku-Kluxism.

It is not to be supposed that an outsider can positively define the aims of a secret organization, but as "actions speak louder than words," those aims may be divined by a diligent attention to their acts. When did the Ku-Klux commence their operations? From diligent enquiry, I believe that it was not until after the election of our state government, in the Spring of 1868. I suppose that I ought to know something of their history, residing as I have done for years in their midst, and being accustomed to hear almost daily of their acts of violence. The first definite information I had of their existence in our neighborhood, was not long after the April election in 1868, at which time a colored man from an adjoining county, who had taken an active part in the election, showed me a large sheet of paper, on which was written in letters of blood, various threatening messages, warning him to leave the country under penalty of death. The sheet was embellished with various bloody devices of "raw head and bloody bones," pictures of gallows, coffins, &c., and signed in large letters, "Ku-Klux Klan." The reader was benevolently advised to wash his hands after handling the sheet, as it was poisoned. I have never heard the consequences of the black man's temerity in refusing to leave his home, at the bidding of these anonymous scribblers. He found the missive nailed to his door, he said, but he seemed determined to maintain his rights. From that day, until after the presidential election, the whole talk of the blacks was of the Ku-Klux and their threats.

I learned that it was the custom of these noble-hearted fellows, so eager to defend their neighbor's honor, to dress themselves up at night with hideous masks, and various kinds of white garments thrown over their persons; or more usually, large sheets, which were thrown over them and their horses, and in this disguise to visit the cabins of the colored people. Sometimes they would rap violently at their doors, and when opened, would demand in a hollow voice, "water! water!" to quench their thirst, exclaiming in sepulchral tones, "I have had no water since the battle of Manasses." When water was given them, they would seem to swallow a whole bucket-full of this refreshing element, having an apparatus contrived for carrying the water off, unperceived in the darkness of the night. This, of course, astonished the affrighted blacks, and prepared them for the assertions of these ghosts, that they were dead people come back to tell the negroes, not to vote the "radical ticket at the next presidential election." Sometimes they would pretend that they were the ghosts of the former masters of the blacks whom they visited, and that they were slain in battle; at other times they would assume to be "simon-pure" negro ghosts, who had come on the disinterested errand, of persuading their colored brethren to vote as the white people wanted them to vote. As is well known, the colored people are all exceedingly superstitious, and easily frightened at any thing of a supernatural character. It is difficult to persuade them to enter alone a room containing a dead person. Accordingly, when these ghosts first appeared, the poor creatures were more frightened, than if they had seen "an army with banners." They usually fled precipitately from the pale forms of these supposed celestial beings. At one time the ghostly visitants were attracted to a prayer-meeting being held in our neighborhood, which visit of theirs was a signal for the hasty flight of all but one of the praying ones. He, a little more valiant than the rest, was so presumptive as to fire at the heavenly visitors, although the white lady of the plantation had warned them not to fire at them; for if they did, they would fall dead themselves. To the surprise of all, after one or two shots had been fired, a groan, like that often heard from live mortals similarly situated, was heard to proceed from the company of celestials, and then the remainder of the company put spurs to their horses, and galloped away, leaving some of their celestial robes behind them; which, on examination, proved to be made originally, of such cotton, as the darkies themselves had picked on this mundane sphere. The next day, a well known citizen of our neighborhood was found to be severely wounded, so that the ghost hallucination speedily came to an end. Previous to this *denouement*, it was confidently believed by the colored people all around us, that the Ku-Klux were actually inhabitants of the other world.

In Carolina, not far from here, some twenty or thirty Ku-Klux, arrayed in their accustomed garb of white, posted themselves in a grave yard, near which a prominent colored man was intending to pass during the evening. They threw themselves upon the ground, in different parts of the cemetery, where they remained until they heard the footsteps of their intended dupe, whose approach was watched for by a comrade, divested of his robes; when they arose simultaneously, and gathering their robes about them, slowly approached the undaunted traveller, but he failed to be persuaded, even if "one should arise from the dead," and walked away, with slightly accelerated steps, but silently.

As far as my knowledge of this gentry is concerned, I take them to be the more adventurous portion of the Southern people, who, after dreaming over the terrible effects of negro domination, can restrain themselves no longer, but in true imitation of Don Quixote, don their armors, and rush to battle with windmills, or whatever else may oppose their progress. I have no doubt that the love of fun, which is a strong element in Southern character, enters largely into the composition of these "Klans," and that to frighten the darkies by their ghostly appearance, was rare sport to the original perpetrators of these deeds; but as no notice was taken of their midnight dissipation, and as they saw how easily frightened "Sambo" was, other and darker counsels entered into their plans, and at length they conceived the idea of controlling the elections by disguised force. I do not believe they designed to commit deeds of blood, until impunity in their fun-loving proceedings, had emboldened them to extend their objects, and multiply their designs. I am more inclined to this opinion from the fact, that well known citizens of this county, belonging to the fraternity, are neither better or worse, than the average of the population; but simply young men, with plenty of leisure on their hands, and with a great love of adventure in their souls, and intensely rebel in their proclivities. It is not by any means true, that they are either ineligible politicians, or their particular friends exclusively, although some of each of these classes, undoubtedly belong to them; but they are certain persons taken indiscriminately from the community at large, like the members of a fire engine company, or an old-fashioned Northern military organization.

They are not desperadoes by profession, nor more inclined to deeds of violence than some of their quieter neighbors, who as "gentlemen of property and standing,,' fully endorse their proceedings. I should say they were rather the exponent of the average Southern sentiment, than an exceptional class of any nature whatever. They may be regarded as the *working force* of the great body of Southern politicians. They are not outlaws in any sense of the word, and the "good and true men in the Southern States" who are represented by some wily politicians as sufficient to put them down, are but as "a drop in the bucket," in comparison to the immense majority that sustains them. If the opinion of these political owls is true, why do we never hear of the least attempt on the part of these "good and true men" to have the Ku-Klux arrested?

I am safe in saying, that no Southern court has ever attempted to take cognizance of their actions. Unmolested alike by judge and jury, they roam over the country accomplishing their nefarious tasks, with none to molest them or make them afraid;" and are as perfectly safe from all danger of this kind, from the "good and true men" at the South, as are the "night police" of the city of Boston. They are in fact, *the* government of the Southern States, fully as much as the California "Vigilance Committee" were that of the gold regions at a certain period in their history.

What then is their object? To answer this question, is but to point to their acts. On whom do they wreak their vengeance? On those who differ from them politically. It is my candid opinion, that bad as are the Ku-Klux, and savoring as their conduct does of unmitigated rascality, there is yet, as there is for the worst of men, some apology to be offered. Of course this apology is not offered for the purpose of shielding the miserable creatures from punishment, but for the purpose of our arriving at a full understanding of what seems to some such inexplicable conduct on the part of the Southerners. Are they not our brethern of the human family, and were they not for many years loving members of our great political institutions, and how can they justify these enormities? is well asked by numerous sincere people at the North. This is true, but Cain *did* kill his only brother, and fathers *do* sometimes murder their own children, unaccountably strange, as it may seem. I will therefore attempt to explain the fearful mystery. The great bug-bear of the Southern people is, *negro domination.* The idea that an irresponsible class of men, formerly their slaves, and for whose abilities they entertain the most sovereign contempt, should become their rulers, is well calculated to arouse their direst apprehensions, and to fill their souls with unutterable madness. I cannot but sympathize somewhat with this feeling, although I so thoroughly detest the means taken to avert what they consider so dire a catastrophe. I am sure, that Northern man as I am, and a life long friend of the colored race as I have been, defending them everywhere at all hazards to my person and my purse, as I have been in the habit of doing; still with my present knowledge of the incapacity of the *uneducated* blacks, I could not consent for them to be rulers over me and my children. With what melancholy forebodings then must the proud Southerners, always looking upon the blacks as but little removed from the animal creation, have surveyed the prospect before them, of being entirely controlled in all their governmental affairs by these "pesky niggers" as they call them; and their "detestable supporters," the Northern "carpet baggers." I must be permitted to say, that I am sorry for our Southern friends, and I lament the dire necessity that caused this domination to be forced upon them. I fought against it, previous to the adoption of our State constitution, contending for an insertion into that instrument of a clause, limiting office holders to those who had been *loyal citizens* of the United States for *twenty years;* thus excluding both rebels and blacks, until each class had served a proper tutilage under the new political dispensation. But wiser men than I am, decided that the colored vote could not be secured to our party, if such a provision was adopted. I question however, if more would have gone over to the rebels, than have already done. Some of the staunchest friends of the colored man have assured me that this love for office, was the great bane of the colored people, and that if they were deprived of office, their political loss would not equal their moral gain. Of course, other things being equal, the black man has the same right to office that any other man has, but considering the necessary political ignorance of the great masses, it seems to me that the part of true wisdom would have been, to have held before the admiring gaze of the black man, the prize of political preferment, at such a time as his mental improvement qualified him for such onerous duties; and thus placed before him a powerful incentive to the acquisition of political wisdom. These remarks are intended to apply solely to the Southern freedmen, and not to those enlightened colored men at the North, who have been "loyal citizens of the United States," for a long number of years. It is a burlesque on legislation to elect any man, black or white, to the dignified position of law-maker, who cannot read the bill presented to him, to receive his vote upon. With what chagrin must such a man contemplate his own conduct, when he afterwards ascertains that the bill for which he has voted is one diametrically opposed to the interest of his constituents; he not having been present at its first reading, and the second and third reading having been dispensed with by vote of the house. Nearly thirty of the colored members of our Legislature, actually voted for a measure that finally resulted in their own ejection from the halls of debate. Would they have pursued this course, if possessed of that political wisdom, that comes from political acquaintance with the history of our own and other nations?

But while I am thus disposed to make allowance for this awful horror of negro domination, on the part of the Ku-Klux, and their friends; still the truth compels me also to admit, that they themselves were responsible for this very state of affairs. Very few negroes would have been placed upon the republican ticket, at the time of our obtaining possession of the State government of Georgia, if competent white men could have been found who were willing to fill the desired positions. We ransacked our county in vain, for white republicans, and even for moderate Southern men, who would consent to serve, if elected as republicans; but the pressure of public opinion was so great, that even those who had no objections personally, to such a course, were afraid thus to jeopardize their temporal welfare, in other respects. In Lincoln county, we could find no white Union man to fill the office of "Ordinary," and we were obliged to nominate and elect a black man, utterly unqualified for that office. Now if our Southern friends had buried their animosity to the United States government, and had manfully come forward to sustain the party laboring for their political renovation, no colored man would have been elected to any office whatever, in Georgia; but they persisted in "breathing out threatenings and slaughter," against our party, and our government; and what else could we do, than put into office, loyal black men, even if they were intellectually unfit for their posts? Was not moral unfitness, a little worse than intellectual incapacity? But the opposition of the Ku-Klux was not limited to negro rule; they also hated political equality with the blacks, even as voters, and especially did they hate the domination, of their victorious conquerors in the war, from whose effects they were striving to recover. So that the whole object of the renowned Ku-Klux, can be stated in one single sentence; *opposition to radicalism*, or republicanism. For the purpose of making this opposition practicable, was the whole horrible machinery of Ku-Kluxism set in motion. In this they were manifestly wrong, for the negro had the same right to vote, that the ignorant foreigner in New York had. The right to vote, by no means includes the right to hold office; all men who are entitled to the one, are by no means qualified for the other. And here the rebel democracy displayed a vast amount of political folly. If it had imitated the action of the Northern democracy, in securing the votes of Irishmen, it might to-day, have held unlimited sway over the entire South, as completly as the Northern democracy "sweeps the course," with a certain class of laborers. But instead of thus imitating the political wisdom of its Northern allies, it fell to beating and abusing the negro unstintedly, almost as soon as the new political boon was conferred upon him, without his being at all to blame. Southern democracy thus almost immediately drove from its folds those, who under a different political regime, would have proved its best friend. At first, the negro did not know with which party to cast his lot, but the democrats began to curse him, and the republicans to comfort him; and human nature, being as it is, he could not hesitate long, in choosing his political mates.

Thus has the pride of the Southerners gone before their political fall, and to-day, all over the South, nothing but the direst political vandalism on the part of the thus rejected democracy, prevents overwhelming majorities of black men from voting the republican ticket. By this time the negroes have learned who are their best friends, and have found that they are certainly not those who maim, wound and kill them, but those who seek to protect them by every means in their power. Many of the negroes now declare, that they will die before they will thus strike hands with the murderers of their brethren; and every renewed attempt of this kind to convert them to the democracy, only results in their still further estrangement from the democratic fold. Elsewhere, persuasion is the grand electioneering weapon, wielded by all parties. Here it is "the knock-down and drag-out principle." "You vote as I tell you, or I'll kill you." This is the present language of Ku-Kluxism, and this is its great object: to frighten men into entering their political fold, as cattle are driven on board a steamboat, with immense clubs, and by using terrific oaths.

It is needless to say, that such a party is digging its own political grave, a thousand fold faster than could be done by the most determined efforts of all its enemies. But why does Ku-Kluxism flourish so vigorously at the South? Because an infatuation seems frequently to seize on the enemies of virtue, and induce them to shorten their own reign by the detestable lengths of vice to which they are driven, as the Spartans placed before their children the vilest debauchees, that they might witness for themselves the horrible effect of drunkenness. So the Ku-Klux "are made mad by the gods who would destroy them," in order to arouse within the whole nation, such a detestation of their conduct as shall eventually cause them to be swept from existence. Ku-Kluxism may wade to its knees in the blood of its murdered victims, for a season, but as sure as the laws of the universe are based on justice, so sure will its bloody reign terminate, and posterity will execrate the memory of its actors, as it does now that of the sanguinary heroes of the bloody days of the French Revolution of 1789. That in a free country, where every party has an equal political chance, any one party should choose to promote its ends by terror and bloodshed, is monstrous, is terribly infamous; and yet the democratic party at the South, essays to do that very thing, and its Northern allies look on approvingly, pat it on its head, and say, "good fellow." I do not charge upon the rank and file of Northern democracy, complicity with rebel Ku-Kluxism, but I do say that the leaders of this party, are "hale fellows well met," with the rebels, in all their nefarious schemes to upset our republican institutions. Southern Ku-Kluxism "lives and moves, and has its being," in the brains of such men as Frank Blair, Horatio Seymour, and *et id genus omne.* Seated on the platform in Tammany Hall, is the sachem, whose talismanic wand vibrates through the whole land, South and North; and as its Northern extremity comes in contact with the great heart of the Irish population, arousing within it all its latent hate of the negro, and of Protestantism; so does its far reaching Southern point, penetrate the great cesspool of Southern hatred of radicalism, creating a stench not to be endured by Northern olfactories, but gratefully inhaled by those of the Southern Ku-Klux. One word from Tammany, and both Irish hate, and Southern anger, are more fully aroused, and each wing of the great democratic army rushes to the conflict; the one to the pulling down of negro houses, and the burning of colored orphan asylums, the other to the wholesale slaughter of Union men, both black and white. Truly has Benj. Butler said, "That one word from the leaders of Northern democracy to their Southern allies, would put a stop to all this terrible effusion of Union blood."

The question then arises, *how shall the Ku-Klux be* overthrown? I answer, first, by such a mighty revolution in public opinion at the North, as shall render it impossible for the habitual allies of this accursed band, to control our Northern elections. This battle must commence at the North. Who then, are the allies of the Southern Ku-Klux? Let the records of the Congressional debates on the Ku-Klux bills, and their enforcement, reply! Every man, woman and child at the North, who endorses the efforts that will be made at the coming session of Congress, to prevent the re-enactment of that portion of our present Ku-Klux bill, that expires by its own limitation next July, is upholding the Ku-Klux. Previous to that time, a mighty, a satanic effort will be made, to sweep that bill out of existence, under the rotten plea, that it endangers the liberties of the South; and who are those who thus cry out, "forget the past, and let by-gones be by-gones?" Are they not the identical persons and papers, that attacked the lamented Lincoln, and termed him a monster of oppression, because he was crushing the rebellion? So it will be, with the opposition to the re-enactment of the only clause in the Ku-Klux bill, that renders it valuable. Deprive the President of the power to enforce its provisions by military power, and it ceases to be anything but a dead letter, as far as protecting Union men at the South is concerned. If the writ of habeas corpus is not suspended, the Southern civil law will infallibly deliver the culprit from the officers of justice; and not one of the Ku-Klux villains will be brought to punishment. I repeat the assertion that every one at the North, who endorses this opposition to the Ku-Klux bill, as it now stands, is a *friend to the Southern Ku-Klux*, and an enemy to those of us who are now being protected by the wise provisions of that bill. Deceive not yourselves, my friends. I have been in the hands of the Ku-Klux. I have lived among them for years, and I know that they stand in fear of no power on earth except the *military power* of the United States. If that cannot be used for their suppression, then farewell to all attempts to control this nefarious organization. O friends, follow me to the graves of the thousands of victims of these maddened men, and reflect that if it had not been for these rogues, those who now lie beneath the clods of the valley, might have been blessing innumerable homes with the smiles of their presence, homes which are now bereft of every earthly protector. Follow me to the sick chambers of thousands more, whose bodies are racked with pain, and their dislocated limbs tortured with indescribable anguish, the effect of the awful wounds inflicted by these vindictive men, and perhaps you will relent in your sad determination to give these rebels a new lease of power, and a prolonged furlough to inflict renewed vengeance on their helpless victims.

O, if you had endured what it has been my lot to endure, of torture, of mental agony, as I closely scanned every place of retreat, that I thought my house afforded, as a hiding place for my beloved ones, when Ku-Klux bullets flew thick and fast around me, you surely would not endorse these unfeeling men, who could take delight in pouring their shot into the premises of a single person, lying apparently in the agonies of death. Words can not express the sorrow I feel while I write these bitter words of condemnation, of many whom on many accounts, I highly esteem for their upright conduct, and for their friendship towards myself; but I cannot allow any personal feeling to deter me from discharging my whole duty towards the "scattered and peeled" ones, whom I came here to protect and benefit. Ask any Southern negro, who he fears more than any other person on earth, and his invariable reply will be, "The

Ku-Klux, sir." Take from him the terrible fear of these midnight assassins, and his life, now a series of terrors from early dawn to late at night, on account of these "spawn of hell," will become a bright and beautiful thing, gilded with the rainbow of promise, whose many colored beauties will then be indicative to him, of that joyful state on earth, that was so long the object of his fond anticipations during the terrible days of slavery. Ask the colored matron, as she gloomingly gazes into the distant twilight, and fancying she sees a shadow approaching, hastily gathers the coarse garments into which she is attempting to put a few hurried stitches, ere the light of day has fully vanished, why she thus leaves her important labors, and she responds with a heavy groan, "O, sir, the Ku-Klux, the Ku-Klux will see me;" and entering her rude cabin she shuts and bars the door behind her, as our fathers barred their doors against the wild Indians. Now this, dear reader, is no fancy sketch, but a living and dread reality, to one half of the 10,000 negroes in this county. One year from this time, rival candidates for the office of president of the United States, will be brought before you. Who they will be, of course no one can tell, but I beseech you, ye friends of the Southern freedmen, not to cast your votes for any of them, not open and pronounced enemies of the Southern Ku-Klux. Be not deceived by the cry of magnanimity towards the Ku-Klux. As well cry out forbearance towards the midnight robber, who plunders your house and murders your wife, and then sets the house on fire to conceal his villainy. When the "era of good feeling" is ushered in towards the rebels, and the Ku-Klux, let its dawning be hailed by kind words and good deeds towards your *own brethren*, who now reside in this unfortunate country; and towards the poor colored men, whom they have come here to protect. But it is unnecessary for me to add any more to this appeal. If you would hear no more of the outrages of the Ku-Klux, cease to uphold any party that endorses those outrages; and labor for the overthrow of all political organizations and candidates that would strike hands with Southern rebels. But if you cannot make up your mind thus to act, then will the sound of these outrages continue to ring in your unwilling ears, until the lurid light from the Southern sky tells of burning dwellings, and towns laid in ashes, by those who tired of waiting for you to avenge their wrongs, have undertaken the task themselves.

The next step for the overthrow of Ku-Kluxism, is to sustain the efforts, now being made at the South, to bring these villains to punishment. We must thoroughly divest ourselves of the foolish notion, that each state should be allowed to take care of its own criminals. Did not the United States government station soldiers in Kansas in the sanguinary days of '56, for the purpose of protecting its inhabitants from home outrages? To be sure, Kansas was then a territory, and not a state; but is not the government under as much obligation to protect its citizens in one part of the land, as in another? I do not understand that Congress received these rebel states back into the Union, with power to crush their loyal citizens. It was understood that the rebels had repented of their unjust acts; and obedience, on their part, to the laws of the Union was implied, if not expressed. As I write these words, I can look out upon a broad highway in front of my house, over which hundreds of Ku-Klux miscreants have passed; and from which have often sped the rebel bullets, just alluded to, as aimed at my house and the residents on my place. Supposing, before this ink is dry, I should hear the familiar sound of their bullets whizzing past my ears. What is my redress? To apply to the State authorities? As well might I apply to the authorities of Pandemonium. Satan is not divided against himself; and no sheriff, or constable of our county would aid in arresting a Ku-Klux. But if a few soldiers are stationed in this county, their known presence would prevent this firing, and other outrages; for then, a messenger could be dispatched to their camp, and soon, two or three of Uncle Sam's brave boys would be in hot pursuit of the marauders. In Kansas, the presence of the United States soldiers saved Lawrence from destruction, when attacked by 2300 men in Sept., 1856, and no one thought of condemning the expense thereby occasioned. The democratic party, although ridiculing our sufferings, yet sent soldiers to Kansas who sometimes protected us; and quite often defended our enemies from our attacks. If the presence of these soldiers shall be the means of preventing another civil war, will not the expense of maintaining them prove to be a good investment? Is not "an ounce of prevention worth a pound of cure"?

The present Ku-Klux bill, we fear, will never effectually quell these outrages; because it is limited in its provisions to those cases where the civil power has tried to suppress these disorders and has proved ineffectual. While we all admire and respect the noble men who procured its passage, we rejoice with trembling, lest on account of the above mentioned provision, it should prove ineffectual in those cases, where no "insurrection" exists.* I repeat that, in my opinion, nothing short of *permanent military occupancy* of the disaffected Southern regions, can render existence tolerable on the part of the hapless victims of the Ku-Klux outrages. Could their progenitors, the *Tories* of the Revolution, be guarded against by the people or the State government of South Carolina? Supposing this execrable doctrine of unqualified State rights, had been in vogue then, where would have been our Revolutionary ancestors of that State? It is well known that during the Revolution, South Carolina was kept from being overrun by the Tory Ku-Klux of those days, only by the constant occupancy of her state, by United States soldiers. As the well-disposed people of that state were then powerless in the hands of this organized Tory Ku-Klux mob, so *to-day*, those who would be friends of our government, are kept in awe by the descendants of these tories, whose hellish instinct for innocent blood they seem to have inherited. Did Massachusetts complain of the expense of thus protecting her revolutionary brethren? Did she not rather rejoice at being able to rid the country of its Tory oppressors? Did Samuel Adams, John Hancock, and Benjamin Franklin cry out against this "unwarrantable interference" in the affairs of the South? No, and why? simply because Adams, Hancock and Franklin were in earnest, and wished to have the British tyrants driven from the country. And do you think our "South

* The above lines were written just after the passage of the Ku-Klux bill in 1871 At the completion of this book in March, 1872, I am happy to state that our fears were not realized; but the bill was so grandly enforced, that life and property became comparatively secure. even in the worst portions of the state of Georgia. All honor to him who kept his promise made in the spring of 1869, that, "you shall be protected."

side" republican politicians would utter this cry to-day, if they were equally in earnest, in wishing to destroy rebel domination at the South? Whenever I hear the cry "hands off, don't punish the villains," I know from whence it comes, no matter what outward garb of republican sanctity the utterer may wear. Was Andrew Johnson any less an enemy of the Southern Unionists, because he professed to be a republican?

What would be said of a Methodist bishop who should cry out against an examination into the affairs of the "Book Concern," on the ground of "unwarrantable interference" in its rights? And of an orthodox clergyman who should publicly declare that an attempt to enforce the seventh commandment, was an "unwarrantable interference" with the rights of debauchees? And what shall we say of a professed republican, who "makes the welkin ring" with his shouts of opposition to the protection of Southern loyalists? But it is unnecessary to multiply words on this subject. Satan never was in favor of punishing his liege subjects, and his followers will always be opposed to the same "oppression!"

You are aroused at midnight by the cry of fire. You open your chamber window, and the lurid flames have lit up the whole earth around you, and the overhanging sky. Stalwart men are rushing to and fro, in frantic eagerness. The cry is everywhere heard "where is the engine? why don't it come?" You open your door and pass quickly to an adjoining engine house, and instead of beholding the frantic horses just ready to start on their benevolent errand, you see them unhitched, the doors of the engine house shut and barred, and sentinels pacing to and fro, to guard the building. Astonished beyond measure, you cry out, "why don't you open these doors and hurry to the fire, don't you know that the whole city is in danger?" The faithful guardians of the engine reply, "Yes, the fire ought to be put out, that's certain, but see here," and taking from his capacious pocket a printed document, one of them begins to read to you a clause from the constitution of the engine company, which expressly forbids an engine company acting, except under the orders of one of the officers of the company. "Swear in a new one, if there is no one here" you excitedly cry, "that fire *must be put out.*" Reluctantly and perceiving your earnestness, the men begin to comply, not without muttering a few curses against this "unwarrantable interference." They elect their captain in haste, and proceeding to the fire, aid effectually in subduing the angry element.

So now, the red and lurid flames of Southern hate, encircle the whole region, and dazzle its whole atmosphere. Brawny men of a dusky hue, rush from one point to another, crying out lustily for help. "Can't these flames be quenched?" they cry. "Yes," replies an honest Yankee teacher, "the government of the United States can quickly subdue them, and I will immediately apply to it for your protection." But some Southernized friend of that government, exclaims, "Not so fast, my friend, it is necessary to proceed with caution in these delicate matters. Perhaps the originators of those flames will not quite like our interference. You see we are only 'a congeries of states,' and not a consolidated government. We must act according to the genius of our institutions, and consult the Southerners first. If they say, 'Put out these fires,' we will quickly do it; but we dare not move *without their consent;*" and the flames leap higher, and shine more brilliantly, as they sweep over vast areas of ground, and their rapid crackling is heard, even up to the throne of the Most High.

But what can be done? You say, "Must not the Constitution be obeyed? And what is the Constitution? Is it not a facile instrument, ever yielding to the powerful touch of its most skillful manipulator? Gen. Jackson could say, "The Constitution as I understand it," and the whole democratic party said, "Amen." Does not every political party that has ever been founded, base its contradictory action, upon "The Constitution"? Did not the Southern rebels secede in obedience to its provisions? And do not all parties fight under its ample folds? If the constitution makes no provision for the protection of every citizen of the United States, *then it is high time it was altered.* Let this be the rallying-cry of all lovers of their country; *a Constitution that shall protect the meanest citizen*, living beneath its ample jurisdiction.

Said the Hon. Judge Gibson, of the Superior court of our county, "It is impossible for a colored man to obtain justice against a white man, in Columbia and several other counties." Now in all such counties, *martial law must be proclaimed.* Why sport with life and death in this matter? How silly to talk of punishing men for these crimes, when, as is well known, no court will convict them? Complain of Ku-Klux outrages to a Southern court, forsooth? As well complain to the Emperor of Brazil, of outrages inflicted upon the slaves there. He punish such outrages, when, as he believes, they are necessary to uphold slavery? So with a Southern court. They will never punish acts, *considered by them*, necessary to the well-being of society. During the six years that have elapsed since my arrival here, I have yet to learn, of the *first* instance of a white man being punished by our courts, for an outrage committed upon a colored man, and the name of such outrages "is *legion*, for they are *many*."

It is not many days, since a poor miserable victim of a white man's rashness came to my house, hardly able to crawl along, and detailed to me a story of his wrongs; which, he said, he had experienced at the hands of his employer, and which had nearly cost him his life; because, as he said, he had asked the white man to pay him some money, he thought was his due. Nothing whatever had been done to arrest the perpetrator of this deed; and in a feeble voice the poor invalid inquired of me, if there was no protection for him. I frankly told him I knew of none; for no jury would convict his assailant, however great might have been the outrage committed. Such a case as this, is not included in the long list of offences so amply provided for in the Ku-Klux bill, as can be seen by referring to its provisions. I ask, if it is for the white man's interest, or true welfare, that such a state of things should exist?

But as this whole subject will be treated upon under the head of "Protection for the Blacks," I will desist from farther comment. May the great Head of the Church, for the promotion of whose sacred cause, this volume is being written, accompany these truths to the hearts and minds of those who shall peruse them, causing all thus influenced, to re-dedicate themselves to His bleeding cause, as manifested in the sorrows of the least of His brethren. May the truth of that eternal law be recognized, that indissolubly binds together the interests of all mankind, rendering it impossible to trample upon the rights of one, without injuring all, as one block of granite cannot be removed from a church tower, without endangering the safety of the entire structure; and as one of the attributes of the Almighty cannot be annulled without effecting the glorious symmetry of His all-perfect character; so may we all learn, that the splendid fabric of American republicanism, cannot lift its burnished and glittering surface, before the admiring gaze of future millions of the race, unless every stone in that vast structure remains intact, polished brightly, and in harmonious relations with every other component part of the noble edifice. Then shall the great Architect of this Spiritual Temple, who ever operates through the humblest of His children, inspire the latest laborer upon this magnificent pile, as he "brings forth the head stone thereof," to do it, shouting aloud, "Grace, grace unto it;" and thus shall the Temple, once uncouth and marred, because of the substraction of so much of its material, become beautiful beyond description, a "crown of glory in the hand of the Lord, and a royal diadem in the hands of its God," "causing the Gentiles to come to its light, and *Kings* to the brightness of its rising."

END OF PART FIRST.

PART II.

CHAPTER I.

PROTECTION OF LOYALISTS, WHITE AND BLACK.

Having endeavored to present to the reader faithfully, the "lights and shadows" of negro life, and to do justice to the rebel side of the story, adhering firmly to the determination expressed in the first pages of this book, "to extenuate nothing, and to set down naught in malice;" but to tell the plain, simple truth, let who would be offended; I now proceed to explain what seem to me, the measures necessary to "bring light out of all this darkness," and to make this Southern wilderness, "bud and blossom as a rose;" and cause the serpent of Southern hate, to eat the dust of the earth, instead of fattening on the blood of its poor victims.

The preceding pages have been mainly devoted to the arousing the sympathies of the reader, in behalf of the colored population of the South. I now wish to show how these sympathies can be manifested so as to secure the highest welfare, of this unfortunate class of our fellow citizens. Among the several measures essential to the accomplishment of this result, the foremost is *protection* of all classes, black as well as white, and union men as well as rebel democrats.

It is the well established policy of all civilized government to protect all of its citizens alike, without especial reference to the moral or intellectual status of such persons. A Jew has the same claim upon the protecting care of our government, that the most devoted Christian has. A drunkard can call upon our authorities to defend him against enemies, as well as the most renowned doctor of divinity. This being the case, it follows that however base may be the victims of "rebel outrages," they have a right to be protected from those outrages, as much as if they were "saints of the first water." In these days of prison reform, and of anti-capital punishment, when in nearly every locality, petitions are often signed to avert the fate of a murderer, it surely will not answer for us to say, "Well, let the freedmen go, they are too vicious for us to interfere in their behalf. They deserve the hard fate they experience." But such is not the "genius of our republican institutions." Like Him who "sendeth his rain upon the just and unjust," does this government open wide its arms of universal beneficence, saying to Jew and Gentile, to bond and free, to male and female, to saint and sinner, "repose beneath the luxuriant foliage of our mighty trees, bask in the sunshine of our loveliest grassy lawns, inhale the delicious perfume of our sweetest flowers, regale yourselves alike upon the bountiful harvests of our fertile soil, partake of all that distinguishes our country from other countries, and renders it deserving of the appellation "home of the free and land of the brave." You may be undeserving of these rich behests poured into your laps so abundantly, by our all bountiful Mother earth; but they shall not be withheld from you even if you use them but to abuse them, and strive to turn the gifts of God into curses for yourselves. Thus speaks the goddess America to all of every name and clime, who seek a home beneath the magnificent folds of her ever glorious Star Spangled banner, and desire to repose in the broad shadow of her political ægis, the far famed Constitution of America.

" Not the righteous, but *sinners*, " Jesus came to save." " We have all sinned and come short of the glory of God," and when we were without strength, " Christ died for the *ungodly*." Were we all to be weighed in the balance of strict and impartial justice, who shall say, that our scale would hang any lower than does that of the poor imbruted freedman, with the scars of his long night of servitude still visible in every part of his person. With the red sword of justice lifted over our heads, should not we, as well as they, need the benignant form of the angel of mercy to push aside its fiery blade?

But we ask for mercy for those children of sin, on account of the tens of thousands of true men and women, whose fate is indissolubly linked to theirs; and also for the sake of great numbers of the freedmen themselves, who do not imitate the vices of the majority. We also claim it because of our own country's reputation, whose " good name " is everywhere spoken against, on account of its failure to protect those who fled to its rescue, in that solemn hour of trial forced upon it, by those from whose wickedness our wards are now suffering. Manifestly then, we are called upon by every claim of humanity and justice, to do something for the protection of the Southern blacks, and their white friends.

But it may be said by the Northern people, in reply to this statement, " We have done all we could, consistently with the nature of our government, and that having given the blacks their freedom, and the elective franchise, secured by constitutional amendments, our duty to them is wholly discharged." Far be it from me to arraign the republican party as a criminal of the deepest dye, on account of its failure to do the whole of its duty towards the defenders of its country's flag. Parties are no more perfect than individuals, and "he that is without sin" in this matter, can cast the first stone at the republican party. No one can discharge his whole duty, while much of his time is occupied in beating off the dogs howling around his track. Ever since the war, its enemies have barked and howled, at every movement of this party in favor of the freedmen. Step by step, every wise and decent measure for the protection of the freedmen, has been disputed by the warm allies of the South, and one after another of the republican strongholds, have yielded to this incessant political bombardment. The republican party would have been more than human, if, under these circumstances, it had never failed in its duty to the black man. To be sure, it may be foolishly said, that the republicans, being in the majority, had all power in their hands, and should never have hearkened to the "mad dog" cry of its opponents. This is undoubtedly true; but, nevertheless, in its failure to do so, it has only followed the example of the "ins" every where, who are more afraid of the "outs," than of their own consciences. Let us, then, bestow the true meed of praise upon that party, that saved the Nation from the horrors of a long continued civil war, by the simple, but noble act, of emancipation, which raised up four millions of stalwart defenders of its country's flag, in the very heart of its enemy's country. Let us also applaud that party, who, in the face of the direst democratic opposition, placed the ballot in the hands of the emancipated ones, and altered the constitution to guarantee them in its possession. We will not forget, also, its noble achievements, through the Freedmens' Bureau, and all of its efforts in behalf of the education of the blacks. Still less, any more than "our right hand shall forget its cunning," will we ever forget its earlier efforts, in behalf of bleeding, and dying Kansas, when a little handful of "Free-State" men were hemmed in on every side by the myrmidons of the slave power, gathered from the purlieus of every Southern city; and were finally plucked from the jaws of these insatiate monsters, by the timely interference of this noble party.

But while endeavoring to do justice to the republican party, it will not do for me, as one of its truest friends, to bolster it up in its short-comings. "Faithful are the wounds of a friend." As such, I must be permitted to avow my convictions, that this party has lamentably failed in doing *all* of its duty towards the emancipated slaves, and needs to be exhorted to return to its "first love." If this party could only remain as single-hearted in favor of the right, as it was in the days of its "first espousals" to Christ, in the form of bleeding humanity, all would yet be well. Let us trust that its vitality "is not dead, but only sleeping," and that it shall yet experience a "time of refreshing from the presence of the Lord," that shall cause it to outdo all its former efforts, in behalf of "Christ's brethren," remembering that "in as much as it does it to one of the least of them," it does it to Christ himself.

It is impossible, for one not a resident of this country, to form an adequate conception of the perfect powerlessness of the colored race before their oppressors. Time would fail me, and expediency would forbid my detailing more minutely, the outrages so common at the South. The Northern press teems with their melancholy recital; and the pages of the N. Y. National *Standard*, for more than a year, have been crowded with the sad tales. If anyone desires more positive information, than I have already given, he is respectfully referred to the printed testimony given before the "Reconstruction Committee," in the case of Georgia, of which Sec. Boutwell was chairman, and published in the spring of 1869; which pamphlet can be obtained by application to the proper United States authorities, perhaps to Ex. Gov. Boutwell himself. I can only say a few words in explanation of the *reasonableness* of the stories so minutely narrated.

Imagine a person cowed down by long years of the most abject thraldom! His manhood denied by law, and he classed among goods and chattels. "A slave can do nothing, possess nothing, nor acquire anything, but what belongs to his master." (Louisiana Slave Code.) "Slaves shall be deemed, sold, taken, reputed, and adjudged in law, to be chattels personal in the hands of their owners and possessors, to all intents, constructions, and purposes *whatsoever*." (South Carolina Slave Code.) Mark the completeness of the subjection, "to all purposes whatsoever." Could anything be any more sweeping? This was the condition of the slaves before emancipation.

Has emancipation altered the slaves' nature one whit, except to disabuse his mind of the fact, that his master had the right thus to control him? The idea of his inferiority had been enstamped upon his mind from time immemorial, and how could a few years of freedom efface it entirely? There it still remains, burning into and blistering his inmost soul; and effectually neutralizing all his aspirations after equality with his white brethren. While a slave, he rebelled inwardly against this assumption of power, as a worm squirms when trodden upon; but, he nevertheless fully believed, in the existence of this inferiority on his part. He knew that he was powerless as a child, in the strong grasp of his tyrannical master. This belief of his own inferiority, then produced abject submission in the vast majority of cases. The heavenly influences of religion were invoked in the service of this same falsehood; and he was taught that God had made him inferior to the white man. Now as "like causes produce like effects," so the continued belief of this dogma, must perpetuate the false reign of the master over the freedman. It is true, that over-weening self-conceit, has been described as one of the characteristics of the black man; but this conceit seldom manifests itself in the presence of a genuine, "lord of the whip and spur." Whatever pretensions the black man may have made of skill or excellence, they all "vanish into the air" as one of these knighted "lords of the manor" approaches. It is seldom, that in the face and eyes of his former master, that a freedman will dare repeat the story of his past or present wrongs. On this account, their testimony cannot always be relied upon, when most needed. Multitudes of outrages are only witnessed by the black hands of the oppressor; and it is nearly impossible to persuade them to testify against him. Often, will they deny the statements they have made a moment before, when a rebel approaches, only to reaffirm them after his absence.

Truth compels me to state, that the black race at the

South, is mostly an abject race, notwithstanding the innumerable provoking acts they commit. These acts are, almost always, committed behind the backs of their employers, and seldom in their presence. And it is not to be denied, that they have more respect for a loud-mouthed Southern declaimer, who boasts of having yesterday fired at two of his negroes, than they have for the gentle-minded Yankee, who approaches them with love in his heart, and uses only, words of a mild and tender accent. Like Topsy, they say to such an one, "La! Miss Ophelia, you can't hurt a 'skeeter." All rude natures, stand in awe of physical, much more than of moral or intellectual power. I well recollect while in Kansas, a certain pro-slavery doctor, who constantly "defied all the armies of the living God," in the shape of Free-State men, so that none dared to question his word. I saw him one day, cut the face and head of a lawyer in Lawrence, because he *refused to admit* the truth of some proposition he had made. But one day, "Davy Evans," from Missouri, came to Lawrence, and learning of the fear that this brow-beating doctor everywhere inspired, he marched boldly up to him, and poured out such a hurricane of terrible epithets, into the affrighted man's ears, as I never thought it possible for a man to utter; and when he had finished, he flourished his bowie-knife in his face, and said: "There now, help yourself if you can, you foul whelp of hell!" The braggadocia doctor turned as pale as a sheet, and from that day onward, was never heard to utter an uncivil, or scarcely a loud word in the streets of Lawrence. It is so with the Southerners, both black and white. The rebels turn pale only, when Uncle Sam precipitates himself upon them; and the blacks are only awe-stricken, in the presence of the rebels.

Now, who can wonder that the rebels exercise this power, that they are so conscious of possessing over the blacks? It would be contrary to human nature for them not to avail themselves of its influence. Their object is to rule over the blacks. This they perceive they can do by force, far better than they can do in any other way. Consequently, the law of force prevails largely, and far outshadows in magnitude, every other law thought of in relation to their treatment of the colored population. As the blacks live under the force of the same law of fear that they formerly did, and are not changed in their mental habits in this respect, so have the rebels failed to change one whit in their disposition to use the same force that they did in the days of slavery. They perceived its excellent results *then*, they are fast learning of its equally important influence *now*. The abolition of slavery neither infused nobleness of character into the hearts of the emancipated ones, nor kindness of disposition into those of their masters.

Under such circumstances, what else can be expected than the exercise of terrific power on the part of the whites? Those who profess to doubt its existence, lack mental perception; and fail to credit the universal operation of the great laws of the human mind.

So far from there being any reason for the wide spread unbelief respecting these outrages, the mystery to my mind is, that they are not ten times more common than they are. The whites would be angelic, rather than human, if under the circumstances of the case, they did not abuse the helpless creatures over whom they possess so much power. The mere voice of the rebels will start the poor blacks from any lethargy, into which they may have unconsciously fallen. Their word of command even now awakens within them, the old sound of the overseer's whip, especially as it is apt to be followed with stinging blows as in the days of slavery. Those of the Northern people who affect to ignore this state of things, remind me of the ostrich, who in the face of danger, hides its head in the sand, fancying that the danger is averted, because it can no longer behold its approach. Some of us at the North have become tired of hearing about the black man's cruel treatment, and so we hide our eyes from the sight, and then go around rejoicing because we can no longer witness his scars. But, dear reader, remember that while you are conjuring up ten thousand other objects of benevolence to occupy your mind upon, and saying, "this and that thing *is the next reform* in the order of God's providence, now that the black question is disposed of," "the black man at the South," still remains bleeding at every pore, and wondering why the fulfillment of the promises you made him of relief, is so long delayed. The infatuation of the American people on this subject is simply amazing, and can be but the prelude to a more terrible awakening in reference to it, than words seem to be destined to accomplish; even such a one as the angel of war only can produce. How any friend of the freedman can for a moment entertain the idea that the black man's condition, as far as the rebels are concerned, is improving, I am at a loss to divine. Here I am every few days delectably engaged in dodging rebel bullets, and my friends at the North are rejoicing over the happy "restoration of concord and harmony" throughout all our borders.

Sitting at a front window in my lonely retreat, penning these lines, suddenly I hear the crackling of musketry. I arise and step outside the door, and behold three colored girls all racing through the yard, with their clothes fluttering in the breeze, and they almost out of breath. Behind their fleeing forms, I notice our front gate wide open, and going up to the oldest of these girls I say, "Docia, why will you always leave that gate open? Haven't I told you ever so many times you must shut that gate. I shall be obliged to fasten it up, if you all will persist in leaving it open."

She replies, "O massa, I done forget all 'bout that ar gate, I'se so busy trying to get away from dem ar rebs. I'll look out next time sure."

I then ask her older brother standing near, what is it about the rebs? and he says, "Didn't you hear them guns a minit ago?" I reply in the affirmative, and then learn, that these three girls were passing peaceably along on a bank near the road, when some white men in a buggy came by, and hallooed to them to know what they were, "democrats or radicals?" "They replied "radicals," when instantly a volley of rebel bullets was poured upon them, which they found it difficult to escape from. I returned to my house, and as I was describing this outrage for future reference, my eye fell upon some passages in a Northern newspaper, lying partly beneath the paper on which I was writing.

Some distinguished friend of "amity" was writing to some other one, whom he seemingly was attempting to hoodwink into believing in his peculiar political faith; and he used words like the following, "Why be forever stirring up these flames of discord between the North and the South? The South are well-disposed; and treat their negroes with all that urbanity of disposition, for which they have been so long and so justly celebrated. It is only the miserable carpet-baggers, who would persuade you to the contrary. Come, friend, let us 'bridge over' this awful chasm that has so long divided those hearts yearning for each other's love. Let us 'clasp hands' over this yawning aperture, and let 'by-gones be by-gones.'" The reader can imagine my feelings towards the miserable political schemer, that was defying heaven with his tissue of misrepresentations.

And then, again, knowing the irascible spirit of the Southerners, and the intensely provoking conduct of many of the blacks, there is still less room for wonder at the black man's fate. I question if the imperturbable spirit of a William Penn, if here, would fail to be wrought upon at times, so as to be tempted to say or do something awful to these provoking creatures, the former plantation-slaves. Innumerable are the instances of their provoking conduct in little affairs, one or two of which, as they have just occurred, I will relate, as an illustration of many others. Day before yesterday, I asked a colored man, who owes me a large sum of money, which will probably always be as large, and one, on whom I had conferred many pecuniary favors, to loan me his mule for an hour or two; when he refused, although I had, not long since, loaned him ten dollars to buy corn with, for this very mule. Another man who also owed me a small sum agreed to go into the woods, and cut a little wood for me on the next day; but failed entirely to keep his promise, although he knew I was entirely out of wood. And then, as elsewhere stated, their habit of never obeying your orders exactly as they are given, is proverbial. Who can wonder at the exasperation of the rebels towards them? It must be borne in mind that the Southern people are none of your patient Jobs, but almost universally fiery Hotspurs; with whom a blow is sure to follow a word, and quite as often to come first. They are irascible by nature, and impetuous beyond conception. No Southern man dare call another a liar, without being prepared for the use of powder and ball.

Then, human life never was considered so sacred, as it formerly was, and is now, to a great extent, in our beloved North. The doctrines of peace never had, even a "corporal's guard" of believers at the South; and non-resistance with them, is the strangest conceivable infatuation.

Now, taking all these things into consideration, is it to be wondered at, that the newly emancipated slave, fares hardly, at the hands of his former master?

It is my opinion that he who saves us from doing wrong, serves us a better turn, than he who encourages us in that wrong, or endeavors to protect us from its consequences. Therefore, I feel that I can truly claim to be a much better friend to the Southerner, than those who cry out, "Let him alone; don't encroach upon his rights." I love the white man at the South, equally with the black man; and my heart yearns over his unfortunate condition, fully as much as it does over that of his miserable victims. I have often told the blacks, that I would shed my blood as quickly in defence of the whites against their outrages, as in defence of the blacks against the whites. I love all men without reference to race or color; and always intend to defend the oppressed against the oppressor, let the former be the proudest, or the lowest of creation. My motto is now, when the *blacks do wrong let them suffer*, and when the *whites do wrong, let them suffer also.* It is as much of a sin, to deprive the whites of their rights, as to do the same towards the blacks. I wish for equal and impartial justice to be done to all, irrespective of race or color.

It is then, because of my love for the whites, and of my intense interest in their welfare, that I advocate this measure of protection for the blacks. It is for the interest of the whites pecuniarily, that they should not be allowed to continue this insane treatment of their former slaves. No Northern man likes to bring his family into such a nation of fighters. Capital is proverbially timid, and can never allow its golden streams to flow into the laps of those who know not how to guard the valuable deposit. The press of the South, that is so continually laboring to foster this turbulent state of affairs, is the greatest enemy the South can possibly have; and is doing far more to curtail its prosperity, than the whole legion of "carpet baggers," multiplied a million fold. If it was once understood at the North, that these outrages had ceased, real estate would increase in value, at least fifty per cent.

But who can say that it is best for the moral nature of the white man, that he should be left to cut the throats of his employees? How wrong for any one to accuse us of injustice to our white friends, simply because we are not willing to allow them to commit murder? I once, by force, restrained a colored woman from doing violence to her boy, and half an hour afterwards, she came to my house, and thanked me for my interference, saying: "I should have felt terribly bad, if I had killed my boy." And so with very many of the whites. An intelligent Southerner, once thanked my sister for interfering in his attempts to 'shoot a negro.' In our better moments we all love the one who rescues us from the power of the tempter, better than the one who tempts us. Like a loving father we would hold the arms of these would be murderers, like the two Southerners who are represented in our picture of the Apling mob, as thwarting a fire-eating Ku-Klux in his murderous intent. Supposing that poor slave of passion, had succeeded in hurling that rock at my head, how much happier would he have been after he had executed his fell purpose; and were not his "oppressors," as he doubtless considered them, his best friends?

I have stated that the black man is utterly powerless in the hands of the whites. Judge Gibson, as already quoted, states that "civil law affords *no security* to the black man in Columbia, and several other counties." I can see no practical difference between his helplessness now, and in the days of slavery. Indeed, I think there are far more murders committed to-day, than there were in those days, for the sufficient reason that then, the slave sustained a monied relation to his master, that is not now the case. To-day, who cares how many darkies are murdered, so long as no white man suffers thereby? In the year 1870, a black man on Hon. J. M. Rice's place, in the edge of this county, was deliberately shot dead by a white man for refusing to go and work for him, when he had agreed to work for some one else. A distinguished planter, who happened to be a strong friend of the colored man, said he would have the murderer punished, if it cost him all of his property, and the murderer was arrested. When the trial came on, after some delay, a letter was produced in court, ostensibly signed by a colored man living on the same plantation, saying, "that the white man killed the black man in self-defence," and the white man was discharged on this testimony. The black man afterwards denied having signed such a letter, or having been questioned at all in reference to the matter. This is the second black man that has been killed in that neighborhood, since I came here. This plantation is eight miles from here, and is under the control of black men, the owner, Mr. Rice, fearing to reside there, on account of the oft-repeated threats against his life, he having been a member of the Georgia Legislature, and a devoted friend of the black man, at all times and places.

It may be asked, if the story of these outrages is true, how does it happen that my life has been spared for so many years? My reply is, that the preservation of my life is as great a mystery to me, as it is to all of my friends at the North. I do not see how it can be sufficiently accounted for, without believing in the interference of God in the affairs of men; but still it might savor of arrogance for me to assert that God had saved my life, and allowed hundreds of others, as devoted to his cause, to perish at the hands of the rebels, and I will therefore endeavor to account for it, from a human point of view. I am sure it is not because of any remarkable good will towards me, on the part of the whites; and still less because I am suspected of any leaning towards the democracy.

But it is well understood throughout this county, that murdering me would not be an altogether safe proceeding on the part of the rebels. It is true that I have never countenanced the idea, that my death should be avenged by the blacks, but nevertheless I feel morally certain that if in an evil hour it should be brought about, it would be the "additional ounce that breaks the camel's back" and scenes not altogether pleasant would be quite likely to follow. At least I gather this from conversation with the blacks, and from their anxiety to destroy Apling, as described by my sister, on her arrival at my apparent death-bed. The blacks, it is true, will and do steal from me, and they do many other things calculated to wound my feelings; but I must do them the credit to believe, that they would defend my life to the last, and many of them would die to save me. I owe my safety then to my unremitted efforts in their behalf, and I know that in my destruction, all their hopes for future elevation in this neighborhood would be so effectually dashed to the ground, that in their despair they would fight terribly. Again if I should be killed, there would be no one about here to counsel moderation, and their anger would find vent in bloody deeds; they being no longer content with the defence words afforded them. Let me therefore warn my rebel friends, who may be displeased at some of my remarks in this book, neither at this or at any other time, to wreak their vengeance on me, or on my property; for I cannot interfere to protect them after my exit from this world.

One evening I was detained on the public road, by conversing with a gentleman until after dark, and before I could reach my house, I met fifteen colored men, armed and in military style marching to my relief, commanded by one who had been a soldier in the Union army; and they returned in triumph, with my person in their convoy. Then, it is also well known, that no attack could be made on our place, without the most determined resistance of men, women and children. Men and dogs are on guard at all hours of the day and night; and woe be to whoever attacks us, unless we are overpowered by a multitude. It is our ability to defend ourselves, and the determination of the brave hearts on our place to do so, that renders my situation at all safe. It is *not* the civil law that affords me any protection whatever.

But I submit to all candid people, if it is right for me to be thus left "to the powers of my own right arm" for protection. Ought not the government of the United States, to afford me protection in the discharge of my *official* duties at least? Does not the Constitution guarantee to every citizen, protection in the discharge of his duties as an officer of the law? To be sure, I hold my present position as an appointee of the Governor of our state; but has he no authority? Has Gov. Bullock never applied to the United States government for protection against domestic violence? No one, who has long been in Washington, since the inauguration of our Governor, and been at all conversant with public affairs there, can deny that long and loud have been the appeals for aid from our state government, backed by the most thrilling ones from a multitude of our citizens; and yet these cries have not been heeded. By what method of reasoning can it be denied that Section 4th, of Article 4th, of the United States Constitution, renders the duty of our government imperative in this matter? As an officer of the law, elected by the people of this county, was I driven from my post, and forced to resign my office, or suffer death. The United States government has been repeatedly informed of the facts in the case, and our executive has, as repeatedly, applied for help to suppress "domestic violence"; but in this, and many other cases, it *has not been granted.* The people of Columbia County, Georgia, are, to-day, precisely as great rebels against the United States government, as they were, when marshalled in battle array, against Gen. Grant, behind the defences of Richmond. Did not the members of that mob defy the power of Congress? And do they not to-day, stand triumphant over the armies of the United States? But my case is by no means a solitary one. Great numbers of other officials are not able to hold the offices to which they have been elected; and especially to visit their homes while they thus hold them. But it matters not to *me*, that I am thus deprived of office; for no earthly power would induce me to attempt to occupy that position at present. I only state facts, to show precisely how matters stand; to let the people of the North know, that in Columbia County, Georgia, to say nothing of other counties, a regularly elected, and appointed officer of the government, can no more hold the office to which he is entitled, than if he was an inhabitant of Europe, and should attempt to fill an office here. Georgia thus *rides triumphantly* over the Union; and yet we are tenderly invited to "let these dear, erring, and repenting, brethren have their own way. Don't trample on their sacred rights! Do be kind to the unfortunate fellows." Sometimes I see it argued in Northern papers, that, the rebellion having ceased at the South, there is no reason why the South should not be left to control its own affairs, the same as Massachusetts, and other Northern states. I can remember when United States soldiers were freely used in Massachusetts, not to suppress a riot, but to guard against an anticipated one; and this by the direction of a democratic administration. Why, then, should it be deemed so unjust, to use United States soldiers to suppress riots of long continuance? The fact is, there has never been an entire cessation of the rebellion at the South. I do not think there is a city, town, or county, throughout the South, where the life of a Union man is *perfectly safe.*

But it may be asked what kind of protection do I demand for myself and others? I reply, simply, that which *will be effectual*, and no other. I ask for no unnecessary expense, for no useless array of military power; but simply for that kind of protection, that will avail to render safe my life and property; and that of all Union men, black, as well as white. And I ask it under those clauses of the Constitution, that are ample in their provisions on this point. In the Section, above quoted, it is made the *imperative duty* of the United States government, to "guarantee to every State, a republican form of government." A republic is defined by lexicographers to be "a government where the supreme power is vested in the people." Of course, not in a small minority of the people, but in the majority.

It is a cardinal principal of a republican government, that the will of a majority of the people as expressed through the ballot box, shall be the law of the land, to which the majority shall submit. Then, whenever a portion of the people shall refuse to submit to the expressed will of the majority, Congress or the Executive is bound to subdue this insurrection; and that *without application from the State Executive.* In the article alluded to, there are three distinct clauses, first "the United States (whoever that may be), *shall guarantee* to *every* State in this Union, a republican form of government;" secondly, "shall protect each of them against invasion;" and thirdly, "on application of the Legislature or

Executive, against domestic violence." Now, as soon as that august power answering to the term "United States," learns of the overthrow of the laws by a mob or otherwise, it is bound to send its soldiers immediately to re-establish those laws; unless it shall be made plain to them that such a step is unnecessary. How comical it would look for a father of a large family not to establish order among his disobedient children, because the disobedient ones do not request his interference? Were our fathers fools when they adapted this wise provision? Says an intelligent commentator on this clause, "It was left as it is, with the presumption that the authority of Congress would authorize an interference to suppress *any* insurrection, violence or revolution, which was so serious or universal, as to *prevent* any Legislature or Executive application for aid." No other than this, can be a common sense view of the case; for if Congress is excused from action, on account of not being requested by the State authorities to act, then the most formidable of all rebellions, where the State government is implicated, cannot be quelled; and this too, if nineteen-twentieths of the State are opposed to the rebellion, provided the State government is in its favor. Verily, such an interpretation of the Constitution would emphatically render it, what it is now deemed to be by the Southern people, a mere "rope of sand" to be blown hither and thither, according to the whims of ever so small a minority of the people; and we are left to that most despicable of all governments, one where the *aristocracy* governs.

If any one doubts that Union men need protection, let him come here and occupy my post. Let him simply engage in teaching the blacks, and in advising them politically and otherwise; and after the knowledge of that fact has been spread abroad, let him travel alone in the upper part of this county, or in Lincoln, and I am of the opinion that he would be on the stool of political conviction, in a short space of time. I have often wished that some of these public men who talk so loudly about the oppression of the Southern people, could be obliged to live here a few months; but the trouble is, while they talk so loudly about the lies of carpet baggars, they keep their own precious selves safely ensconced in snug quarters at home. I may be allowed to say, that during my residence here, I have been much oftener threatened, and have been in much more real danger than I was thirty years ago, when residing in the State of Kentucky. Although I proclaimed my hostility to slavery, yet I travelled alone and unarmed through large portions of that State and Tennessee, and never was attacked by a rebel highwayman, or assaulted by a pro-slavery mob. Never during several years residence there, was a single bullet aimed at my person, or any kind of a deadly weapon used in assailing me, although my life was often threatened. But how has it been here? Not a day or night has passed, for more than one half of the time I have been here, without my fearing an attack from the rebels. Oftentimes, while sitting quietly in my house, has the noise of rebel bullets disturbed my serenity; and men have rode by my house rending the air with their hideous shouts and murderous yells, as if all Pandemonium was let loose. For months and months in succession, I have not passed a single night without springing from my bed at hearing some unusual noise, and at such times hours would elapse before I could rest quietly again. I seldom go any where unarmed, not even on the road leading from my house, unless accompanied by other parties. There are portions of this county, and the whole of neighboring counties, where I should no more think of travelling than among the wildest Indians on our continent. No Union man's life would be safe for a moment, in some counties near here. In one county, not even General Butler, with all his confidence of personal impunity, nor General Grant himself could travel safely. There is no spot in this county, where a Union man would be safe in addressing a political meeting, except at a very few private houses. An attempt was made last Fall, to hold a meeting at Apling, but it ended in the severe wounding of one of the speakers, the Hon. J. M. Rice; and I think all classes agree that free speech is virtually at an end in this region of country.

Now, I ask all reasonable men, if it was for such a purpose as this, that blood and treasure were poured out like water, during our sanguinary struggle with the South? Previous to the war, I could travel unmolested through certain Southern states, with no government to appeal to, in case of an attack; but now, I can go no where, unarmed, except at the peril of my life. Then, my sleep was never disturbed by fear of midnight assassins; but now, hardly a night passes over my head, without my slumbers being aroused from apprehensions of this kind. Then, not a gun was kept at my bedside, nor a revolver ever hidden beneath my pillow; but now, such weapons, with a plentiful supply of ammunition, are every night, placed carefully where they can be easily snatched, at a moment's warning; and they are often grasped, amid the darkness of the night, to repel a supposed attack. Sometimes, our family devotions at night, are disturbed by a rapid discharge of musketry; and, on enquiry, we find that a company of rebels have stopped in front of the house, and discharged their weapons at our abode; and been replied to, by the fire-arms of our valiant boys, who are usually ready for such an emergency.

Men of the Union army, soldiers who braved rebel bullets, and waded through the noxious, miasmatic localities of the South, inhaling the deadly malaria there engendered at every step, in order that you might behold "the flag of our Union" safely waving throughout the entire South; are you satisfied with the result of your perilous efforts? Do you think that you risked your lives for a worthy purpose, if such are the fruits of our "glorious war"? Will you sit supinely by, and hear sycophantic politicians declaim about the "unconstitutionality" and "unnecessary expense," of measures designed to render your services productive of good; and to prevent you from being described as those who have "spent your money for that which is not bread, and your labor for that which satisfieth not"? What have we gained by incurring this tremendous debt, so paralyzing to all branches of industry? It seems to me, as if the possession of a tithe of the spirit, that actuated our fathers at Bunker Hill, would arouse every son of the North, to crush this rebellious spirit, that not content with defeat in battle, seeks by midnight raids, to accomplish what it failed to do in open and fair warfare. Shall we allow our foes to effectually accomplish *secretly*, what they could not at the cannons' mouth? Then the deafening roar of artillery, that, like a mighty earthquake, shook our nation, shall prove to have been, but a deceptive sound, ushering in a fatal triumph, won by our enemies, the fruits of which, they are now enjoying.

I am amazed, and almost petrified with astonishment, as I read the crazy assertions of pretended lovers of their country, that military occupancy of the South, would be a "dangerous precedent," and inimical to republican institutions. Depend upon it, such fearful souls, have been galvanized in their intellectual perceptions, by the power of the Southern *siren*, who so bewitchingly sings in their deluded ears, such soft strains of seducing music, as produces in their emasculated souls, this infatuated love for the monstrous Southern harlot, who is "drunken with the blood of saints, and with the blood of the martyrs of Jesus."

Nothing is so dangerous to our institutions as anarchy and mob-law. I cannot speak calmly of such folly. Dangerous to protect men and women from such brutal outrages, as we fail to find recorded on the pages of history, and as cannot possibly be described on paper; outrages so unusual, that not one in ten of those who hear of them, would believe to be true! One such outrage, was lately described to me by a rebel himself, and excels in intense obscenity, and terrific cruelty, anything occurring in the very purlieus of hell itself. It is my candid opinion, that but comparatively few of the outrages actually committed, ever find publicity in the papers of the land; for I have never seen the remotest allusions to matters of everyday occurrence in our neighborhood. There are vast tracts of territory where no ear, but that of the Almighty, ever listens to the deep throbbings of innumerable souls, who are made "to drink of the wine of the wrath" of these pro-slavery demons, day after day, and year after year. In our county, I know of not a single resident, who would ever make public the story of any outrage upon the black man, however great; and I do not think there is more than one in Lincoln County, adjoining ours. Over all of these vast tracts of land, the stillness of midnight reigns, as far as the voice of an opposer of tyranny is heard; and the unbroken silence, that can be almost felt, it is so profound, is only interrupted by the crack of the demon-like scourge, which is followed by the deep groan of the miserable wretch, to whose back it is applied, crying out, in mournful refrain, "How long, O Lord, how long?" And from whom proceeds this cry of tyranny, but from those rebels, and their allies, who condemned Lincoln's "tyranny," in calling for the first seventy-five thousand men? It comes from men who care not a straw for the Constitution, or its provisions, and who, like a noted rebel leader in Augusta, Georgia, "thanked God that he had once trampled under foot the United States flag, and hoped that he would be able to do it again." These men were then shocked, and are now scandalized, at the use of measures designed to perpetuate the glories of that flag, by making it the synonym with justice and humanity, wherever on earth its starry folds may proudly wave, and

> "Peace and order and beauty, draw
> Round its symbol of light and law."

One word in reference to the expense of military occupancy, of disaffected Southern territory. This could hardly exceed three millions of dollars per annum, allowing fifty men and twenty-five horses to be stationed in each of twenty such counties as ours in Georgia, and the same in each of the other ten states. And what but a "drop in the bucket" is such an item in comparison to the millions wasted annually in listening to long winded speeches in Congress in opposition to such righteous measures? Why, the mileage itself of members of Congress, over and above the amount to which they are legitimately entitled, added to the large sums wasted through the "franking" privilege, would nearly defray the expense of so wise a measure. And then the vast sums expended in carrying on our Indian wars, could be easily lessened enough to sustain a measure, to say the least, fully as rational as the attempt to subjugate by force of arms alone, the vast Indian tribes now hanging upon the skirts of our nation.

Were not forty millions of dollars expended in subduing the brave Osceola and his Seminole subjects? Was any thing then said by the South about the useless expense? Is it not equally important to subdue men not possessing a tithe of Osceola's humanity, and all of his cruelty? In the year 1836, did not the South wring from the pockets of Northern working-men, more than this sum, by having the "surplus revenue" unevenly distributed? And were not twenty-seven millions of the capital of the old United States bank, sunk at the South, without a word of complaining on the part of the North? Ever since this government was founded, has not the great Northern workshop poured its treasures of wealth into the lap of the miserable Southern mistress, who has so effectually captivated the hearts of Northern politicians? One writer estimates this sum as high as several hundreds of millions of dollars; and now is it any hardship for the South to be called upon to reimburse a small portion of this amount. Let the government of every Southern State be obliged to *foot the bill*, for military occupancy of its soil? It is the penalty it should be made to pay for its failure to protect its citizens. But let the property of every open and avowed Union man be exempt from assessment for this purpose. A commission could be appointed, to visit each county and make out lists of all, who would take a solemn oath never to interfere with the administration of justice; and that they are not, and never were members of the Ku-Klux Klan, and never have countenanced them in the least degree. If it shall appear that any persons have taken a false oath, let them be tried for perjury before an United States court. It is not likely that the whole South would perjure itself, to save a little money. Then let the expense of every military trial be borne by the county, excepting those who are known to have expressed their thorough dislike to the operations of the Ku-Klux.

But no matter who bears all this necessary expense, it is cheaper in the end, to *prevent* outbreaks, than to quell them afterwards; and inhabiting as I do one of these rebellious districts, it certainly seems to me far better, to be allowed to sleep in quietness, not expecting every moment to hear a rebel bullet whizzing past my ears, even if it does cost a little money; than it is to live a life of continual terror, never knowing at the beginning of each day, whether I shall see its close in peace or not. But perhaps this is selfishness on my part, and I ought to be willing to endure this constant mental agony, for the sake of saving our worthy uncle a few dollars of expense, in maintaining order throughout his dominions. Or, perhaps I have no business to live here. I was not born in the noble State of Georgia, but was so unfortunate as to inhale the first breath of life, in that "dreary old State" of Massachusetts, whose only exports are said to be "rock, and ice;" and what right have I to leave my own home, and venture to reside in a State so near Heaven, in moral and intellectual acquirements, as Georgia, the "empire State" of the South! The Southerners say, "You are a Yankee, G—d d——n you; and have no business here;" and then to show their vast superiority to us miserable Yankees, they will add what I heard one of them say, "I can whip a dozen Yankees at any time, and I look upon every man that was in the Union army, as a d——d horse-thief." But if I have the right to dwell here, then for God's sake let me be protected.

What is the great argument that is used in opposition to this idea? It is, that "drawing the reins tightly on the rebel steed, will cause him to dash on more vigorously than ever;" or, as Mrs. Davis said to the officer about to arrest her petticoated husband, "don't anger him, he may hurt you!" Now, one could give these cautious politicians the more credit for believing their own creed, if they could ever be heard advocating the same idea with reference to other criminals; but no political party has as yet adopted it, as a plank in their platform, that equal generosity should be shown to the poor woman who steals a loaf of bread, with which to feed her starving children. There is a New York editor, whose lucubrations often meet my eyes, even in this darkened mental region, who professes to be one of the moral lights of the world, and who is exhalted by some of his followers "above all that is called God;" whose advocacy of this fallacy, has caused the South to become a vast Aceldama, and still his sayings are quoted as the embodiment of political wisdom. Now, I would respectfully, and almost reverently, (for I tremble at the thought of questioning the infallibility of such a demigod), ask this paragon of magnanimity, how it happens that the above poor woman does not need his eloquent appeals, almost as much as dear old brother Davis, and our nice cousins, Toombs, Ben. Hill, Quantrell, and the keepers of Andersonville and Florence prisons? Or is it *great* criminals, only, to whom the "olive leaf" of peace is to be extended, on the principle, that "*one* murder makes a villain, millions, a hero!"

Perhaps the example of our Heavenly Father, would not be a bad one for us to follow, who, although he "makes the sun to shine on the evil and on the good," still emphatically says, "except ye *repent*, ye shall all likewise perish;" and who has certainly kindly ordained, that unrepentant rebels, shall never wear the "long white robe and the starry crown." Does nature approvingly smile upon the criminal? Ask that poor soul, who when ordering a magpie's nest to be torn from the top of a very high tree, near his house, gave as a reason, that "it had never ceased reproving him for the murder of his father." Does conscience ever acquit the sinner at its righteous bar, until he has "brought forth fruits meet for repentance?" Why, then, should these Southern sinners be toasted so often, and eulogized beyond measure, as poor unfortunates, on whom the hand of our despotic government has been laid heavily, before they have shown the least sign of repentance? I must be excused for saying, that hypocrisy is the only appropriate name, to give to the conduct of those, who so flippantly talk of pacifying the rebels, by freely pardoning their offences without repentance.

Never, since the conclusion of peace, have the dictates of common sense been applied to our relations with the South. Not content with the result of long years of experience previous to the war, since its close we have been constantly repeating the same lesson, and "reaping the whirlwind by sowing the wind." There never was a better illustration of this folly, than in the case of the chicken-hearted soldier, who, when his comrades were discussing what should be the fate of a rattle-snake, who had intruded into the camp, suggested, "Do with him? Why, swear him, and let him go." So have we been doing, swearing the rebels, and letting them go, to infuse there poisonous virus into the whole community. A distinguished preacher, who doubtless now laments his utterance of such foolishness, shortly after the close of the war, at a celebration at Fort Sumpter, remarked that while there, he was stung by a wasp, and his first impression was to kill the vicious little thing; but he reflected, like uncle Toby, in the case of the fly, that the world "was wide enough for both him and the wasp," and he therefore opened the window, saying, "go, poor devil, go; you will never sting me again." Now this would have been truly Christian conduct on the part of our kind-hearted brother, if he and the wasp were the sole inhabitants of this planet; but when the probability was, that some one else would be stung by the unrepentant wasp, it was cruelty to them to allow the wasp to go in peace.

But the Southern States have been received back into the Union, and what has been done cannot be well undone. They now compose a part of our glorious political fabric, as they did previous to their warlike efforts to escape from the tyranny of this political fold, and they are not content with "taking the back seats" in their old home, but demand rejoicing, on our part, at their return. When I was a boy, I once escaped from the rigor of my grandmother's righteous rule, but after a short absence, as night drew on, I slunk back into the fold, expecting and deserving a severe reprimand at least; but my grandmother, dear old soul, feared she had done wrong in provoking me, and received me with distinguished favor, preparing with her own hands, a nice bowl of white bread and milk, for myself, in place of the brown bread that was usually my portion. So with us. The South has returned from self-interest alone, and we are eager to show her, that we almost regret having driven her away by our unguarded conduct, and we mean to be more careful in future. Poor thing; it is born in her to be rebellious, and we must be more careful about applying a torch to her nitro-glycerine heart, lest a worse explosion than before should ensue.

Supposing one-tenth of the outrages that have been committed at the South had occurred in Boston, upon the persons of the Irish, how many weary months of application, on the part of the Romish priests, would have been required, to induce Congress to interfere? What burning words of eloquence, would have dropped from the lips of every democratic orator in Congress? But because it is the South that plays these "fantastic tricks," every eye must be closed, and every ear shut against the sight and sound of these "irregularities." The South always was a petted child with our government, and bids fare always to remain one, albeit the scars of the wounds she inflicts upon the remaining members of the family, are yet visible, and likely to remain so for a long time to come. Perhaps she will outgrow this refractory disposition, after she has been allowed to nourish it to her satisfaction, upon the blood of tens of thousands of Union men and women, who now lie passive at her feet, waiting her malignant pleasure. But in my opinion, a "straight-jacket" is best for a lunatic, and strenuous efforts to hold a maddened child, are conducive to its highest welfare. Let us, then, imitate a wise father, who will not let his passionate child imbrue its hands in the blood of a brother; and let us calmly say to the South, "you shall not maltreat your brethren, and if reason avails nothing with you, the strong arm of the law shall; for you shall not oppress a single citizen of the United States." An old man once found a rude boy picking apples from one of his trees. He cried out to him, "Come down, my lad; don't touch those apples;" but the youngster only helped himself more plentifully, when the old man cried out, "Sirrah, come down!" and threw tufts of grass at him; but the young thief heeded not the admonition, when the farmer cried out, "Well, young thief, as you will pay no attention to my words, and to soft weapons, I will try what virtue there is in stones;" and he began to pelt the boy liberally with them, when the youngster was glad to descend the tree speedily, and humbly beg the old man's pardon. So let us deal with the South. We have tried words and grass long enough; now let us "see what virtue there is in stones." "The sword is not a terror to good works, but to the evil." "Do that which is good, and thou shalt have praise of the same."

CHAPTER II.

EDUCATION OF THE BLACKS.

The second step necessary for the elevation of the freedmen is *education*. Their being no dissent from this opinion, extended remarks will not be necessary upon this subject. If I was always in favor of the education of the negro, a residence at the South, has only increased my convictions on that subject a hundred fold. No words can describe, nor pen portray the absolute and terrible necessity for the education of this darkened race. A cloud of midnight darkness hovers over the whole South, illuminated only by a few straggling rays of "Northern light," proceeding from the small number of schools established in prominent localities. I say small number, not to depreciate the noble efforts of the martyr teachers, who have dared to brave the wrath of the rebels and to establish schools in every Southern city and large town; but because these schools are so few in comparison to the vast fields utterly unoccupied, and where the rank weeds of ignorance grow in such stately luxuriance, as to defy all attempts to destroy them.

The whole number of Northern schools for the freedmen cannot reach over five thousand, and probably will fall far short of that number, leaving at the very lowest calculation, all of three-fourths of the colored people unprovided with schools. There are four and a half millions of freedmen at least, which would give about one million six hundred thousand children between the ages of five and fifteen; and allowing seventy-five children to a school, a larger number than the schools will average, the number of schools needed would be twenty-one thousand three hundred and thirty-three. This condition of things would be encouraging nevertheless, if the number of schools was encreasing; but instead of this being the case, we are continually told, that it is next to impossible to sustain teachers in the fields already occupied. Ever since I commenced my residence at the South, I have tried in vain to induce some of the many organizations in existence, to send teachers to our locality. Until recently, there has not been a single week-day school in this county for the blacks, except one a portion of the time on our plantation. Every large place is tolerably well supplied with teachers, but this county, containing nearly twice as many negroes as Augusta, has never had a single teacher supported by any Northern organization; and I suppose that this county is only a sample of nearly all the counties of the same character throughout the South. No doubt this was the wisest course to pursue at first, as Northern teachers could not have lived in most of the Southern counties; but as soon as the programme of the preceding chapter is but partially carried out, teachers should be sent into the country, as well as into the cities. The sad example of the Paris Communes, should warn us against an attempt to educate the cities alone. Paris was the center of intelligence. It's people were enlightened, while the country people were ignorant, and

Paris should therefore rule. Now if the country had been educated, this bloody proposition could never have been enunciated.

It is a mistaken idea, to suppose that the city negroes exert an unbounded influence over the country ones. So far as my observation extends, they exert almost no influence over them. On the contrary, there is a narrow jealousy existing between these two classes, almost as much as if they were of a different nation. I have heard black youngsters in Augusta, cry out, as a load of negroes from the country approached, "country niggers!" On my arrival here, our negroes often visited Augusta, and yet their ignorance was as complete as it well could be; still there were eight or ten schools for the freedmen in that place. I do not complain of the past, but it is my candid opinion, that the time has come for more enlarged efforts in this direction, on the part of the Northern people.

It may be said, that the necessity for action on the part of the North, no longer exists, on account of the "free school system" already introduced by the Legislatures of several of the Southern States. Without intending to be *hypercritical* in reference to this "free school system," yet I cannot help regarding it with great suspicion, when upon its face it bears the mark of unjust prescription. In Virginia, no colored child can attend a free school established for the whites; and no white child can be a member of one established for the blacks. In our own State the law says, "The children of the white and colored races, shall not be taught together in any of the sub-districts of the State." Now who can suppose that these separate schools established for the blacks, will deserve the name of free schools?

An extensive movement is now on foot in this State, and advocated by the public press, to *exclude* all *Yankee school books* from Southern schools. A distinguished Southern professor is engaged in *preparing a series of reading books, from which shall be excluded all Union sentiments*, and everything obnoxious to the Southern chivalry! The terrible necessity exists of having these books published for the present, by a Northern house, but when a few more bountiful crops of cotton have been produced, the Southern parents may be able to bear the additional expense of having these emasculated productions printed at the South. Of course, the most distant allusion to freedom, will be excluded from this new-fangled school literature, and no doubt the history of our revolution will be overhauled by these haters of the loftiest flights of the human intellect. No patriotic song will hereafter be sung, and soon no Northern teachers will be employed. But Southern eyes are not always eagle's eyes, and Southern intellects are not always remarkably keen. It would doubly surprise the ghost of Noah Webster, to learn that in lieu of a more pro-slavery book, the Southern matrons now claim his little blue and red immortal speller, as a Southern book. One of our scholars showed a white lady her "Reader," with its pretty pictures, and asked her why she did not obtain one for her child. She took the book with the tips of her fingers, and scanning its pages suspiciously, she at length returned it to the girl, sneeringly remarking, "I don't want any of your old Yankee books," and hugged Webster's old spelling-book to her bosom very complacently. The colored children all call this speller, "the reb spelling-book."

It is the glory of our common-school system at the

North, that it proscribes no scholar on account of race, or condition in society; and why should not the "reconstructed" South follow this impartial example? At the South, any more than at the North, why should a colored child go miles from his dwelling in quest of a colored school, when a white one is to be found near at hand? It may be said, that a "half a loaf is better than no loaf"; but who shall distinguish between the two races? Multitudes of Southern children are so white as to pass for white children; and yet they are to be excluded from white schools because a small amount of negro-blood courses in their veins. Thus, over one half of the population will be excluded from the first-class schools; for no one can imagine, that, having separated the two classes, it is the intention of the Southerners to educate them alike. The idea is preposterous in the extreme. Since emancipation, the Southern mind has manifested signs of mental hydrophobia, at the very mention of negro-education; and, has it experienced a new baptism of love for the African race, that it is now disposed to exert itself for their complete mental elevation? It is hard for "the Ethiopian to change his skin"; and it will be many years, before the Southern mind becomes sufficiently divested of its hatred to negro-education, to tax itself heavily for that education. All seeming pretentions of this kind are delusive. Nothing has occurred to induce the Southerners to change their opinion of the value of education, and especially, of its value for the black man. If they believe more in education for themselves, they believe less in it for the blacks; because they cannot be persuaded to bridge over the intellectual gulf, existing between them and the blacks. Nothing, that I have ever done at the

South, for the blacks, has aroused Southern hostility more, than my feeble efforts for their education. Every one is aware of the large number of negro-schoolhouses that have been burned, and of teachers that have been driven from their schools, in many portions of the South. Said a comparatively well-disposed Southern gentleman to me, "I cannot bear the idea of my children seeing negro children, attending school and learning to read." It is well known, that the sight of a negro-schoolhouse, stirs up the rabid feelings of a Ku-Klux gang, as the sight of water, is said to disturb a mad dog.

Then, the Southern teachers by no means compare, in mental acquisitions, with Northern ones; and, of course, the poorest and cheapest, if any, will be selected for the black schools. Some years ago, the teacher of a white school in Kentucky, assured me that he did not believe in the ordinary doctrine of the earth's revolution around the sun, because his own eyes assured him of the contrary. A teacher of a white school in this county, gave as a reason for not being able to answer some political question, "that she was no politician*er*." The teachers in Virginia, write word that the trustees of the free schools there, openly avow their determination not to employ teachers who are republican. Perhaps I am too suspicious, but it seems to me, that this new-born zeal, in behalf of negro-education, has, for its object, the overthrow of the school-system established by Northern societies; and when that is accomplished, they will quite suddenly lose all their zeal, and the poor negro will be left without any education at all. Intelligent colored people, all around, look at the matter in this light. Sometime since, the whites in this neighborhood, after having severely condemned our efforts to teach the negroes on Sundays, in many instances threatening with loss of employment those who attended, and sometimes executing their threats, all of a sudden, became converts to the doctrine of negro-education, and started a Sunday school near here. They endeavored to persuade the negroes to leave ours, and attend their Sunday school. One day, I asked the blacks in public, why they supposed the rebels had become such friends to their education? With a sly twinkle in the corners of their eyes, they responded with emphasis, "To break up your school, nothing else in the world, and we shall not go to their school."

Will it not prove the same with the week-day schools? Far be it from me to paralyze any well-meant efforts of the whites to educate the blacks. I only state my opinion, to warn our Northern friends, not to relax their efforts, or withdraw their teachers, on account of any law that may be passed by Southern Legislatures, ostensibly, in favor of free schools. These schools, would not be generally attended by the black children, if established.

But it will be asked, if we must always educate the blacks? This brings me to the subject of a national compulsory educational bill. If ignorance is a national evil, and jeopardizes our institutions, then, is it not a part of the duty of a national Legislature, to require the establishment of free, anti-sectarian schools, throughout the length and breadth of the land? We will admit, that many Southerners sincerely desire the colored man's education; still, their faith in his capacity is so small, that, after a few ineffectual attempts to promote it, they will become discouraged, and retire from the field in disgust. It proved so, with those who started the school in our neighborhood. They soon abandoned the task, as a hopeless undertaking. A Northern man does not doubt the capacity of the negro, as the Southern man does. The latter, can never divest himself of the idea, that the negro race is naturally an inferior one; while the observing Northern man, with such bright and shining examples to the contrary all around him, knows its falsity. It is therefore vastly important, that teachers should be furnished, who have full faith in the *natural* ability of the colored race; and can dig through the unpromising outer crust of the negro's mentality, until the pure "hard-pan" of intellectual strength is reached. Teachers, to be successful, must also ardently *desire*, the mental development of the blacks. In the days of Slavery, the masters ridiculed the negroes' efforts to use good language, and become like the whites; and would Southern teachers *now*, be wholly divested of this feeling? They would not be likely to exert themselves much to awaken the dormant energies of their pupils.

It seems necessary, therefore, for our government to step in and demand a national system of education. But, in order to deprive the South of all excuse for forcing education upon them, it would be as well, to allow them a full opportunity to try the experiment in their own way; with the exception of the abolition of caste, and the non-exclusion of school-books, on account of their Northern origin. I would recommend the establishment of a national board of education, composed of both Northerners and Southerners, to whom the selection of both teachers and school-books should be left; and then allow the Southerners to start their own schools. If they refuse to do this, then, let the national government take the matter into its own hands, and compel the establishment of proper schools all over the South. But let our government be generous, as well as just, and ascertain the exact ability of each section to sustain schools, and generously supply the deficiency of means.

It would be hardly just to force virtue upon the vicious, at their own cost, or knowledge upon the ignorant and they pay the expense; but it could not be unjust for the government to force education upon the people, at the expense of the government itself. In New England the whole people pay the expense of instructing the poor, of course a small portion of this expense falls upon the poor themselves. So it should be with our national system of education. The expense of sustaining free schools at the South, if the South refuses to sustain them herself, should be borne by a tax upon the whole people of the United States; and under such circumstances the whole people, through their representatives, should decide as to the character of the schools established. First, allow the South to establish and support schools *free to all*, and without the exclusion of Northern books or teachers. If they refuse to do this, then adopt the other alternative, and let the government establish and support these schools; and in order to deprive the South of all ground for complaint, it would be advisable to make the system universal, taking care, as far as possible, to guard the rights of each State and smaller locality. The benevolent people of New England must surrender some of their private rights, for the sake of promoting the welfare of the whole country.

As is well known, ignorance lies at the basis of nearly all crime. If the negroes were educated, the turmoil and confusion now prevailing at the South, would be considerably lessened. Educate the negro, and he can read his own contracts. Educate him, and he will recognize the binding force of a contract. Educate him, and he will no longer be guilty of the innumerable little offences that now render the planter's life, and his own, a miniature hell. Educate him, and you transform him from a stupid blockhead into a reasonable being. Educate him, and you in reality lend a helping hand to the whites in their efforts to improve their own condition. Educate the negro, and you disabuse his mind of his false religious ideas, and prepare him to receive that religion that is based upon intellectual perfection. Fill his mind with knowledge, and he becomes a humble man, in place of such a bag of self-conceit as he is, in his ignorance. In short, let the negro be educated, and he stands back aghast at the sight of his many imperfections, and gross ignorance; as he beholds shining around him the glorious light of so many illustrious examples, of men rising from a humble condition, to that of poets, scholars, learned divines, scientists, and men of distinguished business attainments. Nothing does the negro lack more, than encouragement to rise from the stupidity of former years. Without education, he was and is but a brute. With it, he can equal the proudest of his white compeers. As has been said, the only difference between the two races, is that of education. Ths difference, as stated between the Augusta negroes and those on our own plantation, was simply that of education. Let then those rays of burning light, forever emanating from that great intellectual luminary of the Universe, the "Spirit of Truth;" who as he moved upon the face of the darkened deep, said "Let there be light and there was light;" and who, according to the inspired penman, was with God, "from the beginning, or ever the earth was, when there were no depths, and no fountains abounding with water, when he appointed the foundations of the earth ;" let those celestial rays of truth and living light, fall in their native splendor, upon the dark abyss of the negro's uncultivated mind, dispelling forever the dank and noisome vapors of ignorance, bestiality, and mental woe.

And to whom is committed the execution of this noble and god-like task? On whom rests the glorious responsibility of this movement? To the Northern people is committed the divine work of remodelling millions of your fellow creatures; of raising from the condition of beasts of burden and thinking animals multitudes of souls, whose hearty thanks shall greet your ears on the great day of final account, as your turn comes to receive your reward from the august Judge of the Universe. God, originally created these souls in his own image and likeness. Slavery obliterated this image. Unto you it is given to restore it to innumerable souls. If the divine mind contemplates with ineffable complacency, throughout the endless ages of eternity, those angelic beings who have retained his handiwork in their natures, and his benevolent heart is filled with holy delight at the sight of the innumerable throngs from whom was never effaced his glorious image, will it not afford you extreme delight to gaze upon another multitude, to whom as the almoners of heavens' bounty, you have restored the divine image intellectually, and fitted them to appreciate the sublime occupations of the intelligent throngs, that surround the throne of the God of infinite wisdom?

CHAPTER III.

KIND OF SCHOOLS NEEDED IN ADDITION TO COMMON SCHOOLS.

The first in importance, under this head, is the *Normal* school. It will be seen at a glance, that this kind of a school is of the utmost importance. Its necessity has already led to the donation of large sums, which have been appropriately expended. On the right character of the teachers employed, depends the whole value of the common school system. It is a grave error, that only the poorer classes of teachers, are needed for this Southern work. It is often said, "He is not much of a teacher, but I guess he will do to teach the niggers." No more ruinous mistake than this, can be made by those having the supervision of our Southern schools. Of course, it is not necessary that a teacher should be versed in the classics; but in other respects, the *very best* of Northern teachers are none too good, to lay, broad and deep, the foundations of the school system at the South. Send inexperienced teachers anywhere else, than to the South. Teaching at the South is no sinecure, but a laborious service, taxing the mental powers of the best minds, to their utmost capacity. What would be said of a General, who should select as army scouts, some of his poorest soldiers, on the ground that they were not to meet the disciplined forces of the enemy, but only to hang upon the outskirts of his camp, and perform whatever odds and ends of service, that came in their way ? It would require no keen prophetic vision, to predict the failure of such a general's campaign.

At the North, a small portion only of the child's education is obtained within the walls of a school-room. The whole Northern atmosphere, is loaded with the rich perfume emited by the fragrant fruit of the tree of knowledge. Every conceivable avenue to instruction is open on all sides, to the inquisitive child ; and angels of intelligence are stationed at their entrance, inviting all to walk in their pleasant ways. But here, there is absolutely nothing but the school, to enlighten the mind of the child. At the North, the street, the shop, the market, the play-ground, and above all, the *home*, unceasingly pour streams of knowledge into the receptive mind of the young. But here, a " thick darkness covers the whole land," and the school house, is the only luminous object visible, amid the surrounding gloom.

The teacher, must not only be versed in the studies taught in Northern schools, but he must be a walking encyclopædia, capable of imparting information on every conceivable topic. Three-fourths of a Northern child's knowledge is obtained from his mates, his brothers, sisters, and parents. But, among us, all are alike in ignorance, and an older brother, is more stupid than the child itself ; and the parents are the most stupid of all. There is absolutely no knowledge, of any kind, among a lot of plantation hands, previous to the establishment of a school among them, except that which relates to the simplest labors of life. If you have not witnessed this ignorance, you cannot comprehend its extent. They, literally, do not know their right hand from their left, their own ages, and scarcely their names. Everything that is known, must be taught them. Even the books put into their hands, they will hold upside down, or sideways, as often as in the proper manner. The name of the most common object around them, they are ignorant of; as they are also of every fact in History, Geography, Astronomy, Natural History, Natural Philosophy, Chemistry, Arithmetic, and Grammar. But they are quick-witted, and will soon begin to ask questions, that will confound the teacher, unless he is a person of varied acquirements.

Then, of course, such minds are wholly undisciplined, and disposed to cling to the few ideas already formed in their minds. Northern children, are used to some kind of discipline from their infancy. They early acquire the habit of fixing their attention, if it is only to listen to the beautiful story Aunt Maria is telling them, or to some of grandpa's funny anecdotes. But the poor colored child, never had an aunt, whose mind is stored with all sorts of baby-lore, wherewith to regale the ears of her childish auditory. This little outcast, never had a kind grandparent, whose stock of funny stories is never exhausted, when the "wee ones" are teasing him for a "new one." Think of this, ye highly-favored Northern children, and learn to pity this poor child of mental want. His aunt, and grandparents, have hardly any more knowledge, than the poor child possesses himself. Consequently, his mind has been undisciplined from the first. Teachers need an infinite amount of skill, to enable them to contrive methods, of arousing within these wandering minds sufficient interest, to induce them to fix their attention on some given point. The opening of a door, the passing of a person by the window, or the slightest motion of any one, will often throw the whole school into confusion, and quickly banish from their minds, the sound of A, B, C, which the teacher is endeavoring to fasten there. Nothing is more common, than for half a dozen scholars to rise and leave the room for a few minutes, and then return. Of course, these difficulties must be overcome, or there is an end to all order and discipline. This, of course, requires considerable tact on the part of the teacher.

Then, the amount of confinement such natures will uninjuriously endure, is another nice point for adjustment. No method, hitherto adopted, in all of these matters, will avail here; and the teacher, to be successful, must be a perfect Napoleon of invention, of "ways and means" to accomplish the desired ends; none of which qualifications can be obtained, without thorough and systematic training.

I pass now to a consideration of the question, where shall these teachers be educated? I answer, if possible, partly at the North, in addition to the term of years necessary here. Particularly is this necessary, with colored teachers born at the South. It is difficult for them, born and reared at the South, as they have been, to comprehend the magnitude of their task, until they have seen some country, on whose fair surface the hideous cloven foot of Slavery, has never been planted. The scenes witnessed in our busy Northern workshops, must be daguerreotyped upon his mind, by an actual observation of them; before he can fully comprehend the illimitable distance between Northern and Southern industrial life, and mental and moral acquirements. He must see for himself Northern industry, must drink in the spirit of Northern intelligence, by actual contact with its fountains of knowledge; he must enter into its hallowed sanctuaries, and witness its unostentatious piety, with his own eyes. Then he will return to his brethren, fired with a holy zeal, to impart to them some of the rich treasures of wisdom and knowledge, bestowed upon him. He may acquire some of this zeal, by a residence of a few years, within a good Normal school institute here; but one year's residence at the North, will do more for him in this respect, than several years study here. Of course, the Norman schools here, are absolutely necessary, only that when possible, the pupils should visit the North for a season.

The next question to be considered is, shall the teachers be white or colored? I should say both. For years to come, the white teachers will prove the most competent; but in the great dearth of such teachers, colored ones must be employed. There is also no disguising the fact, that in many cases they will be better received, than their white comrades; for strange as it may seem, the negro is not wholly divested of "prejudice against color;" or, at least, is not free from suspicious feelings against his lighter complexioned brothers. The black teacher, also, understands more fully than his white brother, the quality of the material he has to mould; and succeeds better than he, in administering reproof to his erring friends. The black teacher is besides a "living epistle, known and read of all men," of the power of education to remodel the human soul.

Next to Norman schools, in importance, is the Manual Labor, or self-supporting schools. Important as they are, even at the North, in aiding indigent students, they are still more so at the South, where all labor has been looked upon as degrading. When labor, and the cultivation of the intellect are united, the prejudices against the former are likely to vanish; especially when it appears that without such labor, education must be dispensed with. A manual-labor school of this kind, could easily be established. A small farm could be obtained, of sufficient capacity to furnish labor for thirty hands. Sixty persons could be employed upon it, one-half of whom could work in the forenoon, and the other half in the afternoon, thus keeping the working force of the farm intact. The labor of these sixty persons, each working one-half of the time, and studying the other half, would be worth seven and a half dollars per month. It would cost four dollars a month for their provisions; and the rent of cabins for their accommodation, allowing four persons to a cabin, would be only fifty cents a month, leaving then a margin of thirty-six dollars per annum for other necessary expenses. The tuition would be necessarily free.

Another advantage of such an institution, would be that young children could be thus taken, and educated away from other influences. It is the opinion, I believe, of most of the teachers, that one great obstacle in the way of their success, is the adverse influences of the homes of the children. These are too apt to be nurseries of vice, as well as of ignorance. I can see no way of dissevering the link, that binds these children to their old slavery-acquired customs, except a total removal from the scenes of their former degradation, and a substitution of an entirely new life around them. You teach a child purity of speech, and after its return home, it will quickly unlearn the precious lesson. Inculcate upon the child lessons of gentleness and kindness, and half an hour's life amid the rude scenes of its home, will banish them from his mind. His parents are rough and boorish ; how can you expect him to become refined and gentle ? His brothers and sisters, cousins and playmates, are immodest in word and action, cruel in their treatment of the brute creation, and uncivil towards each other, and towards their superiors ; how, then, can you expect him to be modest, kind to animals, and civil towards others ? A removal from the untoward influences of a colored child's home, becomes then in many instances, of the utmost importance. Teachers have often told me of the necessity of such a step, and some of them have seriously contemplated the establishment of such a home themselves.

A manual-labor school would effectually accomplish this end, if thoroughly undertaken, and properly managed. There is always plenty of labor on a Southern farm, adapted to the capacities of children, so that they could easily defray the expenses of their food. But this brings me to the consideration of a third kind of school, and one imperatively demanded by the wants of the freedmen. This is, the Industrial School, which differs from a manual-labor, or self-supporting school, in this way. Its object is not to enable the pupil to defray the expense of his mental training, but to teach him how to work, and that in employments new to him. While the manual-labor school, aims principally at intellectual advancement, the object of the Industrial school, is primarily physical or material education. If such a school is needed in Boston, and other large cities at the North, much more is it needed here, where all kinds of industrial arts are neglected by the whole community. It is notorious, that in the days of Slavery, even the scourge and branding iron, were of Northern manufacture; and to-day, almost every article of comfort and luxury, is manufactured away from home. Good mechanics are few and far between, and very many of them are of the colored race. I cannot but regard instruction in the mechanical arts, as a very important step, in the elevation of the freedmen. A nation of farmers only, can never acquire true independence, any more than one of artizans alone. God never intended England to be the "workshop of America," while America is the grand grain-producing country of the world. We must live within ourselves, if we would attain to true and permanent prosperity.

How absurd to raise cotton at the South, transport it a thousand miles to be manufactured, and then return it to our own doors in its remodelled condition. Georgia, especially the middle portion of it, is emphatically adapted to manufactures. It is too far South to be a good grain producing region, and too far North to compete successfully with States farther South in raising cotton. But occupying as it does, a sort of middle ground between the North and the South, it would find a large market for its productions; which would also be furnished to its Southern brethren, cheaper than if they were manufactured at the North. I think here is a fine field for the operations of Northern capitalists. But as I am writing for the benefit of the freedman, I will only consider this subject in relation to their interests. If they are now properly educated in these trades, it may prevent the ingress of a large foreign population, who will soon be needed to carry on the various industrial enterprises now contemplated in our State.

But other Southern States are also turning their attention to manufactures, and the same necessity exists all over the South, for the speedy establishment of *Industrial Schools* for the freedmen. I would have these schools at present, limited in their operations to the colored youth. The plan I would suggest is this. On some suitable farm, let a large building be erected, sufficient to accommodate quite a number of different trades with workshops. Let steam power be provided for this building, and rented out to persons desirous of engaging in the various trades, like similar establishments in Worcester, and other New England towns. There could be a boot and shoe shop, a carpenter's shop with a turning lathe, a sash and blind manufactory, a brush and broom shop, a harness shop, a whip manufactory, a plough shop, and in an adjoining building a large tailoring establishment. Apprentices to all these trades from among the freedmen could be taken, while the great body of the workmen could be good Northern mechanics. In the manufacture of all the lighter articles, children could be employed, and thus taught the first great lesson of civilized life, the science of construction. But if this be deemed too complex an arrangement to commence with, the children could be taught the arts of domestic life, and instructed in the thousand and one things, necessary to the happiness of every well ordered household; trusting to the gradual development of the system to accomplish all that has been described. But we must have well ordered industrial schools, for the education of children, if nothing more is attempted.

The boys could be taught to work on a farm, or in a garden, and to make small articles needed everywhere, and the girls could be instructed in cutting and fitting dresses, making their brother's clothes, and in every kind of useful and even ornamental sewing. A large sum of money would not be needed with which to commence operations. A single house large enough to accommodate fifteen or twenty persons, would suffice to begin with. The school could be kept in one room of the building, another large room could be used for a small workshop, and a few rooms set apart for the teachers; and the remainder used as dormitories for the children. If a manual-labor school is connected with the industrial school, the youth employed would only have to recite in the schoolroom, the eating and sleeping accommodations being elsewhere, as before suggested. Then five hundred acres of land could be obtained to start with, which would be amply sufficient for the employment of the thirty hands above alluded to, and for timber purposes. The whole expense of the farm need not exceed $6000, and it would be necessary to pay only a portion of it down, the remainder being secured by mortgage. There are a plenty of chances of this kind in this county. Besides the amount needed to pay on the farm, about four thousand dollars more would be needed as a working capital, making only ten thousand dollars in all. For this sum, nearly seventy-five human beings could be successfully established, as the nucleus of a great manual labor, industrial and reformatory school, for the whole South; and after the experiment had proved a successful one, there would be no lack of munificent endowments, to make it the model institution of the kind in the world. The whole of this movement could be connected with the far more extensive one of establishing Northern villages throughout the South. This experiment had better be tried on a farm contiguous to one of these Northern settlements; and the isolated farm house, with its hum of busy voices, attuned to a hymn of industrial praise, would afford a grand accompaniment to the loud chorus of the many voiced village; and the two combined, would startle the dull laggards of the South, by the magnificent music of these happy laborers, as the mighty chorus and orchestra of a monster musical jubilee stir the busy inhabitants of a crowded city.

CHAPTER IV.

INTRODUCTION OF TRUE CHRISTIANITY, DETAILS OF THE PLAN, CONSEQUENCES OF THE SAME.

Next in importance to schools, as an agency for the elevation of the freedmen, is the introduction of true Christianity. I place this *next* to schools, because, without some education, it is impossible, to make the blacks comprehend the nature of this grand remedial agent for the world's moral ills. To this end, preachers must be provided of precisely the right stamp. They must be preachers of Christ, and not of creeds; of personal holiness, and not of barren forms. They must be men who, like the primitive preachers of Christianity, feel that "a woe is upon them, if they preach not the gospel," and men who have been "endowed with power from on high" to preach this gospel. "Words of man's wisdom," will fail to reach the sin-encased consciences of these stricken ones. Naught but the power of God, can qualify a man to attack these outposts of the devil; and sustain the pressure that he will endure, while contending with the hideous moral nightmare, brooding over the souls of this people. Exposed alike to rebel bullets, and stolid indifference on the part of the blacks, he must be more than an ordinary well-to-do clergyman, accustomed to gifts innumerable, and abundant sympathy from his hearers. He must be like his divine Master, raised far above the fear of man, and so filled with inextinguishable love to God, as to be happy, although all men turn against him. He must renounce the love of "filthy lucre," and of personal renown; for neither of these rewards will fall to his lot, if he does his Master's will faithfully.

At first, his hearers will shout "hosannas" in his hearing, and perhaps strew the ground with branches of palm-trees, as in Christ's time; but as his mellowed accents are changed into stern denunciation of the violators of God's law, "a change will come over the spirit of the dreams" of his hearers, and he will find himself abandoned by many, who at first, would have "plucked out their eyes and given to him." Then will come his hour of trial; and, if not a true man of God, he will falter in his task, and cry "peace, peace, when there is no peace"; in which case, he will be shorn of his spiritual strength, and become like other men. Thousands of preachers, have thus become emasculated, before the domineering power of Slavery, both here and elsewhere; and thousands of others, will lose all their claim of being the chosen of God, if they fail to declare his whole truth. Northern ministers coming here, need to be especially cautioned on this subject; for no class of religionists are more unwilling to hear the pure gospel of Christ, than the plantation blacks.

The preachers to whom they are in the habit of listening, are infinitely worse than no preachers. Their characters have been already alluded to, and need not again be described. The only particular in which they are above their fellows, is, in their superior audacity. In all other respects, in learning, morality, piety, and intelligence, they are on a par with the weakest of their flock. Of course, such preachers can never reform the people, for "a stream can rise no higher than its fountain."

But how shall a change be produced? In the first place, by the education of devout men among their own number, as teachers and preachers. This vastly important labor, has been auspiciously commenced in several places. A Theological school, under the auspices of Northern Baptists, has been established in Augusta, and has made commendable progress in this highly Christian work. But efforts should be made also, to educate some colored preachers at the North, who would return, bearing not only messages of truth and love in a religious point of view, but also, deeply imbued with the spirit of Northern ideas and customs.

The whole structure of Southern society, is so far removed from a Christian basis, that no education, fully equal to the emergency, can be obtained here. It is impossible to estimate the importance of such a step. While being educated here, the student continues his labors among his flock, and however distasteful to him, he feels obliged to "rave and rant," on a Sunday, instead of reasoning with his hearers; for if he does not thus "speak great swelling words of vanity," his critical flock will cry out, "Oh! he's no got de Holy Spirit, he only de book larning man; we no want sich a preacher." A man educated at the North, will be removed from these vicious tendencies; and will return to this moral waste, with instincts tolerably pure, in comparison to those who have always been surrounded with this vast sea of crime. He will at least, stand something of a chance to get his mind disabused of the popular idea among the blacks here, that a thief can be a Christian.

In my description of the religion of the blacks, I have not exaggerated, but have rather fallen short of the truth, in describing the miserable character of their religion. This being so, no candid person will fail to see the absolute necessity of a change, in order to promote the elevation of the negro. It is true, that education will accomplish much in this respect; but Christianity, its glorious handmaid, must second its efforts, before this moral "desert will bud and blossom as a rose."

By Christianity, I do not mean sectarianism, in any of its forms, but the pure and simple religion, as taught by our Lord himself, in his inimitable teachings while on earth; accompanied by the influence of his own Spirit since his death, to make those teachings efficacious "in pulling down the strong-holds of Satan." And here, may I be allowed to intrude a few thoughts, perhaps not strictly connected with this subject, and yet, forcibly suggested by the condition of my sable flock. In my isolated Southern home, a stray Northern paper occasionally reaches me, teeming with incidents of all kinds; and among other items, I sometimes see allusions to what I should judge to be a new party, termed by its friends, "free religionists." As far as I can learn, this party is inclined to ignore Christianity, or at least, to affect a superiority to its claims. Now, while I would not say that those engaged in this new movement, are not actuated by a desire to do good, yet I would respectfully ask its gifted advocates, if they can point to any community, where Christianity is fully practiced? If not, and I have never heard of such an one, would it not be well to wait until such a community is produced, and its character well weighed, before thrusting Christianity aside, to make way for "another gospel?" It seems to me, that to turn Christianity "out of doors," before its full power has been experienced, in a single town or village, is like failing to allow a president, a single day, in which to test the value of his cherished notions, but to turn him out in the first months of his presidential career. It may be said, that Christianity has had 1800 years, in which to test the. value of its principles, but such is not the case. No nation, as such, has as yet adopted them. They remain almost as unknown, practically, as when Jesus first proclaimed them. It is discouraging, to be sure, to reflect that people will not accept these precepts, but would it not be better for our "free religion" friends, to bend all their energies towards the introduction of these principles, into some one hamlet, at least? And then, if after a few years of trial, they fail to prove "the wisdom of God and the power of God," let them be superseded by something better. I am persuaded, that in this section of country, at least, Christianity has hardly been heard of, much less believed in and practiced. It does seem to me, that Christianity is eminently calculated to fit men for a true life here, and a glorious one hereafter. I cannot conceal my love for its author, and admiration for his precepts, and I would fain do all in my power to introduce this religion into the benighted South. It is a mighty work, and requires all the energies of the most energetic of men.

Both white and colored preachers, can be advantageously used in this work; only let educated white men superintend all efforts of this character. The colored men can more easily find their way to the cabins of the people, and that without arousing the supicions of the whites. The "Methodist Episcopal Church North," is doing a great work, in this matter. Its greatest danger, is in coalescing with its foul Southern sister, whose embrace is spiritual death. Oil and water can as soon mix, as the Northern and Southern religions, only by the former being absorbed by the latter. Whenever the Northern Methodists, unite with the Southern, "Ichabod" will be written upon the walls of their churches, and God will not, and cannot own them as His true and devoted children.

The inquiry will naturally arise in the minds of my readers, what does the author mean, by true Christianity? My answer is, not the preaching of this or that creed, but the simple doctrines taught by Christ himself. He is the author of Christianity, as far as its proclamation to man is concerned, and His teachings must constitute the essence, of what I regard as the "sovereign balm for every wound, the cordial for every fear," in a moral point of view. Christ preached holiness of heart and life, and not adherence to any particular forms, or modes of belief. The grand moral thesis he evolved was, that purity of heart alone, fitted man for acceptance with God, here and hereafter. In thunder tones, as well as with melliferous accents, he proclaimed these startling truths, viz., the unalterable nature of God's law, requiring perfect love to God, and equal love to man; the utter inability of man to obey that law, without divine assistance; and the full and complete provision made in Christ for obedience to that law. "Thou shalt love the Lord thy God with all thy heart, with all thy soul, with all thy mind, and with all thy strength." "On these two commands, hang *all* the law and the prophets." "This do, and thou shalt live." "Heaven and earth shall pass away, but *my words* shall not pass away."

"No man can come unto me, without the Father that sent me, draw him." "As the branch cannot bring forth fruit, except it abide in the vine, no more can ye, except ye abide in me." "Without me ye can do nothing."

"Wherefore he is able also to save them to the *uttermost*, that come unto God by him." "God sending His own Son, in the likeness of sinful flesh, and for sin, condemned sin in the flesh, *that the righteousness of the law might be fulfilled in us*, who walk not after the flesh but after the Spirit." "Likewise reckon ye also yourselves to be *dead unto sin*, but alive unto God, *through our Lord Jesus Christ.*"

Or to sum it up more concisely, sin shall always receive its proper punishment. There is no escape from its power except through divine help. Christ lived, died, and now lives for the express purpose of saving us from sin.

In direct opposition to this system is the religion of the Southern blacks. This system places a light value on forms. "Blessed are the pure in heart for they shall see God." The religion of the blacks delights in them, from immersion in the water, which they make a *sine qua non*, to their heterogeneous compound of shuffling, and dancing, termed by them shouting. Christianity deals with the heart. Their system cannot comprehend such a thing as a *pure motive*. Christianity inculcates disinterested action, as the foundation of purity of heart. Their system knows nothing of other than selfish action. Christianity requires obedience to God, from love. Their system, ignores all action of this kind, and teaches obedience to God from *fear*. Christianity requires knowledge, according to our opportunity for its acquisition. Their system places no value upon religious knowledge, neither historical, doctrinal or practical. Christianity teaches honesty. Their system, makes this of but little value. Christianity makes acceptance with God conditional upon holiness of life. Their system eschews this as utterly unattainable and undesirable, and substitutes therefor, dreams, visions and supernatural sights. In short, Christianity teaches an entire devotion of the individual to the service of God, and to the promotion of the interests of mankind, "That they which live should *live not unto themselves*, but unto him that died and rose again." Their system fails to comprehend the possibility of such self abnegation.

But it is unnecessary to continue this parallel. The intelligent reader can continue it himself from the history heretofore given of the practices of the blacks. It is sufficient to know that the two systems are diametrically opposed to each other. I do not deny that in large towns, there are Christian churches among the blacks, but they are only bright spots on the broad surface of that funeral robe, that covers the whole of the Southern religion, as with a pall of midnight darkness.

In opposition to it, we desire to see the bright resplendent garment of genuine Christianity exhibited to the admiring gaze of the people, expecting that its brilliant colors will allure the beholders from the sombre robes of their own system; and induce them to cast away the blackened covering, and "be clothed upon with our house which is from heaven;" whose immortal sheen shall far exceed all the "tabernacles of earthly houses," ever devised by erring man.

But how shall this change be accomplished? Never was more applicable, our Saviour's direction, "Be wise as serpents, and harmless as doves." Laborers in this vineyard must "lean not to their own understanding," but obtain "wisdom from above." God alone can so direct the steps of the proclaimer of Christianity, as to enable him to obtain a foothold, among the dark systems of false religion. It will be useless to denounce this system in words. All religionists are sensitive to attacks upon their peculiar faith; the Mormon and Mohammedan, equally with the Puritan and the Christian. A man's religion, whether true or false, is his dearest idol. I never knew the most rigid adherent to the "five points of Calvinism," more ardently attached to his peculiar faith, than these poor sons of darkness are, to to their midnight carousals. The preacher of pure Christianity must then avoid, if possible, all direct conflict with these infatuated ones; and direct his efforts to the gradual undermining of their system, by implanting beneath it, those seeds of truth, that shall, as they shoot upward, become the mighty tree of life, whose leaves shall be, for the healing of the nations. This he can only do, by boldly proclaiming the doctrines of true Christianity, and insisting upon it, as did the Saviour, that no religion is worth a farthing, only as its fruits are those of righteousness; and that all creeds, forms, and observances, must be tested by Christ's eternal rule, "By their *fruits*, ye shall know them."

Then, to render attractive this new religion, as his hearers will regard it, let him surround it with beautiful externals; not ostentatiously, or without a due regard to Christian economy, but let the beautiful form be attired in neat and tidy garments; alike worthy of the wearer, and in accordance with the purity of its own character. I would advocate first, the erection of small chapels of a neat and tasty character, painted white outside, or, at least, whitewashed, and the benches fastened inside; so as to prevent the floor being used for their religious dances. Let the walls of this chapel be hung with colored pictures, illustrative of Scripture incidents; inexpensive ones, answering every purpose. At night meetings, let the whole be brilliantly illuminated; argand burners sufficing for this purpose, as their own meetings are often carried on with no other light than a pine-knot, blazing forth from the dingy fire-place. Above all, let instrumental music be added to the charms of the new religion. The minister, if possible, should be a good singer, or he should be accompanied by one; and let him be provided with a small parlor organ, melodeon, or at least, a violoncello. This is very important; for their meetings in the country are wholly destitute of instrumental music, and the blacks are extravagantly fond of music.

Then, let a selection of verses from the Scriptures, suitable for chanting, and containing a high moral lesson, be printed in very large, and perfectly plain letters, on good sized cards, and be kept for the use of the congregation; and let the people repeat them, and sometimes sing them in concert, in connection with the minister. These, they would soon learn to read; and thus their progress in letters would be accelerated. At the close of each sermon, which should be instructive, and not exhortatory merely, let the congregation be encouraged in asking questions respecting the new doctrine; and let the pastor also question the flock, in reference to what they have heard. Then, let the aspiring brethren have a short time in which to exhibit their talents, as they would not patronize a meeting where this was not occasionally allowed; but let them be instructed not to yell when they pray, but to speak to God as reverently and confidingly, "as one friend speaketh to another." Meetings of this character, would not fail to be attractive to the blacks; and thus be the means of rendering them disgusted with their own barren services, and perhaps, at length, result in their acceptance of the new or Christian religion.

But some doubts may be felt, as to the final success of a movement, the object of which is to introduce a religion, so different from the prevailing one. This objection should not be made in the face of the great success of foreign-missions, as will appear from the following considerations. First, the language of these heathen is similiar to our own, and requires no years of laborious effort to comprehend it; which is one of the greatest tasks of the foreign missionary. Secondly, the government of the country is friendly to these efforts, and is not arrayed in bitter opposition, as is so often the case with foreign-missions.

Thirdly, the Christian teacher will be *received with distinguished favor*, by the people whom he wishes to convert, and not be martyred, as is often the case abroad. This is of itself, a sufficient reason, for sending missionaries to this field. The advent of every new preacher from the North, will be hailed with pleasure by the colored people all around.

Then, the great truth remains, that all souls are either emanations from, or creations by, the eternal God of the Universe; and were originally formed in "his own image and likeness." How ever long may have been the soul's journey from its father God, the cord that binds it to the parent stock, is never wholly unwound;

but retains its connection with God, ready to be used in drawing the distant wandererer back to his "father's house," as the cords of love, reaching forth from the heart of his father, to the "prodigal son," served at last to draw that wanderer thither. So that all mankind are susceptible of gracious influences, and only wait the "new creation" taught by Christianity, to be restored to God's favor, and to the pristine beauty of their former glorious condition.

To restore the mental nature, to one from whom it has been well nigh obliterated, is a task worthy of the most superhuman efforts. How much more glorious, is that of extricating a *soul*, from the slough of sin, and error, into which it has fallen; and extending it in our arms of love, before the gaze of our Redeemer, as one of the trophies of his grace, having been transformed by the power of his wonderful love from its former fallen condition, into that of resemblance to the truth and beauty of his own immaculate character? As eternity opens before us, its gladsome secrets, shall we not there behold more than one glorified spirit, belonging to that innumerable throng, who are "saying with a loud voice, worthy is the Lamb that was slain, to receive power and riches, and wisdom and strength, and honor and glory and blessing," who will under God, owe to *us* his ability to join in that rapturous song? And will not a sight of that beatified soul, with our knowledge of the "rock from which it was hewn," and of the "pit from which it was digged," sufficiently recompense us, for our efforts in lifting it from its darkened earthly condition? And as the sound of its rejoicing, echoes and re-echoes through the vast arches of heaven's magnificent temples, shall not its wonderful strains excite within us greater feelings of delight, than if earth had poured into our lap its richest treasures of wealth, pleasure and renown? "Let us then, not be weary in well-doing, for in due season we shall reap if we faint not."

CHAPTER IV.

LAND FOR THE LANDLESS.

From the close of the Feudal ages until to-day, the struggle of human beings has been for homes that they could call their own, free from the tyranny of heartless landlords. Previous to the abolition of the Feudal system, the laborer and the land were sold together. To-day, the land can be sold, the laborer never. Without wishing to burden the great cause of land for the homeless freedman, by the introduction of intense radicalism, I may yet venture to say that the only true model of a laborer's paradise, was the old government of the Peruvian Incas; who acted as the fathers of the people, and held the landed estates of that fine country, in trust for the tillers of the soil, dividing it at stated times among them, according to the needs of each. No grasping monopolist could seek to claim "all the land adjoining his," until he became the owner of millions of acres, while thousands around him did not own a rood. No avaricious father could portion out a vast estate, giving to each of his sons sufficient land to support a hundred laborers; but as each soul was re-committed to its mother's bosom, "earth to earth, dust to dust," it ceased being the owner of more than sufficed to cover its mortal remains.

When a young man married, he came into possession of a certain number of acres of land, which was increased at the birth of each successive child, the whole of which reverted back to the State, on the death of its cultivators. Poverty, that direst physical curse of humanity, was unknown, as was also extreme wealth, resulting in enervating luxury. The nearest approach to this desirable paradise, is when the owner and tiller of the soil are always the same. When he who "eats bread in the sweat of his brow," produces that sweat by labor on his own, and not on another's domain. To dig and delve always on land belonging to another, without the possibility of ever owning it, like many of the farm laborers of England, is an abominable shame. Akin to it, is the fate of those of our laborers, who often die landless, after expending their strength in enriching another person's monopolized acres. Words cannot express the horrors of such a life. The poor laborer sweats profusely, only to feed another, who is not willing to lose any of his precious physical power. Such is the character of the present wages system when applied to land. It is bad enough when machinery is the juggernaut that crushes the life out of the laborer, that stamps its iron foot upon the neck of the working man, and almost grinds him to powder; but it is still worse when God's green fields and fertile vales, overhung by his broad and beautiful sky, looking down so lovingly on all, become the laborer's oppressor. Such is emphatically the condition of the mass of colored farm laborers at the South, and many of the white laborers at the North. Here gigantic monopolists claim all the land, forbidding the laborer to own an acre, and requiring him to work on their land, or submit to starvation. The most cruel laws are enacted to enforce this compulsory state, and woe to the white man who dares to sell to a colored one, an acre or a rood of land. The storms of Ku-Klux wrath begin to rage about him, and he is hissed at and growled at, as an enemy of his country.

And yet this guilty course curses itself as well as others. The "whole land is cursed with a curse." Agriculture becomes the most slovenly and unproductive of all pursuits. Immense tracts of land are but a burden of expense to their owners, yielding them no income whatever. Many Southern land owners claim from two thousand to ten thousand acres of land, which is mostly unproductive, and the remainder cultivated so shiftlessly, as to be poorly remunerative. Notwithstanding the pride of ownership, which stands in the way of improvement in this respect, yet the time must come when the owners will perceive that it will prove vastly more renumerative to them, to dispose of their supernumary acres, and invest the proceeds in some paying enterprise. What can be gained by keeping one thousand acres of land lying idle, and serving no other purpose than to increase the commissions of the tax gatherer? Five hundred acres is sufficient for all practical purposes, of the farmer in this country; and yet that amount would be considered quite a small farm. One of my neighbors owned before he died, four thousand acres, and most of the farms around here, contain from one to two thousand acres. One family in this county own ten thousand acres.

Of course, I do not advocate taking this land by force from its present owners. According to our present laws, they have the same right, that a poorer man has, to his fifty or hundred acres: but, if I could convince these land monopolists of the pecuniary injury they are doing themselves, I should rejoice. During the most of my sojourn here, my mind has been agitated with the question, how shall these swarthy laborers become owners of land? In the spring of 1869, I visited the North with this project in my mind, of providing homes for these landless people. That project was sanctioned, so as to enable me to offer homes to fifty or sixty heads of families, of these landless ones. But only about twenty, or twenty-five, have yet been able to avail themselves of this offer, owing to their poverty, and the bitter opposition of their rebel employers, to their becoming owners of land. It seems absolutely necessary, to the well-being of the black man, that he should become a land-owner; and if temporary assistance could be afforded him, in making a crop, many more would gladly avail themselves of this privilege. A few would prefer the easier way, of working for wages; but numbers would gladly own land of their own, if they possessed means for its cultivation. To remedy this want, while at the North, it was proposed that we should form a society for the purchase of land, to be sold on time to the blacks; who also should be aided in cultivating the same. In this latter project I was unsuccessful; and some of those who have taken land have been compelled to abandon it, for want of means for its cultivation: while others have struggled on, with what little assistance I could render them. It does seem as if the great Northern public was not sufficiently awake on this subject. While many admit that the colored man should have land, very few are willing to aid him in obtaining it; and still fewer, in furnishing means for its cultivation. There are some, who favor the adoption of the co-operative principle among the blacks; but my experience is, that although co-operation is the grand remedy for the ills complained of by workingmen, yet the freedmen are not sufficiently advanced, intellectually, or morally, to render its adoption among them, a practicable thing: although, it is to be hoped, that after the lapse of years, that desirable end can be obtained. At present, the very best that can be done, is to furnish land to small squads of five or six, — all members of the same family, or related to each other. If others, however, see fit to risk their funds in a co-operative experiment here, I have not a word to say, only to warn them beforehand, that co-operation certainly requires an amount of business talent, and self-abnegation, that is not to be found among the plantation-blacks; if indeed it is, among the whites of the South. We found that a large portion of those engaged in this enterprise, would inevitably shirk their portion of the work, leaving it to be performed by those more honest; and yet would claim an equal share in the profits with others. This, of course, created dissatisfaction among the industrious ones, and jangling and disputes followed; until it was apparent that those most needed in such an enterprise, preferred working for themselves. After this matter had been pretty well tested on our place, I put it to vote to a large company, assembled from all the neighborhood, to hear the result of my Northern mission; and their voice was unanimous in favor of each man having twenty-five acres of his own, in preference to their working together.

Accordingly, I proceeded to supply them land in the way they preferred. Many united together in small squads, admitting none but near relations. One company of five persons, consisting of a father, three sons, and a son-in-law, took one hundred and twenty acres of land, and worked it together quite harmoniously, considering their natural selfishness which would some times leak out. Others, in bands of two or three, took smaller amounts of land, and worked amicably together.

They usually prefer working with others, if all will do their share of the work, but the industrious ones have no notion of working hard, while others are listlessly performing their task; and I cannot possibly blame them. One man, this year, felt obliged to give his own son a tremendous beating, for not performing his due share of the labor devolving upon him.

It is difficult to perceive, why the rebels should so object to the freedmen becoming land owners. One of my neighbors declared at one time, that "if the niggers get land, I shall leave the country." The argument they use is, that if the negroes have land of their own, they would not cultivate it, but would depend on stealing for a living. But my experience proves the reverse to be true. I have known men who were idle and trifling to a proverb, while working for others, and yet would cultivate a little patch of their own, with heroic industry. One man, named Levi Reed, took twenty-five acres, and planted fifteen in cotton, and the remainder in corn, performing all the labor with the assistance of his wife. His cotton was separated from mine, by only a fence, the soil of both fields being of the same quality. From his fifteen acres, he obtained nearly three times as much as I did from double that quantity, worked by several hands on shares. His cotton was half as high again as mine, and entirely free from weeds, presenting a beautiful appearance, while mine was choked with weeds, which greatly retarded the growth of the cotton. I have already alluded to being prevented from visiting my farm by sickness in my family, and this was the result thereof.

This contrast was seen in other fields, showing that they will work far better for themselves, than when only partially interested in the crop. When the land is theirs, they feel that every blow is struck for themselves alone, while on any other principle, some other one is receiving partial benefit from these blows.

The spur of having a home of their own, enables them to overcome some of these most inveterate of their evil habits; and they will become saving, and even very penurious, under its magic influence. While extravagance and recklessness are the general rule among the freedmen, .under this new influence, they become worthy rivals of "poor Richard" himself, for the prize of industry and economy.

It is also á grand school for sharpening their wits. It is amusing to witness their skill in devising "ways and means" to compass their ends, under this new arrangement. I think greater progress will be made in mental development, from the necessities imposed upon them, than even in mastering the mysteries of the ordinary sciences. Said an old man to me last year, "I never studied so hard in all my life afore as I have dis year, in 'triving how to git along," While slaves, of course they were spared all of this "studying." If they wish to pay for their land, they must study "mighty hard."

By becoming land owners, they are much more likely to be honest. It is rare, that a colored man will betray a thief of his own race, as has been already stated; but not long since, a colored man owning land near me, heard some one in the night in his white neighbor's cornfield, and immediately informed his neighbor of the fact. His interest now is united to that of other property holders, and he makes common cause with them; whereas before it mattered not to him, how much stealing was practiced. He now feels the same indignation at the thief that the white man feels.

At the South the mania of the white planter is to add "field to field." This spirit is soon developed among the colored owners of land, and often in a very amusing manner. One man at first, bought fifty acres of land, and the next year he purchased ninety-one more. Between him and another colored man, there was a field of twenty-five acres, which he became extremely anxious to possess also, and he was very much "hurt in his feelings" as he said, because I would not let him have the whole of the twenty-five acres, but wished to reserve a portion of it for his neighbor. No freedman wishes to be outdone by his comrades, in the amount of land he possesses.

But it may be said in reply to all this, "very well, we admit the importance of the colored man's having land, but it is equally important that the white man should be the owner of land. Why waste your energies upon the black man, and leave the white man landless? When is this everlasting prating about the black man's right to cease? We are tired and sick of hearing so continually of the black man's necessities. Let him learn to take care of himself." This objection is sometimes offered by those who in more favorable spiritual moods, professed to be the black's friend, and have in reality made sacrifices in his behalf, and is therefore entitled to respectful consideration.

I will briefly adduce eight principal reasons, why the

Southern black man is likely to be benefited, by the successful result of these efforts in behalf of his becoming the owner of land.

First, at the North no one objects to the laboring man becoming the owner of land. Here, nearly every one is thus opposed. If a farmer's son at the North wishes to buy a farm, almost a hundred hands are stretched out to aid him in so laudable an undertaking. Rich men stand ready to assist him with their capital, because they expect a return from it in the shape of interest. All are confident of his success, and one foot quickly follows the other in the road to agricultural excellence. No aristocrat fears any encroachment by the ambitious youth, upon his peculiar domain, that being surrounded by still more insurmountable inner walls. But here, the great aristocrat is the land owner. Even the merchant and professional man seek to enter the aristocratic enclosure more easily, by adding to their other possessions, the ownership of many broad acres.

Previous to the war, as great efforts were made to prevent the "poor white" from becoming a land-owner, as are now to debar the negro from this aristocratic step. Now, this objection has ceased; and the "poor white" is welcomed to this landed enclosure, if he will join in the crusade, against the negro's reception therein. *He*, must be debarred therefrom, at any rate. I know of but one other enterprise than ours, in all this region; and that is on the part of another Northern man. It becomes therefore necessary, to aid the black man in acquiring land, as the odds arrayed against him are so formidable; and not because he is deserving of more sympathy, from the mere fact of his color. Both white and black laborers should own the land they work upon.

There is no objection now made to the white man's success in this particular, while there is very great to that of the black man. He should therefore be helped.

Secondly, there is a political necessity for this movement, which does not exist in the case of the Northern laborers. In this county, out of some seventeen hundred colored voters, only one vote was cast for the republican ticket in the last presidential election, as has been already stated. About two hundred voted elsewhere. Of the balance, a few voted the democratic ticket, under duress, but the mass did not vote at all. It is true, that at the North, a laborer is sometimes discharged for voting contrary to the wishes of his employer; but such a man is met on every side with sympathizing friends, and his ill-treatment redounds to the welfare of his own party, who consequently, either toast, or lionize him. But how is it here? "Vote as I tell you, or I will not hire you another year," says the plantation owner. The laborer refuses; and his case is immediately reported all over the county, and every planter's gate is closed against him; unless there happens to be a great scarcity of hands, which is not often the case. Said Gen. Wade Hampton, in an address in Charleston, South Carolina, a few years ago, — "Agree among yourselves, and act on this agreement, — that you will not employ any one who votes the radical ticket."

How can we expect the negro to stand up, under such a pressure? What little moral principle he may have acquired since emancipation, is effectually crushed out of his soul by this process. In some few cases, men have said that they would die, rather than to yield to others upon this point; but such cases are "few and far between," as the results of such elections abundantly prove. In 1868, there were eighty thousand colored voters in the state. Not twenty thousand of them voted at all, in the presidential election of that year. In our Senatorial district, out of three thousand colored voters, only eighty-six voted for Grant; and yet, nine-tenths of the colored people of Georgia are decided republicans. In an adjoining county to this, out of seven hundred or eight hundred republican votes, not one was cast for Grant. As has been shown, the last state election was carried overwhelmingly for the democrats. To be sure, physical intimidation was everywhere used; but behind all this violence, stood the demon of poverty viewing the freedmen with angry looks, and threatening to pounce upon them, if they dared to disobey the will of their employers. Great efforts have been put forth, to import both white and Chinese laborers, to supply the place of the contumacious ones, who are consequently filled with terror, as the black man's home instincts are very great; and, on this account, these threats possess a peculiar power over him. He is not naturally a "wandering Jew," or even a "travelling Yankee," but a great lover of home. It is not probable, that these new-comers, would prove one whit more subservient to the whites, than are the blacks; but yet, it is a rod that can be, and is, held over the heads of the blacks, to deter them from exercising their political rights.

Now, if the black man owned land of his own, he would not be exposed to the tender mercies of a domineering landlord. He might, indeed, be killed for exercising his political privileges; but that will be prevented, when our government does its duty in the matter. The danger to him industrially will still exist, even if our government contemptuously hurls from it, the ineffably mean accusations of hair-brained political demagogues; and marches boldly up to its lawful work, of protecting all men, despite the sneers of assassins and murderers; some of whom, for the sake of office, would consign every black man at the South, to the regions of black Tartarus forever, along with every Union man, who dares protest against the black man's wrongs. The black man must be placed on a firm industrial pedestal, as well as on a sure political foundation; and this can only be done by furnishing him with *land.* It may be said, that it would take a long time to remedy this evil, in this manner; that the few aided, would hardly be missed from the ranks of the great *landless* masses. Of course, this is partially true; but in such a county as this for instance, in favorable seasons, the demand for, and supply of laborers, are nearly equal. If the supply falls short of the demand, great injury will result to the planter. Now, supposing I say to one hundred men, "You can have land of your own, and a little assistance in making a crop if you wish," and they accept the proposition. There is immediately created a deficiency of hands, amounting to the number of those thus furnished with land. Some of the planters will vainly search for hands in their places; and such disappointed persons will exaggerate the deficiency, until a little panic about laborers will be produced in the county; all from the simple fact of one hundred men having been furnished with a little land of their own. Then the Southerner, being prone to imagine evils in the future, wherever the negro is concerned, will say, "next year, every nigger will have land, and our farms will have to lie idle." Acting under the influence of these fears, he determines to break away from his political obligations; and he goes secretly, to several very radical negroes, known to stand in fear of their employer, and says to them, "come and work for me next year, and you may vote for whoever you please." The negroes, highly elated with this idea, forthwith engage themselves to the "new departure" planter, and he chuckles over his success, to his neighbors. One by one with secret steps, they apply in the same manner, to some fire-eating rebel's hands, and make the same bargain with them; so that it turns out, by next election time, that at least, two hundred more votes are added to the small republican vote. Now, I know the truth of what I affirm; for the negroes do not hesitate to unbosom themselves to me, and I know they are ready to resume their *old places in the republican ranks*, just as soon as these two movements are made in their favor: first, protection against rebel bullets, and secondly, the ability to furnish food for their children, without reference to their rebel employers.

Even the small movement that with the aid of a few Northern friends has been here inaugurated, has had a perceptible effect, in the matter of increasing the wages of the laborers, which have risen from fifty and seventy-five dollars, per annum, to one hundred, and one hundred and twenty, and many of them are promised political immunity also. It's a little amusing, to see the deference with which some of the most rabid of the rebels, will approach our place with smiles on their faces, and words of smooth-flowing accents, to see if we have any hands to spare; when before this movement, they had said, "I wouldn't hire one of Stearns' d—m niggers to save them from hell."

If one fourth of the negroes in this county, could be

supplied with land, *Ku-Kluxism would hide its hateful head*, and flee to some other community; for irascible as are the Southerners, they will learn to govern their fiery natures, when they ascertain that the negroes can refrain from working for them if they please.

A third reason for this movement is, that now, the poor laborer is almost a slave in the hands of his employer, although the legal relation of Slave is perhaps forever abolished. In this state, if a laborer is hired, without the consent of those for whom he has agreed to work, the one hiring him, becomes *liable to a fine of two hundred dollars*. This law is a rod continually held over the freedman's head, to deter him from fleeing from unjust treatment, and is peculiarly oppressive in its operation. At the North, if a man is treated badly by his employer, he is at full liberty to seek employment elsewhere, rendering him liable to a suit for damages at the most. But here, if a man comes to me, with scared visage, and mangled form, followed by his frightened wife and screaming little ones, and begs me to give them a home, and protect them against the wrath of their employer; pretty soon, I shall behold this employer in hot pursuit, and with vengeance in his heart, he rides up to me, and threatens me with a fine and imprisonment, if I offer a home to the unfortunate family.

I know this by experience; and the case is the same if I do this ignorantly, not knowing that the man was hired elsewhere. I can hire no man, except at the close of the year, without first ascertaining that he has not hired himself to another; and as the negro will not always tell the truth, extreme caution is necessary. At one time, a neighbor rode all around, to forbid any one hiring a woman, who had been abused by his family.

The excuse of the framers of this infamous law is, that without it, their negroes will leave on every slight whipping, and all wholesome discipline is at an end. It is of course an evil for a man's hands to leave him, but why subject innocent men to punishment for hiring them? The planter escapes from the obligation to pay his hand for past wages, whenever he thus leaves him, and he also has the delectable privilege of imprisoning him, conferred upon him by the same, or by a similar law. What would be thought of a Massachusetts Legislature, if it should pass a law, fining a corporation two hundred dollars, if it hired a person who had left another corporation? Is this much better than Slavery? Think of it ye arrant humbugs, who prate about permitting the Southerners to *act as they please!* This law has been in operation evér since my first arrival here, and I have never heard of any attempt being made for its removal.

Now supposing our colored friends had a little land of their own, on which they could work, when these whippings became "immoderate," would not their condition be somewhat improved? At present his employer may beat him, stab him, set the dogs upon him, or fail to give him his regular rations! He may force him to occupy one corner of another man's cabin, with no place of privacy on all the premises; or he may oblige him to change his cabin every week! He may forbid his sending his children to a Sunday, or week-day school, or attending himself! He may prohibit him voting any ticket, but the one pleasing to him, and he may insult him to his heart's content! It matters not. If the black man leaves his employer, without his consent, the person who hires him, *is liable by law*, to the above mentioned fine, of two hundred dollars,—thus the poor creature is almost entirely at the mercy of his employer. Well may the black man reproachfully exclaim, "Is this the liberty for which we fought? Is this the freedom conferred upon us by the immortal Lincoln?"

The *fourth* reason for this movement is, that in this way, can the black man obtain a more comfortable living, than by working for wages. There have been years during my residence here, when the sum total of a black man's wages for the year, was from fifty to seventy-five dollars, besides his rations. Now, what possible progress can a laborer make in pecuniary elevation, with only such a pittance for his subsistence? It will only suffice to furnish food for a few of his children, leaving him utterly destitute of the means to clothe himself and them. And if he receives one hundred dollars, the present price of labor, there cannot be a very large margin left at the end of the year, unless all of his family are able to work. Very few black people find themselves in possession of any great sum of money, at the end of the year. I have heard a planter boastingly say, "I never mean to let a nigger have over ten dollars at Christmas." He said he should charge him a dollar a plug for his tobacco, and every thing else in proportion, and charge him well for absences, so that there would not be much his due at the end of the year; for said he, "it will do a nigger harm to have much money coming to him; it will make him proud and overbearing."

Every year negroes come to me, complaining bitterly of their employers withholding from them their dues; and particularly when they have been to work for a share of the crop. It is possible, that in some of these cases, they may not state the exact truth; but I have repeatedly asked them for all the items of their labor;

the number of acres cultivated, amount of corn and cotton raised, the price it brought, and the amount they had received; and in a multitude of cases I was forced to admit, that they had been shamefully robbed, unless they are the greatest liars in existence. But there is the more reason for not doubting their statements, when we reflect upon the probable fate of many laborers at the North, if their masters were amenable to no law in the pecuniary treatment of their employees; and especially if these hands could neither read nor write. Perhaps this is one reason why the planter's evince so much opposition to the instruction of their negroes. An intelligent Irishman, of whom I once inquired, as to the reason of this opposition to education, replied, "because if the negro is educated, they cannot cheat him so well." If the negro had land of his own, he would at least avoid this cheating process, and of course would be likely to receive all he earned.

One colored man, to whom I sold twenty-eight acres of land, has this year rented that same land for two hundred dollars, besides making good crops elsewhere. Whoever receives himself the entire profit of his own labor, is better off pecuniarily than if that profit had to be shared with others.

It is certain that by working for wages, the negro may labor to the end of his days, and die penniless. His whole life will have been spent in adding to the wealth of another. While I shudder at confounding moral distinctions, such as those between slavery and freedom, yet I cannot help believing that there is not such an heaven-wide difference between the principle of wages, and chattel slavery, as we would be glad to believe. When the black man was a slave, his master speculated upon his labor. He gave him his food and a few clothes. Now, he gives him his food and a few more clothes, and perhaps a few dollars in money. But he enriches himself from the labor of others, as he did before. Of course he does not compel any one to work for him without he first agrees thus to work. He does not buy and sell God's image, and does not control him in every respect, but he is guilty of robbing him of his earnings as surely, although not as extensively, as in the days of slavery. Having spent so much of his life in enriching others, ought not the black man to be allowed at least, to own land enough to afford a final resting place for those weary limbs that have toiled so incessantly, and have been scourged so unmercifully during his life long pilgrimage?

A *sixth* reason for engaging in this enterprise is, the poetic justice of the matter. The black man has toiled unremittingly on these vast estates, and his labor has given them their principal value. Now as the wheel of fortune turns, why should he not become the owner of some of this land, by just and honorable means? At the North every one feels that it is right for a son to inherit the soil he has labored upon for many years, and that at his father's death, no stranger should take possession of the acres, endeared to him by long years of their cultivation. Why should it not be so with the negro? His sweat has enriched that soil, his sinewy arm has stirred up its hardened surface, his hands have gathered its bountiful crops; why should he not now be permitted to continue those labors in his own behalf, and in behalf of future generations of his children?

But *seventhly*, I advocate this measure because it is necessary to the black man's elevation. It is the only impetus that will arouse him from his mental stupidity, and make him a keen contriver of ways and means to enrich himself; and thus impart to him a self-respect, and nobility of soul hardly attainable in any other way.

The *eighth*, and last reason which I shall adduce in favor of this important enterprise is, that here, the laborer is seldom a mechanic, while at the North he is, in the great majority of cases. There, multitudes of working men would hardly cultivate the land if it should be given them, while here, agriculture is the principal occupation of the freedman. It is necessary for the negro to be instructed in the mechanic arts, in order to promote his highest elevation; but while the great body of laborers are agriculturists, it becomes important that he should be furnished with the opportunity to compete with the same kind of laborers in other parts of the world, or at least to guard against the rapacity of agricultural employers. It is true, that the negro will live and die as a tiller of the soil, that being the occupation for which he is at present better fitted than for any other. And there is no degradation in this kind of life. If any man on earth deserves the thanks of the community, it should be the one whose labor lies at the basis of all wealth, the genuine and original producer. But if the black man could easily engage in mechanical employments, there would not be so great a necessity for providing him with land, as there is at present.

It is unnecessary to multiply these arguments. It must be apparent to all, that our brethren of the colored race, pre-eminently need to become the owners of land themselves. But it may be asked, if white laborers do not also stand in need of homes of their own? I answer in the affirmative, and in the next chapter, these claims in connexion with those of the colored man will be considered.

CHAPTER VI.

NORTHERN EMIGRATION OF WHITE LABORERS.

I may be allowed to state that during the whole of my residence here, it has been the anxious enquiry of my mind, "how shall these poor creatures be delivered from the multiplied evils of their present condition?" No one can dwell among them and not be affected even to tears, at the sight of their unfortunate situation. I came here to learn for myself, the whole story of their degradation, and having learned it, to proclaim to the world the result of my observations, and if possible to point out a true and sufficient remedy for their woes. I may be mistaken in supposing that I have discovered this remedy; but if my scheme shall prove a successful one, then shall I feel recompensed for all the losses and privations it has been my lot to endure, during this to me terrible sojourn, among a people so entirely distasteful to me in all of their mental and moral acquisitions, as well as absolutely repulsive in their physical surroundings. If I can but see these enemies of the colored race, fleeing from before the new order of things I would fain have introduced here, then I shall feel like exclaiming, in the words of the immortal Nelson, "I die happy."

The plan I would propose is as follows. Let our

Congress appropriate ten millions of dollars, in the form of a loan to an incorporated society, whose object shall be the purchase of lands at the South, on which shall be allowed to settle the poor Northern laborer, and the Southern freedman. Let these lands be deeded to the U. S. government, so as to guard against all loss, and let this society obligate itself to pay annually to the government, four or five per ct. interest, on all the money advanced. This sum to be advanced only so fast as the land is procured, which might not be more than a million of dollars annually ; and for several years, perhaps considerably less. The officers of this society must be responsible men, who will be good for the amount of the interest, and whose word can be relied upon, to return the deeds to the government, as fast as the land is obtained. In places where the government owns suitable land, in the Southern states, that could be used for the same purpose, instead of purchasing elsewhere. Then, let a farm of one thousand acres be purchased in as many counties as possible, the object being to obtain that number of acres, in *every Southern county.* In Georgia, there are one hundred and thirty-two counties. In some other states not so many, so that the whole number of Southern counties is not far from 1000, which would give one million of acres for the whole South, at the rate of one thousand acres to every county. Land can be bought on an average, of about ten dollars an acre, which would amount to ten million of dollars for the whole South. Now let this land be divided into farms of twenty-five acres each, which is about the amount that can be cultivated here by one man, besides leaving enough for timber. Let this land be offered to proper persons on the following terms.

Let ten or twelve dollars be paid in advance by each settler, which will be sufficient to pay the interest to the government; and let the remainder of the interest, and one-tenth of the principal, be paid at the end of each year, which would be $25, on the principal, and as much more in the shape of interest, as the society deem expedient. Ten per cent. per annum, would cover the whole expense of interest to the government, of purchasing the land, superintending the farming operations, and collecting the amount due at the end of the year. On each farm of one thousand acres, it would amount to $500, besides paying the government five per cent. interest. One agent could superintend the farms in a number of contiguous counties; so that the income derived from this source could be made to cover the whole expenses of the society, and make it a self-supporting institution. Or, if agents could be found benevolent enough to perform this labor gratuitiously, or a part of it, the amount thus saved could be deducted from the interest of the poorest ones.

Let the society then raise a sum of money to be used as a loan to the settlers, and in *no case* to be given to them. This money would be expended under the supervision of the superintendent, who would in all cases, secure its payment in the fall, by a *lien on the crops.* The society would thus be able to guard against all losses, and could charge the settlers as low a rate of interest on the loans, as its conscience might require, Some of those thus settling, would require no asistance after the first year or two, while others might, for a series of years.

But previous to securing the aid of the government, which might be delayed for a season, the society could purchase a few farms in adjoining counties, in some state near the Northern line, Virginia, for instance, and commence operations independently of the government. If the society could raise $20,000 at first, one half of it could be expended in purchasing farms, and the remainder in aiding those wishing to embark in the enterprise. Thus $10,000 would purchase land sufficient for forty persons, and $10,000 more would be all that they would need, to enable them to raise their first crop.

Then, let every effort be put forth, to secure the emigration of the right sort of Northern men. They should be honest, intelligent, upright, and hard-working men; those used to labor, and capable of setting an example worthy of imitation, to the shiftless Southerners, white or black. Their object should be, not merely to enrich themselves, but while they are provided with homes on easy terms, they should be determined to exert a good influence on all classes. This, they should do first, by imitating the example of our Puritan fathers, when they first landed in New England, and established schools for the free education of their children. These schools should be open to all classes, thus affording an opportunity to try the experiment of mixed schools, and offering at once, a partial solution of the problem, how shall the colored children of the South be educated? The schools should be of the highest practicable character, fully equal to the average of our New England public schools; and teachers possessed of the true missionary spirit, should be employed in them. In due time, these schools could be multiplied, as opportunity is afforded for their introduction, outside of the New England village, which would grow up on every plantation. Then, let a hall for all kinds of lectures and meetings, be erected in each village, and let it be dedicated to free discussion on all important topics. In this hall, there should be religious services held every Sunday, and the pure gospel preached free to all classes. If possible, sectarianism should be excluded from the infant colony, and preachers of all denominations should be invited to occupy the hall alternately. Of course, a union Sabbath school should be established for all classes; and every week a lecture of some kind should be delivered, or a debate be held, on some subject appertaining to the welfare of man; which should be made simple enough to be comprehended by the darkened minds around.

Then let the strictest attention be paid to order and neatness in every department, so that the colony shall be in this, as in other respects, a model settlement. Every member should realize that the great object of his mission is to set an example worthy of imitation to all around. The influence of one such Northern village, in every Southern county, would be incalculable. From such a colony, would flow forth streams of intelligence and morality, that would eventually cleanse the whole Augean stable of the South, filled as it is, with every kind of impurity. Knowledge, with its beneficent wand, would beckon the slaves of ignorance to come to its sacred feast. Religion, shorn of its immorality and vindictive spirit, would lovingly invite all people to repose beneath its life-giving shade. Industry and economy, twin sisters of prosperity, would extend their arms of invitation to the wasteful sloths around them, asking them to behold their virtues, so opposite to their own indolence and extravagance; and above all, the sun of temporal prosperity, would shine in unwonted splendor all over the new colony, enlightening "the dark places of the earth, so full of the habitations of cruelty," with the brilliant light, reflected from the burnished roofs of these new temples of industry, morality, knowledge and religion.

This is taking it for granted, that New England fashion, these forty families will choose to build their houses in proximity to each other, instead of scattering them all over the large farm. The village thus created, would be like quarters of the black people, on every plantation, although much larger. If extra aid is needed in cultivating land, it could be obtained from the colored people around, although each family should go prepared to perform all of its own labor; for we do not want a colony of gentlemen, but of honest laborers. We want to show the dilatory blacks what true labor is, and what it can accomplish. We want to show them how much more labor can be performed by Northern working men, and thus produce true emulation on their part. Mechanics will also be needed in this new enterprise. We propose the establishment of a flourishing Northern village in each Southern county; and of course mechanics will be needed. But as we have already alluded to this point while describing industrial schools, it is unnecessary to add any more. The true Yankee settlement must contain its rows of mechanic shops, as well as its tasty dwellings for all classes. It would be better for each mechanic to understand farming, and then the two classes of laborers could be united in one. Then, during the hotter portion of the day, and in rainy weather, the work of the shop could be progressing, while Nature is performing her allotted part. Mechanics of all classes are needed here, carpenters, blacksmiths, wheelwrights, masons, painters and glaziers, boot and shoe makers, tailors, and among the women dressmakers, would all find ample employment here to-day. There is no doubt that the planters around the new settlement would gladly avail themselves of the skilled Yankee laborer in lieu of those whom they are obliged to put up with now.

Every such colony would be amply able to protect itself, for no Ku-Klux band in Georgia would dare attack a settlement defended by forty stout Northern arms. Such is not the genius of Ku-Kluxism. It prefers conflicts with unarmed men, with defenceless women and children; and retires affrighted from the sight of a few bristling bayonets. Neither would they be inclined to do this, for the colonists would instruct their children gratuitously, and would labor to impart to all the treasures of wisdom and knowledge they possess; and I do not think the Ku-Klux would find it in their hearts to molest them, especially as the colonists would not interfere in the matter of hiring their hands, and would be ready to lend a helping hand to their Southern brethren, in time of industrial need. The colonists would be friendly to all, and the enemies of none, and it would not be long before the white Southerners would come to them for instruction in a multitude of things, which their benevolent hearts would always prompt them to give. Thus would be gradually healed the virulent sore so long festering in Southern hearts, and they would come to see that Northern men, so far from being their deadly enemies, as they now believe, are their truest and best friends.

Of course this little colony, would all be staunch Union men, and would march to the polls, and deposit their votes for truth and justice in the face of all the Ku-Klux hosts around them.

But could land be obtained for this purpose? I have called upon several of my neighbors, and stated our plans, and they have appeared highly pleased with them, and have informed me of five or six thousand acres of land, that could be obtained not far from here, at an average of about fifteen dollars an acre. They say that if white men come here and labor for themselves, it will disabuse the colored people of the idea, that they only can cultivate the soil, which idea, the whites say, is one cause of their insubordination as laborers.

But can Northern whites successfully labor under the hot Southern sun? During my residence here, I have never known the thermometer to rise above ninety-eight degrees in the shade, and I do not think that in this locality, the heat is ever so intense as it is at the North. A large portion of the country is covered with trees, and numerous springs everywhere abound, which cause a humidity in the atmosphere, that modifies the heat very sensibly; and at about half past ten o'clock of every hot summer day, a gentle breeze usually arises, besides the nights being always cool and pleasant. I have labored through many a warm summer's day, in the open air, without experiencing any inconvenience. The great drawback here, is the chills and fever, but by proper attention to the laws of health, this disease, like all others, loses the most of its terrific nature. I do not think that Northern people are any more subject to it than the natives. During the last two years, no member of my family has had an attack of this disease, and my boy of fourteen, has been exposed to the climate, at all hours and in all weather.

It is customary for the negroes to abstain from labor

about two and a half hours during the heat of the day, and Northern men could do this very easily, and still accomplish much more than the negroes can, so great is the difference between skilled and unskilled labor. The chills and fever do not prevail in every Southern locality. In selecting a site for a colony, care should be taken, especially, to guard against miasmatic localities. I would urge this upon all Northerners, going South, in whatever capacity. Use your common sense, and read medical works upon the subject, and never buy a place exposed to fever and ague, if you can get it for one dollar an acre. Guard against all swampy localities, as you value your health. But should you be unfortunate in this respect, then strictly avoid going out of doors just about sunrise and sunset, and build a fire in the evening in your houses during the summer. And then on the first appearance of a chill, go to bed immediately, and place warm flat-irons at your feet, and drink freely of *composition* tea; and if all this does not answer drink tea made of the *seeds of red pepper*, steeped in boiling water. Above all, watch for the first symptoms of *congestion*, and apply to different parts of the body applications of mustard; and call in a physician as soon as possible. By following these directions, I think you can escape falling a victim to this terrible scourge of all new countries, and of some older ones.

But lift up your drooping heads, ye victims of consumption in its incipient stages? Here you can be cured of this dire disease. Not far from here is a famous strip or belt of land, extending through the state of Georgia, called the "piny woods region," and celebrated for its entire exemption from chills and fever, and from most other diseases. The celebrated watering place of Aiken, South Carolina, is embraced in this region, and it is said no more healty locality is to be found on the face of this green earth. Consumption is almost un-unknown here. During the first year of my residence here, an old gentleman died in the neighborhood. I asked my overseer, a Southerner of thirty-five or forty years of age, what was his disease. He scratched his head, looked puzzled, and at length said, "Well, I can't remember, its some curious name; I never hearn on before." I then named several diseases, but he shook his head, until I at length mentioned consumption, when he said, "O, yes, that's it. What kind of a disease is that any how, Mr. Stearns?"

Warm weather commences here two months earlier, and lasts one month later than at the North. It is now the fifteenth of November, and we have had but one slight frost. Oftentimes at Christmas, the air is as warm and balmly as it is in May at the North. We have some cold spells, usually in January and February, but snow never remains on the ground more than one night. Ploughing usually commences the first of February. Vegetables usually live in the ground through the winter. But Northern people should never come here without their thick clothing, as our houses are built more for purposes of ventilation, than for comfort during the winter. They can be plastered of course, if the inmates so elect. The climate is, however, enervating, and not bracing like that of New England. One cannot overcome slight bodily ills here, by mere force of will, as at the North; but if you are slightly indisposed you must succumb, until rest has recuperated your system. The negroes go coatless and hatless, at all seasons with impunity.

But have I not said enough in favor of colonizing this county with Northern working-men? Will not the good sense of every reader, respond to the truth of these suggestions? The whole earth has been lifted from its degradation, more through colonization, than in any other way. What was England, previous to its settlement by Roman, Saxon, Danish, and French colonists? What was our country, previous to its occupation by foreigners, but a vast howling wilderness, inhabited by wild beasts of every description, with here and there the red man's footsteps, to break the vast monotony of the scene? What would the beautiful and exuberant West have been, without Eastern emigration? How was Kansas rescued from the dominion of the Slave power, except by streams of Eastern and Western men, which poured in upon its fertile prairies, and swept away the incoming myrmidons of pro-slavery wrath, about settling upon its rivulets? And shall not *this* fair land, come under its benign influence? Why should the South be left to stumble on, in its own crooked way, while other portions of the land are made broad and beautiful, by the genius of improvement? Why should there not be "a highway of the Lord cast up *here*, in which the ransomed may walk," as well as elsewhere, in this vast and broad extent of territory? The reader, and its author, will excuse me, for an alteration of Whitter's inimitable "Kansas songs for emigrants," to suit this new scheme of Southern emigration.

We cross the rivers as of old
  The Pilgrims crossed the sea,
To make the South, as they the North,
  The homestead of the Free.

We go to plant the working-men
  In freedom's Southern clime,
And press from out the cotton-tree
  The polished Northern dime.

We're flowing from our native hills
  As our free rivers flow;
The blessing of our mother-land
  Is on us as we go.

We go to plant her common schools,
  On distant mountain swells,
And give the Sabbaths of the South
  The ring of Northern bells.

Upbearing like the ark of old,
  The Bible in our van,
We go to test the truth of God
  Against the fraud of man.

We'll cross the rivers as of old
  Our fathers crossed the sea,
And make the South, as they the North,
  The homestead of the Free.

CHAPTER VII.

THE FUTURE OF THE COLORED RACE, FEARFUL CONSEQUENCES OF THEIR DEGRADATION, THEIR FINAL DELIVERANCE.

It was said by one of old, "To everything there is a season, and a time to every purpose under the heaven." Some twenty years ago, the claims of the working classes were urged upon the attention of the American people; but in the providence of God, the time had not fully come, for those claims to be duly considered. A system of tyranny, exceeding in iniquity, all the wrongs inflicted upon the white laborer, as Mount Blanc towers above the other Alpine heights around it, attracted the attention of the friends of the human race. That system has happily been levelled to the earth. Naught remains to mark the spot of its bloody throne, but the terrible debris of the fallen citadel. The poor victim of its Satanic rule, has, however, only partially escaped from the dominion of the hated tyrant. He still lies bleeding at the feet of his former master; who, with whip in hand, forbids his rising only to a certain elevation. But having tasted of the precious morsel of freedom, his appetite has only become whetted for a larger slice of the loaf of perfect liberty. He cannot see why he, any more than his white compeer, should be beaten with cruel stripes, and subjected to countless indignities. He, imploringly, asks for the same protection of law, that is accorded to his Northern brother.

On the wings of every Northern wind, there is borne to his ears, the sound of innumerable voices, lifted up in behalf of the laboring classes; and, with his dull intellect, he fails to perceive why he, as a laborer, should not be included in the category of those, whose wrongs are being righted. Eloquent men make the "welkin ring," with shouts in behalf of the poor son of toil; and conventions of all classes are held to right their wrongs, and reconcile the difficult-to-be-adjusted differences between labor and capital; but, in all these meetings, he hears not the faintest allusions to his own melancholy condition. Orators who denounced his wrongs while a slave, now that he is ostensibly free, forget him, in their pleadings for his lighter colored brother; albeit the wrongs of the latter, are infinitely less than his own. Shall this apathy in reference to his case continue, until the sun of American freedom has again set in blood? or shall we all awake to a proper consideration of his claims? I pause for a reply!

From my acquaintance with the present relations existing between the white and black man at the South, I can come to no other conclusion than, that a *worse war than our last one, will break out at the South*, unless measures are speedily taken to rectify the wrongs now being heaped upon the black laborer! Numerous incidents have occurred, to justify me in this belief; and no intelligent man can long remain at the South, without being forced to adopt the same conclusion. Moodily and stealthily, does the thinking negro move about, treasuring in his mind, the remembrance of every new outrage inflicted upon him ; but, confidently gazing towards the bright " North star " in hopes of deliverance. Wearied with his midnight vigils, and that star only shedding its cold and placid light upon his maddened soul, he at length grinds his teeth together, closes his lips firmly, and says to himself, " well, there is no hope from them, dis nigger must fight for hisself " ; and soon the fiery light of burning dwellings will illuminate the sky, and the piercing shrieks of helpless women and children, will stun the ears ; for it is this kind of a war, that is sure to be the result of the present contempt of the negro's claims, on the part of the American people. Indeed, during my residence at the South, it has been no slight task always to appease the angry souls who have come to me with the story of their wrongs. It has been my unceasing effort to prevent every outbreak on the part of the negro ; but sometimes, it has required all the nerve we all possessed to prevent such an outbreak, as in the case mentioned by my sister, on her second arrival from the North. I candidly believe, that if I had not been here, a large portion of this county would have been laid in ashes ere this. The fact that the republican party is so nearly dead in our state, is one of the worst omens for the future. While men can rectify their wrongs by the ballot, the danger of a public outbreak is but small, that operating as a safety-valve, through which can escape the pent-up streams of wrath, which would otherwise collect in sufficient force, to cause a terrific explosion. It is on this account, that the English government constantly dreads a popular uprising of the elements opposed to its measures, and usually succumbs to the popular will. Where neither of these processes obtains, the wrongs of the people will be righted in a more sanguinary manner.

When men are allowed to meet and discuss their real or fancied wrongs, there is but little danger of riots; and when they can by the simple instrumentality of the ballot, protect themselves, there is no need of standing armies to awe them into submission. But where neither free speech nor a free ballot is allowed, as is the case all over the South, and a large class of the people is oppressed, then let the perpetrators of these outrages "stand from under," for the temple of oppression they themselves have reared, has already begun to crack from capstone to basement, and soon the whole stupendous pile will come tumbling down upon the heads of the unfortunate supporters of this villainy. I give this as my opinion. The Southern and Northern people can take it for what they deem its real value.

But allowing that this ruin will not speedily follow our present course, who is to be benefited by this disregard of the assertion of God, that "Righteousness exalteth a nation, but sin is a reproach to any people?" The laws of Jehovah apply to nations, as well as to individuals; and in both cases there is no escape from the fiery mandate, "The soul that sinneth, it shall die." We have already received the first installment, of the wages due for our sins, in the shape of the terrible war from which we have so recently emerged, and still we do not cast those sins from us. Still is heard in the ears of an avenging God, the cries of those who "are ready to perish." Pharaoh was punished ten times for his disobedience to God, each punishment being severer than the last, until he and his vast hosts were engulphed beneath the dashing waves of the mighty current, that overwhelmingly rushed to their destruction

Jefferson "trembled for his country, because God was

just." His justice sleepeth not, and is not changed since the days of slavery, and it is never more thoroughly manifested than in letting nations and individuals "be filled with their own doings." To give men up to "blindness of mind and hardness of heart," is the greatest of all punishments. When God says, "my spirit shalt not always strive," he says a more terrible thing than if he should precipitate upon that nation, all the hosts of war, and deluge its land with streams of blood. What more loathsome sight can meet the eyes, than that of a miserable drunkard expiring in the agonies of his own debauchery?

So with our county. Allowing that we shall escape the fiery wrath of the avenger of all transgressed laws, how shall we avoid the inevitable consequence of our own acts? What more dreadful fate than to live surrounded with the instruments of our degradation, a reeking, bloated carcass of corruption? We ask to be allowed to strike hands of amity, over the bloody form of our wounded colored brother, and while he is writhing in the agonies inflicted upon him, by these "repentant brethren," we wish to hold a Saturnalian feast with the harlot, who seeks to fold her wanton arms around our unsuspecting necks. Listen while we depict the consequence of this foul matrimonial union!

No two European countries can more widely differ than the two extremes of our beloved land. Do we wish to transmit to our children, the Northern or the Southern phase of our present civilization? Look at it first politically. Here are 600,000 voters, with whom manifestly rests the balance of political power? Whichever scale of the political balance they are found in, that scale inevitably causes the other to "kick the beam." On whichever side of the great political battle field they range themselves, there will the fortune of war be found to turn favorably. These negro voters, if possible, are far more ignorant then the devoted adherents of Tammany at New York. Ignorance will then rule our nation. Who can do otherwise than shudder, as he contemplates the political fate of our nation, under such auspices? The South are allowed to govern themselves, or, in other words, to debase the negro to their heart's content. These negroes wield the political destinies of our nation. Adieu then, to our common schools, to our intelligence, to our virtue. Dismal clouds of inky blackness will gird our Southern horizon, until they are rolled together into one vast pall of such terrific darkness, as brooded over the "face of the great deep," when God detained from his new creation, the rays of celestial light, so essential to the beauty of its young existence.

The Southerner claims the right to treat the negro as he pleases. It is evident what that pleasure is, viz., to degrade the negro far beneath his own mediocre intellectual and moral attainments. Will such a state of things add anything to our reputation, or safety, as a nation? Can a people be otherwise than doubly cursed, whose laboring population are extremely degraded? If they are thus degraded, will they not easily become the tools of despicable villains, who will seek to use them to compass their own diabolical ends? Who burnt the orphan asylum, in N. Y., but a degraded mob, used by more enlightened but as vicious leaders? So with the South. Let them accomplish their present aim, and what terrific tools are put in their hands, for the accomplishment of the worst,—the most Satanic of behests!

I tremble when I think of the probable fate of this beautiful country, when it is again ruled over by the Southern aristocracy, as it is bound to be, if the present political "status" of the black man is preserved. Let the schemes of Northern politicians prove successful, and soon will the South be able to marshal on its side, nearly the whole of these 600,000 voters, and with their aid, march to the conquest of Northern refinement, as the Goths and Vandals marched to the destruction of Rome and Italy. Yea, more, as the Crusaders butchered their yielding enemies, so will these new cohorts of iniquity, stamp the life from the vanquished forms of their foes, as the records of Andersonville, Salisbury, Florence, and Libby prisons, abundantly testify. Do we want these tyrants of the South, to ride over us, as they did over our prostrate comrades in those vestibules of hell?

Remember the Southern character has not changed one whit since the war. The records of the Ku-Klux outrages teem with proofs of this assertion. I "speak that which I do know, and testify of that which I have seen." There can be no exaggeration of the *bloody purposes* of Southern leaders. Allow them to govern themselves, without any interference on our part, and in less time than has elapsed since the close of the war, we shall find ourselves bound hand and foot, and tied to the car of the miserable juggernaut of Southern rebellion. The animus and spirit of the South are the same, as when it first surrendered its sword to our valiant general. I have seen it, at every step of my Southern life. It burns and boils over, wherever you direct your steps at the South. There need be no hesitation about believing this assertion. Examine almost any Southern paper, and the truth will be revealed to you. The purposes of the South are as distinct to-day, as they were just before the rebellion. The "lost cause," still retains its firm and devoted adherents; as the *lapsus linguæ* of Jeff. Davis in his recent speeches in this region abundantly proves. The spirit of secession is "not dead, but sleepeth," ready at a favorable moment to assert its rights, and march in battle array to their maintainance. I can assure my Northern readers, that during my residence here, my eyes have not been shut, nor my ears closed; and I am as certain as I am of my own existence, that to-day, would witness the marshalling of the Southern hosts in hot haste, if there was any reasonable hope of their success. To-day, the spirit of the rebellion is no more crushed than it was at the battle of Gettysburg, or when our armies retreated from the vicinity of Richmond.

Ignorance in the hands of vice is a fearful weapon. Allow the vicious whites to control entirely the ignorant blacks, and you may look for a high carnival of crime, that shall make angels weep, and demons turn away in disgust. This can be avoided by the elevation of the negro. Educate him, and he is no longer the tool of designing men. Enlighten him, and he ceases to be a power for evil in the hands of revellers in deeds of blood. And again, enlighten the negro, and you enlighten the white man. Education alone enables us to control the educated. This is one of the strongest arguments in favor of the education of the blacks. Educate him, and he can no longer be controlled by ignorant men. Will the whites allow their children to grow up in ignorance, while the black youth around them, are emerging into the ranks of scholars, and philosophers? Will Southern young men relish the idea of associating with their former slaves, now far advanced above them, intellectually? Then educate the blacks, because in so doing, you are causing the god-like blessings of education, to descend upon the whole country, transforming a "waste howling wilderness" into an intellectual garden of the Lord.

It is unnecessary for me to present facts in reference to the ignorance prevailing at the South. The statistics of the nation furnish ample proof of this point. Some twenty years ago, one-fourth of the adult population of Virginia could not read and write, and in 1837, Gov. Clarke, of Kentucky, publicly declared, that one-third of their adult population could not write their own names. In Ohio, the scholars in the primary schools, out-numbered all the scholars in fifteen slave states and territories, by 17,000. The number of pupils in the primary schools in the free states, was 1,627,028, while in those of fifteen slave states and territories, there were only 201,085, or about one-eighth. The libraries of all the universities and colleges in the slave states, numbered but 223,416 volumes, while those of the free states numbered nearly 600,000 volumes. This was twenty years ago. In 1834, there were six times as many Sunday school scholars in the free as in the slave states. In one year Massachusetts voted a tax of a million of dollars for the support of common schools, which to-day is no doubt increased four fold. Many of her school-houses then, cost $25,000, and some $75,000. How many millions of dollars have the whole South ever voted for education in a single year?

To be educated here and at the North are quite different affairs. Here, no man loses the respect of his neighbors for the lack of that which so many lack; while at the North, we all know how an ignorant man is regarded. I have repeatedly seen an high officer in this state, who could not sign his name to documents requiring his signature, and he was obliged to do it by proxy. As corroborative of my opinions, I will introduce the testimony of Mr. Wm. Gregg, of North Carolina, given many years ago, on the occasion of a flying visit to the free states. He says, "My recent visit to the Northern States, has fully satisfied me, that the true secret of our difficulties, lies in the want of energy on the part of our capitalists, and ignorance and laziness on the part of those who ought to labor. * * * It is only necessary to travel over the sterile mountains of Connecticut, Massachusetts, Vermont and New Hampshire, to learn the true secret of our difficulties, to learn the difference between indolence and industry, extravagance and economy. We there see the scenery, which would take the place of our unpainted mansions, dilapidated cabins, with mud chimneys, and no windows, broken-down rail-fences; fields overgrown with weeds, and thrown away, half exhausted, to be taken up by pine thickets; beef-cattle, unprotected from the inclemency of the weather, and so poor as barely to preserve life;" with much more of similar language.

Horace Greeley, some twenty years ago, gave as the result of his observations in Va., the following sketch. "At this moment, not one-fourth of the soil in the counties I have visited, is under any sort of cultivation, while the portion cultivated, is but wretchedly skimmed over. Not one-eighth of what the country ought to produce, is produced, although agriculture is almost the sole business carried on. Such an entire dearth of manufactories, and mechanical arts, a Yankee can hardly realize, and the churches and school-houses, at best are scarcely equal to Dutch barns. The schools are all private, and I wish the admirers of the voluntary system of education, would come here and see it in operation. I think not half the children (out of the few and straggling villages) attend school, as much as three months per annum, and many of those who do, have to travel from two to three miles, often overtaken in the long stretches of wood, by violent thunder storms, and compelled to ford suddenly swollen streams, at the imminent peril of their lives. Of twenty streams that you will cross in a day's ride, not two will have any sort of a bridge, and this in a country that has been well settled for more than a century, and was probably almost as populous in Washington's prime as it now is. No work or next to none is done on the roads, which are consequently all but impassable, except after days of bright, dry weather. Indolence, improvidence and ignorance of the main comforts of civilization, are displayed in the squalid, narrow, wretched log tenements which mainly serve for habitations, and on nearly everything else. This should he a joyous, populous, thrifty, wealthy region. It has the sun of Greece, and the sky of Italy. Man has known no healthier clime, no purer atmosphere. The soil naturally fertile, and easily cultivated, there are water power and timber in abundance; and the gold mines, must soon create extensive and steady home markets. A lovelier land lies not beneath the summer sun, nor one more inviting to effort. Yet you ride through miles and miles of forest of oak and pine, which serve but as covers for game, though equal in beauty and fertility to the ducal parks of England. And in the midst of these interminable forests, you will frequently pass the falling chimney, the scraggy apple tree, the weedy patch of grass and briers, which tell where the home of a family once nestled. Adieu, land of buried greatness. I could not think otherwise than regretful of the soil that embosoms the ashes of Washington and Patrick Henry."

It is from such a sad condition, that we propose delivering the South, and it is into the arms of such a miserable fate that our whole country is in danger of being plunged, by allowing Southern supremacy in the councils of our nation. Look closely at this picture of the South, and behold as in a glass, the reflection of our fate when Southern governments are allowed full sway, subject to no interference on the part of the national government. Are we prepared for the supremacy of such ideas? Is "negro supremacy" about which we hear so much, one whit worse than Ku-Klux, and Andersonville prison supremacy? And remember as we have stated, that if we allow the South to "manage her own domestic affairs," we shall have both Ku-Klux domination and negro rule combined. But our plan proposes delivering the South from her worst enemies, her own ungovernable passions. We would fain extricate her from the horrible maelstrom into which she seeks to plunge the negro, soon to be whirled herself into the terrible vortex; and would place all her citizens on the delectable shores of purity, intelligence and material prosperity. Is not such a task a glorious one, and one that angels will behold approvingly?

There is much that is noble and pure in the true Southern character. I have never met with greater sympathy, and more ardent friendship, from those who harmonized with me religiously, than in Kentucky. Like the ancient Jews, the Southerners are the most devoted of friends, as well the bitterest of enemies. There is a whole-souled generosity of feeling towards and absorption in the interests of a friend, that is not so common at the North. I am able to speak of the thoroughness of this friendship, from the experience of twenty-two years of matrimonial intimacy with one of the daughters of the South. I can therefore have no prejudice against the home of some of my dearest friends. It is because I love the South, that I would not leave her like a wayward child, to compass her own destruction.

But what shall be said of the poor victims of our misguided brethren, over whom the long night of slavery has so fearfully hung, leaving scarcely one bright spot on their blighted souls? If it is god-like to rescue their former masters from the consequences of their crimes, is it not doubly so to "snatch as brands from the burning" the poor imbruted ones, on whom the whole of this storm of sin and woe has burst with unmitigated fury? In the just balance of an impartial God, it is true that his sins may outweigh his virtues, but will not the "Judge of all the earth," regard them with leniency, as he reflects that their moral perceptions have been well nigh obliterated, by the Satanic pressure of slavery's iron hoof upon their souls? And I would not forget also, that the crimes of their masters, may seem less heinous to Him who "knoweth the hearts of all men," than they do to us from whom their temptations are hidden. I wish to do justice to all men. I therefore must express my sympathy for the Southern whites, as for those who have brought upon themselves "swift destruction." Never was a nation more thoroughly punished for its sins, than they have been for theirs. They have "sowed the wind," and now are engaged in "reaping the whirlwind." They have created the miserable laborer whose faults are so constantly before them. He is the manufacture of their own wicked hands. They have themselves caused to be wound around them, the folds of an anacondic monster, from whose slimy grasp they can no more extricate themselves, than the unfortunate traveller can escape from the crushing power of the far-famed South American serpent. The Southerner has "given and it has been given unto him," but of curses, and not of blessings. The poisoned chalice, that he has prepared for the lips of others, is now being drank of by himself; a fearful mixture of the " wine cup of the wrath of God." Still we pity him in our heart of hearts, and would fain do something to deliver him from the terrible consequence of his own violent dealings, that have emphatically " fallen upon his own pate."

Four millions of Caspar Hausers, passed in melancholy retinue before the eyes of President Lincoln, as he signed the proclamation that will immortalize his name in the annals of the world. Caspar Hauser, as our elder readers will remember, was a youth released from a long imprisonment in Nuremburg, Bavaria, some forty years ago. A brilliant writer thus describes him: " Though seventeen years old, he could not walk or talk. He heard without understanding, he saw without perceiving, he moved without definite purpose. It was the soul of an infant in the body of an adult. After he had learned to speak, he related that from his earliest recollection, he had alway been kept in a hole so small, that he could not stretch out his limbs, where he saw no light, heard no sound, nor ever witnessed the face of an attendant who brought his scanty food. For many years conjecture was rife concerning his history, and all Germany was searched to discover his origin. After a long period of fruitless enquiry, and speculation, public opinion settled down into the belief that he was the victim of some great unnatural crime, that he was heir to some throne, and had been sequestered by ambition; or the inheritor of vast wealth, and had been hidden away by cupidity, or the offspring of criminal indulgence, and had been buried alive to avoid exposure and shame."

The treatment of this unfortunate lad was termed the "crime on the life of a soul"; and such crimes were the South continually guilty of, in shutting out the light of education from the souls of the black race. Shall we not endeavor to atone for our share in this awful act of villainy, at the sight of which, holy angels drop their harps in dismay, as they quickly turn from the fearful object, by co-operating with all who are endeavoring to lift this curtain of ignorance, from the souls of these millions of Caspar Hausers?

While I do not aspire to prophetic knowledge, I can yet behold in the illimitable future stretching far before me, the fulfillment of the glorious prophecies of Holy Writ, respecting the down-trodden of the earth, which, although not originally intended to apply especially to the African race, may yet be considered, as a description of their future glory. "Thou shalt no more be termed Forsaken: neither shalt thy land be termed Desolate: but thou shalt be called Hephzibah, and thy land Beulah." "For brass I will bring gold, and for iron I will bring silver, and for wood brass, and for stones iron." "Thy sun shalt no more go down, neither shall thy moon withdraw itself: for the Lord shall be thine everlasting light, and the *days of thy mourning shall be ended.*"

Or, in the words of a distinguised poet, —

"Hear what God the Lord hath spoken,
'O my people, faint and few,
Comfortless, afflicted, broken,
Fair abodes I build for you;

Thorns of heartfelt *tribulation,*
Shall no more perplex your ways,
You shall name your walls salvation,
And your gates shall all be praise.'

"God shall rise, and shining o'er you,
Change to day, the gloom of night;
He, the Lord, shall be your glory,
God, your everlasting light."

And as this race has already under God been the means unwittingly, of increasing the depth and power of that regenerating influence, that the American church was established for the spread of, so shall it still continue to shed abroad from its purified form, those holy streams of benignant grace that shall wash away the old errors and sins of its former despotic abode; as the waters of Niagara, in their distant influence, wash the shores of many an infected region. Then shall the South present to the admiring gaze of the whole earth, the beauty and moral loveliness, so appropriate to its land of "sunny fountains," and where,

"In vain, with lavish kindness,
The gifts of God are strewn."

Then shall "*violence* no more be heard in its land, wasting nor *destruction* within its borders," but its "officers shall be made *peace*, and its exactors *righteousness.*"

"The tyrants of the plain,
Their savage chase give o'er,
No more they rend the slain,
And *thirst for blood* no more;
But infant hands
Fierce *tigers stroke*,
And lions yoke
In flowery bands."

"Amazing, beautious change,
  A land created new,
My thoughts with transport range,
    The lovely scene to view."

Then shall the precepts of Him who came to "break every yoke and let the oppressed go free," be beautifully reduced to practice by a nation redeemed by the power of his love, from their former vicious habits, and

"By such shall He be feared,
  While sun and moon endure,
Beloved, obeyed, revered;
  For He shall *judge the poor*,
Through changing generations;
  With *justice*, mercy, truth,
While stars retain their stations,
  Or moons renew their youth."

I feel as if this was destined to be the work of this generation, and I call upon all lovers of Jesus, to unite in the glorious enterprise of thus placing upon the crown of our Saviour, one of its most brilliant gems. The colored race is eminently religious as no other race is, albeit its present form of religion is so different from the benign system of our holy Redeemer. But when we find a race so immersed in the religious element, there is certainly great hope for that race. They all believe theoretically in the One God of the American nation, and it is only necessary to convince them of his true character, and of the nature of his requirements, to convert many of them to true Christianity. Their vices exist because they are not yet satisfied, that God is a pure and holy God, and utterly opposed to all sin. Even the most debased of them, have moments of religious exaltations, when they seem transformed into pure beings, but the power of evil habits is too great to be escaped from immediately. The continual preaching of God's law, and the certain consequences of its violation, together with the glad news of a Saviour from sin, must eventually free them from the trammels of vice, and regenerate their degraded natures.

But no nation ever redeemed itself. This task of its redemption, is under God left to others. Why should we fold our arms in moody silence, and say, "we have done enough for the black man, remove the story of his wrongs from our surfeited ears!" Will not the picture of his degradation as drawn in these pages, arouse within you feelings of the deepest compassion for this afflicted race?

And are we not all of us somewhat to blame for this terrific degradation? Did we always do all in our power to deliver him from the hands of the oppressor? Has not God "concluded us all under sin," in this matter? And are we not all "verily guilty for the blood of our brother?"

Reader, I have purposely drawn for your consideration, a sombre picture of those whose claims I have endeavored to defend, and in whose behalf I would fain interest all who may read this book. Behold in panoramic view before you, all the traits of this forlorn race. Look upon their degradation and reflect upon its causes, and say if there is not sufficient reason, why you should not enlist in the little army who are yet battling in their behalf? And you, Mr. Copperhead, if you should chance to read these pages, pray do not increase the guilt of your hatred of "God's image clothed in ebony," by parading before the world this record of the black-man's faults, as a justification for the "outrages" committed upon him. When you speak of the delinquencies here portrayed, be so kind as to specify their cause, and denounce not merely the helpless criminal, but unite with all his friends, in introducing a "new departure," indeed, into our whole public policy respecting him.

And as the long retinue of blood-washed ones marches in joyful array, before and around the throne of "Him, that liveth and was dead, and behold is alive for evermore," on that dread day when "the books shall be opened, and another book be opened which is the book of life;" shall we not rejoice "with joy unspeakable and full of glory," when the heavenly scribe shall turn to our name, occupying some humble place

"Beneath my Lord the Lamb,"

in that brilliant catalogue, of those "who love their fellow men?"

And if the just angel of record, discovers the tracing of some darkened lines on the glowing page, some former error of our lives and hearts depicted there, may we not reverently hope, that a loving tear will blot out the unseemly record, as he perceives there the story of our prayers and tears in behalf of God's most suffering ones, as "charity covereth a multitude of sins." And will he not triumphantly escort us, to one of heavens' glorious mansions, proclaiming to all as we joyfully follow his steps, "Inasmuch as he did it unto one of the least of these the brethern of the Lord, he has done it unto heavens' King himself;"and as the portals of the pearly gates are thrown wide open for our admission, will he not turn and address us, with these soul inspiring words, "Enter ye into the joy of our Lord." And there,

> "No bleak cliffs upward towering,
> Shall bound our eager sight;
> No tempest, darkly lowering,
> Shall wrap us in its night.
>
> Love, and unsevered union
> Of soul with those we love,
> Nearness and glad communion,
> Shall be our joy above.
>
> No death, our homes o'ershadowing,
> Shall e'er our harps unstring;
> For all is life unfading
> In presence of our King."

THE END.

www.ingramcontent.com/pod-product-compliance
Lightning Source LLC
LaVergne TN
LVHW021230110826
845150LV00002B/288

* 9 7 8 1 4 2 5 5 6 2 9 0 8 *